Michal Vít, Magdalena M. Baran (eds.)

TRANSREGIONAL VERSUS NATIONAL PERSPECTIVES ON CONTEMPORARY CENTRAL EUROPEAN HISTORY

Studies on the Building of Nation-States and Their Cooperation in the 20th and 21st Century

ibidem-Verlag
Stuttgart

Bibliografische Information der Deutschen Nationalbibliothek
Die Deutsche Nationalbibliothek verzeichnet diese Publikation in der Deutschen Nationalbibliografie; detaillierte bibliografische Daten sind im Internet über http://dnb.d-nb.de abrufbar.

Bibliographic information published by the Deutsche Nationalbibliothek
Die Deutsche Nationalbibliothek lists this publication in the Deutsche Nationalbibliografie; detailed bibliographic data are available in the Internet at http://dnb.d-nb.de.

Cover picture: V4 Summit + South Korea in Prague on 3 December 2015 by P. Tracz/KPRM.
Source: Wikimedia Commons. Public Domain.

∞

Gedruckt auf alterungsbeständigem, säurefreien Papier
Printed on acid-free paper

ISSN: 1614-3515

ISBN-13: 978-3-8382-1015-5

© *ibidem*-Verlag
Stuttgart 2017

Alle Rechte vorbehalten

Das Werk einschließlich aller seiner Teile ist urheberrechtlich geschützt. Jede Verwertung außerhalb der engen Grenzen des Urheberrechtsgesetzes ist ohne Zustimmung des Verlages unzulässig und strafbar. Dies gilt insbesondere für Vervielfältigungen, Übersetzungen, Mikroverfilmungen und elektronische Speicherformen sowie die Einspeicherung und Verarbeitung in elektronischen Systemen.

All rights part of this publication may be reproduced, stored in or introduced into a retrieval system, or transmitted, in any form, or by any means (electronic, mechanical, photocopying, recording or otherwise) without the prior written permission of the publisher. Any person who does any unauthorized act in relation to this publication may be liable to criminal prosecution and civil claims for damages.

Printed in the EU

Soviet and Post-Soviet Politics and Society (SPPS) Vol. 170
ISSN 1614-3515

General Editor: Andreas Umland,
Institute for Euro-Atlantic Cooperation, Kyiv, umland@stanfordalumni.org

Commissioning Editor: Max Jakob Horstmann,
London, mjh@ibidem.eu

EDITORIAL COMMITTEE*

DOMESTIC & COMPARATIVE POLITICS
Prof. **Ellen Bos**, *Andrássy University of Budapest*
Dr. **Ingmar Bredies**, *FH Bund, Brühl*
Dr. **Andrey Kazantsev**, *MGIMO (U) MID RF, Moscow*
Prof. **Heiko Pleines**, *University of Bremen*
Prof. **Richard Sakwa**, *University of Kent at Canterbury*
Dr. **Sarah Whitmore**, *Oxford Brookes University*
Dr. **Harald Wydra**, *University of Cambridge*
SOCIETY, CLASS & ETHNICITY
Col. **David Glantz**, *"Journal of Slavic Military Studies"*
Dr. **Marlène Laruelle**, *George Washington University*
Dr. **Stephen Shulman**, *Southern Illinois University*
Prof. **Stefan Troebst**, *University of Leipzig*
POLITICAL ECONOMY & PUBLIC POLICY
Prof. em. **Marshall Goldman**, *Wellesley College, Mass.*
Dr. **Andreas Goldthau**, *Central European University*
Dr. **Robert Kravchuk**, *University of North Carolina*
Dr. **David Lane**, *University of Cambridge*
Dr. **Carol Leonard**, *Higher School of Economics, Moscow*
Dr. **Maria Popova**, *McGill University, Montreal*

FOREIGN POLICY & INTERNATIONAL AFFAIRS
Dr. **Peter Duncan**, *University College London*
Prof. **Andreas Heinemann-Grüder**, *University of Bonn*
Dr. **Taras Kuzio**, *Johns Hopkins University*
Prof. **Gerhard Mangott**, *University of Innsbruck*
Dr. **Diana Schmidt-Pfister**, *University of Konstanz*
Dr. **Lisbeth Tarlow**, *Harvard University, Cambridge*
Dr. **Christian Wipperfürth**, *N-Ost Network, Berlin*
Dr. **William Zimmerman**, *University of Michigan*
HISTORY, CULTURE & THOUGHT
Dr. **Catherine Andreyev**, *University of Oxford*
Prof. **Mark Bassin**, *Södertörn University*
Prof. **Karsten Brüggemann**, *Tallinn University*
Dr. **Alexander Etkind**, *University of Cambridge*
Dr. **Gasan Gusejnov**, *Moscow State University*
Prof. em. **Walter Laqueur**, *Georgetown University*
Prof. **Leonid Luks**, *Catholic University of Eichstaett*
Dr. **Olga Malinova**, *Russian Academy of Sciences*
Prof. **Andrei Rogatchevski**, *University of Tromsø*
Dr. **Mark Tauger**, *West Virginia University*

ADVISORY BOARD*

Prof. **Dominique Arel**, *University of Ottawa*
Prof. **Jörg Baberowski**, *Humboldt University of Berlin*
Prof. **Margarita Balmaceda**, *Seton Hall University*
Dr. **John Barber**, *University of Cambridge*
Prof. **Timm Beichelt**, *European University Viadrina*
Dr. **Katrin Boeckh**, *University of Munich*
Prof. em. **Archie Brown**, *University of Oxford*
Dr. **Vyacheslav Bryukhovetsky**, *Kyiv-Mohyla Academy*
Prof. **Timothy Colton**, *Harvard University, Cambridge*
Prof. **Paul D'Anieri**, *University of Florida*
Dr. **Heike Dörrenbächer**, *Friedrich Naumann Foundation*
Dr. **John Dunlop**, *Hoover Institution, Stanford, California*
Dr. **Sabine Fischer**, *SWP, Berlin*
Dr. **Geir Flikke**, *NUPI, Oslo*
Prof. **David Galbreath**, *University of Aberdeen*
Prof. **Alexander Galkin**, *Russian Academy of Sciences*
Prof. **Frank Golczewski**, *University of Hamburg*
Dr. **Nikolas Gvosdev**, *Naval War College, Newport, RI*
Prof. **Mark von Hagen**, *Arizona State University*
Dr. **Guido Hausmann**, *University of Munich*
Prof. **Dale Herspring**, *Kansas State University*
Dr. **Stefani Hoffman**, *Hebrew University of Jerusalem*
Prof. **Mikhail Ilyin**, *MGIMO (U) MID RF, Moscow*
Prof. **Vladimir Kantor**, *Higher School of Economics*
Dr. **Ivan Katchanovski**, *University of Ottawa*
Prof. em. **Andrzej Korbonski**, *University of California*
Dr. **Iris Kempe**, *"Caucasus Analytical Digest"*
Prof. **Herbert Küpper**, *Institut für Ostrecht Regensburg*
Dr. **Rainer Lindner**, *CEEER, Berlin*
Dr. **Vladimir Malakhov**, *Russian Academy of Sciences*

Dr. **Luke March**, *University of Edinburgh*
Prof. **Michael McFaul**, *Stanford University, Palo Alto*
Prof. **Birgit Menzel**, *University of Mainz-Germersheim*
Prof. **Valery Mikhailenko**, *The Urals State University*
Prof. **Emil Pain**, *Higher School of Economics, Moscow*
Dr. **Oleg Podvintsev**, *Russian Academy of Sciences*
Prof. **Olga Popova**, *St. Petersburg State University*
Dr. **Alex Pravda**, *University of Oxford*
Dr. **Erik van Ree**, *University of Amsterdam*
Dr. **Joachim Rogall**, *Robert Bosch Foundation Stuttgart*
Prof. **Peter Rutland**, *Wesleyan University, Middletown*
Prof. **Marat Salikov**, *The Urals State Law Academy*
Dr. **Gwendolyn Sasse**, *University of Oxford*
Dr. **Jutta Scherrer**, *EHESS, Paris*
Prof. **Robert Service**, *University of Oxford*
Mr. **James Sherr**, *RIIA Chatham House London*
Dr. **Oxana Shevel**, *Tufts University, Medford*
Prof. **Eberhard Schneider**, *University of Siegen*
Prof. **Olexander Shnyrkov**, *Shevchenko University, Kyiv*
Prof. **Hans-Henning Schröder**, *SWP, Berlin*
Prof. **Yuri Shapoval**, *Ukrainian Academy of Sciences*
Prof. **Viktor Shnirelman**, *Russian Academy of Sciences*
Dr. **Lisa Sundstrom**, *University of British Columbia*
Dr. **Philip Walters**, *"Religion, State and Society"*, Oxford
Prof. **Zenon Wasyliw**, *Ithaca College, New York State*
Dr. **Lucan Way**, *University of Toronto*
Dr. **Markus Wehner**, *"Frankfurter Allgemeine Zeitung"*
Dr. **Andrew Wilson**, *University College London*
Prof. **Jan Zielonka**, *University of Oxford*
Prof. **Andrei Zorin**, *University of Oxford*

* While the Editorial Committee and Advisory Board support the General Editor in the choice and improvement of manuscripts for publication, responsibility for remaining errors and misinterpretations in the series' volumes lies with the books' authors.

Soviet and Post-Soviet Politics and Society (SPPS)
ISSN 1614-3515

Founded in 2004 and refereed since 2007, SPPS makes available affordable English-, German-, and Russian-language studies on the history of the countries of the former Soviet bloc from the late Tsarist period to today. It publishes between 5 and 20 volumes per year and focuses on issues in transitions to and from democracy such as economic crisis, identity formation, civil society development, and constitutional reform in CEE and the NIS. SPPS also aims to highlight so far understudied themes in East European studies such as right-wing radicalism, religious life, higher education, or human rights protection. The authors and titles of all previously published volumes are listed at the end of this book. For a full description of the series and reviews of its books, see
www.ibidem-verlag.de/red/spps.

Editorial correspondence & manuscripts should be sent to: Dr. Andreas Umland, Institute for Euro-Atlantic Cooperation, vul. Volodymyrska 42, off. 21, UA-01030 Kyiv, Ukraine

Business correspondence & review copy requests should be sent to: *ibidem* Press, Leuschnerstr. 40, 30457 Hannover, Germany; tel.: +49 511 2622200; fax: +49 511 2622201; spps@ibidem.eu.

Authors, reviewers, referees, and editors for (as well as all other persons sympathetic to) SPPS are invited to join its networks at
www.facebook.com/group.php?gid=52638198614
www.linkedin.com/groups?about=&gid=103012
www.xing.com/net/spps-ibidem-verlag/

Recent Volumes

162 *Natalya Ryabinska*
Ukraine's Post-Communist Mass Media Between Capture and Commercialization
With a foreword by Marta Dyczok
ISBN 978-3-8382-1011-7

163 *Alexandra Cotofana, James M. Nyce (eds.)*
Religion and Magic in Socialist and Post-Socialist Contexts I
Historic and Ethnographic Case Studies of Orthodoxy, Heterodoxy, and Alternative Spirituality
With a foreword by Patrick L. Michelson
ISBN 978-3-8382-0989-0

164 *Nozima Akhrarkhodjaeva*
The Instrumentalisation of Mass Media in Electoral Authoritarian Regimes
Evidence from Russia's Presidential Election Campaigns of 2000 and 2008
ISBN 978-3-8382-1013-1

165 *Yulia Krasheninnikova*
Informal Healthcare in Contemporary Russia
Sociographic Essays on the Post-Soviet Infrastructure for Alternative Healing Practices
ISBN 978-3-8382-0970-8

166 *Peter Kaiser*
Das Schachbrett der Macht
Die Handlungsspielräume eines sowjetischen Funktionärs unter Stalin am Beispiel des Generalsekretärs des Komsomol Aleksandr Kosarev (1929-1938)
Mit einem Vorwort von Dietmar Neutatz
ISBN 978-3-8382-1052-0

167 *Oksana Kim*
The Effects and Implications of Kazakhstan's Adoption of International Financial Reporting Standards
A Resource Dependence Perspective
With a foreword by Svetlana Vlady
ISBN 978-3-8382-0987-6

168 *Anna Sanina*
Patriotic Education in Contemporary Russia
Sociological Studies in the Making of the Post-Soviet Citizen
With a foreword by Anna Oldfield
ISBN 978-3-8382-0993-7

169 *Rudolf Wolters*
Spezialist in Sibirien
Faksimile der 1933 erschienenen ersten Ausgabe
Mit einem Vorwort von Dmitrij Chmelnizki
ISBN 978-3-8382-0515-1

Table of Contents

Foreword 9

Rick Fawn
Introduction: The Historical Difficulties
of Regional Cooperation in a Space
Where My Hero is Your Enemy 11

Petr Pithart
The foolish dream of a clean slate?
A common past acting as both a burden
and an inspiration. What to do with borders
and with minorities? 21

Pavlína Janebová and Dominik Želinský
What Does It Take to Become a Hero:
Perspectives of Cultural Sociology and Political Science 37

Milan Hauner
The Legacy of Central Europe 1918–1945 47

Oľga Gyárfášová
Historical Consciousness in the Visegrád Four 73

Ivo Budil
History of Modern Central Europe, Anthropology,
and Theory of Mimetic Rivalry 99

Joanna Mysona Byrska
My Enemy – The Best Opportunity
to Build One's Own Identity. Carl Schmitt Again. 105

Dorota Pietrzyk-Reeves
Civic and ethnic nationalism and the identity
formation of Central European societies
in the interwar period 117

Miklós Zeidler
A Heritage of Historic Hungary — Remembrance and
Revisionism as an Approach to Hungarian
Nation Building in the Inter-war Period 129

Ákos Bartha
From Myths to Reality: the Regionalism
of Endre Bajcsy-Zsilinszky (1886–1944) 139

Michal Kšiňan
Štefánik's Death and the Czecho(Slovak) Identity 149

Jiří Němec
Kamil Krofta and Czechoslovak Identity among
Czechs, Slovaks and Germans and Others 161

Ágnes Tamás
New States — Old-new elements
of nationalism in caricatures (1919–1921) 175

Jan Rychlík
Jozef Tiso: My Enemy — Your Hero? 189

Milan Zemko
Jozef Tiso, Patriot or Traitor? A Slovak Debate
That Has Been Carried on from
the Second World War to the Present Day 215

Miroslav Michela
Welcoming the Admiral on a White Horse:
The Depictions of the Horthy Regime in
Slovak Historical Culture 233

Ignác Romsics
Changing Images of Miklós Horthy 253

Kristina Kaiserová
Edvard Beneš and His Image: 'Hero or Villain'? 269

Piotr M. Majewski
**Freemason, Coward, Russophile, Schemer:
Edvard Beneš in the Eyes of the Poles, 1918–45** 281

Paulina Codogni
'A Wasted Year': Władysław Gomułka and 1956 307

Zoltán Ripp
Imre Nagy — Hero or Victim? 321

Stanislav Sikora
Alexander Dubček, the Best-known Slovak Politician 335

Oldřich Tůma
Alexander Dubček, a Czechoslovak Politician 357

Paweł Ukielski
**'Havel on Wawel!'
or a Prophet is Not without Honour,
but in His Own Country** 371

Tomáš Zahradníček
Wałęsa's Absence from Czech Society 387

Magdalena M. Baran
**Summary: Factors Driving Nation Building Processes
after 1918 and Their Implications** 395

Paul Gradvohl
Persons who became myths 399

Andrea Pető
How to teach history today? 403

Dominika Kasprowicz
**What is the role of history
in contemporary political discourses?** 407

Michal Vít
**How to ask about the V4 identity
from historical and contemporary point of view?** 411

Bibliography 417

Index 447

Foreword

Main idea of the conference that was realized in 2012 was relatively simple: to compare various positions towards historical personalities and events in Central European countries. Rather provocative title of the conference *My hero, your enemy* was based on the fact that a successful politician in one country or an important and celebrated event in its history can often provoke an ambiguous reaction in neighboring country or countries. Particularly, inside of such close space as the Central Europe is.

The realization of the project was considered for a relatively long time. There were concerns that the topic was rather dangerous and conference may end up with a sharp clash of Visegrad historians. There was also a problem with title which was taken as too irritant. During one discussion on other variants of the title, original compromise proposal emerged — to put at the end of the title a question mark as a sign of historical optimism… Particularly this sophisticated joke set the wheels in motion.

We can meet controversy embodied in the title *My hero – your enemy* in any historical period but approaching our times the topic is becoming more and more sensitive. Neighbouring countries are able *to forgive* Czechs for their Hussites, however, personality of former Czechoslovak president Edvard Beneš has been able to provoke controversies till today. Discussion on role of such *complicated* persons has sometimes even explosive political potential.

The second conference *National Identities in Central Europe in the Light of Changing European Geopolitics 1918–1948*, organized in 2015, develops the idea of the first discussion on the mentioned topic. As its organizers announced: *In a similar way to its predecessor the conference will focus on national histories. Moreover, it will also try to build a bridge and to identify links between historical events and the contemporary identity politics in the Visegrád countries.*

Both conferences, supported by the International Visegrad Fund, were based on *modest* wish expressed by organizers in subtitle of the first conference: *Listening to Understand.* Vivid but very correct exchange of opinion led during these conferences demonstrated that it is possible to discuss very delicate topics, if people are prepared not only to speak and promote their opinion as the only right but also to listen. Particularly this moment has been one of the most important results of these two meetings of experts who managed to leave various historical animosities, sometimes accompanied with political ambitions, at the door.

Another important contribution of both conferences, let's hope that they will have continuation, lies not only in cultivated and meaningful *multilog* of experts from various branches; it also lies in dialogue with our common history, with our traditions. Whether we like it or not, history has had its impact on our present and such dialogue can help us to understand this influence better. At the same time, we should understand that such dialogue will not often lead to mutually acceptable results because in various society it has various grounds.

The question what historical truth is, if it exists, would be an issue for very serious methodological discussion, but let it be only said here that history can be *a good servant but a bad master.* Relativity of historical explanations, falsification of history or its misuse can have a very negative impact on the relations between nations as we can, unfortunately, see in contemporary world as well. Evenhanded and factual character of most of contributions presented in this book shows the way how to deal with history, no matter how complicated. And it should be not only another result of both conferences but also an example worth emulating.

No doubts that readers will make their own conclusions but it is not enough because it is necessary to disseminate them if we want to have our world more secure and friendly.

Petr Vágner, former director of International Visegrad Fund

Introduction:
The Historical Difficulties of Regional Cooperation in a Space Where My Hero is Your Enemy

Rick Fawn[1]
University of St Andrews

Let's not take Visegrad cooperation for granted. Of course, it cannot and has not solved every issue; arguably, it avoids embracing issues which already lack pre-existing consensus—let alone serving as a mechanism to forge consensus on, and strategies for more vexing issues.

But it also has done a great deal not only to stabilise, but also to strength relations among its four member countries, and then among them with others. Casting back now more than a quarter of a century, so much at that time suggested that the Visegrad format that we now know would be unthinkable, let alone durable.

Part of that improbability was because if Central European regional cooperation had any pedigree on which to build, it was negative. Far from providing collective defense, the Warsaw Pact distinguished itself in 1968 by becoming the first military alliance to attack itself. The CMEA was jokingly referred to as an antithetical common market, one that fostered shortages; a veteran observer of Soviet bloc economies called its trade 'an exchange of inefficiencies'.[2] On the interpersonal level, Slovak dissident and legal scholar Miroslav Kusý

---

1   Email: rick.fawn@st-andrews.ac.uk
2   Hanson, P., *The Rise and Fall of the Soviet Economy: An Economic History of the USSR* (London: Routledge, 2003), p. 120.

lamented before 1989 that what seemingly societal interactions occurred only strengthened mutual distrust among the region's nationalities.[3]

If the post-WWII and socialist eras corrupted the idea of regional cooperation as a practice of mutual of benefit, the post-World War I, interwar period witnessed its antithesis. The new-founded Czechoslovakia and Poland briefly flirted even with federation, a fleeting contemplation also made after the other international-systemic changes of the twentieth-century, following the Second World War and the revolutions of 1989. But in each case, the pre-eminent impulse of state sovereignty quickly reasserted itself. Otherwise, the new order emerged as one where zero-sum calculations predominated. Post-World War I liberal institutionalism embodiment in the League of Nations provided only short-lived aspirational hopes of collective security, undermined by the 1930s by inability even verbally, let alone practicality, to resist the revisionist policies of the defeated powers of the Great War. The League, of course, could not even retain membership of the revisionist or revolutionary states of Fascist Italy, Nazi Germany or the USSR. At least its, eventual successor, the United Nations, countermanded that fateful leagues by entrenching Great Power interests by granting them a veto on the Security Council, an organ uniquely empowered to enact the use of force in international politics.

The hopes of collective security notwithstanding, interwar Central Europe's real efforts at inter-state regional cooperation were invested in classical state-centric alliances: of the Little Entente of Czechoslovakia, Romania and Yugoslavia against the revisionism of the much-reduced Hungary. When possible, extra-regional Great Powers were enlisted also, foremost for Czechoslovakia with, first, France and then the USSR.[4] And when a status quo power most needed help —

---

3   Kusý, M., 'We. Central-Europeans-Western-Europeans', in George Schopflin and Nancy Wood (eds), *In Search of Central Europe* (Cambridge: Polity Press, 1989). When I raised that piece with him in 1994 he said, importantly, that it was 'written a long time ago'.

4   Among the leading literature is Piotr S. Wandycz, *The Twilight of the French Eastern Alliances, 1926–1936: French-Czechoslovak-Polish Relations from Locarno to the*

Czechoslovakia, truncated after Munich — neighborly recourse was its further occupation by Hungary and Poland in 1939 once that country had been liquidated.

The international level of non-cooperation was heightened and reflected by internal dynamics of these new polities. The successor states sought, like any other state, to construct a national rational, but one complicated by their multi-ethnic tapestry. National narratives were created, but often in contradistinction to and in exclusivist terms of other states and of other peoples, even and often especially of those found within the young states' borders. And these processes of identity-creation come to the heart of the present collection. Narrative were forged that relied on heroes who, while naturally representing some, were anathema to others. Those legacies find new political lives today, and demand rigorous scrutiny and mutual understanding.

Thus, apart from the negative, Soviet-era experience of regional cooperation, the intensity of negative historical legacies in the periods analysed by the papers in this collection mitigated further against prospects for post-communist regional cooperation. True, this previously ethno-linguistically heterogeneous region had become far more homogenous — in contradiction to the multiethnicity of interwar period, by 1993, three nation-states having the 90 percent ethno-linguistic homogeneity that, if arbitrary, social scientists take to constitute a contemporary nation-state. That was achieved through mass murder, force expulsions and redrawn borders. Nevertheless, and partly because of that ominous history, historical legacies of insecurity and animosity remain. And dealing openly and honestly with such unsettled — indeed, exploitable and thus malignant — legacies are fundamental to the roles of socially-engaged historians.

Remilitarization of the Rhineland (Princeton: Princeton University Press, 1988). More broadly, see the Czechoslovak émigré historians Igor Lukes, *Czechoslovakia Between Stalin and Hitler: The Diplomacy of Edvard Benes in the 1930s* (New York: Oxford: University Press, 1996); Jiri Hochman, *Soviet Union and the Failure of Collective Security, 1934–1938* (Ithaca, NY: Cornell University Press, 1984).

That is all the more important because unsettled historical issues fed Western perceptions that post-Cold War Central Europe's new future would actually be a return to its conflictual past. A few examples suffice. Prominent international security scholar John J. Mearsheimer postulated the possibility (deciding otherwise, if only out political expediency) that the 'minor' states between united Germany and (the still existing) USSR would likely not seek nuclear weapons. As oddly reassuring as that might have sounded, in an intentional throwback to the 1930s, he nevertheless submitted that 'because the results of local conflicts [in post-communist Central and East Europe] will be largely determined by the relative success of each party in finding external allies, Eastern European states will have strong incentives to drag the major powers into their local conflicts'.[5] Voices from within the region projected exactly that pessimism outwards. Wrote a Hungarian in a leading US broadsheet in 1992, 'it is not difficult to foresee an unprecedented diplomatic fervor for creating alliances and counter-alliances, wooing the great powers, and playing them off against each other the possibilities are limitless'.[6] If such sentiments were insufficient to indicate the obstacles to regional cooperation among former Soviet bloc states, a British study identified over two dozen ethno-linguistic, disputed border or population displacement flashpoints across the region.[7]

How did Visegrad help to transcend these pessimistic scenarios? Now we know Visegrad has lived for a quarter-century Before we (again) take Visegrad for granted consider that another seasoned Western observer of communist-era Eastern Europe could write in 1991 of regional cooperation initiative that 'they usually consist of countries most likely to be antagonistic toward one another, and often include only states that are weak individually and, together, are even

---

5   Mearsheimer, J., 'Back to the Future: Instability in Europe after the Cold War', *International Security* Vol. 15, No. 1 (Summer 1990).
6   Antal, L., *The Wall street Journal Europe*, 8 July 1992.
7   Dick, C., Dunn, J F, and Lough, J.B.K., 'Potential Sources of Conflict in Post-communist Europe', *European Security* Vol. 2, No. 3 (Autumn 1993), pp. 386–406.

weaker'. One might expect then to be given Visegrad as the counter-example. Instead, it is the 'Pentagonale'.⁸

Such analysis suggests that Visegrad's prominence—let alone survivability—was minimal, even if others detected Visegrad's early significance. And indeed Visegrad has had hard times. Well-known is that it effectively disappeared in the mid-1990s due the consciously denigrating efforts of the Czech Republic's Klaus government, and by the erratic domestic and foreign policies of Slovakia's Mečiar government. But survive Visegrad did. Now seemingly-forgotten was the Czech and Slovak instrumentalist boycott of a Visegrad summit in Hungary in 2002 to protest the Orbán government's (unsuccessful) demands to have the Beneš Decrees annulled. And after the 2004 EU accession Visegrad determinedly defied expectation of a death, instead showing renewed vitality and an expanded agenda, including activism towards the Western Balkans and Eastern Partnership countries. By 2016, and coincidentally its quarter-century anniversary, the Group has gained still more recognition—and perhaps its greatest moment of international attention by its standing on the 'migrant' issue.⁹

But casting again back to the post-1989 period, what Visegrad embarked upon then was foremost to rewrite and recast the historical image of the region in the Western mind. The 1991 Visegrad Declaration astutely used 'Western' and 'European' language and declarative planted Central Europe in those values. The Declaration further reassured the still-skeptical Western interlocutors that, after the peaceable revolutions of 1989, the region would return to practice of those values; xenophobia, hatred and intolerance and were banished.¹⁰

---

8   Nelson, D., 'Europe's Unstable East', *Foreign Policy* No. 82 (Spring, 1991), p. 151.
9   For example, 'Illiberal Central Europe: big, bad Visegrad', *The Economist*, 30 January 2016. Anecdotally, people who have never spoken to me of Visegrad noted in from media appearances. Visegrad featured by name on the BBC's News Quiz, one participant explaining that the Visegrad Four was not referring to group of fugitives. BBC Radio 4, broadcast 19 February 2016.
10 *Declaration on Cooperation between the Czech and Slovak Federal Republic, the Republic of Poland and the Republic of Hungary in Striving for European Integration*, available

This expression of a progressive, truly European Central Europe, and the evidence of tangible cooperation among then-three countries, rapidly gained the Visegrad countries positive reputational traction (aided, of course, by the efforts of political leaders who carried esteem in the West). The Visegrad brand — seemingly unintended as the name for the group, but as Havel later explained it was put into circulation by Hungarian journalists,[11] and fortuitously so — established those countries in the Western political mind as reliable, historically-settled states. That reputation also earned the nascent Visegrad the enduring jealous of neighboring states, from those with far less claim to those, for historical (as it Austro-Hungarian imperial heritage) and proximity to the Western Slavic languages.[12] By the end of 1991, the Visegrad group countries uniquely were meeting with the European Community and signing, albeit individually, the EC's first Association Agreements with post-communist states. The distinctiveness of Visegrad continued so that in January 1994, by name, US President Bill Clinton referred to them as such, and not only to them and with them in Prague, but before that historic visit, just before to all of NATO. And, in a momentous evolution of US policy, Clinton announced that it was no longer a question of whether but nearly of when those four countries would become Alliance members.[13]

The transformational influence of Visegrad on the region's accession into European and Euro-Altantic institutions is unambiguous among those who worked for it. Again, may but a pair of examples be sufficiently

---

      at: http://www.visegradgroup.eu/documents/visegrad-declarations/visegrad-declaration-110412-2.
11   Havel, V., *To the Castle* (London: Portobello Book, 2009), p. 156
12   Accounts of what we might call Visegrad envy are detectable since the Group's inception and continue. Some outline of those perceptions in the 1990s is attempted in Rick Fawn, 'The Elusive Defined? Visegrád Cooperation as the Contemporary Contours of Central Europe', *Geopolitics*, Vol. 6, No. 1 (Summer 2001), pp. 47-68.
13   'The President's News Conference With Visegrad Leaders in Prague, 12 January 1994, available at: http://www.presidency.ucsb.edu/ws/?pid=49832.

indicative? The Czech Republic's Michael Žantovský summarized Visegrad as 'a powerful negotiating tool' for gaining NATO membership.[14] Slovakia's Martin Bútora explained that Visegrad quickly found favor with the West, because it was a positive, sensible, stabilising, and constructive concept. Positive symbols are essential in politics and public diplomacy, and Visegrad quickly became just that.'[15]

These achievements are all the more impressive when we recall that NATO and the EU did not initially want to open their doors to post-communist states. They certainly would not have had they the convenient and viable excuses of finding in Central Europe a lack of democratic development and the enflaming of ethno-national issues (as the rejection of Slovakia for negotiations by organizations in 1997 demonstrated).

Establishing new historical records in foreign policy brings us back to the continuing and essential role of confronting history. Here, too, Visegrad has played a role. When Visegrad could relaunched itself in 1998 and 1999, it foresightedly established the International Visegrad Fund (IVF). That body, with ever-increasingly but still relatively limited funds, has made tremendous and distinctive strides to facilitate inter-societal dialogue and mutual understanding. Supporting reconsideration of the most divisive aspects of recent history is essential for societal well-being, on a domestic, bilateral and regional basis. True, not only divergent interpretation can be reconciled. Heroes will remain that for some, while continuing to be the embodiment for others of enduring harm.

But understanding those differences, at the most basic, and expressing divergent interpretations, including associated feelings of injustice, can be a significant contribution. Confront difficult parts of history is noble, notable and necessary. Keeping and strengthening lines of communication and interactions among peoples is essential. Visegrad in foreign

---

14 Žantovsky, M., 'Visegrad Between the Past and the Future', in Andrzej Jagodziński (ed.) *The Visegrad Group: A Central European Constellation*, (Bratislava: International Visegrad Fund, 2006), p. 85.
15 Bútora, M., 'The Spirit of Visegrad was Revived in Washington', in Jagodziński (ed.) *Visegrad Group*, p. 143.

policy and the IVF in society have built bridges. This is, naturally an ongoing, even unceasing process. And new (mis)perceptions risk being prompted by more recent, and extraneous factors. Unimagined in, say 2012, but graphically real soon after are annexation and war in Ukraine, and massive refugee/migrant influxes which prompt new questions of identity and belonging, of inclusion and exclusion. Dialogue about history and identity become even more essential.

The Visegrad meeting convened in 1991 drew intentionally on the historical analogy of the 1335 meeting of Hungarian, Polish and Czech kings. The enlightened, truly 'European' thinking, the new form of relations that 1991 pronounced was not—thankfully—a reflection of 1335, which included practices unthinkable today, quite apart from being a quintessential expression of balance-of-power *realpolitik*—an alliance against the Hapsburg.

Should not positive use of historical myths be applauded and welcomed? After all, another Visegrad, but 500 kilometers south of the Hungarian and but one year after the 1991 Summit, became an early victim of ethnic cleansing. Those atrocities were spurred by the application of another fourteenth-century historical episode—defeat in 1389 at Kosovo Polje—to the late twentieth-century. If we are engaging in the use of historical myth I know which version, which use, of the fourteenth century I applaud.

We all have a long road still ahead to deal with all historical grievances, ignorance and misperceptions. But Visegrad cooperation and the IVF need to be commended for enabling the platforms for developing new possibilities. The contributions that follow in this collection—dynamic and informative in themselves—also speak well to the health of governmental and societal support for collaboratively confronting dark and difficult chapters of history that, left unaddressed, risk giving fodder to more contention today.

Central Europe:
Social, Political, and Historical Consequences

The foolish dream of a clean slate? A common past acting as both a burden and an inspiration. What to do with borders and with minorities?

Petr Pithart, Prime Minister of Czechoslovakia (1990–1992)

I will pose the question here of whether or not it is ever possible to somehow overcome the past, or rather, whether it is possible to "come to terms" with it, at least in the sense that it would not constantly give us, the neighboring nations and states in Central Europe, sticks in our hands; that it would release our minds from prejudice and idiosyncrasies; and that it would not force us to continue with old regrets, mistrusts, and hostilities. I am mainly considering the Visegrad member countries and their surrounding areas, and especially discussing disputes over borders and over minorities.

Most likely, we will find out about the chances and threats before us when we take on the task of investigating our past sine era et studio, i.e. when we primarily look upon ourselves critically and also attempt to look at the past from the perspective of others. This is the most difficult task. I can already see how in the Czech Republic, upon hearing such words, people will speak in resistance—self-inflicting harm, flagellation. Flagellation, however, gives me the least cause for concern in regards to my country: here it is the exact opposite. We are rather preserving ourselves and planting the seeds of our wounds so that they can continue to hurt for a long time.

There was, is, and most likely always will be, the same foolish illusion, old as civilization itself: the illusion that there are moments when it is possible to start over, with a clean slate, to be for a moment as if paradise—innocent, freed from the burdens of the past. A fresh start! People will believe in something like this for a time following big coups, revolutions—after big changes. The path which we have followed can be forgotten following the fall of communism, some said in late 1989: old regrets, idiosyncrasies ingrained under the skin, stiff hetero-stereotypes will hopefully not stand in the way next time. We are staring anew, starting to build a new world from the ground up. Specifically, a new Central Europe, the place that was once culturally and spiritually the most colorful and productive. We, the new generations, unburdened by the past. Generations that were active during times when old regimes collapsed. We will now build it not just for ourselves, but for all of Europe, which had in the past allowed for its center to be kidnapped?

I remember the very first foreign visit of the delegation of the Coordination Center of the Civic Forum in December of 1989. As its representative, I led it into Polish Těšín without hesitation, where we met with Adam Michnik. My first trip as chairman of the new government again without much hesitation led right into Hungary in March 1990. Moreover, I was in Bratislava right the next day after my nomination (unlike Václav Havel). So we perceived our path into Europe: together with our neighbors, with whom we have a shared experience of a post-war past. This will now strengthen us and bring us together.

In the spring of that year, a conference of politicians, historians, and philosophers was held at the Bratislava Castle regarding the future of Visegrad. The presidents at the time were Vaclav Havel, Lech Walesa, and soon to join them Arpád Gonz. A shared past full of misunderstanding and strife was in no way being pushed out of our minds at the time, but we, the people of opposition or dissent, did not need to irritate it in order to gain favor with the electorate. We had at least the illusion of a clean slate. Dissent and exile during many long years opened up the most sensitive, painful pages of particularly recent histories existing in all three of our countries. We were prepared to discuss and act upon them, but we were the exclusive minority that at first refused to admit its exclusivity.

It turned out that the cruel, graphic image of Jacques Rupnik was correct regarding what we would discover at the bottom of the freezer. Once upon a long time ago there were deposited pieces of still bloody meat. Meat is, after all, always bloody. Some remember that something like that was indeed there, but then totalitarian or authoritarian regimes turned the freezer up to the highest degree- to total forgetting. Now we will open that freezer, take out its contents, and throw it out into a landfill. Then, however, comes the shock: what we take out is something completely different and much worse than that what was put inside in the first place. Time in people's minds simply worked and substances of rot and decay took their effect on the meat, even through the frost. Old wounds did not heal under totalitarian and eventually post-totalitarian regimes. Inside them, new and old pus has been collecting, and now it all quickly melts in the free air. A clean slate was once again shown to be an illusion — a dangerous illusion.

What was it, what was the "bloody meat"? Following the Great War (I will refer to it as such because at the time it was not yet known that it was only the first of the world wars) there were new, respectively old-new states: Czechoslovakia, Poland, and Hungary. Even the new Austria and the Kingdom of Serbs, Croats, and Slovenes, as well as Germany in somewhat diminished borders.

Czechoslovakia was brand new. On allegorically styled maps from the end of sixteen century, Europe was artificially captured in the form of a female figure and the Czechs were her heart. After the war, Czechoslovak statesmen felt a big responsibility due to this. Yet, it's possible they felt more of an opportunity than a responsibility. They did not mention the complete truth about the ethnic composition of the population of the state to the representatives of the winning states of the Treaty — that a third of the population was German. This was due to the fact that according to that, they would have had to be the second state-forming nation of the country. Negotiators at the Paris Peace Conference had reached almost the maximum limit and it was important not to show that the Czechs did not have the strength to govern such a diverse state.

They rather wanted to set an example, more than others. Beneš promised that we would be "something like Switzerland" in seven places of his memoranda, which he submitted to the Paris Peace Conference. He meant by this that we would be a state of national and religious tolerance, just like the Swiss. Even though the adjective was not yet in circulation at the time, he could have meant by this that above an ethnically varied, even most colorful state of nations and nationalities in Europe, we would be able to vault over to the higher floor of a political nation. Was it possible?

Czech historian Jan Rychlík, however, claims that creating a political nation from two or more nations has never been accomplished by anyone and that had someone done so, they would have received a Nobel Prize for it by now. He adds that if such states exist, then only because they have existed as such for at least several hundred years. He is thinking of Switzerland, which has been working on this for over seven hundred years. Creating a political nation from a freshly comprised state of ethnically and religiously diverse base of people is supposedly impossible. This is not to say that it should not be worked towards, but rather that it is not a task to be accomplished in only a number of election terms.

Postwar ratios were not created only according to how and where the war fronts finally stopped, although apparently mainly according to this criterion. However, they were also created from ideas, or rather slogans. Oddly enough, the creators of catchwords that were convenient for arranging post-war Europe, met in Paris and included the idealistic American democrat Wilson and the cynical Russian pragmatic-dictator Lenin—both of whom postulated as a catchword the right of all nations to self-determination. Lenin added, since he knew that this was merely propaganda and that matters wouldn't be settled with mere words, that it was "self-determination up to secession". And so both the Czech democrats and Czech communists (the ones with a catchword "without the October Revolution, had it not been for October 28, 1918") appealed to, if we are considering the merit of the creation of the independent state, two antipodes with an equally dysfunctional but still zealous catchword—that is to Woodrow Wilson and Vladimír Iljič Lenin.

The statesmen of two empires at the time badly advised smaller ethnic islands in the center of Europe, but also wrongly advised the winners in Europe. This resulted in the second act of the Great War. I would also add the Enlightenment German philosopher Herder to these two politicaly motivated advisors, as he had already one hundred fifty years prior inspired the thought in the minds of Germans and Slavs that a nation is made up of those who speak the same language. The triad of Herder—Wilson—Lenin seems far-fetched, but these three truly decisively stepped into our Central European destinies.

Wilson was then a decisive authority, upon whom our politicians in exile relied on the most. However, the noble principle, confirming the right of every nation to its own state, could not have worked even for a moment; nor did it work. A nation here in Central Europe is something different than in Western Europe. It is something natural, a tribe which one cannot choose. People are born into their nations. Wilson had never been in Europe before, i.e. not in Central Europe and even less so in the Balkans. Furthermore, he had no awareness of the principle of the Russian Matryoshka. He had no idea that inside the big doll was a smaller one, also in some kind of a costume, and that inside that one was yet another one! And once more in some kind of a different costume! Yet even then there isn't an end to the dolls! And all of them in some kind of costume! On Žitný island between two streams of the Danube, in the middle of the Hungarian minority in the South of the Slovak Republic, there are islands of Slovak minorities, but in that Slovakian village in the middle of the Hungarian neighborhood are certainly several buildings in which Hungarians live, and when there are more than 20% of them, they are bound to want to assert their national rights and assure that the Slovakian mayor speaks to them in Hungarian. And there are many other places like this in the center, east, and south of Europe.

Wilson was an idealist professor, deeply convinced that ideals work. Masaryk was in many respects similar to him, but he knew that ideals don't always work. Yet, he also did not mind sometimes pretending that he believed in them. When he signed the Pittsburgh Agreement at the end of May 1918 with the Slovaks, agreeing that they would have their own assembly in a shared state, the more sober Beneš did not add his signature. "You will not be able to fulfill that which with your signature you had promised", dared to oppose Masaryk's otherwise loyal and devoted student. All the while Beneš claimed that until the end of his life, he would not believe in the existence of a distinctive Slovak nation.

After years and decades, Beneš suffered from the fact that at the time, during negotiations regarding the borders of the state, he succumbed on the one hand to the idealists such as Wilson and on the other hand to vengeful victors. At first he refused to accept the northern borders of the new state, those of the Frýdland and Šluknov kind, andperhaps he did not even want the Cheb, Eggrensis kind, but he was told exactly the same thing that the Hungarians and Germans were told: those who lost in this war cannot gain anything, but rather, can only lose. They can never gain territory. In other words, the right to self-determination is only reserved for the winners. That was almost rather Lenin's conception, which of course means that this so-called right to self-determination was never a true right, but merely a phrase to sugar-coat revenge, especially that of the French. This is understandable, but in no way justifiable. It is worth noting that Beneš never publicly admitted to his formerly realistic attitude toward imposed maximum borders—only in the weeks prior to Munich, when he indicated that he had already then offered what was being asked of him by Henlein. He did not admit it because it would have been very unpopular at the time and Beneš was not only a statesman, but also a politician. The voters therefore lived under the illusion that one could and should want everything.

Even Masaryk wasn't as much a foolish idealist as he appeared to be. Even in 1924, he dared to write to Peroutka's weekly Presence a letter that he did not sign and in which he contemplated whether or not the southern borders of Slovakia should be reconsidered, by which he meant that the border should be pushed to the north, ceding land to Hungary. It was realistic, yet completely inappropriate. The president wanted to reduce the territory of his own state! Supposedly, it was prime minister Švehla who recognized and rebuked the author.

Wilson's ideals regarding Czechoslovakia did not even begin to work. German minorities around the borders of Bohemia, Silesia, and Moravia demanded the right to self-determination to their own little states based on Wilson's promises—provinces that intended immediately after to "determine themselves" as part of Austria. They claimed that the same way Czechs had the right to secede from Austria, they themselves have the right to secede from Czechoslovakia. It was immediately explained to them that what had not been mentioned was that the ideals of self-determination did not apply to the losers. This was a logical explanation, but had nothing to do with ideals. The logic needed to be supported by shooting at German civilians. A similar situation unfolded in Southern Slovakia.

This was then already the new Czechoslovakia, at war with the Hungarians and the Poles. Without the help of the French army and their generals, it would have likely not been possible to handle a war on two fronts. The Czechs even wanted the French army to fight a battle for their own new borders. Legions were still far away in easternmost Russia.

Never were disputes over the borders resolved in a manner that satisfied both sides. The worst part is that they were once again revived during a time when Czechoslovaks and Poles could and should have stood together against Hitler. Instead, the Czechs fought with the Poles once more, in 1938.

The beginning of the existence of independent states in this region did not promise peaceful coexistence or alliances: all states of the later Visegrad—Poland, Hungary, and Czechoslovakia—were in constant conflict with all their neighbors following the Great War! The first two due to far too great ambitions, the Czechs supposedly out of worry. Poland was, until the spring of 1921, in a latent or open war conflict with all of its neighbors. All brought up territorial claims with all others. Peace treaties were simply not successful. Could they ever have succeeded?

The linking of the idea of national rights to national self-determination by the idea that the winner gets the spoils created an explosive mix that initially deceived due to the fact that after the war, it was soaked with the blood of tens of millions of casualties. So thereby the philosopher Emanuel Rádl could already in the year 1927 (!) predict that a second Great War was awaiting Europe and that it would break out due to the circumstances in the Czechoslovakian Sudetenland. Rádl was the one who insisted that we finally start building a political nation, but he was almost all alone.

The precarious situation following the first war unfortunately did not change and rather lasted until the beginning of the second war: Czechoslovakia did not have any allies beyond its borders during critical times. Indeed, it did not even have a loyal population within its borders. It seems as if it didn't even make attempts to change anything about this state of being. Edvard Beneš relied on more generous concepts — on the construction of collective security, reinforced skillfully by a system of interdependent treaties with France, Great Britain, and the Soviet Union. Next to all of this, the issues with border disputes probably seemed petty- issues not only with Těšín, but more so with several little-known villages in Javorina and mountainous Spišsko, on the disputed border with Poland. These problems, however, might decide that Czechoslovakia would not stand against Hitler with the Poles, which could avert the war. I daresay that the other Great War perhaps might not have had to break out had the Czechs and the Poles stood side by side, and perhaps all it would have taken were several generous gestures regarding those villages on Spišsko. Yet, it would have had to be gestures from both sides and these gestures could not have been held off until the last minute. Beneš's confidence in the last days before Munich suggests that he had a kind of guilty conscience and therefore a rescue plan and it should have been regarding the relations with the Poles. At this time, however, it was already too late. Beneš tragically overestimated his own diplomatic abilities, and his cold chess-like approach to world diplomacy evidently did not take something like neighborly relations and simple, needless disputes between people over their garden fences into account.

Czechoslovakia was therefore throughout its entire inter-war existence surrounded by enemies and behaved accordingly in response, with the exception of unfortunately useless neighboring Romania. The enemies, however, saw it completely differently. In any case, a small agreement, called the Little Entente, was a military coalition for defense against the supposedly expansive Hungarians, who according to common judgement at the time caused the first World War. They had, of course, felt unjustly punished. The Czechs did not wish to include the Poles in the Treaty, despite the wishes of the French, because they seemed to be too close to the Hungarians.

This hostility was created and maintained at the onset by the impractical ideal that each nation had the right to have its own state. It was created from this ideal then sugar-coated on the maps of meeting halls in Versailles, Saint Germaine, and Trianon, but born however abroad and modified by the understandable worry and revenge of the winners. It is a paradox, and to this day instructive: the ideals were not invented in the minds of apolitical thinkers. They were communicated by the president of a democratic state that already had behind him a respectable stretch of road towards a political nation, toward a state of citizens, loyal to the constitution, the rule of law, the army, and the state symbols. Even this state was still missing a lot in its ideals and remains to this day. These were, however, not only impractical but also pernicious ideals for Europe, and particularly for her central and eastern parts: its consequences after the war resulted in legitimizing the expulsion of the Germans and even almost the Hungarians. Why do I say that this paradox is instructive to this day? It is because the USA has not yet abandoned its foolish attempt from time to time to spread its ideals in places where it instead causes disruption and catastrophe.

The Second World War and the subsequent occupation of large parts of Central Europe by the Soviet Empire petrified all of the old problems and created new ones. They were, of course, put away in the aforementioned freezer. Sooner or later, strategies of national communism were created and functioned in all countries of the Soviet Bloc, which did not bring us closer to Europe, although they gradually counterbalanced us from the superpower grip of Moscow. The worst of it was that public reflection of the Central European situation did not continue. Reflection of dissenters and exiles within, and even across nations, could in their participants give the impression that things were changing for the better. Today I do not think so. That which was changing was the growth of distances between involved members of exclusive debates of dissenters and exiles, and untouched by the public. For example, the Czech Republic today is not willing to invalidate a so-called amnesty law in post-war legislation absolving those who after the war carried out, in the words of the law, "just retribution". Progress in this direction is, for a quarter of a century, small.

I will return to the idea of a political nation. Was there hope? Many of us return to it not only as an ideal, but also as a practical guide. So where, other than in Switzerland, has it been fulfilled? Apparently also in the United States of America, but then we would have to abstract from racial issues. In multiethnic Canada? And what about the mass ethnocide of local Native Americans, Inuits, which is only in recent years coming to the surface? Recently, my Canadian friend told me about his childhood, showed me a little town on the map in the state of Alberta, and insisted upon the fact that he experienced there firsthand the same circumstances that were present in Alabama.

The French political nation? Yes, sure, but what preceded it? Rough, violent assimilation of Bretons, Aquitaines, Picards, the people of Gascony and of Provence, creating already a long time ago a political nation in France; therefore, the happy ones have no idea about the difference between the word state and the word nation. They merge them into one. This no longer quite applies to Corsica, where the local people do not always uphold this ideal, similarly to Catalans and Basques, who destroy the concept of a Spanish political nation, and it may be even that Scots do the same to the concept of a

British political nation. Belgium is being held together perhaps only by the glue of Brussels as the headquarters of the institutions of the European Union.

Or is then the viable way to a political nation only separation and secession? Are the Bohemians, Moravians, and Silesians a political nation, now alone without the Slovaks, Hungarians, Germans, and Rusyns? And, of course, even the Jews? Hardly, since we did not get to our current, so-called internal ethnic peace by overcoming national conflicts, but rather by mechanical, collective detachment. We had a blessing in disguise: the border with Slovakia was ancient and therefore non-conflictual, and compact minorities did not live on either territory of the now independent states. When the nations of former Yugoslavia were seceding, a lot of blood was spilled because the borders ran through strips along the borders and islands of minorities. People were ousted through mass expulsions and chunks of land were destroyed. This is certainly not a viable path.

That which was overcome only mechanically, with separation or assimilation, even perhaps without blood, lives on in the minds of the people, merely manifesting itself differently. For some things it is simply too late.

Hopefully that for which it is not too late and is rather instead high time is for the creation of bigger units — from states, not from nations in the Central European sense of the word. Nations are almost always being born, maintained, and internally reinforced through negative feelings. Identity, the obvious, unappreciated identity, always needs the Other, but needs it as an enemy, a threat. We cannot do anything about all of this.

There is therefore only a future in a strong supranational grouping, which with its mere existence and its daily functions relativizes the importance of borders and thus even the problem of minorities. It is for this reason that I was such a decisive supporter of the Euro-region after November 1989, foreshadowing the Schengen area. It would be worth taking into account how strong were the opponents of this pioneering experience in the Czech Republic.

Otherwise, of course, these larger units, perhaps including the EU, should pose only moderate, gradual goals for themselves. They may have maximal ambitions, but it will be better if they fulfill them very carefully and gradually. I would like to read in this context comparative studies of all possible attempts to create a commonwealth, personal union, federation, or confederation in Central Europe. Maybe such a study exists. Many such attempts have been made. I can simply recall Masaryk and Beneš under different circumstances, Milan Hodža even under more different ones, Coudenhove-Kalergi, and more. What did they all have in common? Correct instinct commanded them to attempt something that isn't a better, more just, or more accurate guidance of borders because that will never be accomplished. What does this otherwise insoluble problem with borders, and naturally also with minorities, relativize? It simply gradually reduces its urgency. Why did all the previous, traditional attempts have to fail? It would be useful to know.

I would say that Europe, the founding core of its Union, was not reasonably prudent nor modest, especially after 1989. It should have opened its gates to us Central Europeans only after we had come together, consolidated, say, like the Benelux countries. Integration was rushed: both deepening and enlargement almost at the same time, maybe even because behind all the haste were economic interests in new markets. The fundamental meaning of the Union is grounded in the gradual desensitization of old, unhealed wounds, minorities, and borders, and was and still is threatened today by this haste.

Today, under the impression of an influx of refugees and immigrants, as well as through the consequences of the financial sector of the economy, which has gotten out of hand, many intend to back out of achieved standards and abolish the gains made toward a Europe without borders. It is a dangerous state of mind, reviving old wounds. So what then?

What then, when in building political nations, states of citizens, there was initially too little time and now it is instead too late? In many places, there is nothing to build from when here in Central Europe we are merely the sum of purified islands of homogeneity. Yet surprisingly, the old wounds are once again beginning to resurface. In the medical field, this is called phantom pain—we feel the pain of part of the body, which isn't even there anymore. This is due to the fact that we are missing a common European consciousness, and moreover a Central European identity. This consciousness, this identity, cannot be conceived from the green table, nor in the workrooms of thinkers. The consciousness of something in common arises only from a common story, and a common story cannot lack the dramatic decision-making regarding what is more important and what is less important. What will we give preference to and over what? In other words, it cannot be done without sacrifices. Only the victim establishes the order of values because some values are exclusive, one is at the expense of another, and it is precisely this common alignment of values that is then his or her story, establishing his or her identity. Europeans are facing far too many problems at the same time, and thus, there will be increasingly more opportunities for victims. Yet, are we going to be at all willing to undertake any? To give something up that we have already achieved? In the name of maintaining the Union? Or in the name of upholding the area of free movement? Or in the name of achieved and ever-increasing prosperity?

I have always been shy to repeat the Patočka-Havel challenge to "live in the truth". Not that I would run in the face of truth, rather the opposite, actually. Yet, I simply don't know what the truth is, seeing as I, just like you, am still searching for it. Therefore, I have always felt closet to Solženicyn's more modest idea of not living in a lie because I sometimes dare to discover the lie. This is what we Central Europeans can do. We cannot and we do not desire to change or fix borders any longer. We do not know where the right ones belong, nor if they exist at all, but we can choose not to live a lie; to get rid of all possible illusions and lies, but to not fall victim to cynicism and despair; to return to the past, so that we can see more clearly, from places upon which we will agree, both in the present and hopefully even in the future. Yes, we are still conquering former firing sites, old mined fields, and rusted border barricades, but now not only so we can move on from them fighting, but so that we could use them to understand both the present and hopefully also the future together.

Moreover, if we are considering the unsurprising shortage of common heroes, we should make attempts to increase their familiarity. Rather than soldiers or resistance fighters, which we all usually have for ourselves, they will rather be thinkers, statesmen, politicians, and economists—those who discerned a common enemy and those who saw him not only beyond their borders, but also within them. They do not have to be renowned heroes. For our Czech team, I nominate our very own philosopher Emanuel Rádl and exile publicist Pavel Tigrid; for the Hungarians I dare suggest János Esterházy and István Bibó; for the Slovakians, Imrich Karvaš and perhaps even Milan Hodža come to mind; and for the Poles, Jerzy Giedroyc and Andrej Wajda. These and similar other lists can surely be created in greater quantity.

Epilogue

We Czechs, Slovaks, Poles, and Hungarians do not have a common hero, which is to be expected, but it seemed for a long time that we don't even have common enemies. We all had our own national enemies. This was, of course, a symptom of ideological and especially geopolitical blindness. Ethnic interests tend to be blind, selfish, and petty. They are preoccupied with border disputes over a few meters, a percentage, over the founding or denying of the rights of minorities.

In reality, we have had common enemies from the first years following the First World War. Our enemies were Hitler and Stalin. Maybe many saw it as such, but did not have enough strength to influence the states and nations of Central Europe to act accordingly.

Even for this reason, we observe the developing relations with Poles, Hungarians, Slovakians, certain Germans, and last but not least, even our relations with Putin's Russia with tension and sometimes uneasiness. Peripherally, we register shifts in the political optics of Austrians, understand that Serbs do not have problems with Russians, etc. We keep track of who is clearly committing to the Euro-Atlantic West.

A clean slate has, therefore, following the year of miracles in 1989, not arrived. Once again, monologues are being initiated and interests diverge. At least, however, we have stopped chasing such decisive slate, which I regard as progress; it is nevertheless important to have more of them, but smaller, down to earth, mobile. We do not negotiate new contracts or new borders at these tables, but everyone uses them to tell their story and others try to understand it, even though they will probably never make it their own. It is impossible. These tables are always needed. Even small ones: they form the now so-called small Visegrad. The governments of the four states may even pass each other, but the small Visegrad in the future, supporting cross-border activities and living off the Visegrad Fund, which after all connects thousands and thousands of people, especially the youth from our four states.

The table will therefore never be completely clean, but it will have to be larger in a sense so that it can include a larger part of Europe and encompass bigger stretches of time. Our European world will then be able to be more understandable at least in the sense that we will be able to predict and avoid further unnecessary conflicts.

I hope that even our presumably unending and wandering conference about our heroes and our enemies, and about what unites us, but also about what separates us, is attempting to achieve something similar, something like a solid slate, opened to the civil society, with a transparent agenda. The fact that it is already today aware that it will not one day be closed by a definitive court or resolution, but rather that it will continue wandering around the entire region, deserves both encouragement to persevere and wishes of good luck in acquiring both good subjects and good participants.

What Does It Take to Become a Hero: Perspectives of Cultural Sociology and Political Science

Pavlína Janebová[1], Dominik Želinský[2]
EUROPEUM Institute for European Policy

Abstract: The text offers an attempt to present theoretical perspectives of the disciplines of cultural sociology and political science on the phenomenon of national heroes. It lists and discusses some of the specific factors that are necessary for a person to become a political leader/hero. The crucial aspect of becoming a hero is the acceptance by one's followers, resulting from charisma, public performance and participation in the key rituals. The factors affecting one's ability to perform political leadership depend crucially on the external context, i.e. the character of political systems, potential states of cries etc.

According to its title, the present book aims to tackle on the issue of heroes in the region of Central Europe. Taking a look at the list of contributions, it is obvious, what does the term "hero" mean for the authors — and probably few readers would object against the historic personalities analysed in this book deserving the label, if only in their national contexts. The following text will offer an attempt at presenting specific factors that are necessary for a person to become a political leader or a hero in the eyes of her followers, using the resources offered by cultural sociology and political science.

Performing Heroism

How do ordinary people become political 'heroes'? What is the social situation that transforms individual agent into a walking and talking

---

1   E-mail: janebova@mail.muni.cz.
2   E-mail: zelinskyd@gmail.com.

symbol, a "personification of community"[3] that functions as a crucial element in the identity of her followers?

In his analysis of Hitler's success[4], the German psychoanalyst Wilhelm Reich contended that at the basis of leaders success is a specific state of what he called 'sex-economy'. The sex-economy, according to Reich, is the structural interconnection of the systems of gender relations (e.g. kinship system) and economic production. To understand Hitler's emergence as a leader of the German nation — and a hero still pertinent to some collectives today — for Reich it seemed enough to know the social situation and state of sexual frustration of their audience. And indeed, there are certain conditions that perhaps engender significant heroic personas more often than others. These are often what Habermas termed 'crisis of legitimation'[5], the moments when old structures are destabilized and a new order has to be established. This was undoubtedly so after 1918 when the Austro-Hungarian empire lost its position as a legitimate state and fell apart into national projects, producing several 'heroes' — fathers of nations — for instance Józef Piłsudski and Tomáš Garrigue Masaryk. Similar situation took place seven decades later when in 1989 Communist regimes fell, leaving the new east-European democracies with heroes like Lech Wałęsa and Václav Havel.

Yet, a 'hero' cannot be suasively reduced to a contingent personality surfacing in the public discourse due to a momentary people's propensity for being led. Heroes are charismatic personalities[6] because they articulate, through meaningfully concocted chains of symbols, crucial cultural content with which the audience can identify — they perform. According to J. C. Alexander, performance is a social

---

3   Voegelin, E. *Modernity without Restraint: The Political Religions; The New Science of Politics; And Science, Politics and Gnosticism.* London: The University of Missouri Press, 2000, p. 54.
4   Reich, W. *The Mass Psychology of Fascism.* New York: Orgone Institute Press, 1980.
5   Habermas, J. *The Legitimation Crisis.* Cambridge: Polity, 1992.
6   For theory of charisma see Weber, M. *Economy and Society: An Outline of Interpretive Sociology.* Berkeley & Los Angeles: University of California Press, 1978, pp. 1111–1156.

process through which agents display meaning of their social situation; a meaning they want others to believe as true[7]. What sets political heroes apart from other performers is that their actions, gestures and speeches aim at externalizing not only their own social situation, but a situation of whole collective. To become heroes, heroes symbolically — and performatively — devise what Benedict Anderson called 'imagined communities'[8], discursive constructions that their audiences can relate to and utilize as functional elements of their social identity. Theodor Herzl spoke of Zion, Tomáš Masaryk of Czechoslovak nation and Adolf Hitler of German Volk. Of course, not all performances are successful. As Alexander argues, there must be a mutual understanding between the performer and her audience. Symbolic content she articulates must be congruent with the audience's systems of 'background symbolic representation' — she must articulate ideas that do not significantly diverge from the cultural patterns and codes her audience lives by. And if so, she must adequately justify it.

Still, political heroes are radical. They symbolically distinguish themselves from their rivals. An apt perspective was recently developed by Patrick Baert[9] in his 'positioning' theory. According to Baert, public intellectuals performatively seek a position in the discourse — they distance themselves from particular authors or thought systems, and approximate themselves to others, with each speech, paper or book. Said with Baert, every 'intervention situates locates the author(s) (…) within (…) a broader socio-political (…) arena (…) while also situating other(s) (…), possibly depicting them as allies (…), predecessors (…) or opponents.'[10] The same is true of political heroes who often

---

7   Alexander, J. C. 'Cultural Pragmatics: Social Performance between Ritual and Strategy' in Alexander, J. C., Giesen, B., Mast, J. L. (eds.) *Social Performance: Symbolic Action, Cultural Pragmatics and Ritual.* New York: Cambridge University Press, 2006, p. 32.
8   Anderson, B. *Imagined Communities: Reflections on the Origin and Spread of Nationalism.* London & New York: Verso, 2006.
9   See Baert, P. *The Existentialist Moment: The Rise of Sartre as a Public Intellectual.* Cambridge: Polity, 2015.
10 Ibid., p. 166.

are themselves public intellectuals of sorts. What is different is that those who aspire to acquire a status of a hero must distinguish themselves by articulating novel or radical ideas—usually to advocate for new political and social system, or at least forcefully opposing the existent order.

As Alexander highlights, however, the symbolic content of performance is not the only component that participates in creation of its meaning. Performances are complex nexuses that encompass also other elements—social power, material and spatial context (or mise-en-scène), the means of symbolic production[11]. These elements have to be in balance with the symbolic content of the performer's action and the audience's system of background representation. Importantly, they usually reach the most effective equilibrium during public rituals.

It is perhaps not too much off the mark to say that it is through rituals that political heroes are made in modern societies. Be it marches (like those on Rome, Munich or Washington), or mass celebrations of regime, rituals are, as conceptualized by the late Émile Durkheim[12] powerful integrative and cohesive moments through which social agents retain their sense of belonging to a community. During rituals, people experience mutual corporeal proximity, unity and a sense of shared focus on a common symbolic centre. They feel as parts of a larger body. Religious person is stronger[13], because, as phrased by Randall Collins, she is charged through his participation in the ritual[14].

Importantly, rituals are events when the social structure is demonstrated visibly and tangibly—they manifest the structure of power in society[15]. In rituals, the spatial and symbolical organisation

---

11 Alexander, J.C., 2006.
12 Durkheim, É. *The Elementary Forms of Religious Life*. New York: The Free Press, 1995.
13 Ibid., p. 430.
14 Collins, R. *Interaction Ritual Chains*. Princeton & Oxford: Princeton University Press, 2004.
15 Apart from Collins, see Lukes, S. 'Political Ritual and Social Integration' *Sociology* 9, 1975, pp. 289-308.

makes hierarchy visible. But rituals are also the effervescent moments in the course of which new meaning are attributed[16]. Agents can acquire a new meaning – and become heroes. An apt example of attaining such position is the ritual of army medal awarding. Those deemed worthy are selected from the mass of laymen and receive, from hands of an authority, a sign meant to denote their heroic qualities. Without symbolic recognition of one's merit in ritual context, even a microscopic one, there would be no heroes.

Major public rituals are, moreover, fecund ground for documentation – both visual and textual. Such data (photographs, footage, or articles) can petrify the ephemeral meaning of ritual, originally accessible only to the relatively limited number of direct participants. The process of dissemination of information and meaning negotiation is crucial for heroes to become recognized on a broader scale. Their discursive image as leaders and heroic interpretation of their acts must be perpetuated through public media to ensure that the maximum of potential receivers will be exposed to the meaning. Undoubtedly, educational system is a priceless instrument in construction of political heroes. The meaning of personalities can be inculcated through textbooks, instruction and also other, less apparent means such as photographs, prayers or vows.

This process of ex post discursive construction is a key element in creation of a 'hero' because it enables the personality, limited by a span of one life, to have a lasting impact on the society. Heroes, in the end, become iconic signs, characteristic by strong surplus of meaning[17]. Through textbooks and historiography they enter the realm of community's myths and key narratives. Normative re-interpretation is not uncommon. Heroes might later end up as villains – like the president of Slovak war-time state, Jozef Tiso.

---

16   Durkheim, ibid. 217–218.
17   See Ricoeur, P. *Interpretation Theory: Discourse and The Surplus of Meaning*. Fort Worth: The Texas Christian University Press, 1976.

To become a political or national hero is not an easy task. Rather, it is a complex social process cannot be reduced to a one element. Heroes tend to appear in difficult times, when the erstwhile social and political authorities lose their legitimacy. However, to rise to the position of a hero, or a leader, is not contingent and depends crucially on abilities of the individual. Above all, it is necessary to perform publicly — to communicate radical cultural content that allows the members audience to identify themselves as a collective. Performances are usually delivered in a ritual context that, if successful, contributes to the feeling of unity and symbolically as well as spatially distinguishes the performing leader from the crowd. And lastly, the figure of a hero must undergo processes of meaning negotiation and fixation that result in attribution of a stable meaning (such as a place in community's history) and a lasting effect on its future.

Leaders and heroes

Speaking about politics, the concept of "heroism", presented in the previous part of this chapter, comes close to the concept of political leadership. Alistair Cole[18] provides a list of personal characteristics that are considered crucial for a person to be able to become a political leader and possibly a (national) hero. According to Cole, a potential leader should of course have a high level of political and communication skill, together with political[19] intelligence, clarity of goals, capacity for mobilization and personal attributes (e.g. courage). It seems

---

18 Cole, A. 'Studying Political Leadership: The Case of François Mitterrand', *Political Studies*, XLII, 1994, pp. 453–468.
19 Interestingly enough, intelligence as measured by the IQ level does not seem to be considered the most crucial here. Rhodes and t'Hart support their argument by pointing out that the popularity of US presidents does not correlate with their intellectual capacity, giving the example of R. Reagan, one of the most highly-rated people in this function, who relied rather on his emotional intelligence (Rhodes, R. A. W., t' Hart, P. 'Puzzles of Political Leadership', in Rhodes, R. A. W., t'Hart, P. (eds.) *The Oxford Handbook of Political Leadership*. Oxford: Oxford University Press, 2014, pp. 1–27.).

reasonable to assume that the capacity for mobilization is closely related to the personal attributes, one of them certainly being the above mentioned charisma.

James MacGregor Burns distinguishes between two types of political leaders—the *transactional* and the *transformational* leaders [20]. While the transactional leader's interaction with her followers is of a rather "routine and patterned manner" and responds to their needs and requirements on ordinary basis, the transformational leader's activity and interaction with her followers has the ability to change them and "lift both the leader and followers to a new plane of action". It is clear that it is especially the latter category that corresponds to the notion of a "hero", even more when it comes to heroes spoken about in this book who in their time certainly proved an exceptional ability to inspire, persuade and mobilize followers.

Indeed, in the region of Central Europe, it were national political leaders who, while heroes (although not always unreservedly) for their own nations, became villains for the other—take the example of E. Beneš, M. Horthy or J. Piłsudski. In the turbulent times of the first half of 20th century, when empires fell apart and new states emerged from their ruins, and at the end of 80s, when the communist systems were crashing, the role of national political leaders became ever more crucial. Political leaders who get subjected to analyses in this volume played their heroic roles during the times of crises and can for sure be categorized as "transformational". States of emergencies (in a broader sense, i.e. not as used in the area of public law) obviously have implications for political process and the role of the leadership. According to András Körösényi, political opportunities for political leadership are different at times of crises and states of emergency, as opposed to states of "normalcy"[21]. Emergencies result in political instability, with the position of incumbent governments and political representations

---

20 Burns, J. M. *Leadership*. New York: Harper and Row, 1978.
21 Körösényi, A. 'The Impact of Crises and States of Emergency on Political Leadership', Paper presented at the 7th ECPR General Conference, Section on *Elites and Transatlantic Crisis*, Bordeaux, 4–7 September 2013, pp. 5–31.

deteriorating. The feeling of uncertainty among citizens will increase a desire for strong leaders, thus making it easier for a new person/people to acquire political positions and play the role of a hero. It applies especially to the context of crises that not all the elected representatives are leaders (let alone heroes) and not all the leaders necessarily have to be elected representatives. It is however worth to mention that, especially in the context of Central European countries, those personalities who proved to be true leaders in extraordinary times, became democratically elected "institutionalized" leaders afterwards — and it is the same people we tend to label as national heroes: for example V. Havel, L. Wałęsa or L. Sólyom.

Leaders and Democracy

Regarding the relation between democracy and leadership, there are two main interpretations of democratic political process in relation to leadership. The "classical" view[22] (in Schumpeter's terms) presents democracy as a bottom-up process, i.e. ensuring that public policies are based entirely on the will of the people, with public office holders being only delegates and executives of the popular will and having no space left for asserting their own political visions. The concept of "leader democracy" on the other hand assumes that policy programs originate on the side of aspiring politicians rather than on the side of citizens. The premise of leader democracy is that instead of the public policies being based on issue-preferences of rational and autonomous citizens, the citizens merely participate in the *selection of leaders*. In the political competitions, the prospective leaders try to win the support of citizens by means they have at their disposal — their image, charisma, ideological appeal, etc. [23] The concept of leader democracy thus assumes that the role of the leader is not limited to the states of crises or emergencies but instead we can conclude that a

---

22 Schumpeter, A. J. *Capitalism, Socialism and Democracy*. New York: Harper & Row, 1942.
23 Körösényi, A. 'Political Leadership: Between Guardianship and Classical Democracy', For the ECPR Workshop on *„Political Leadership: a Missing Element in Democratic Theory'*, Helsinki, 7–12 May 2007.

presence of a leader in the political system is an integral part of democracy itself.

It would however not be accurate to assume that exclusively those can become great leaders and heroes, who acquire their position in the hierarchy through "free and fair" democratic election process. As Roderick A. W. Rhodes and Paul T Hart point out, it is possible to find a lot of historical examples of "great" leaders who did not always (if at all) use democratic means to achieve their goals. Adopting an explicitly normative perspective, it is possible to draw a distinction between leaders who, in interaction with their followers and their exercise of power, use legitimate methods that are in accordance with democracy and the rule of law on one hand and leaders who use force or manipulation on the other[24]. And taking a look back in history, it is not difficult to notice that some of the people we tend to consider the biggest political leaders—Napoleon, Stalin or Hitler—fall precisely in the latter category. Furthermore, not only that a political leader does not necessarily have to be democratically elected. It is not even necessary for her to hold an institutionalized function. According to Jean Blondel[25], it is necessary to distinguish between formal institutional hierarchies and the exercise of real (i.e. behavioural) leadership, because a real leader of a constituted organization may well be someone who does not occupy a formal position in it.

Conclusion

Based on the above mentioned, it is apparent that some common points can be identified in the sociology and political science perspective on the issue of political heroism/leadership. What does the integration of the perspectives possibly bring to the study of the subject? When assessing the evolution of a personality into a hero, we need to consider various

---

24 Rhodes, t'Hart 2014.
25 Blondel, J. *Political Leadership*. London: Sage, 1987, p. 13; see also Rhodes, R. A. W., t' Hart, P. 'Puzzles of Political Leadership', in Rhodes, R. A. W., t'Hart, P. (eds.) *The Oxford Handbook of Political Leadership*. Oxford: Oxford University Press, 2014, pp. 1–27.

dimensions, on both individual (agent) and external (structure) level. Becoming a hero depends crucially not only on one personal features but also on the relation she can establish with her audience and last but not least on the momentous *demand* for leadership on the side of the people. Furthermore, this fact can then bring some valuable insights for the study of the emergence of leader in different political systems and considering specific historical conditions. Are there some common individual features shared by political leaders of 1920s and 1980s? How does the performance of heroes, based on their individual features, change through time and in different societal and political settings? Embarking upon both of the perspectives while studying the emergence and performance of political heroes can be particularly beneficial for example in the research of legitimacy of political leadership and its relation to democracy.

The Legacy of Central Europe 1918-1945

Milan Hauner[1]
University of Wisconsin-Madison

Abstract: The text examines the phenomena of Central Europe from various points of view and emphasizing several contextual factors affecting the historical position and development of this region in the history of the whole continent. It is of key importance to assess the role of Germany and Russia, especially during and after the WW2. The chapter concludes on a rather gloomy note, claiming that the consequences the WW2 and holocaust had for the region, followed by forty years of Soviet occupation, are immense and tragic.

Central Europe from Traum to Trauma and back

Does Central Europe (*Mitteleuropa*) still exist? Meaning Central Europe, as a contemporary experience and a concept for the future? This question has been repeatedly asked by many contemporary writers and answered with skeptical nostalgia, if not outright repudiation (Timothy Garton Ash, Jiří Gruša, Tony Judt, György Konrád, Milan Kundera, Adam Michnik, Czesław Miłosz, etc.) We are stuck here with the ideologically heavily overloaded term *Mitteleuropa*, which on the one hand can be identified with the notorious eastward expansionism (*Drang nach Osten*), and on the other also with the cultural richness of Austro-Hungarian heritage. Its more accurate geographical designation is East-Central Europe, *Ostmitteleuropa*, i.e. that of the "other Europe," which after the Second World War and the ensuing Cold War became the western buffer of the Soviet Eurasian empire. We cannot, however, speculate over the term "Central Europe" before defining its position between East and West within the relevant time frame. This could be carried out jointly by historians and geographers.

There is a wide range of possibilities on how to interpret the phenomenon of Central Europe. Some authors have dwelled on cultural rather than political geography in trying to rediscover the lost

---

1 E-mail: mhauner@wisc.edu.

Traumlandschaft Mitteleuropa,[2] which would overcome the East-West bloc mentality that characterized Europe during the Cold War. This nostalgic trend of the idealized but defunct *k.u.k.* monarchy was inspired in the 1970s by an Italian *Movimento Mitteleuropeo*, headed by Claudio Magris. In the 1980s, however, the dream (*Traum*) turned quickly into *Trauma*. While images of a bygone cultural landscape from Czernowitz to Trieste began to fill the agendas of international conferences, Milan Kundera and György Konrád, to name the most audible East European voices, repeatedly accused the West of abandoning Central Europe to sovietization.[3] During the past two decades, several wake-up calls have reminded us that the nostalgic coffee houses of the Habsburg monarchy lay too close to or even astride of the ideological fault line cutting across Central Europe between the Western (Catholic & Protestant) and Eastern (Orthodox and Islam) civilizations, which produced another bloodbath when Yugoslavia fell apart.[4] For my part, I consider which geo-politico-historical framework is best suitable for investigating and explaining the fate of *Mitteleuropa* in what Eric Hobsbawm would call the Age of Extremes.[5]

The implosion of Russian Communism and German unification opened radically new perspectives. The Russian withdrawal from Eastern Europe was paralleled by the eastward shift of Germany's capital from Bonn to Berlin, which raised fears in some quarters of the revival of Germany's hegemonic intentions. The short-lived "Pentagonal," launched in 1990 by Italy, may have been a reaction to that. It

---

2 Lendl, E. *Die mitteleuropäische Kulturlandschaft im Umbruch der Gegenwart*. Marburg: Elwert, 1951; Burmeister, H.-P. (ed.) *Mitteleuropa, Traum oder Trauma*. Bremen: Temmen, 1988.

3 Kundera, M. 'The Tragedy of Central Europe', *The New York Review of Books*, 26 April, 1984, pp. 33–38; Konrád, G. *Antipolitik. Mitteleuropäische Meditationen*. Frankfurt: Suhrkamp, 1985; Ash, T.G. 'Does Central Europe Exist?', *The New York Review of Books*, 9 October 1986, p. 46.; Jaworski, R. 'Die aktuelle Mitteleuropadiskussion in historischer Perspektive', *Historische Zeitschrift*, No.247, 1987, pp. 529–550.

4 Huntington, S. P. 'The Clash of Civilizations?', *Foreign Affairs*, Summer 1993, pp. 22–49; and *The Clash of Civilizations and the Remaking of World Order*. New York: Simon and Schuster, 1996.

5 Hobsbawm, E. *The Age of Extremes*. London: Michael Joseph Publs., 1994.

was an attempt to revitalize the interwar experiments with Danubian federation, consisting of the former regions of the Habsburg empire plus Romania, from which Germany was to be excluded. Even Pentagonal's enlargement by Poland, to become a "Hexagonal," did not prevent this experimental alliance from vanishing within a year. Its core survives in the *Visegrád* group of four East European countries, Czech Republic, Hungary, Poland and Slovakia, which could appear somewhat anachronistic given the prevalent tendency of these countries to integrate within the larger structures of the EU, in which Germany had already acquired a dominant economic and financial position.[6] Nevertheless, Visegrád is the last remnant of a non-German alliance of countries in Central Europe, surviving since 1991. Renamed CEFTA (Central European Free Trade Agreement), the group lacks the votes to block EU decisions, but it can constitute a serious nuisance factor, as has occurred in the ongoing flight of refugees from the Middle East to Central Europe.

Germany? But where is it situated? I don't know how to find this country. Where the scholarly starts, the political ends.[7]

To understand what Central Europe is before defining its relations with East and West, one must delineate the position of Germany properly, as the biggest country in the middle of Europe, and one with a turbulent history. Schiller's quote has been frequently used to demonstrate that some two hundred years ago, Germany as a political entity did not yet exist. Only two elements then held Germany and Central Europe together. These were culture rather than the political unit of a state and the 'Imperial Idea', derived from the legacy of the Roman Empire in combination with the medieval idea of universal Christendom. This legacy was going to be radically revised in the

---

6   Hauner, M. 'Mitteleuropa' in *Encyclopedia of Contemporary German Culture*. London: Routledge, 1998.
7   "Deutschland? Aber wo liegt es? Ich weiss das Land nicht zu finden. Wo das gelehrte beginnt, hört das politische auf." (Schiller, F., von Goethe, J. W. *Xenien*. Leipzig: Weber, 1852.)

course of the 19th and 20th centuries with the arrival of ethnic nationalism. However, it was still widely understood that 'Germany' represented a geographic entity in the centre of Europe whose western boundary had been well delineated since Roman times as running along the Rhine, in contrast to the eastern boundary, which remained fluid.

The publication, in 1915, of Friedrich Naumann's book *Mitteleuropa* did not introduce the term for the first time. An argument in favour of creating an economic bloc in Central Europe, stretching from the Netherlands all the way to Bulgaria, centered on the political axis of Berlin and Vienna, was already developed in the 1903 book of Josef Partsch.[8] In reality, attempts to define *Mitteleuropa* preceded Naumann's book by a good one hundred years. They appeared about the same time as the definitions of 'Greater Germany'. Thus, since the French Revolution the two terms, *Mitteleuropa* and *Grossdeutschland,* had become inseparable.

Today, Central Europe finds itself at the crossroads of three extraordinary processes. The gradual progression of European integration, which among the original six EEC members (1958) included a portion of Germany then known as the Federal Republic. By 2013 the enlarged European Union (EU) reached 28 member states, thereby bringing Eastern and Western Europe together under one flag. The precipitated unification of Germany after 1989 was a second important event. Finally, a third event was the disintegration of the Soviet Eurasian empire since 1991. All three events brought Central Europe together under one roof politically. The debate has now shifted to the next stage about where Eastern Europe starts and ends, how much of it can be called Central Europe or *Mitteleuropa*. Can, for instance, Ukraine belong to Eastern Europe? How much of it? The de-

---

8   Naumann F. *Mitteleuropa*. Berlin: Georg Reimer, 1915. Also Partsch, J. *Central Europe*. New York: D. Appleton, 1903; and *Mitteleuropa*. Gotha: J. Perthes, 1904; Meyer, H.C. *Mitteleuropa in German Thought and Action*. The Hague: M. Nijhoff, 1955, p. 246.

bate is not an entirely academic one. It is not merely a question of geography. It is also a question of ideology, of our beliefs. Where do we belong? With which history, language, territory, do we identify ourselves? In his epigram Schiller asked two fundamental questions: *What* and *where* is Germany? These two questions contain, in a nutshell, the so-called German Problem, to which Europe has tried to find an answer during the last two hundred years. [9]

The terms *Mitteleuropa* and *Grossdeutschland,* emerged shortly after the French Revolution and have since then become inseparable. The German War of Liberation 1813-14 fused geography with ideology. The French model of the *Grande Nation*, unified by one language and territory, inspired many German intellectuals who were mesmerized by the vision of a homogeneous German nation-state, reaching, according to the poet Ernst Moritz Arndt, "as far as the German tongue can be heard" (*Vaterlandslied*, 1813). The Prussian reformer Karl vom Stein offered in 1813 a geopolitical concept in which *Grossdeutschland* merged with *Mitteleuropa* into one vast space stretched between France and Russia.

If the entire space between France and Russia was to be filled out with a single superstate, later called *Grossdeutschland*, what should happen with those many non-German nations and countries left in between? What should happen, in the first place, with the multi-ethnic Austrian Empire? On the other hand, could at least Germany's natural borders be delineated in the physical sense? This was the job of geographers. One of them, August Zeune, delimitated Germany's natural 'ancient borders' (*Urgrenzen*) for the entire space between the Alps, the North and Baltic Seas, and the rivers Rhine and Oder. Zeune used the term *Mitteleuropa* for the larger topographic space that stretched from the Atlantic coast all the way to the Black Sea.[10]

---

9   See Calleo, D. *The German Problem Reconsidered: Germany and the World Order, 1870 to the Present.* Cambridge: Cambridge University Press, 1978; Verheyen, D., Soe, C. (eds.) *The Germans and Their Neighbors.* Boulder: Westview, 1993.

10 Zeune, A. *Gea–Versuch einer wissenschaftlichen Erdbeschreibung.* Berlin: Wittich, 1808, quoted in Schultz, H.-D. 'Deutschlands "natürliche" Grenzen', *Geschichte und Gesellschaft,* No. 15, 1989, pp. 248–281.

Geographically *Mitteleuropa* covers the Central European plain, stretching from the Rhine to the mouth of the Danube, and from the Baltic to the Adriatic. Politically, *Mitteleuropa* is inseparable from the key problem of European history of the 19th century, the German Question, i.e. the formation of an unitary German State through its political struggle between Prussia on the one hand, Austria and France on the other, until the victory of Bismarck and the era of German *Weltpolitik*, including the two world wars, interpreted as the German drive for world dominion (*Weltherrschaft*), and their aftermath (the occupation and partition of Germany, the liquidation of Prussia as a state, the reunification of two German States until today).[11]

The Great War of 1914–18

The Great War of 1914–18 brought about a decisive turn in the conceptualization of *Mitteleuropa*. Epitomized in the publication of Friedrich Naumann, *Mitteleuropa* (1915), which advocated a voluntary fusion of the East-Central European nations under German leadership into a loose confederation (*Staatenbund Mitteleuropa*), which was to extend along the Berlin-Vienna-Constantinople-Baghdad axis as far as the Black Sea and Asia Minor. In fact, the argument about creating a united economic bloc, stretching from the Netherlands all the way to Bulgaria, had already been developed in a 1903 book by Joseph Partsch. Other Austrian and German geographers followed suit, including Albrecht Penck, Hugo Hassinger, and the Swede Rudolf Kjellén, the author of the nascent discipline of *Geopolitik*.[12]

Naumann's *Mitteleuropa* was meant to be directed by Germany and Austria-Hungary as equal partners, though the Germans obviously regarded themselves as "more equal" than anyone else. The design caused alarm among the Slavic peoples, whose leaders found in the *Mitteleuropa* scheme the confirmation of their fears that German

---

11 Excellent survey in Geiss, I. *Die deutsche Frage 1806–1990*. Mannheim: BI Taschenbuch, 1992.
12 Partsch (1903). Meyer (1955) remains the best critical survey on *Mitteleuropa*.

imperialism had started the war in order to subjugate the Slavs and to rule over the vast spaces between Berlin and Baghdad. In order to counterattack German *Mitteleuropa,* professor R. W. Seton-Watson from London and the Czech exile leader T. G. Masaryk, launched in England the periodical *New Europe,* in which they championed the independence of Europe's small nations, located primarily between Finland and Greece.[13] However, *Mitteleuropa* was wrecked not by Allied propaganda from Paris or London, but from within by the militarist clique and the ideologues of Pan-Germanism. The victorious generals Hindenburg and Ludendorff held more aggressive views about the future of East-Central Europe than the liberal politician F. Naumann. From the conquered territories in the East, consisting of Lithuania, Courland and several large chunks of Poland, they carved out their own mini *Lebensraum,* known as *Ober-Ost*.[14] Eventually, it was to embrace the Ukraine and the Black Sea region and would inspire so profoundly and decisively Adolf Hitler, then serving in the German army in the West. Their vision seemed to be partially fulfilled in March 1918 when Germany forced the Bolshevik government to sign the Brest-Litovsk Peace Treaty.[15]

Even after the publication of Naumann's bestseller, the benefits deriving from this utopian Central European "Common Market" were still mere talk, since an effective economic coordination with Austria-Hungary, Bulgaria and Turkey in the middle of the war remained wishful thinking. True, many Germans and Austrians welcomed the idea as a device to prop up Germanic influence[16] — despite Naumann's

---

13 Hanak, H. 'The New Europe, 1916-20', *The Slavonic Review,* Vol. 39, 1960/61, pp. 368-399.
14 The term *Lebensraum* was first introduced in 1901 by Friedrich Ratzel (1844-1904). Smith, W. D. *The Ideological Origins of Nazi Imperialism.* New York: Oxford University Press, 1986. On *Ober-Ost* see Meyer 1955, p. 255.
15 Lange, K. 'Der Terminus 'Lebensraum' in Hitlers 'Mein Kampf', *Vierteljahrshefte für Zeitgeschichte,* Vol. 13, 1965, pp. 426-437.
16 Especially Ernst Jäckh and the hyperactive Paul Rohrbach in the periodical *Das größere Deutschland,* carried the notion of *Mitteleuropa* far beyond Naumann's original intention. These journalists, however, were not Pan-Germans. See Meyer 1955, p. 235; also Mommsen, W. J. 'Die Mitteleuropaidee und -Planungen im

constant warnings that all East Europeans, even those without nation-states, must be treated as equals. The East European collaboration was vital and Naumann appeared to be moderately successful in initiating dialogues with social democrats from among the Austrian allies (Karl Renner, Bohumír Šmeral, Wilhelm Feldman).[17] Only the Hungarians (e.g., Oskar Jászi) would collaborate; the Czechs temporised. Renner, having been attacked by fellow socialists as "Social Imperialist," was chiefly responsible for keeping the socialist vision of *Mitteleuropa* alive.[18] Because — with the exception of a few Czech and Slovak politicians — the attitude of the Austrian Slavs was overwhelmingly negative to the *Mitteleuropa* concept, Naumann had to concentrate on winning over the Poles, since they held the key position. Throughout 1917, the Poles (e.g. W. Feldman) remained indecisive. When the peace terms of Brest-Litovsk had been revealed, the Poles flatly refused. Thus, the Polish veto put the final seal on Naumann's *Mitteleuropa*.[19]

Mitteleuropa between the Wars: German and non-German plans

Certain historians and political thinkers prefer to contemplate the entire era of the two World Wars, 1914-1945, as another *European Thirty-Year War* or *European Civil War* of thirty of maybe even of fifty years' length. [20] If *Mitteleuropa* should remain the focus of our analysis, then

---

Deutschen Reich vor und während des Ersten Weltkrieges' in Plaschka R. G. (ed.) *Mitteleuropa-Konzeptionen in der Ersten Hälfte des 20. Jahrhunderts*. Vienna: Verlag der österreichischen Akademie der Wissenschaften, 1995, pp. 3-24.

17 Plaschka (1995, pp. 25-150), especially articles by J. Kořalka and I. Diószegi. Apart from the social democrat Šmeral, Naumann met other Czech politicians: Jaroslav Goll, Zdeněk Tobolka, Karel Mattuš and František Udržal. Naumann also met the Slovak politician Milan Hodža. See Renner, K. '*Deutschland, Österreich und die Völker des Ostens*'. Berlin: Verlag für Sozialwissenschaft, 1922.

18 Meyer 1955, pp. 165-166; Stirk 1994, pp. 9-10.

19 For Naumann's own despair and admission of failure, see his pamphlet, Naumann, F. *Was wird aus Polen?* Berlin: Georg Reimer Vlg., 1917. It had been held up by censorship for over two months. See Meyer 1955, pp. 269-71.

20 E.g. Nolte, E. *Der europäische Bürgerkrieg 1917-1945. Nationalsozialismus und Bolschewismus*. Berlin: Herbig, F. A., 1987. See also Hobsbawm 1994. In 1993 Prof. Hobsbawm told students of the Central Euopean University in Budapest: "In my

we cannot escape the observation that it was the First World War that left such lasting changes upon the region and its inhabitants and that the coming of the second "Great War" must be related to it, especially as it became obvious that the roots of Adolf Hitler's radical programme lay there too.[21]

What happened to the *Mitteleuropa* concept during the interval between the two devastating catastrophes? In contrast to the period of the First World War, when the German initiative in conceptualizing *Mitteleuropa* was challenged by the ideologues of "small nations," there is no real juxtaposition between the two camps during the interwar period. Each group, i.e. the "German" on the one hand, and the "Non-German" on the other, seemed to operate in deliberate isolation without referring to the other. The immediate reason for this conceptual chaos was the break-up of the four historical empires in the region, with Germany as the leading military and economic power that was no longer present. Fearing the real possibility of Germany forming a post-war alliance with Russia, Sir Halford Mackinder, the father of modern geopolitics, suggested in 1919 that "Eastern Europe" (which equalled *Mitteleuropa*), instead of Russian Central Asia, should become the new pivot of the dual continent of Eurasia.[22]

In fact, a number of counter-schemes to the German *Mitteleuropa* project had emerged already during the war. They were characterized by the absence of Germany in the Central European scheme. In 1918 for example, the Romanian Premier Take Ionescu proposed the creation of an eighty-million-strong Central European confederation,

---

own lifetime every country in your part of Europe has been overrun by war, conquered, occupied, liberated, and reoccupied. Only six of the 23 states which now fill the map between Trieste and the Urals were in existence at the time of my birth [*1917], or would have been if they had not been occupied by some army..." (Hobsbawm, E. 'The new threat to history', *The New York Review of Books*: December 16, 1993, p. 62).

21   Hillgruber, A. *Germany and the Two World Wars*. Cambridge: Harvard U.P, 1987, p. 41.
22   Mackinder, H. *The Democratic Ideals and Reality*. New York: H. Holt and company, 1919; see also Hauner, M. *What is Asia to us? Russia's Asian Heartland Yesterday and Today*. London: Unwin & Hyman, 1990, p. 141.

formed by all the states situated between Germany and Russia. Thomas G. Masaryk, the founder of Czechoslovakia, developed similar ideas on behalf of the "small nations" located between Germany and Russia. In October 1918, while he was still in the United States, he hurriedly convened a conference of East European delegates to Philadelphia in order to proclaim the "Democratic Mid-European Union," which was to replace the German *Mitteleuropa*. Within two weeks of the armistice, the Polish and Yugoslav delegations walked out, unable to reach an agreement with the rest of the negotiators. By Christmas, the "Mid-European Union" was dead.[23] As he was sailing to Europe, Masaryk carried with him the manuscript of a book entitled *New Europe*, which he had composed as a response to the German *Mitteleuropa*. It carried the subtitle "from the Slavic standpoint." Its principal message was still strongly flavoured by Masaryk's wartime propaganda, which was centred on the black-and-white thesis that "theocratic" forces of darkness, represented by the Pan-German ideology, must be opposed by the "forces of light," namely the exploited Slav peoples allied with Western democracies.[24] Such an approach offered little hope for a dialogue between the winners and losers inside a devastated and chaotic Central Europe.[25]

Edvard Beneš, Masaryk's pragmatic assistant and co-founder of Czechoslovakia, initiated a defence alliance of three Danubian countries — Czechoslovakia, Romania and Yugoslavia — known as the *Little Entente*, against future attempts, specifically Hungarian, towards a Habsburg restoration (two foiled attempts by the ex-Emperor Charles in 1921). Schemes proposing a *Danubian federation*, but separated from

---

23 Meyer 1955, p. 340.
24 English and French editions published in 1919, German edition in 1922. First Czech edition appeared in 1920. Cited from 4th Czech edition, Masaryk, T.G. *Nová Evropa: Stanovisko slovanské*. Brno: Doplněk, 1994, pp. 182–183.
25 Jaworski, R. 'Tomáš G. Masaryk versus Friedrich Naumann. Zwei Europavisionen im Ersten Weltkrieg' in Pousta, Z., Seifter, P., Pešek, J. (eds.) *Setkání, Begegnung. Sborník k 65.narozeninám Jana Křena*. Prague: Karolinum, 1996, pp. 123–34.

Germany, propounded in particular by the untiring Hungarian professor Elemér Hantos, or the Slovak statesman Milan Hodža,[26] remained on the drawing board before even tackling the problem of Austrian membership.[27]

Most ambitious in the category of non-German projects were those designed by the Poles. This was understandable under the new circumstances. The Poles defined their *Europa Sródkowa* as a region under Polish political and cultural influence, dominated for centuries by the Poles as the historic defenders of the *Antemurale Christianitatis* against Asian invaders. Here the Poles, not the Germans, were supposed to be the dominant force. The Polish historian Oskar Halecki opened the debate on "What is Eastern Europe" in 1924 by defining it as the sphere of Polish political and cultural expansion. Halecki included in his "Eastern Europe" the regions inhabited by Poles, Balts and the "Eastern Slavs" (Russians, Ukrainians, Belorussians), without defining the easternmost geographic delimitation of this space. Clearly, a German-dominated *Mitteleuropa* would have run up against the Polish scheme and had to be rejected. It was a classical conflict of "either us or them". Realizing that they would be defeated if fighting the Russians and the Germans simultaneously, the Poles tried other combinations.[28] They were, for instance, ready to double up with the Hungarians against the Czechs. The metamorphoses of the Polish Central Europe realm could be traced back to the multi-ethnic *Rzecz Pospolita* before partition. By contrast, the Hungarians were the losers. Having lost over sixty percent of their population and territory in the Treaty of Trianon, the Hungarians remained absorbed in their uncompromising revisionist claims. Interwar Poland, aspiring to lead a

---

26 Hantos, E. *Der Weg zum neuen Mitteleuropa*. Berlin: Mitteleuropa Verlag Berlin, 1933; Hodža, M. *Federation in Central Europe*. London: Jarrolds Limited, 1942; expanded Slovak edition: Hodža, M., Lukáč, P. (ed.) *Federácia v Strednej Európe a iné štúdie*. Bratislava: Kalligram, 1997. Also Lukáč, P. *Milan Hodža v zápase o budúcnosť strednej Európy 1939–1944*. Bratislava: Veda, SAV, 2005.
27 Suppan, A. 'Mitteleuropa-Konzeptionen zwischen Restauration und Anschluss' in Plaschka 1995, p. 195.
28 Studnicki, W. *Polen im politischen System Europas*. Berlin: Mittler, 1935.

North-Eastern Baltic federation 'between two seas', known as *Miedzymorze* or *Intermarium,* found a noble geopolitical vocation in defending Christian Europe against Asian and later Bolshevik invaders.[29] The anachronistic revival of the Jagiellonian federation under Polish leadership however, which was the dream of Józef Piłsudski (1867–1935), could have been resurrected only on the ruins of the German and Russian empires.

Although East-Central Europe, especially Poland, had been economically devastated in the course of the Great War, the peace conferences offered the new countries no economic remedies except the illusion of territorial aggrandizement. It should not be forgotten that the economic chapters of *Mitteleuropa,* which in fact constituted the bulk of Naumann's book, found an unexpected response among the victors when the economist John Maynard Keynes, a member of the British delegation, proposed to establish a free trade zone under the auspices of the League of Nations, comprising all Central European countries plus Turkey and Russia. Losers and winners were to be treated alike. Keynes' major concern was to prevent the further sinking of Germany into anarchy and civil war. He realized that she needed to restore her capacity to pay through restarting her industries and trade, especially with impoverished Russia, which in turn would restore her grain exports. Keynes exposed the hypocrisy of the Allies, who preached adherence to the Wilsonian idea of national self-determination and universal peace but who were about to impose on Germany a "Carthaginian Peace." "Let us encourage and assist Germany to take up again her place in Europe as a creator and organizer of wealth for her Eastern and Southern neighbours," proposed Keynes.[30] His compatriots thought Keynes had gone mad. Seeing that no one wanted to take his economic proposals seriously, Keynes resigned in protest. A quarter

---

[29] Wojtecki, A. *Sprawa Europy Srodkowej.* Warsaw: Skład główny Gebethner i Wolff, 1939; Halecki, O. *The Limits and Divisions of European History.* New York: Sheed & Ward, 1950.

[30] Keynes, J.M. *The Economic Consequences of the Peace.* London: Penguin, 1988, pp. 265–269.

of a century later, when Germany lost for the second time, Keynes was chosen to represent Britain at the Bretton Woods Conference that established the International Monetary Fund. This time, the Allies had taken him seriously and adopted his basic ideas in a plan that became known as the Marshall Plan.

Among the rare projects that did not discriminate between the losers and winners was the *Paneuropa* scheme, conceived by the Bohemian nobleman Count Richard Coudenhove-Kalergi.[31] The plan was to comprise twenty-six European countries with their French, Dutch, Portuguese, Spanish and Danish colonies. This Pan-Europe would coexist in peace with four "international complexes": the British Commonwealth, the Soviet Russian Federation, East Asia (China & neighbours, Japan with colonies) and Pan-America. In 1921 Coudenhove-Kalergi visited Masaryk to tell him that he would make the ideal president of Pan-Europe. The old man declined, saying that in his opinion it was too early. However, he could not resist telling Coudenhove how he himself, with the premiers of Greece and Romania, had once tried to organize a federation of "United States of Europe," designed to absorb thirteen states situated between Germany and Russia, and how he had failed in the end. As far as Beneš was concerned, he found the idea of Paneuropa attractive but not pressing; he was not prepared to do more than sign the preface in Coudenhove's book.[32] It seemed as if neither economic nor geopolitical solutions could have succeeded in reorganizing and reconstructing *Mitteleuropa* without the involvement of Germany. The prewar economic links and regional infrastructures, which had been the result of decades of political stability in the region, were destroyed by the war and the peace settlements. Geopolitical reality indeed pointed not to federalization but towards disunity and intra-regional conflicts.[33]

---

31 Coudenhove-Kalergi, R. N. *Pan-europa*. Wien: Paneuropa Vlg., 1923.
32 Coudenhove-Kalergi R.N., *Crusade for Pan-Europe*. New York: Putnam, 1943, pp. 60, 75, 89; Coudenhove-Kalergi 1924, p. 115.
33 Stirk 1994, p. 16.

Turning now to the defeated Germany, between 1919 and 1933 *Mitteleuropa* as a concept seemed to be only remembered as Friedrich Naumann's failed dream (he died in 1919). The term remained in general usage in those succession states and border regions inhabited by contiguous or scattered German minorities, estimated in excess of seventeen million.[34] Their ancient political allegiances to the Habsburg and Romanov rulers were shattered after 1919. The previous *Großdeutsch* ambition was replaced by the *Gesamtdeutsch,* incarnated in the merger (*Anschluss*) of Austria by Germany, which the majority of Austrian voters had desired after the collapse of the monarchy but which was prevented by the Allies.[35] "If the French can turn *Mitteleuropa* against us," warned Martin Spahn in 1925, "our historical function will be ended, for we shall lose the area in which by nature we must exert ourselves. But if, instead, we can give *Mitteleuropa* form and function, then we shall again become the leading nation of Europe."[36]

After Hitler's seizure of power, a new regional trading model called "*Grossraumwirtschaft*" took shape, which would allow Germany to first economically penetrate most of the countries in South-eastern and Northern Europe, before she could dominate them politically.[37] It was a non-free trade system of mutual dependence, whereby a dozen

---

34 Over 6.5m in Austria, 3.5m in Czechoslovakia, over 0.2m in the Baltic States, 0.4m in Danzig, 1.5m in Poland, 0.6m in Hungary, 0.75m in Romania, 0.6m in Yugoslavia, 1.5-2m in the USSR—not counting Switzerland.
35 This could be best demonstrated in the works of German and Austrian historians, such as Wilhelm Schüssler, Martin Spahn, Hermann Ullmann, Harold Steinacker, Josef Pfitzner, Wilhelm Wostry and Kleo Pleyer (the last three were strictly speaking Sudeten-Germans). This is discussed up in Sweet, P. 'Recent German Literature on Mitteleuropa', *Journal of Central European Affairs.* III.1, 1943, pp. 1-24.
36 Sweet 1943, p. 3; Spahn, M. 'Mitteleuropa', *Volk und Reich.* Berlin: Politische Monatshefte, 8., 1925.
37 Matis, H. 'Wirtschaftliche Mitteleuropa-Konzeptionen in der Zwischenkriegszeit' in: Plaschka 1995, pp. 229-255; Berend, I. *Decades of Crisis: Central and Eastern Europe Before World War II.* Berkeley: University of California Press, 1998, pp. 146-51, 273-77; Chodorkowski, J. *Niemiecka doktryna gospodarki wielkiego obszaru (Grossraumwirtschaft) 1800-1945.* Wroclaw: Zakład Narodowy im. Ossolińskich, 1972.

small food and raw-material producing countries entered in clearing or barter agreements with Germany and were promised manufactured goods in exchange. During the world depression, the Danubian cereal exporters became deprived of their traditional markets and eagerly accepted the German offer. Within a few years, Germany became the major trade partner in bilateral trade agreements over the entire Central European region—with the exception of Czechoslovakia whose exports consisted mainly of manufactured goods and were much more diversified.[38]

Finally, what was Hitler's vision of the Greater German Empire and how did he acquire it? Hitler's *Lebensraum,* must have been inspired by Ludendorff's *Ostimperium* of 1918, based on the original *Ober-Ost* of 1916 and incorporated in the Peace of Brest-Litovsk whose provisions carried German troops as far as Trans-Caucasia in 1918. Thus, Hitler's vision went far beyond the classic *Mitteleuropa.* It aspired to reach world dominion, to be achieved stage by stage in the name of the ultimate racial superstate, the "Greater Germanic Empire" (*Großgermanisches Reich*). Hitler insisted that the *Lebensraum's* primary criterion should be "blood-related".[39] Naumann's *Mitteleuropa* was rejected by the chief ideologue of National Socialism Alfred Rosenberg as being too liberal and "pseudo-socialist." Naumann's major shortcoming was said to be the absence of racial awareness. Indeed, Naumann's association with Jews was in itself a sufficient flaw to make his concept unacceptable in Hitler's Third Reich.[40]

National Socialism did not favour a liberal economic order—but self-sufficiency or autarky, with the ultimate purpose to sustain a long war. A vital extension of the domestic drive towards self-sufficiency of the Third Reich was to be the acquisition of the Ukraine and the

---

38   Barsch, A. *The Danube Basin and the German Economic Sphere.* Boulder: Columbia University Press, 1943; Milward, A. *The German Economy at War.* London: Athlone Press, 1965; idem, *War, Economy and Society, 1939–1945.* Berkeley: University of California Press, 1979.
39   Picker, H. (ed.) *Hitlers Tischgespräche im Fuhrer-hauptquartier, 1941–1942.* Stuttgart: Seewald, 1965, p. 45.
40   Meyer 1955, p. 317.

Crimea, which acquired almost the status of myth in Hitler's *Mein Kampf*.[41]

World War II: The Lebensraum Obsession and the End of Mitteleuropa

The Molotov-Ribbentrop Pact, signed on 23rd August 1939, one week before the German attack on Poland, and four weeks before the Soviet invasion, was an imperialist contract that divided *Mitteleuropa* between the Soviet Union and Nazi Germany. It reestablished the common border between Russia and Germany and removed the "middle tier", whose existence T. G. Masaryk had advocated so eloquently on behalf of "small democratic nations of Europe" in his *New Europe*.

What happened to the *Mitteleuropa* concept? The war of racial extermination, which Hitler unleashed in June 1941 upon the Soviet Union for the German *Lebensraum* in the East, unmasked Hitler's war in the East as a different one from the war Germany conducted in the West or in North Africa. In the East, Hitler was conducting two wars. One was the customary military campaign, a kind of a giant *Blitzkrieg* that was stopped before Moscow in December 1941. The other was a racial war against the "Judeo-Bolshevist" enemy. In the East, these two wars merged into one. Since *Mitteleuropa* lay on the invasion path, the whole region experienced massive transfers of population in connection with German resettlement policy and racial cleansing during 1941–45, and the Soviet cleansing of "class enemies" during 1939–41 and again after 1944.

Hitler and Himmler dreamed that within twenty years ten million German and Germanic settlers would repopulate the agricultural land of European Russia. The so-called *Generalplan Ost* of 1942 foresaw the deportation of 31 (51 with the Poles) million Slavs and Jews from *Mitteleuropa*: 80–85 % of Poles, 65 % Ukrainians, 50 % Czechs, together with the rest of the Russian population, were destined to end

---

41   Milward 1979, p. 261; Overy, R. J. *War and Economy in the Third Reich*. Oxford: Clarendon Press, 1995, p. 227.

up in Siberia; the rest was considered suitable to ruthless Germanisation.⁴² The monstrous "racial restructuring" (*rassische Neugestaltung*) was to include the obliteration of Leningrad and Moscow, whose entire populations Hitler intended to starve to death. A network of German settlements was planned to emerge from this vast space laid waste by the *Wehrmacht* and deprived of population by special execution squads (*Einsatzgruppen*) or mass deportation.

Already in his prewar speeches Hitler kept complaining about the fundamental socio-economic injustice of the contemporary world system that provided only a pitiful quantity of land per head to every German, but eighteen times more land to every Russian.⁴³ Together with the *Lebensraum* dream, the "Blood and Soil" *(Blut und Boden)* issue provided the major theme for Hitler's second volume of *Mein Kampf*. Hitler used these ideas while adapting the idea of *Großraumwirtschaft* and urging Germany to regain her lost status of world power.⁴⁴ By October 1941, Hitler's relentless war machine held under occupation a space of 7 million km², that was in size between British India and the United States and which contained 360 million subjects under direct or indirect German rule.

"Once we are masters of Europe," boasted Hitler, "we can dominate the entire world. We'll have 130 million in the Reich, 90 in the Ukraine, and together with other nations of the New Europe we'll reach 400 million. We can easily take on 130 million Americans".⁴⁵ "We have undertaken the construction of roads that will lead to the southernmost point of the Crimea and to the Caucasus," said Hitler on another occasion, "in twenty years the Ukraine will already be a home

---

42 Heiber, H. 'Der Generalplan Ost', *Vierteljahrshefte für Zeitgeschichte*, 6, 1958, pp. 319–320; Benz, W. 'Der Generalplan Ost. Zur Germanisierungspolitik des NS-Regimes in den besetzten Ostgebieten 1939-1945' in *Die Vertreibung der Deutschen aus dem Osten*. Frankfurt: Fischer, 1985, pp. 39–48; Hoensch, K. 'Nationalsozialistische Europapläne im Zweiten Weltkrieg' in Plaschka (1995, pp. 307-25).
43 Milward 1979, p. 134.
44 Hitler, A. *Mein Kampf*. Munich: Franz Eher Vlg., 1927.
45 Heim, H. *Monologe im Führer-Hauptquartier 1941-1944*. Hamburg: A. Knaus, 1980, pp. 110.

for twenty million [German] inhabitants besides the natives [...] As for the natives, we'll have to screen them carefully. The Jew, the destroyer, we shall drive out [...] As for the rest, let them learn to read just enough to understand our highway signs, so that they won't get themselves run over by our vehicles!"[46]

The main transportation artery between German-controlled Europe and the Ukraine, later to be extended to the Crimea and the Caspian Sea and beyond, was to be the giant three-meter gauge railway, carrying double-deck trains at speed of 250 km/h.[47] It immediately appealed to Hitler's megalomania, for he readily envisaged how the appearance of these giant trains on the Russian steppe would shock and overwhelm the eastern *Untermensch*. The racial megalomania of the Third Reich reached its ultimate horrifying proportions in the creation of extermination camps with gas chambers in the very heart of Central Europe. The name of Auschwitz must thus be included in the ghastly legacy of *Mitteleuropa* as the symbol of utter debasement and corruption of the human race.

No other nation suffered more in World War II than the Poles, especially Poland's Jews. Nazi genocidal programmes selected Polish Jews as their main target. Out of 3.3 million almost 3 million perished between 1939 and 1945. Of Poland's non-Jewish population between 2.4 and 2.7 million died of causes inflicted by German occupants. The genocide was selective. It was aimed to liquidate the Polish elite. Every second Polish university graduate did not survive the war.

The defeat of Hitler's Third German Reich in 1945 also meant the end of German-dominated *Mitteleuropa* and its costly experiment with the *Lebensraum*. Mass deportations and ethnic cleansing followed, replicated by the Soviets as they replaced the Germans. *Mitteleuropa* was to be either German or Russian: there was no third option. *Tertium non*

---

46 Trevor-Roper, H. (ed.) *Hitler's Table Talk 1941–1944*. London: Weidenfeld & Nicolson, 1973, pp. 68–70; Hauner, M. *Hitler. A Chronology of His Life and Time*. London: Macmillan, 2005, pp. 68–70.

47 Joachimsthaler, A. *Breitspurbahn. Das Projekt zur Erschließung des groß-europäischen Raumes 1942–1945*. Munich: Herbig, 1985.

datur. After the Soviet victory over Germany in 1945, *Mitteleuropa* was turned into a Russian-controlled region and thoroughly de-Germanised. Between 15 and 17 million ethnic Germans were expelled from the Soviet-occupied territories of Eastern Europe between 1944 and 1966; German sources claim that during the expulsion 2.1 million Germans died.[48] In 1939, over 4 million Poles fell into Soviet hands were killed. Tens of thousand were deported to the Arctic camps or to Siberia and Central Asia, where most of them perished. In the following year, the Red Army moved into the three Baltic States and to Bukovina and Bessarabia. Their citizens, too, faced now the full force of Stalinist terror. Arrested and deported were not only the obvious so-called class enemies. The NKVD feared also such dangerous elements as stamp collectors and Esperantists.

Central Europe has been designated by the historian Timothy Snyder as the greatest killing field of the twentieth century.[49] This is a dreadful privilege. Snyder's *Bloodlands* comprises the northeastern portion of *Mitteleuropa* (known during World War I as *Ober-Ost*), consisting of the Baltic countries, Poland, western Ukraine, Belarus, within which over a period of 14 years, 1933-1945, 14 million, largely non-combatant people perished. This figure encompasses ten million civilians and prisoners-of-war (POWs) killed by the Nazis, including six million Jews killed in the Holocaust and 4 million civilians and POWs killed by the Soviets. It includes three million estimated Ukrainians starved 1932-1933, as well as three million Soviet POWs starved by the Nazis 1941-1942.

One of the first acts of cold-blooded genocidal mass murder in the Second World War was the grisly execution of some 25 000 Polish

---

48 According to German sources, 17 658 000 Germans lived in 1939 in the former German territories and in the adjacent regions of Eastern and South-eastern Europe. Of these 1.1m lost their lives during the war due to unnatural causes, mostly as soldiers in the armed forces. From the remaining 16.6m about 11.7m were expelled. Until 1966 further 2.5m Germans came to FRG, GDR and Austria. Source: Heinsohn, G. *Lexikon der Völkermorde*. Hamburg: Rowohlt, 1988, pp. 115-117, 346.

49 Snyder, T. *Bloodlands. Europe between Hitler and Stalin.* New York: Basic Books, 2010.

POWs by the NKVD in the spring of 1940.⁵⁰ Until 1992 the Soviet government kept accusing the Germans of having committed this horrific crime. When the war ended, huge-scale deportations and relocations were recommenced by the Soviets. Soviet POWs returning from Germany were rearrested in their own country and despatched to the Gulag. The enclave of East Prussia, which was emptied of its German population, received one million Russians and Ukrainians. Up to three million Poles from the eastern regions occupied by Soviet troops were driven out to the new Polish territories in the west.⁵¹

Thus, it was the combined negative impact of the lack of stability during the interwar period, caused by the imperfect peace treaties of 1919–1923, the shock of the Nazi-Soviet partnership 1939–41, the brutality of the Nazi-Soviet war of 1941–45, that forced the East Europeans in exile in London to discuss confederation plans. The division of East-Central Europe between Germany and Russia in 1939–41 meant a de facto elimination of *Mitteleuropa* as a geopolitical entity. At the same time, the temporary vacuum encouraged the planners and dreamers to figure out an imaginary post-war Central Europe that would be miraculously freed from both German and Russian control.

Hubert Ripka, who was the acting foreign minister in the exile government of President Beneš, referred to *Mitteleuropa* as "the Baltic-Aegean region".⁵² The advance of the Russians to the river Elbe signaled however the end of the lofty (con)federation projects that had been developed during the war years by East European exiles under British supervision, e.g., between the Czechs and Poles, the Greeks and the Yugoslavs (Balkan Federation), and the Danubian nations.⁵³

---

50 According to the key document of 5th March 1940, signed by L. Beria and countersigned by J. V. Stalin and five other politburo members, which was finally released by the Yeltsin government in 1992. See Materski, W., Wosik, E. (eds.) *Katyń-Dokumenty ludobójstwa... przekazane Polsce 1992r.* Warsaw: Instytut Studiów Politycznych, 1992, pp. 34–39.
51 Heinsohn 1998, pp. 279-83; Davies, N. *Europe – A History.* Oxford: Oxford University Press, 1997, pp. 1002–1005.
52 Ripka, H. *The Central European Observer*, London: 30 May, 1941, p. 130.
53 See Bán, A. D. *PAX BRITANNICA – Wartime Foreign Office Documents regarding Plans for Postbellum East Central Europe.* Boulder: Columbia University Press, 1997;

Stalin, the true victor over Hitler, prevented all such designs by keeping the Red Army in Central Europe after the defeat of Nazi Germany. Ripka understood that and adjusted his Central European perspective to the requirements of the new masters.[54]

The direct consequence of the advance of Soviet troops into Central Europe and the defeat of Nazi Germany was the 'de-Germanization' of East-Central Europe. Germany as an entity was to vanish for considerable time from future *Mitteleuropa* concepts.[55] Federation plans in Central Europe would mention Czechs and Slovaks, Poles, Hungarians, Serbo-Croats, Slovenes, and Romanians, occasionally the Baltic nations, and very rarely Austrians — but never Germans, not even the "good ones" subject to de-nazification and re-education. The liquidation of Jews during the Nazi occupation was followed during the advance of the Red Army by the flight and forcible removal of Germans as historical inhabitants of *Mitteleuropa*. In the ensuing Cold War, Soviet-occupied East-Central Europe assumed the function of a strategic buffer or fortified bulwark in the anticipated confrontation with NATO.

President Beneš, the most resourceful statesman among exiled leaders who congregated in London during the war, was not very happy having the Poles as senior partners in the planned confederation. In spite of supportive declarations in 1940 and 1941 in favour of the confederation, and to please the British who championed the idea, he made the Czechoslovak participation conditional on a Soviet-Polish rapprochement. That made sense only after Hitler's invasion of Russia, when it became also Britain's strategic aim. Many Poles, however, continued to believe that the Russo-German war would end with

---

Wandycz, P. *Czechoslovak-Polish Confederation and the Great Powers 1940–43*. Bloomington: Indiana University Press, 1956; Nemeček, J. *Od spojenectví k roztržce 1939–1945*. Prague: Academia, 2003.

54 Ripka, H. *Russia and the West*. London: New Europe Forum, 1942; idem, *Small and the Great Nations*. London: Czechoslovakia MFA Information Service, 1944; idem, *East and West*. London: Lincolns-Praeger, 1944.

55 For more details see Kühl, J. *Föderationspläne im Donauraum und in Ostmitteleuropa*. Munich: Oldenbourg, 1958.

the paralysis of both great powers for the benefit of Polish territorial demands, which had remained not only inflexible regarding the old Polish territories, but which increased with regard to German territories in the East, such as Danzig, East Prussia, Pomerania and the whole of Silesia, and included the former Czechoslovak region of Těšín (Cieszyn). In any case, regardless of constant British pressure, it was unimaginable that after the Katyń massacre any Polish leader could shake hands with Stalin. And yet, this was exactly what the Anglo-Americans demanded from the London Poles. By contrast, the pragmatist Beneš could do that. He retreated quickly from the joint project with the Poles when he was confronted with the Soviet veto in July 1942.[56] Furthermore, he accepted the Soviet version of Katyń after the German revelations in April 1943. He would go to Moscow in December of the same year to embrace Stalin and to sign the Soviet-Czechoslovak Friendship Treaty. Beneš welcomed the Soviets in Central Europe for two main reasons. First, as an investment in security so that he could call upon the Red Army to prevent another Munich in the event of a repeated German invasion. Second, that the Soviets would support his plan to expel Czechoslovakia's German and Hungarian minorities.

If one of the most pronounced characteristics of *Mitteleuropa* was its ethnic mixture and the coexistence of minorities, this was going to be radically changed. Under the brutal practices of totalitarian regimes, Beneš decided to get rid of the minorities for the sake of homogeneity. He saw only two options available: either assimilation or expulsion/transfer. Through tireless intervention, first with the British, then the Americans, and finally the Soviets, Beneš was able to per-

---

56 Štovíček, I., Valenta, J. *Czechoslovak-Polish Negotiations 1939–1944*. Prague: Karolinum, 1995, p. 229; Kaminski, M. K. *E. Benes kontra gen. W. Sikorski*. Warsaw: Neriton, 2005.

suade the Big Three that the transfer of German and Hungarian minorities from Czechoslovakia, re-established in her pre-Munich borders, was necessary for the benefit of peace in Central Europe.[57]

The Soviet take-over of *Mitteleuropa*, replacing the German occupation, brought about the anticipated Soviet territorial adjustments, which had been passively accepted by the Western Allies in the middle of the war and confirmed at the Potsdam Conference. It was the Red Amy which was to become the principal vehicle of the Soviet *fait accompli* in East-Central Europe and for the lasting post-war political arrangements. Those applied especially to Poland. Her population was pushed westwards behind the so-called Curzon Line. Poland's underground movement was crushed in the Warsaw rising by the Germans and bled in a prolonged civil war by the Soviets. A lonely group of East European intellectuals, mostly Hungarians (e.g., Oszkar Jászi, László Németh, István Bibó), would continue to discuss the Central European idea under the harsh realities of the post-Yalta arrangements.[58]

The failure of British-sponsored federation projects in Central and Southern Europe taught the West European politicians, Paul Henri Spaak, Jean Monnet and Robert Schuman, a useful lesson. The

---

[57] Beneš, E. 'The New Central Europe', *Journal of Central European Affairs*: Vol.I.1, April, 1941, p. 2; idem 'The Organization of Postwar Europe', *Foreign Affairs*, January, 1942, pp. 226–242, idem, 'Postwar Czechoslovakia', *Foreign Affairs*, April, 1946, pp. 397–410. For Beneš' adherence to neo-Slavism see Beneš, E. 'The New Slav Policy', *Free World*, May 1944; Beneš, E. *Úvahy o slovanství*. Prague: Čin, 1947.

[58] In contrast to Beneš, who remained diplomatically cautious as the head of exile government throughout the war, the Hungarian expert on nationalities Oskar Jászi, appeared to be the only intellectual representing *Mitteleuropa* who openly discussed the German and Russian options while contemplating the future of Central Europe. He felt obviously free to do that from the academic oasis of his American professorship. Jászi, O. 'The Future of Danubia', *Journal of Central Europan Affairs*, July, Vol. I.2, 1941, p. 128; Jászi, O. 'Central Europe and Russia', *Journal of Central European Affairs*, April, Vol. V.1, 1945, pp. 1–16; Jászi, O. 'The Choices of Hungary', *Foreign Affairs*, April, Vol. 24.3, 1946, pp. 453–465. Further Litvan, G. (ed.) *O.Jászi: Homage to Danubia*. Lanham: Rowman & Littlefield, 1995; Bibó, I. *Misère des petits États d'Europe de l'Est*. Paris: L'Harmattan, 1986; Borsody, S. *The Tragedy of Central Europe: The Nazi and Soviet Conquest of Central Europe*. New York: Collier Books, 1962.

realization that they were out of the Soviet sphere of control must have encouraged them to go ahead with their own projects of West European integration. Though formally restored in 1945 as independent states, all of the "middle tier" countries behind the Szeczin-Trieste line, epitomized in Churchill's "Iron Curtain Speech" of March 1946, had become outer buffers of the extended Soviet empire.

Strategic lessons can be read in different ways. The Allied victory over Germany in 1945, mainly obtained thanks to colossal Russian sacrifices, made the Soviet position incomparably more advantageous than in 1939–1941. Due to the unmitigated defeat and subsequent dismemberment of "Greater Germany" (including Austria), the Soviet Union could annex (together with Soviet-controlled Poland) one fifth of the former German territory, and occupy another one-fifth until 1990.

What happened to the fantasy *Landschaft* once upon a time called *Mitteleuropa*? In his melancholic book, *The Centre Lies Eastwards*, Karl Schlögel gives the following gloomy but vindicated judgment:[59]

"Six *Wehrmacht* years were long enough to completely shatter centuries of settlers' time in the construction of *Mitteleuropa* cities. How could the fine cultural web be so quickly and utterly destroyed? [...] With the liquidation of Central European Jewry, and the Germans as the integrating element in the region, the old *Mitteleuropa* was doomed to die [...]The era of settlers was reversed by the era of deportations [...] Next to the old capital cities in the region new ones were constructed: Next to Vienna, Mauthausen. Next to Munich, Dachau. Next to Berlin, Oranienburg. Next to Danzig, Stutthof. Next to Prague, Theresienstadt. Next to Wilna, Ponary. Next to Riga, Kaiserwald [...] A secretive new capital of this giant region was selected, Auschwitz, which is located at the fault-line of three former empires that had divided *Mitteleuropa* among themselves. [...] It has become the capital of the secretive empire of death [...] reproduced in the mi-

---

59 Schlögel, K. *Die Mitte liegt ostwärts. Die Deutschen, der verlorene Osten und Mitteleuropa.* Berlin: Siedler Verlag, 1986.

crocosm of the death factories: Maidanek, Chelmno, Treblinka, Sobibor, Auschwitz. These were the virtual capitals of the empire, the *Lebensraum* of the empire of death."

I wish I could provide a less desolate picture of the geo-cultural *Landschaft* once called *Mitteleuropa*, but, alas, this is also my stocktaking of the "Thirty-Year European Civil War." Other contributors, no doubt will, and so they should, present a more cheerful vision of the Central European legacy.

Historical Consciousness in the Visegrád Four

Oľga Gyárfášová[1]
Institute for Public Affairs, Bratislava

Abstract: Is the shared past reflected in the historical consciousness of citizens of the Visegrád Four countries today? What are the narratives within each society in the region? What are the images of 'us' and 'them'? Firstly, the text presents Historical consciousness and collective memory as theoretical concepts. Then it moves to the results of a public surveys that focused on historical consciousness and related questions and were conducted in all four Visegrád countries in October 2011. Results of the surveys have shown that the national history of the Visegrád Four countries has more heroes than anti-heroes, however large gaps appear in neighbours' knowledge of each other.

Central Europe has traditionally been a geographical area characterized by ethnic and cultural heterogeneity, where national/ethnic minorities co-existed, sometimes at war, sometimes in peace. Is this shared past reflected in the historical consciousness of citizens of the Visegrád Four (V4) countries today? What are the narratives within each society in the region? What are the images of 'us' and 'them'? We know very well that common history can be a double-edged sword: it can strengthen mutual understanding and cohesion, but it can also lead to negative stereotypes and prejudices. What are the effects of common history among the Visegrád nations? The question was recently put not to historians, other experts, or politicians, but to the general public, ordinary people, who have learnt this history at school (often years ago and under a Communist regime that manipulated the facts and interpretations). Collective historical memory is also influenced by the mass media, politicians, and family narratives. Public opinion surveys that focused on historical consciousness and related questions were conducted in all four Visegrád countries in October

---

1   E-mail: olga@ivo.sk.

2011.[2] The project was initiated and funded by the International Visegrád Fund and was coordinated by the Institute for Public Affairs (IVO) based in Bratislava together with national partners in the Czech Republic, Hungary, and Poland.[3] The survey was part of a wider project entitled 'My Hero—Your Enemy: Listening to Understanding', which brought together historians from V4 countries to discuss this common history.

Historical consciousness and collective memory as theoretical concepts

One objective of this article is to present the empirical findings of the surveys. But that is impossible without at least a rudimentary theoretical conceptualization of historical consciousness, collective memory, and related terms, and a clarification of how we understand them for an empirical survey.

Memories are social, cultural, and political constructs that change over time and have their own history of development. Making Aleida Assmann's ontological distinction, we may usefully distinguish among individual, social, cultural, and political memories.[4] Whereas social memory consists in the coordination of individual memories transmitted by means of communicative exchange, cultural memory is made up of experience and knowledge that have been disconnected from their human bearers and are transferred to material

---

2   The surveys were conducted on a representative sample of the adult population (about 1,000 respondents in each country) by professional polling agencies. The interviews were conducted face to face.
3   Jiří Vinopal and Jiří Šubrt (Institute of Sociology, Czech Academy of Sciences, Prague), Gergő Medve-Bálint (Central European University, Budapest), and Małgorzata Fałkowska-Warska (Institute of Public Affairs, Warsaw). See e. g. Fałkowska-Warska, M. 'Die Geschichte aus der Perspektive der Bürger der Visegrád-Staaten—Verklärung der Vergangenheit oder gesellschaftliche Amnesie?' Available on-line: www.laender-analysen.de/polen/pdf/PolenAnalysen102.pdf [accessed 9 June 2012]. I thank all the partners for their comments and insights from their home countries.
4   Assmann, A. *Der lange Schatten der Vergangenheit: Erinnerungskultur und Geschichtspolitik.* Bonn: Bundeszentrale für politische Bildung, 2007.

transmitters. Assmann points out the ways that lead from an individual construction of the past to a collective one. Where history is at the command of identity-formation, where it is being evoked by politicians and taken on by citizens, it is fair to talk of national or political memory. Whereas social and cultural memory is memory 'from below', transformed with the change in generations, national memory is intentionally constructed to last, and tends to be a much more homogeneous construction. It is anchored in political institutions, supported by symbols, evoked during commemorative events, and thus influences society 'from above'.[5]

In this regard, we have to talk about the politics of memory (and forgetting) which underlines the role of politics in shaping collective memory by instrumentalizing and highlighting specific historical events and personalities, while neglecting others, which can cause collective amnesia. Assmann examines the tensions between personal experience and official remembrance, suggests standards of an appropriate culture of remembrance, and advocates 'giving memory a common space' for expression. Other authors, too, remind us that the politics of memory or the politics of history draws our attention to the discursive negotiations in a society fragmented along political and ideological lines, where memory appears to be always only a temporary result of the permanent battle of history.[6]

Consequently, the national historical memory is not a stable construct. It changes depending on current social and political conditions and is continuously adapted to contemporary needs and values. The bigger the discrepancy between the experience of the past and the value-system of the present, the greater the pressure usually is on politics and society to adjust the past to the norms of the present. The development and the transformation of the framework for interpretation of both the perception of the present and the memory of the past,

---

5 Ibid., pp. 33-37.
6 Uhl, H. 'Memory Culture—Politics of History: Some Reflections on Memory and Society', in Wahnich, S., Lášticová, B., Findor, A. (eds.) *Politics of Collective Memory*. Vienna: LIT, 2008, pp. 57-65.

which in turn determines the elements that are going to be remembered and in what form, depends largely on pressures exerted by different internal and external factors. These factors include changes in the structure of society, which resulted from the change in generations and their perceptions of the past, changes in political régimes, each of which may have their own narratives, often even opposing ones, or international constellations. Similarly, according to the Czech sociologists Jiří Šubrt and Jiří Vinopal, historical consciousness is an entity that is co-created by the interaction of several components: experienced historical events (lived or mediated experience), 'state ideology' (each regime uses history and historical argumentation for its own legitimacy), knowledge produced by history as a field of study, and by collective memory.[7] Moreover, collective memory is selective, constructed by the same factors as historical consciousness.

Šubrt and Vinopal point out that there are two approaches to the content characteristics of the historical consciousness in the Czech discourse. The first is based on understanding as the summary of knowledge of history available to a certain group or community of people. The second approach underlines the broader understanding of historical consciousness as a general term from history or a mental stage of society, depending on the characteristics, and must necessarily be unstable.[8]

Historical consciousness is a constitutive part of national identity, which has been usefully described as 'one of the most successful constructs of collective identity in human history, comparable only with religious identity. Its success is based on the fact that it addresses archetypal components of human sub-consciousness. It works with the

---

7   Šubrt, J., Vinopal, J. 'K otázce historického vědomí obyvatel České republiky', *Naše společnost* (periodical of the CVVM Sociologického ústavu AV ČR), Vol. 8, No. 1, 2010, pp. 9–20.
8   Ibid.

opposites 'us' and 'them'. In consequence, the construct of national identity is given mythological features'.⁹

Instead of aiming to achieve a holistic view, we have decided, in keeping with the idea of the project and conference, to approach the perception of national history and the history of the 'other' by means of historical figures. Each nation has its Pantheon of historical figures who represent the 'glory days' of national history, the heroes depicted in stories. As the Slovak historian Dušan Kováč has neatly put it: 'In certain moments of national agitation, national heroes cease to be historical figures and play the part of national symbols'.¹⁰

We have examined national histories, but the main added value of the project is the exploration of mutual perceptions of the history and historical personalities of the Visegrád countries. This aspect had not been surveyed before and the current volume represents a unique improvement over earlier research on mentalities and mutual perceptions in the V4 countries.¹¹

National Pantheons

National heroes are a source of national pride and national identity. We sought to find out who the heroes are in the countries surveyed. To explore the 'top-of-mind' awareness of historical figures, we opted for open-ended questions.¹² The 'personality perspective' in analyzing the historical consciousness also corresponds to the central idea of the conference 'My Hero—Your Enemy: Listening to Understanding', great figures in history.

---

9   Kováč, D. 'Identita a národ', in Kiliánová, G., Kowalská, E., Krekovičová, E. (eds.) *My a tí druhí v modernej spoločnosti*. Bratislava: Veda, Vydavateľstvo SAV, 2009, pp. 338–342.
10 Ibid., p. 341.
11 E.g. Gyárfášová, O. *Visegrad Citizens on the Doorstep of the European Union*. Bratislava: Institute for Public Affairs, 2003.
12 The question reads: 'When thinking about Czech/Hungarian/Polish/Slovak national history, could you please name people you are proud of? Give three names at most.

Let us start with Czech history. Among the figures regarded by the respondents as a source of national pride were Charles IV (47 %), Tomáš G. Masaryk (44 per cent), and Václav Havel (26 %)[13]. (Table 1) The findings correspond to earlier surveys on the perception of historical events and periods: the reign of Charles IV., the first Czechoslovak Republic with Tomáš G. Masaryk as President, the era of Great Moravia, and the era of the Přemyslid dynasty are each seen as the 'golden age' of Czech history.[14] Also in the list are Comenius, the 'teacher of nations' (19 %); Jan Hus (16 %); Jan Žižka (8 %); Saint Wenceslaus, a patron saint of Bohemia (5 %), and Maria Theresa, Empress of Austria (5 %).

At the top of the list of figures that the Hungarians are most proud of are their greatest politicians of the nineteenth century: Lajos Kossuth, the leader of 1848 revolution (31 %) and István Széchenyi (28 %) (Table 3). Number three is Matthias Corvinus (20 %), King of Hungary and Croatia (*reg.* 1458–90). He was the most powerful monarch of medieval Hungary before the Ottomans conquered the country in the sixteenth century. He appears in many folk tales and legends, something that has greatly contributed to his persistent popularity. The fourth place in the list is held by Stephen (18 %), the first king of Hungary, crowned in 1000. He is the founder of the Kingdom of Hungary and the man who established Christianity there. He is still hugely popular; 20th August, the Feast Day of St Stephan, is the great national holiday in Hungary. He is followed by Sándor Petőfi (13 %), a Hungarian romantic poet and revolutionary who died during the War of Independence in 1848–49. He is the most popular Hungarian poet of

---

13 Since Václav Havel died on 18 December 2011, the public's perception and assessment of him may have changed for the better.
14 Hampl, S., Vinopal, J., Šubrt, J. 'Reflexe novodobých českých dějin, sametové revoluce a současného vývoje v názorech veřejnosti', *Naše společnost* (CVVM Sociologického ústavu AV ČR), Vol., 9, No. 1, 2011, pp. 19–29; Šubrt, J., Vinopal, J. 'K otázce historického vědomí obyvatel České republiky', *Naše společnost* (periodical of the CVVM Sociologického ústavu AV ČR), Vol. 8, No. 1, 2010, pp. 9–20.

all time. Ferenc Rákóczi (9 %) was the leader of the unsuccessful uprising against the Habsburgs between 1703 and 1711. Also among the top ten personalities are Ferenc Deák (6 %), János Kádár (5 %), and Imre Nagy (4 %), the martyr prime minister of the 1956 Revolution.[15]

The Polish respondents most frequently mentioned Pope John Paul II (48 %), the inter-war statesman Józef Piłsudski (26 %), and the leader of the Solidarity movement, Lech Wałęsa (14 %). They were followed by Tadeusz Kościuszko, the leader of the eighteenth-century uprising against Imperial Russia and the Kingdom of Prussia (9 %); the scientist Marie Curie (Maria Skłodowska-Curie; 7 %); John III Sobieski (5 %); the Renaissance astronomer who first formulated a comprehensive heliocentric cosmology Nicolaus Copernicus (4 %), and Władysław II Jagiełło (*reg.* 1386–1434) (4 %). (Table 5)

The list of top ten figures that Slovaks are most proud of comes as no surprise. The first two on the list, Milan Rastislav Štefánik and Alexander Dubček, have been at the top of such lists since the 1990s. They have the special aura of national martyrs: Štefánik died in an aeroplane crash in May 1919 on his return home from Italy to the new Czechoslovak Republic, which he had helped to establish together with Tomáš Masaryk and Edvard Beneš. Dubček died in a car crash in November 1992 on his way to Prague (he was a member of the Federal Assembly). (Table 7)

Historians have argued that the image of a golden age of Slovak history is related to early medieval pre-Hungarian history. In the nationalistic discourse the primacy of Great Moravia is unquestioned. It is also because in the context of Slovak-Hungarian relations this historical event can help to legitimate the primacy and cultural maturity

---

15 In 1999, a Hungarian commercial TV station and a left-wing daily, *Népszava*, conducted a straw poll on the most popular Hungarian personages. Eight people from the current representative survey appeared in the top twenty of the list (with their ranking in parenthesis): St Stephen (1), István Széchenyi (2), János Kádár (3), Matthias Corvinus (5), Lajos Kossuth (10), Sándor Petőfi (12), Ferenc Deák (14), and Ferenc Rákóczi (18).

of the Slovaks.[16] At the individual level, however, one also sees identification with more modern historical figures, such as Dubček, Ľudovít Štúr (the leader of the Slovak National Revival in the nineteenth century), and Štefánik. The historian Peter Macho sees the causes of this phenomenon in the discontinuity of historical development in Slovakia.[17]

National antiheroes:
Figures that citizens in V4 countries are ashamed of

The negative side of historical memory is represented by eminent figures perceived as antiheroes, whom people are ashamed of.[18] In the Czech Republic, the first five places on the list are occupied by Klement Gottwald, the first Communist President (30 %), Gustáv Husák, the President of the re-established hardline Communist regime after the crushing of the Prague Spring (19 %), Václav Klaus, the former President (7 %), Emil Hácha (7 %), the puppet President of the Protectorate of Bohemia and Moravia, and Miloš Jakeš, the General Secretary of the Communist Party after the crushing of the Prague Spring (6 %). (Table 2)

In Hungary the list contains only twentieth-century figures: Mátyás Rákosi, a Stalinist politician, and Ferenc Szálasi, the leader of the National Socialist Arrow Cross Party, Head of State and Prime Minister of the Kingdom of Hungary's 'Government of National Unity' for

---

16   A recent political gesture in this line was Prime Minister Robert Fico's government erecting a statue of Svatopluk I (*reg.* 871–894) at Bratislava Castle in 2009. According to politicians tending towards nationalism, the Great Moravia Empire is a source of Slovak culture and a symbol of national self-confidence. The inscription on the plinth of this equestrian statue reads: 'Svatopluk, King of the Ancient Slovaks', and quotes the opening salutation from a papal bull sent to Svatopluk by Pope John VIII in 880. The statue was designed by Ján Kulich, a sculptor prominent during the Communist era in Czechoslovakia.
17   Findor, A., Kiliánová, G., Macho, P. 'Symbolické aspekty národnej identity', in Kiliánová, G., Kowalská, E., Krekovičová, E. (eds.) *My a tí druhí v modernej spoločnosti*. Bratislava: Veda, Vydavateľstvo SAV, 2009, pp. 285–337.
18   In full the open-ended question asks: 'And on the other side, could you name historical personages you are ashamed of? Give a maximum of three names.'

the final three months of Hungary's involvement in the Second World War. Among the top five anti-heroes appear another two figures, though less antagonistic: Miklós Horthy, the emblematic figure of the post-First World War right-wing authoritarian system, and János Kádár, the leader of the oppressive post-1956 Socialist system. The contemporary left-right political division of Hungary is well reflected in the fact that both the former Socialist (Ferenc Gyurcsány) and the current right-wing prime minister (Viktor Orbán) rank close to each other near the top of the list. (Table 4)

The dark side of Polish history is represented by recent politicians: Jarosław Kaczyński (8 %), Prime Minister from July 2006 to November 2007, and currently Chairman of the Law and Justice Party, and Wojciech Jaruzelski (7 %), who was the last Communist leader of Poland from 1981 to 1989, and introduced martial law; they are followed by Bolesław Bierut (5 %), a Polish Communist leader and hardline Stalinist who became President of Poland after the Communist takeover, and Władysław Gomułka (4 %), a later Communist leader in Poland. The frequencies of these anti-heroes in such polls nevertheless remain low. (Table 6)

Among the figures Slovaks are the most ashamed of are Vladimír Mečiar, three times Prime Minister between 1990 and 1998, who is now seen as an 'historical figure' (he was mentioned by 19 % of the respondents), and Jozef Tiso, a Roman Catholic priest and President of the Slovak State during the Second World War (mentioned by 16 % of the respondents). In the 1990s, Tiso used to be perceived more controversially, but today there is a broader consensus on assessing him negatively.[19] (Table 8)

Amongst the figures representing the dark side of history, there is a pattern common to all the Visegrád countries. The percentage for anti-heroes is much lower than that for heroes. Moreover, the percentage for the options 'such a figure does not exist' or 'I do not know' or both is much higher. Above all, 67 % of the Polish respondents did not

---

19   See e.g. Gyárfášová, O., Krivý, V., et al. *Krajina v pohybe: Správa o politických názoroch a hodnotách ľudí na Slovensku*. Bratislava: IVO, 2001.

mention anyone. In Hungary that was 60 % and in Slovakia the proportion of ambiguous responses was 50 %. The most structured in their responses regarding anti-heroes were the Czech respondents— 34 % mentioned no one. The positive figures seem to be more visible, more recognizable in the popular perception of national history. This finding is fully in line with hypotheses of 'heroization' of national histories and the thesis that positive heroes cease to be authentic historical personalities, becoming instead symbols and myths, which makes them more present in the collective memory.

Another common feature shows that people tend to draw their heroes from the more distant past, ranging from the nineteenth century to just before the Second World War, whereas the anti-heroes are often current or almost current politicians whose images are vivid in the collective memory (Klaus, Kaczynski Mečiar, Ján Slota). The group of anti-heroes in each of the V4 countries includes the principal actors from both the totalitarian régimes that the countries were under in the twentieth century. It is of particular interest to see how they share the dark side of the history in each country. Gottwald (a representative of the Stalinist years in Czechoslovakia) and Husák (an incarnation of the years of re-established hardline Communism in Czechoslovakia). In Slovakia, the list is headed by Mečiar and Tiso, in Poland by Jaruzelski and Bierut (a similar pattern to the Czech), and in Hungary by Rákosi and Szálasi.

The findings in all four countries demonstrate that pride and shame may appear side by side: each country has a figure that may be present in both lists. In the Czech Republic it is Havel who in spite of his charisma had opponents as well (26 % of those polled chose Havel as a positive figure, compared to 4.8 % who chose him as a negative figure). A controversial figure in Hungary is Kádár (4.8 % of those polled chose him as their positive figure, compared with 5.5 % who chose him a negative figure). In Poland, it is Wałęsa (14 % positive, compared to 3.4 % negative), and in Slovakia, Tiso (16 % of those polled chose him as their negative figure, versus three per cent who chose him as the positive figure).

Who knows whom of their neighbour's history?

A considerable part of the survey focused on citizens' knowledge of other countries' history. Applying the 'personification approach', we asked about historical figures. Though we had expected a large *terra incognita* in recognition of historical figures in other countries, the extent of mutual indifference and 'amnesia' surprised even the greatest sceptics amongst us. The least known history among other central Europeans turned out to be Slovak, which is not represented by any widely shared historical figure. When asked the open-ended question 'When you look at the neighbouring Visegrád countries and their early and modern history, which important figure comes to mind? You may give a maximum of three names regardless of the positive or negative role in the history', nine out of ten Poles and Hungarians were unable to give any concrete name connected with Slovakia. Naturally, the situation between the Czechs and Slovaks is different because of the long past they had in common. Many Czech respondents mentioned the following historical figures from Slovak history: Mečiar, Jánošík, Dubček, Tiso, and Husák. On the other hand, the Slovaks most frequently recalled Havel, the first democratic and also the last Czecho-Slovak president (1989–92); Tomáš G. Masaryk, Charles IV., Jan Hus, and Edvard Beneš.

Unlike Slovakia, the other Visegrád countries have one generally valued figure whose recognition goes beyond national borders. In the Czech Republic it is unambiguously the late Havel, who holds a place not only in the Czech, Czechoslovak, and central European Pantheon, but also in the global Pantheon of distinguished figures who are highly respected and represent a widely shared ethos.

Similarly, Poland has Pope John Paul II. (born Karol Wojtyła). The Hungarian number-one was quite surprising, since the respondents of the other three Visegrád countries most frequently recalled Kádár, the representative of 'goulash socialism' of the 1970s and 1980s. Though the percentage of those who mentioned him was lower than the percentage of people mentioning a Czech and a Polish top personality, Kádár is the lowest common denominator in the minds of members of the other nations. Perhaps it is mostly the older generation that remembers the excellent Hungarian food and colourful markets in the period when the rest of the East bloc was predominantly grey and lacking in taste. One may wonder why they did not mention the current Prime Minister Viktor Orbán, who frequently makes headlines in the international press. But he is not yet seen as a historical figure.

In any case, the mirror of mutual awareness has one unquestionable winner — Mr. Nobody, or Her Majesty Collective Amnesia, or Indifference. In view of these results, the title of the conference could be reformulated as 'Your Hero–My Ignorance'. An interpretation of this state of affairs could usefully elaborate on a variety of factors, including unsuitable methods of teaching history, political manipulation, the use of history to meet current political 'demand', and a concentration on national history taken out of its central European context. The survey has clearly revealed that the history of the neighbouring countries is unknown and invisible. But that is not the fault of the mirror.

A new beginning

The survey also focused on the perception of events that took place over the last two decades and on mutual trust amongst the Visegrád countries citizens. In recent years, several important events occurred in central European countries or nearby. The respondents were asked to assess some of these events, and to say whether it was good or bad that they had happened. We have got unison responses across all four countries with regard to the fall of the Communist régimes in the late 1980s and the V4 countries joining the European Union and NATO. This historical re-start was difficult, with transition costs being high, but the change was worth going through the 'Valley of Tears'. Concerning the fall of the Communist régimes in the late 1980s, 76 % of the Poles, 71 % of the Czechs, 56 % of the Slovaks, and 54 % of the Hungarians who were asked, believe that it was a very or a rather good thing that it happened.

We also asked how the public perceived the establishment of regional cooperation within the Visegrád countries. The overwhelming majority responded positively: 61 % in Poland, 56 % in Slovakia, 54 % in Hungary, and 52 % in the Czech Republic. The other side of the coin was not a negative, but yielded the neutral or indifferent response 'I don't know'. The current findings may legitimately, at least indirectly, be compared with the findings of a similar survey conducted in 2003, shortly before the Visegrád countries joined the EU. At that time, the perception of Visegrád cooperation looked different: the most eager were the Slovaks, and one should recall that in the late 1990s Slovakia was the driving force of this regional platform, since regional cooperation was important for catching up in the integration process. Slovak politicians have frequently stated that the Slovak road to Brussels was through Visegrád. Today the establishment of Visegrád cooperation is most positively perceived in Poland. Is that because Poland is a regional leader? Or because it is the biggest and strongest Visegrád country, with assertive regional and European policies? Polish self-confidence could also be demonstrated by other statistics: Of V4 members, Poles are the proudest of their national history (76 %), compared to 43 % of Slovaks (the lowest percentage among the V4 countries). Moreover, 54 % of the Polish respondents believe that the overall course of history has mainly been upward, that is, making progress. In this respect, the most similar to them are the Czechs, with 53 %, followed by the Slovaks (39 %). The gloomiest interpretation is—as could be expected—amongst the Hungarians (with only 23 % of them seeing history as progress). In Poland, a unique pattern appears: pride in national history (some would say an 'obsession with history') combined with an optimistic outlook and high self-esteem.

The general perception of history: Are there any national patterns?

Pride in national history clearly prevails everywhere, but mainly in Poland. By contrast, most Hungarians see the general course of history as a decline. The Slovaks are the least proud of their national history, a reflection of the short period of being an independent country and the controversy about what constitutes 'national history'. Is it the history of the Slovak nation within other state entities or the history of the territory of Slovakia — which is of course also the history of other nations, above all Hungarians. (Table 9) On the other hand, however, Slovaks today see the course of history in a more positive light than Hungarians — 39 % of the respondents in Slovakia see human history as an upward course, as progress, whereas in Hungary such an opinion is shared by only 23 % of the respondents. (Table 10)

The cultural patterns of national pride and the way the course of human history in seen reveal interesting combinations: Poles are proudest of their national history and hold the lead in being optimistic about the future. The Czechs are slightly less proud, but do not lag behind the Poles when it comes to the course of history in general. Hungarians are proud, but profoundly pessimistic. The Slovaks are less proud, but more optimistic than the Hungarians. We anticipate that the attitudes have been affected not just by perceptions of the past but also by the present situation in the country.

Who trusts whom, or social capital in the Visegrád 4

When asked, 'To what extent could we trust and rely on the following nations?', the respondents could choose from a list of nations comprising the other three V4 countries, the USA, Russia, and three major European countries. Our survey revealed two extremes within the V4. The first was the clearly positive relationship between the Czechs and the Slovaks: 82 % of the Czechs trust their Slovak neighbours, and 81 % of the Slovaks trust their Czech neighbours, each considering the other the most trustworthy nation among the other eight. The figures seem to confirm the words of the Czech Foreign Minister, Karel Schwarzenberg, who recently quipped that the Czech and Slovak republics are the luckiest divorced couple he had ever met. The originally mutual distrust and accusations turned into a feeling of being the closest friends and allies. A long common history and cultural closeness won over mutual scepticism between the elder and the younger brothers.

The second extreme revealed by the survey is less encouraging. Distrust between the Slovaks and the Hungarians, with only 26 % of the Slovaks trusting the Hungarians (the only nation less distrusted are the Americans), and only 19 % of the Hungarians trusting the Slovaks (the only less distrusted nation are the Russians). The results reflect centuries of mutual relations and stereotypes. The trauma of some historical events played up by today's politicians has to be reflected in one's perceptions. One can only hope that the Most-Híd (meaning 'bridge' in Slovak and Hungarian) will be built not only between the Slovaks and the Hungarians living in Slovakia but also between Slovakia and Hungary.

Conclusion

Our surveys have shown that the national history of the Visegrád Four countries have more heroes than anti-heroes. Clear majorities (particularly in Poland) are proud of their national history. The golden era of these nations are most often considered to have been in earlier times, whereas the dark side of history is the years of the two totalitarian régimes that the countries experienced in the 20th century. Also, unpopular and untrustworthy contemporary politicians are often perceived as negative 'historical' figures. On the other hand, we see that the new beginning after the Changes of 1989 is judged very positively in all four countries — the citizens almost unanimously appreciate the collapse of the Communist régimes in the late 1980s, and the V4 countries' joining the European Union and joining NATO.

Our project also focused on mutual perceptions and the awareness of the history of the other countries. Regrettably, large gaps appear in neighbours' knowledge of each other. This presents a challenge not just for history teachers but also for Visegrád elites in the broadest sense. A popular adage has it that 'history is the teacher of nations.' Yet we can only learn from history if we know it. With close relations, a shared past, and common borders, we should clearly have much more empathy and understanding for our neighbours' histories.

Appendix

FREQUENCY TABLES (in percentages)

Eminent figures in national history — Czech Republic

Table 1

When thinking about Czech history, could you name figures you are proud of?[20]

Charles IV	48
Tomáš Garrigue Masaryk	43
Václav Havel	26
Comenius	19
Jan Hus	16
Jan Žižka	8
Saint Wenceslas	5
Maria Theresa	5
Božena Němcová	5
Edvard Beneš	5
No such figure exists	1
Don't know/NA	5

---

20 Give a maximum of three names. OPEN-ENDED QUESTION. (10 most frequent names, percentage of cases.)

Table 2

Could you name historical figures you are ashamed of?[21]

Klement Gottwald	30
Gustáv Husák	19
Václav Klaus	7
Emil Hácha	7
Miloš Jakeš	6
Václav Havel	5
Antonín Zápotocký	4
Edvard Beneš	4
Miroslav Kalousek	4
Ctirad and Josef Mašín	3
No such figure exists	8
Don't know/NA	26

21　Give a maximum of three names. OPEN-ENDED QUESTION. (10 most frequent names, percentage of cases.)

Eminent figures in national history — Hungary

Table 3

When thinking about the Hungarian history, could you name figures you proud of?[22]

Lajos Kossuth	31
István Széchenyi	28
Mátyás Király	20
Saint Stephan	18
Sándor Petőfi	13
Ferenc Rákóczi	9
Ferenc Deák	6
János Kádár	5
Imre Nagy	4
Lajos Batthyány	4
No such figure exists	9
Don't know/NA	11

---

22   Give a maximum of three names. OPEN-ENDED QUESTION. (10 most frequent names, percentage of cases.)

Table 4

Could you name historical figures you are ashamed of?[23]

Mátyás Rákosi	18
Ferenc Szálasi	12
Miklós Horthy	8
Ferenc Gyurcsány	6
János Kádár	6
Viktor Orbán	4
Béla Kun	2
Gyula Gömbös	2
Artúr Görgey	1
Ernő Gerő	1
No such figure exists	34
Don't know/NA	26

---

23 Give a maximum of three names. OPEN-ENDED QUESTION. (10 most frequent names, percentage of cases.)

Eminent figures of national history — Poland

Table 5

When thinking about the Polish history, could you name figures you are proud of?[24]

Karol Wojtyła (Pope John Paul II)	48
Jozef Pilsudski	26
Lech Wałęsa	14
Tadeusz Kosciuszko	9
Marie Curie (Maria Skłodowska-Curie)	7
Jan Sobieski	5
Nicolaus Copernicus	4
Władysław Jagiełło	4
Casimir III the Great (Kazimierz III Wielki)	4
Frédéric (Fryderyk) Chopin / Adam Mickiewicz	3
No such figure exists	6
Don't know/NA	19

---

24 Give a maximum of three names. OPEN-ENDED QUESTION. (10 most frequent names, percentage of cases.)

Table 6

Could you name historical personalities you are ashamed of?[25]

Jarosław Kaczyński	8
Wojciech Jaruzelski	7
Bolesław Bierut	5
Władysław Gomułka	4
Lech Wałęsa	3
Lech Kaczyński	3
Janusz Palikot	3
Donald Tusk	2
Felix Dzerzhinsky (Feliks Dzierżyński)	1
Aleksander Kwaśniewski	1
No such figure exists	29
Don't know/NA	38

---

25 Give a maximum of three names. OPEN-ENDED QUESTION. (10 most frequent names, percentage of cases.)

Personalities of national history — Slovakia

Table 7

When thinking about Slovak history, could you name figures you proud of?[26]

Milan Rastislav Štefánik	32
Alexander Dubček	32
Ľudovít Štúr	24
Juraj Jánošík	6
Tomáš Garrigue Masaryk	5
Pavol Országh Hviezdoslav	3
Pavol Demitra	3
Jozef Tiso	3
Saints Cyril and Methodius	3
Anton Bernolák	3
No such figure exists	9
Don't know/NA	17

---

26 Give a maximum of three names. OPEN-ENDED QUESTION. (10 most frequent names, percentage of cases.)

Table 8

Could you name historical figures you are ashamed of?[27]

Vladimír Mečiar	19
Jozef Tiso	16
Ján Slota	14
Gustáv Husák	6
Mikuláš Dzurinda	5
Robert Fico	4
Vasiľ Biľak	2
Andrej Hlinka	2
Iveta Radičová	2
Klement Gottwald	2
No such figure exists	11
Don't know/NA	38

---

27 Give a maximum of three names. OPEN-ENDED QUESTION. (10 most frequent names, percentage of cases.)

Table 9

In general, looking back on the history of the Czech/Hungarian/Polish/Slovak nation, would you say that you feel:

	Czech Republic	Hungary	Poland	Slovakia
Very proud	10	14	24	7
Rather proud	48	43	51	36
Neither proud nor ashamed	37	37	20	44
Rather ashamed	2	3	2	6
Very ashamed	1	2	0	1
Don't know/NA	2	1	3	6

Table 10

How would you describe the course of human history overall? Is it mainly:

	Czech Republic	Hungary	Poland	Slovakia
An upward course, progress	53	23	54	39
A downward course, decline	13	34	11	25
A course that is neither upward nor downward	24	36	23	27
Other	2	1	1	2
Don't know/NA	8	6	11	6

Theoretical context of Central Europe

History of Modern Central Europe, Anthropology, and Theory of Mimetic Rivalry

Ivo Budil[1]
University of West Bohemia

Abstract: The text emphasizes the importance of modern anthropology, its methods and tools of conceptualization for the study and understanding of history. Besides the microhistorical perspective of the investigation of historical anthropology there is a macrohistorical, or holistic dimension of contemporary anthropological thinking, enabling us to see the world as a whole and to study the interactions and mutual relationships among different parts of the world. Using these tools, the author looks at the emergence of totalitarianism and its related ideologies in the region of Central Europe.

The main purpose of this paper is to emphasize the importance of modern anthropology, and its methods and tools of conceptualization, for the study and understanding of history. In past decades many historians belonging, for instance, to the French *Annals* school or to the movement of *New Cultural History* have utilized anthropological methods in their regional research of local history or in the interpretation of human social interactions in the past. But besides the above-mentioned microhistorical perspective of historical anthropology there is also a macrohistorical, or holistic dimension to contemporary anthropological thinking, enabling us to see the world as a whole and to study the interactions and mutual relationships among different parts of the world.

The encounters of the various regions and civilizations could have deep and profound consequences in social, technological, political, or ideological domains. For instance, Hannah Arendt tried to explain in her book *The Origins of Totalitarianism*,[2] published shortly after

---

1 E-mail: budil@khv.zcu.cz.
2 Arendt, H. *Původ totalitarismu*. Prague: OIKOYMENH, 1996.

the Second World War, the political radicalization of Central European societies culminating by the emergence of modern totalitarianism by establishing a now famous dichotomy between older and traditional *colonialism* and a newer and more aggressive *imperialism*. Whereas colonialism included an extension of the laws and political ideology of the mother country to the colonial context, imperialism did not attempt to extent these laws and to assimilate the foreign territory, but focused rather on sheer exploitation and pure dominance though racist ideology and excessive violence. In this sense, imperialism was a direct precursor to totalitarianism, having presented the application of the methods of imperialism to dominate European society itself[3].

Hannah Arendt coined the phrase "boomerang effects" to characterize the mutual interaction between the West and the conquered territories which initiated dramatic changes and transformations in Western political culture. Therefore, it is impossible to understand the emergence of totalitarianism without considering the historical interaction between Europe and the non-European world, particularly Africa. Totalitarianism should be contextualized within the global European imperial endeavor. The experience gained by Europeans in the colonies, which was fed by a psychology of dominance and superiority, had far-reaching effects back in Europe. The idea that imperialism played a crucial role in creating the conditions of possibility for totalitarianism in Europe was not new. Similar views to those of Hannah Arendt were expressed for by William Edward Burghardt Du Bois and Aimé Césaire, for instance, who assumed that fascism was "European colonialism brought home"[4]. These scholars argue that it is unlikely that the Holocaust could have taken place without the precedent of colonial massacres.

---

3   Ibid., pp. 201–204.
4   King R., Stone D. *Hannah Arendt and the uses of history: imperialism, nation, race, and genocide*. New York: Berghahn Books, 2007, p. 4.

Despite the attempts of the above-mentioned authors, the global aspect of the interpretation of totalitarianism has been largely neglected in Western scholarship, which has preferred an entirely Europe-focused explanation for the emergence of totalitarianism. Totalitarianism has traditionally been considered to be a consequence of a long intellectual development of Western political ideology, a particular hidden aspect of German or Russian culture or perverse side of Western rationalism and the Enlightenment.

The historical distinctiveness of Central European societies and their particular historical path consisted in the relatively late establishment of the national state based on the ethnic homogeneity. The region had been dominated by the large traditional multinational states whose collapse enabled the expansion of totalitarian movements, fascism, Nazism and communism. From the economic point of view, the region had presented a periphery in contrast to the core located in North-Western Europe. Therefore, the clash of local identities shrouded in ethnic idioms with political aspirations constituted a never-ending game in the geopolitical space of Central Europe. Some Central European societies suffered significant territorial losses after the First World War and went through the traumatic experiences of revolutions, civil wars and political terrors. These events also created strong anti-Semitic sentiments. The local nationalist and populist political movements and parties exploited and ideologically manipulated selected historical symbols, traditions, and personalities to legitimize their territorial demands at the expense of their neighbors and rivals, or to initiate national revitalization. Sometimes, new political mythologies closely linked to a legendary past emerged. For instance, the Party of Racial Defence, founded by Major Gyula Gömbös in Hungary in 1919, proclaimed a mystical belief of the legendary Turanians who worshipped a War Lord called Hadúr[5]. The Legion of Archangel Michael established by Corneliu Zelea Codreanu in Romania assumed

---

5 Carsten, F. L. *The Rise of Fascism*. Berkeley: University of California Press, 1982, p. 175; Payne, S. *A History of Fascism, 1914–45*. London: Routledge, 1995, p. 286.

a strong semi-religious character and emphasized the peasant's unspoiled soul and the primitive values of the past[6].

I consider it quite impossible to understand the role of symbols and imagination in the course of ethnic, ideological and political rivalry without an anthropological perspective. French anthropologist René Girard assumes that people who compete with each other in the course of history are constantly imitating their rivals or their aspirations and collective desires. Participants in various historic events attempt to imitate and take possession of effectual and prestigious historical patterns and episodes, thus gaining an advantage over their rivals. The identification with a certain symbol, character, archetype or a more or less historical episode releases deep resources of collective psychic energy[7].

I am convinced that the Western collective imagination had been highly captured by the so-called the Eurasian revolution taking place approximately from 1750 to 1830, which brought radical change to relations between the West and the rest. The traditional non-Western civilizations were not able to face the mighty growth of Western economic, military, political and symbolical power caused by industrial revolution and other socio-economic changes in European society. The system of racial hierarchy, as developed in Western visions in the first decades of the 19th century, represented a global metaphor, originating in the Eurasian revolution, and subsequently became an important tool in mimetic rivalry[8].

After 1848, when the liberal expectations related to European revolutions had not been fulfilled, a biological understanding of race as a fatal predicate justifying the historically privileged status of a specific population was asserted. The frustration stemming from the unfulfilled goals of the 1848 revolution "biologized" the Western political

---

6   Ibid., p. 186; 279.
7   Girard, R. *O původu kultury*. Brno: Centrum pro studium demokracie a kultury, 2008.
8   Budil, I. *Úsvit rasismu*. Prague: Triton, 2013; idem, *Triumf rasismu*. Prague: Triton, 2015.

and ideological thinking as the confidence in the potential of public space dropped. That is what enabled the war between France and Prussia, which had broken out as a traditional fight for hegemony in Europe between two leading powers, but was soon interpreted as fatal racial conflict between the Germans and the Celts. The race category represented a way of emphasizing the continuity of contemporary political rivalry from ancient times. Political thinking dressed itself in myth and confronted Gaul and Germania. If the Mexican-American war demonstrated unambiguously the racial superiority of the Anglo-Saxons over the Latin mestizos, the Prussian-French conflict showed the triumph of the Germanic element over the romanized descendants of the Celts, in compliance with the widespread idea of racial hierarchy. The Anglo-Saxons and the Germans, two superordinate Nordic races, started controlling the world in the collective imagination and historical consciousness.

War and race constituted the two main components of the Nazi worldview. Konrad Heiden means that Adolf Hitler's actual goal was not Germany but unification of the Aryans and anti-Semites in order to achieve world dominion, predicted by Houston Stewart Chamberlain. In Hitler's speeches and dreams of "millennial empire", we can sense a remote echo of the "great geopolitical turn" from the period of 1756 to 1815, in which the balance of powers among traditional Eurasian great powers was disturbed. The global fight for hegemony set in, and Great Britain emerged as the winner. That empire presented itself externally as a "moral empire" with a special "civilizing mission" based on liberal and late-Enlightenment values. But we should not forget the relatively complicated ethnic development of the British Isles where, in the fifth and sixth centuries, the Celtic element clashed with the Anglo-Saxon and later with the Norman element. This conflict, including colonization of Ireland and violent subjugation of Wales and Scotland, was presented at the turn of the eighteenth and nineteenth centuries by romantic writers and historians as a racial one, concluded by triumph of the Anglo-Saxon race that had assumed control of the world. That seemingly illustratively that the way to build an empire was through purity of race, with elimination of "inferior" elements. Social Darwinists suggested that racial revitalization could be performed outside a lengthy historical process, through rational reforms and tools of modern science freed from hindering moral "prejudices" and sentiments. Adolf Hitler, admirer of the Anglo-Saxons, imitated the British example in the spirit of the genocidal amorality of social Darwinism in the political and ethnic conditions of Central European space. Central Europe, unlike the British Isles, was inhabited, side by side with the Germans, not by Celts but by Jews and Slavs. The German empire could emerge only by their elimination in Hitler's vision. Nazi ideology attempted to capture an imaginary Aryan and Germanic past and use it as an alternative symbol pattern during its confrontation with modern liberal Western civilization. Aryan ideology was meant to be the final word and ultimate triumph of the symbolic rivalry which had been present between the rivals of Eurasian civilization since at least the early Modern Era. Therefore, for the political and ideological development of the modern West, it was extremely important that German-speaking Central Europe was unified on an ethnic basis in the era of Great Britain's triumphant power. Traditional Germanism, which was revived at the turn of the 18th and 19th centuries, did not look only towards Tacitus's Germans, but also to Aryans as a higher and more prestigious incarnation of Germanism. Aryan ideology expressed the subconscious desire for a rise to power through imitating the prestigious Aryan model which was exemplified by Great Britain.

My Enemy — The Best Opportunity to Build One's Own Identity. Carl Schmitt Again.

Joanna Mysona Byrska
Pontificial University of John Paul II, Krakow

Abstract: This article aims to put the Carl Schmitt's Freund — Feind identity-building dilemma under scrutiny by introducing Józef Tischner's views on identity-building as a by-product of in-group solidarity into the contemporary discussion on forming of a common Visegrad identity. Furthermore, it raises questions on whether or not the work within and for a certain group of people is more productive as compared with work within a certain group and against another group.

Most people want to be "somebody" in life. To be somebody is connected with having the respect of your peers (those around you). Being someone is definitive. The man who is "somebody" has a clearly defined identity, he knows who he is and is usually proud of it. However, becoming "somebody" requires making an effort, it means working on oneself and often requires years of learning and aspiring towards the designated objective. After many years all of this produces the sought after effect and the man finally becomes "somebody". However, there is no guarantee. All this effort can be wasted and result in nothing — the man's efforts can be foiled and he will become no more than he already is, still a nobody, still insignificant.

As it turns out there is a much easier way to build one's own identity and that is by identifying who is your enemy — the one whom we consider alien, evil, harsh or disturbing. Identifying an enemy allows a person to acquire friends — that is, getting to know the people with whom we share a common enemy. Having a common enemy allows me to quickly and easily determine the total of who I am — because I have an enemy, which I share with others, I can also determine who is my friend — it is very simple — the one with whom I share an enemy.

It is worth asking who is this enemy that allows you to specify a group of friends, a group of "we". Carl Schmitt, who is the author of famous pairs of opposites: Freund—Feind (enemy—friend), wrote that the enemy (Feind) is an enemy by his very existence.[1] I decide who is my enemy, I identify the enemy—this type situation is optimal. If someone defines themselves as my enemy—and builds both his and my identity by identifying me as the enemy—the situation is more difficult. I am not completely sure why this man has identified himself as my enemy. He is my enemy and he fights against me. I bother him, according to Carl Schmitt, through the very fact of existing and filling the existential space which my enemy could have if I did not exist. Defining the enemy in these terms is similar to that of a war of aggression, or preventive war, when the attacker chooses the time, the place and the type of weapon with which to carry out the attack. In this way the aggressor can be well prepared and the war is carried out on someone else's territory and he is therefore able to defend his own terrain.

Having an enemy is, in an interesting way, connected with the postulate of tolerance. With enemies one does not need to be, nor should be, tolerant. Enemies are not tolerated. Enemies are fought. Tolerance—that is, tolerating the enemy in the name of the higher value, peace—may prove disastrous in the long run. The enemy will grow in strength and be a much greater threat. As Carl Schmitt wrote, fight the enemy, the enemy must be removed, the enemy is a threat that cannot be tolerated. By definition the enemy is evil.

Having an enemy simplifies a lot of things. The enemy—as this evil—is responsible for our failures and can be blamed for everything. It is not until the enemy has been definitively eliminated that the situation can heal, with the condition that another enemy does not appear making the effective action impossible. With an enemy I do not feel responsible for my own fate, what happens is, after all, a result of hostile action.

---

1   Schmitt, Carl. "Pojęcie Polityczności." In *Teologia polityczna i inne pisma*. Znak ed. Kraków, Kraków / Polska: Znak, 2000.

Defining oneself in opposition to someone or something — determination through negation or through denial — is easier than through what is positive. The perception of the world through "no" changes the individual, changes me. Here, the positive appears as a negative, and feelings characteristic of the negative image of the world such as hostility, hatred, resentment, fear, misunderstanding, intolerance, and lack of acceptance dominate. It's difficult to escape from the spiral of negative feelings into which a man falls when defining himself by the negative, by identifying the enemy. This person is changed not only emotionally but also changes everything around him by his negative emotion. Friends are then found among those who share enemies. People connect with each other not because of a common desire to experience nice moments together but through a common feeling of fear, hatred and danger. When the enemy disappears, changes, or offers an attractive solution to their existing supporters, the people connected only by negative feelings often and relatively quickly lose their sense of having something in common, the sense thing that unites them. They scatter because they lack the thing that untied them, the thing that was common. There is no enemy and it is not clear what can effectively take its place, perhaps a new enemy?

In the group which identifies itself by having a common enemy, there is also often an unusual understanding of what is accepted as solidarity. The Polish priest and spiritual guide of the Polish Solidarity movement, Józef Tischner, gave one of the most interesting expressions of what is meant by solidarity. Tischner defined solidarity in these words: "shouldering each other's burdens."[2] It was a call for cooperation, mutual assistance and the willingness to make sacrifices for other people. Being in solidarity is being together with others, sharing in their fate and cooperation, which should, according to Tischner, take the form of a conversation, a dialogue about what is essential and what is very practical and mundane.[3] For the group gathered around

---

2   http://www.wszechnica.solidarnosc.org.pl/?page_id=1410
3   Sperfeld, Enrico. *Arbeit Als Gespräch: Józef Tischners Ethik Der Solidarność*. Orig.-Ausg. ed. Freiburg I. Br.; München: Alber, 2012.

a common enemy being in solidary often only means joint operations against the enemy, and mutual aid, which is the core essence of solidarity Tischner's definition, seems to be peripheral.

Finally, there is a very interesting and at the same time disturbing category of "them" — "them" that is not ours, not us, not our own people, strangers. You do not have to respect "them" because they are not "ours", you can make them responsible for all our failures, or our unwillingness to act ("they are against us, they do not agree with us, they are not allowed" etc.) They are strangers, or bad, they are not like us, and therefore the best, and at the same time the easiest way, is to recognize them as enemies — the foreign, not ours, that is to say: bad.

When there is the above-described method for identifying who I am by what I am against, the situation is usually filled with negative feelings. It is very difficult to change and seems very easy to imitate.

The situation is greatly complicated when my or our enemy turns out to be a friend of someone who, until now, belonged to the group "we", who was at one time our friend. In a simple world, divided into enemies and friends at this time there is someone completely different, someone who wants to belong to both groups, someone who can mediate, mediate and change the way you identify with both sides. This task is difficult but not impossible.

The person who wants to be with "us" and "them" does not have an easy life. An obvious uncertainty that arises in a world divided into enemies and friends is that if a person likes "us", adheres to our principles and is like we are, then how is it possible that this same person is able to be a friend of our enemy? They are, after all, different. They are not us. One day they might attempt to destroy "us" because of this difference. In other words, the enemy is a permanent, potential threat. The enemy is different and because of that difference they aren't with us. They are strangers and pose a threat to us. Making friends with them is dangerous and suspicious.

Someone who wants to be a friend to everyone in a world that is divided into friends and enemies — a polarized world — can, for the group to which they thus far belonged, quickly become someone completely different than they want him to be. He will become a suspicious person for "us" and for "them." This person will become someone who each group is reluctant to trust. He will become an outsider. In order to prevent this type of situation, he must have great charisma as well as the ability to act and talk to other people. He must be someone who is able to handle the "phenomenon of tribalism." Richard Sennett, a student of Hannah Arendt, believes that this phenomenon is well characterized by contemporary social groups. He writes: "tribalism couples solidarity with others like yourself with aggression toward those who differ." The problem is that the tribal group only accepts and helps its own. It does not accept outsiders and does not provide them with assistance. The tribe defends its territory from intruders, is closed to others and treats them as enemies. Mistrust is the basic quality of the tribe which has a hostile attitude toward strangers. This behavior protects the tribe from threats which come from outside and allow it to survive during times of trouble.

As described by Sennett, the tribal phenomenon of being closed to others, hostile toward the other, and a refusal to give help when needed, appears to be justifiable in today's world. The group defends its members, they are afraid of others and this results in an increased chance of survival for the group.

For this reason a very sensitive and talented mediator will be able to win the trust of polarized groups who submit to this tribal phenomenon. For Carl Schmitt, there is no room for a person like this in a world divided into friends and enemies (Freund—Feind.) If a person like this were to appear he or she would be a great mediator, a natural negotiator or... a spy who is happy to gain the trust of both sides. Hostile groups would try to exploit this type of person for their own gain.

A world divided into friends and enemies, a world full of the political phenomena beyond the borders of ones own country, is a dangerous world. Of course the whole time we are speaking about the reality of the life of the person who builds his or her identity by identifying his or her enemies and being in opposition to them.

Within the limits of the state described by Carl Schmitt, the political phenomenon—that is a sharp division into groups of enemies and friends who are ready for armed combat with each other—does not appear in a country at peace. However, the person who forms his or her identity based on an attitude toward a potential enemy does not feel well, simply cannot feel good in a country at peace. Although the country is at peace and people are not shooting at each other in the streets there remains a sense of danger for this person. The conviction that the enemy is somewhere and might appear at any moment is rooted in his consciousness. This belief accompanies this type of person constantly. It is even possible to say that it poisons his or her thoughts and will. Carl Schmitt spoke about countries and their mutual hostility. The phenomenon of politics would concern only the countries themselves. However, today the divisions between friends and enemies do not only exist between countries. The dividing lines run between countries, cultures, religions, or simply between people who have different social status.

The human being is an intelligent animal and has instincts just as animals do, even if they are only residual. Every animal looks for a safe place to rest. And this safe place for the human is their home. A safe, warm home has been a constant theme throughout history and literature as well as the dream of every person. The home must be a safe haven, a friendly place where one feels good. The (unfortunately common) feeling of insecurity causes people to try to make their homes safe. It is quite normal to see a sign "protected by..." with the name of the company on homes in Poland. These companies, for a small fee, protect the possessions of the owners and allow them to sleep peacefully.

Another expression of this sense of danger is the desire for people to isolate themselves from what is hostile or ugly in monitored gated communities. Inside the walls of these communities it is safe — there is a guard, paid for by the residents, who ensures that only the owners or their guests enter. A closed monitored housing estate becomes an isolated, safe, and prosperous island, which can arouse hostile feelings among those who are not allowed to go there. Jealousy of inaccessible space can be a first indicator for the potential build up of hostility.. Just as often jealousy can be what motivates people to action—a jealous man might "want that too" and will begin to work hard to achieve it. The public sphere—the space of the community when it is surrounded by a wall and closed, is, however, appropriated. The interior streets are available only to the residents. Non-residents must avoid the area entirely. Even as a result of this simple fact animosity and small animosities may appear and from small animosity open hostility may not be far off. A closed, monitored housing estate is certainly richer than one that is not monitored. They are nicer and better. And, after all, why is it closed? People who isolate themselves must surely have some kind of reason. Envy might develop among those who do not have access to the space, which is a good basis for the development of hostility.

Another problem in a world in which some people build their identity based on the divisions of friends and enemies (us—them), and which is also present in the phenomenon of tribalism is in the work place. Real work, as described by Jozef Tischner who died in 2000 and was the spiritual guide of Solidarity, is cooperation. We work surrounded by other people and we produce for other people. Through work a person puts down roots into the world in which he or she is working, is changing this world and is building—or destroying it. Whether the man builds or destroys through his work depends on his basic attitude to the world and the purpose of his work.

Work is good work if the person is working "for"—for oneself in order to support oneself and one's family or for other people, that is, to deliver products or services that they need. It is also essential that the person works in a place that he respects. Through work, writes Tischner, a person "is rooted in the world" he is building the world around himself and in the process is also creating himself. If the person doesn't respect this world, is looking only at the profit—his or her work will be a type of robbery and the working person will be a kind of thief. However, if it is not, work can and should become a cooperation, work as a type of conversation, an exchange between people and the world.

Joseph Tischner wrote:

> "Work is a dialog. People who are working are having a conversation. Work is born out of a conversation and its further development. The internal understanding of the human conversation is also the internal understanding of the work. The external understanding is called agreement. The conversation approaches its essence when it becomes an agreement. It is similar with work. That too approaches its essence when it becomes cooperation. As argument is a speech pathology, so conflict is a work pathology."

According to Tischner work is based on an agreement, understanding, sharing of responsibilities and openness to the other, a kind of invitation for joint action. In other words, it is the opposite of everything we associate with the phenomenon of tribalism mentioned above.

However, if the working person senses a constant threat, is a member of a distrustful tribe and his reality has undergone a polarization between enemies and friends it will be visible in his work. Full of fear and having enemies, people will work primarily to protect themselves and their family, to protect themselves from attack. If the people with whom he or she is working share his or her fears and have a common opponent—an entire group of working people can appear "against" the enemy. The change of work "for" to work that is "against" causes the work, as Joseph Tischner writes, to become sick. Sick work loses its cooperative character—it works against itself, it becomes a struggle, it takes prioity over the work and it becomes necessary to mobilize forces against those who threaten it.

The work "against" allows a person to bypass these issues that are important when they work 'for'. When a person works "against" there is always an enemy in the background—a threat that must be avoided at all costs. The existence of that threat allows for the omission of secondary issues, and for the encouragement of people to maximum effort—after all, through the work they are defending themselves against the enemy, they are actively serving on the front lines of work. In an atmosphere of danger it is possible to require employees to make their strongest effort. This applies not only to the "against" work situation, but to every job performed in a threatening atmosphere. From the employees who are afraid (e.g. afraid of losing their job) it is possible to require more effort for less compensation.

Fear, as the Stoics argued, is the worst emotion that can affect man because it paralyzes reason and will. People who are afraid often lose understanding of their situation. Fear limits their ability to be prudent and take rational action. Most people work hard in order to protect themselves and their family from danger. An employee working in fear of an external threat or of losing a job is someone who is easily controlled.

For the man who builds his identity based on the enemy he fears, there is another problem. The problem that proves that loyalty to this so-called "us" may prove, in spite of everything, to be a disadvantage. It is a problem that can tentatively be called the problem of the shrewd man. The shrewd man is an intelligent man but one who is not guided by right reason. He is not prudent. The shrewd man is cunning and has the ability to benefit from any situation. This shrewdness differs from the wisdom classified among the cardinal virtues in that it does not and cannot contain the famous eight abilities that make up the virtue of prudence. The shrewd man takes his own good into account above everything else. He is an egoist who won't limit his possibilities on account of other people. He is driven by a shrewdness that allows him to exploit the weaknesses of others and does not take into account the adverse effects that his actions have on other people.

In order to understand why the shrewd man wins over the prudent man, we should imagine this situation. Two people are going after something that is very important to them both. They can share it, it is not something indivisible, but it would be worth less divided than undivided. They walk together side by side until they come to a fence surrounding a large area. There is a sign on the fence which states that the area is dangerous and one should not go in. It is a low fence that can easily be jumped. The shortcut is much quicker than the path around the fence. The desired item that is good for both the shrewd man and the virtuous man is just on the other side of the enclosed area. And thus appears the question: Which road to choose? The long one which goes around the dangerous area or the short one through the unsafe terrain?

The shrewd man will choose the shorter road. He will choose it because he knows that the virtuous man is next to him and the shrewd man can safely assume, knowing his companion, that in case of emergency the virtuous man will assist him. After all they belong to the same group and should be loyal to each other and help each other in difficult times. The shrewd man leaves the virtuous man behind and goes through the dangerous area. What happens as a result of being driven by shrewdness is that the possibility of achieving the desirable good is supposedly greater than the possibility that he will be killed. If nothing happens to him while taking the shortcut, he'll be the first one there. He will not share with the other, the one who went around and got there later, because he will not feel it is necessary and will not want to wait. Waiting is a waste of time for the shrewd man.

But if something bad happens to our shrewd man in the dangerous area he will call for help, which is completely natural. The virtuous man who is going the long way round will hear the cries for help. He will hear and, because he is virtuous and right thinking, will hurry to help. He is not in a mental state to not help. The other man is calling for help and is someone who also belongs to the same group. He will expose himself to danger but will try to help. After all the other man is calling for help. After providing assistance they, the shrewd man and the man who provided help, will go together for the good on the other side of the enclosure. Together they will reach the destination and the shrewd man (who is not bad, but merely shrewd) will share with the one who saved him.

In every possible variant of this story, apart from the variant with the tragic death of the shrewd man in the dangerous area, the shrewd man wins. He will either be quicker or will arrive together with the virtuous man.

The virtuous man seems to be at a disadvantage. However, he is not completely. He is a loyal member of his group. When he reaches the target after the shrewd man, who has not divided the good but taken it all for himself, the virtuous man can tell his group. Much depends on how the group with a strong tribal character will react. They might condemn the shrewd man and give full support to the virtuous man. However, they might also consider that the virtuous man showed weakness, did not rise up to the challenge and did not take the risk. Both situations are possible. For a man who builds his identity based on the character of the enemy, the latter possibility seems as equally probable as the first. This is a world in which there cannot be many who are weak because it is necessary to protect them. The strong group will survive, the weak one will not necessarily.

To build one's own identity by identifying ones enemies is very complex. The permanence of such an identity depends on the strength of the image of the enemy, to the extent that it is hateful, dangerous and real. The loss of the enemy will require the need to rebuild ones identity. But keep in mind that the enemy is — as Carl Schmitt wanted it to be — an existential enemy, you do not have to dislike him, he simply must occur in a place that would be "mine" or "ours". When one disappears, another worthy enemy will be found to replace him very quickly.

People taught to build their identity and define themselves by reference to the enemy quickly replace one with another. This is a very simple mechanism. One that is easy to reproduce. It does not require great effort or difficult work. It is sufficient to simply take a negative stance toward somebody and to look for other people who have similar opinions.

The national identity can be also constructed in an easy way by appealing to character of the enemy, created for that purpose. Our enemy may be a specific group or a different attitude. The enemy is evil, we should be afraid of a foreigner/stranger. In such a case the national identity can shape the basis of feelings insecurity and promote nationalism.

To some extent, this phenomenon can be observed in building the identity of Visegrad countries. This image is slightly exaggerated, but it captures the crux of the problem. The Poles are a big nation, strongly linked to the Catholic church. When Poland was divided between the three partitioning powers, the national identity was simple: Poles are Catholic. Polish Catholicism is national, with strong libertarian movements in the past. Poland's southern neighbors are the Slovaks, a small nation and country of many mountains in the center of Europe. Slovaks perceive Poles as having expansionist tendencies and are also able to take the advantage of the situation. The Czechs are more numerous than the Slovaks, with a sense of superiority. They are closer to the Germans. Finally—the Hungarians, the former imperial country, important in Europe. In the Visegrad countries only Hungarians speak a language completely incomprehensible for Poles, Slovaks and Czechs.

The building of a common identity of the Visegrad Group without any form of enemy, which could be consolidated in a sense of a danger, is a long process. An external threat that would endanger all four countries should be consolidating for them. But it is not so easy as it turns out. When the enemy is identified, they will first look for help elsewhere before looking to the other countries of the Visegrad Group. However, there is a motivation to work together.

Civic and ethnic nationalism and the identity formation of Central European societies in the interwar period

Dorota Pietrzyk-Reeves[1]
Jagiellonian University in Krakow

Abstract: The aim of this paper is to re-examine the well-known distinction between civic and ethnic nationalisms and its application to the Central European context after the First World War. Although scholars associate ethnic nationalism primarily with this part of Europe, the establishment of multiethnic states such as the Polish Republic, Yugoslavia or Czechoslovakia after 1918 suggests that what was at stake was civic nationalism: a nationhood that reflects common citizenship of political community rather than common culture and ethnicity. However, the question is why there was so much tension on ethnic grounds between different national groups and why in some cases ethnic nationalism prevailed. This is too complex an issue to be explained in one paper, my aim is more modest and concerns the validity of the distinction between civic and ethnic nationalism in Eastern and Central Europe in the interwar period.

The aim of this paper is to re-examine the well-known distinction between civic and ethnic nationalism and its application to the Central European context after the First World War. Paradoxically, although scholars associate ethnic nationalism primarily with this part of Europe, the establishment of multinational or multiethnic states such as the independent Polish Republic, Yugoslavia or Czechoslovakia after 1918 suggests that what was at stake was civic nationalism: a nationhood that reflects common citizenship of political community rather than common culture and ethnicity. However, if that was the case, the question is why there was so much tension on ethnic grounds between different national groups and why in some cases ethnic nationalism prevailed. This is too complex an issue to be explained in one paper, my aim is more modest and concerns the validity of the very distinction between civic and ethnic nation/nationalism in Eastern and Central Europe in the interwar period. To address this question we need

---

1   Email: d.pietrzyk-reeves@uj.edu.pl

to examine the process and conditions of identity formation, especially national identity formation in the societies of the region.

When the Great War ended, many phenomena were taking place in Central and Eastern Europe including the national awakening of some ethnic groups, statehoods being regained, nation-states being built, struggles for national identity and its protection, divisions between "us" and "them"s, and the rise of national minorities and their struggle for recognition. Nation-building policies were designed to promote cultural unity and unconditional loyalty to the state[2]. For the complex histories of Central European nations — Czech, Slovak, Polish and Hungarian — the year 1918 signified a starting point, the beginning of the twentieth century, a new stage in their political, social and national development. It is never easy to deal with completely new challenges, something we know very well, bearing in mind the experience of 1989 and the early 1990s. Some of these challenges in 1918–1920 were the questions of how to consolidate a new statehood, what is the most appropriate way of dealing with multinational societies, or whether nation-state building is the only available strategy and if so, what principles it should be based on. The collapse of multinational states such as Austro-Hungary initiated the process of nation-state building when "nations" in this part of Europe had to define or redefine themselves anew. It was the triumph of the nation-state, as many scholars emphasize. National identity formation played a significant role in this process, and arguably was reinforced by the new opportunities for political self-determination that emerged at the end of the war. Of course not all historical or nominal nations could create their own nation-states. Some like Ukrainians ended up living within borders of more than one nation state, which has had long-term consequences visible even today. In addition, the rise of national minorities

---

2   Green, A. Education, Globalization and the Nation State. New York: St. Martin's Press, 1997, pp. 29–40.

and their struggle for recognition was to become one of the most difficult and unresolved issues in the interwar period[3].

The analysis that follows will focus on the well-known distinction between civic and ethnic nationalism and its applicability to the Central European nations after the First World War. According to the traditional approach[4], civic identity is an inclusive identity that lacks a strong ethnic attachment and civic nationalists are relatively tolerant of other ethnic groups living within the territorial boundaries of the state while ethnic nationals place importance on the history, cultural values, religion and promotion of their sub-group to the exclusion of others. How far do the processes of identity formation in Central Europe support this distinction? Can it be reformulated to be a valid category of analysis of this region or should it be abandoned altogether?

The distinction in question was reinvented[5] by Hans Kohn in his *The Idea of Nationalism. A Study of Its Origins and Background* (1944). Civic nationalism was premised on Enlightenment values of reason and precedence of the state over ethno-cultural appeals to solidarity. As Kohn stressed, it was "predominantly a political movement to limit governmental power and to secure civic rights. Its purpose was to create a liberal and rational civil society representing the middle-class and the philosophy of John Locke"[6]. It was associated with democracy, liberalism and constitutional rule and its aim was to liberate the individual. As it was adopted by peoples in Central and Eastern Europe, according to Kohn, 'nationalism became there first a cultural move-

---

3   Chlebowczyk, J. Między dyktatem, realiami a prawem do samostanowienia: prawo do samookreślenia i problem granic we wschodniej Europie Środkowej w pierwszej wojnie światowej oraz po jej zakończeniu. Warszawa: PWN, 1998.
4   Kohn, H. Nationalism: Its Meaning and History. Princeton: N.J. Van Nostrand, 1955, and Plamenatz, J. 'Two types of Nationalism' in Kamenka, E. (ed.) Nationalism: The nature and evolution of an idea. Canberra: Australian National University Press, 1973, pp. 23–36.
5   Scholars find this distinction already in a 1868 work of Émile de Laveleye, Belgian economist and academic.
6   Kohn, H. The Idea of Nationalism: A Study of Its Origins and Background. New York: The Macmillan Company, 1944, p. 29.

ment, the dream and hope of scholars and poets'. This new nationalism 'looked for its justification and differentiation from the West to the heritage of its past'[7]. The problem with ethnic nationalism, in this view, is that it stressed group interests over individual liberty and was considered to have a tendency to illiberalism and authoritarianism. Margaret Canovan goes even so far as to stress that "from a theoretical point of view, liberal-individualist' and 'romantic-collectivist' nationalisms are very different and probably incompatible"[8]. In many ways, president Woodrow Wilson's Fourteen Points promulgated in 1918 represented, if only symbolically, the high point of liberal nationalism in so far as they stressed 'the absolute sovereignty of the national state, but sought to limit the implications of this principle by stressing individual liberties — political, economic and religious — within each nation state' (Vincent 2002, 88). The key theme was the right of self-determination by nations, with the proviso that such self-determination would inevitably lead to constitutional, liberal, democratic rule. This proved extremely difficult to implement as the example of Ukrainians on the one hand and Hungarians on the other clearly prove. There was no solution for resolving conflicts between liberal national states and even more problematically, secessionist movements *within* liberal or illiberal nation states. But of course this was not Wilson's problem.

The implications of this dichotomy for explanations of nationalism are mainly indirect, but it suggests something worth considering for our discussion. If Kohn is right, civic nationalism was a project of the state, aiming to disseminate a sense of nationality that was essentially political, and coextensive with the state. Ethnic nationalism is the result of a completely different process; state seeking and state consolidation; and often was a protest against existing state forms, expressed initially largely in cultural terms, and was 'a venture in edu-

---

7   Ibid., p. 30.
8   Canovan, M. Nationalism and Political Theory. Cheltenham: Edward Elgar, 1996, pp. 6–9.

cation and propaganda rather than in policy shaping and government'⁹. After the First World War the emphasis on ethnicity in Central and Eastern Europe might be explained as a prerequisite for the building of a nation-state rather than because it promised mere ethnic solidarity. The demand for a political nation was associated with the popular demand for the political right to vote in Western nation-states, whereas in Central Europe demands for national unity and independence were of crucial importance.

In order to illustrate how this dichotomy may work in the context we are interested in, I will briefly discuss two contrasting views of the nation and the state that we find in Roman Dmowski and Józef Piłsudski, two rivals and giants of Polish modern history and the most significant politicians both before and after 1918. They disagreed fundamentally on the question of how to define the Polish nation and its relationship to the Polish state. Dmowski, the leader of the right wing Narodowa Demokracja (National Democracy) advocated a compact homogenous Poland comprised only of the territory in which Polish Catholics were the majority. Ethnic minorities in Eastern Poland were welcome, but were to be subject to "Polonization"[10]. Pilsudski, the chief of state and the Polish leader who gained prominence as the father of Polish independence, sought to establish a Polish-led democratic federation of independent states, an *Intermarium* ("betweensees"), in the vein of the Polish-Lithuanian Commonwealth. It was to be a federation of free states stretching from the Baltic to the Black Sea. Resurrected Poland was to be a multinational and multiethnic, civic rather than an ethnic state.

It is Piłsudski's view of the Polish nation that particularly complicates the clear distinction between civic and ethnic nationalism. Polish post-Romantic nationalism, — which Piłsudski did not

---

9   Kohn, H. Nationalism: Its Meaning and History. Princeton: N.J. Van Nostrand, 1955, p. 330.
10 Polonsky, A. Politics in Independent Poland 1921–1939. Oxford: Oxford University Press, 1972, p. 59.

share[11] — nurtured the vision of united Polish nation defined in linguistic or ethnic terms and rejected the Commonwealth (multiethnic civic state) as a basis for Polish identity[12] and it led later to the vision of Polishness defined by language, religion and ancestry. Pilsudski, who was both Polish and Lithuanian, envisaged the nation not in ethnic terms as a particular collection of people but rather as a historical force[13]. Unlike Dmowski, he was concerned with Poland understood as a state and not as a nation or a people[14]. In that sense it seems that Pilsudski's view of the nation and the state was closer to the ideals of civic nationalism, seeing the nation in political rather than ethic terms, as a territorial and historical entity[15], with its people sharing common citizenship and belonging to a political community, but not necessarily the same blood, language or religion. Dmowski viewed the state as an instrument of the nation for its liberation, survival and development whereas for Piłsudski the state was in a sense above the nation or prior to the nation.

It seems easy to classify Dmowski's nationalism as ethnic, however, it was not only exclusivist, but also assimilationist; he welcomed other nationalities such as Ukrainians or Belarusians and Jews (the three biggest national minorities in Poland in the inter-war period) as long as they were willing to fully assimilate into the Polish nation. Pilsudski's vision was inclusive and non-assimilationist, although he

---

11 Walicki, A. 'Intellectual Elites and the Vicissitudes of the 'Imagined Nation' in Poland', East European Politics and Societies 11 (2), pp. 227–253.
12 Ibid., p. 348.
13 Brykczynski, P. 'A Poland for the Poles? Józef Piłsudski and the Ambiguities of Polish Nationalism', PRAVO: The North American Journal For Central European Studies 1:1.
14 Kulesza, W. T. 'Myśl Polityczna Józefa Piłsudskiego', Przegląd Historyczny 74 (1), 1983, pp. 49–73.
15 Ibid., pp. 254–255.

expected members of different national groups to pledge unconditional loyalty to the Polish state[16]. Yet he was still very much concerned with an imagined vision of the state, the state that should be as his geopolitical conception presupposed. This was not the existing Polish state with its borders defined in 1918-1919. He hoped for the resurrection of the Commonwealth of the Two Nations, with considerable devolution of power to Ukrainian, Belarusian and Lithuanian territories, although with Poles retaining a leading role. This vision, romantic as some scholars say, proved to be unrealistic. Therefore, as Brykczynski rightly points out, Piłsudski's nationalism was not entirely civic either[17].

The key problem is that this dichotomy may well overstate the implications of these two types of nationalism; especially since nationalism everywhere may be seen to contain different mixes of these two conceptions of the nation. As Rogers Brubaker pointed out, sharp contrasts between Western civic nationalism and Eastern ethnic variant leads to 'a dubious series of linked oppositions — between universalism and particularism, inclusion and exclusion, civility and violence, reason and passion, modern tolerance and ancient hatreds, transnational integration and nationalist disintegration'[18]. Ethnic nationalism should not be seen only in the Central and Eastern European context as if it never existed in the West[19]. The term civic nationalism makes sense only in reference to citizenship and statehood but without excluding culture, as the examples of France and the USA indicate. "The nation is conceived in language not in blood" and is joinable in time

---

16 Zubrzycki, G. 'The Classical Opposition Between Civic and Ethnic Models of Nationhood: Ideology, Empirical Reality and Social Scientific Analysis', Polish Sociological Review 3 (139), pp. 275-295.
17 Brykczynski, P. 'A Poland for the Poles? Józef Piłsudski and the Ambiguities of Polish Nationalism', PRAVO: The North American Journal For Central European Studies 1:1.
18 Brubaker, R. 'The Manichean Myth: Rethinking the Distinction between 'Civic" and 'Ethnic' Nationalism, in Kriesi, H., et al. Nation and National Identity: the European experience in Perspective. Zurich: Ruegger, 1999.
19 Shulman, S. 'Challenging the Civic/Ethnic and West/East Dichotomies in the Study of Nationalism', Comparative Political Studies 35 (5), 2002, pp. 554-585.

(Andreson 1991, 145). Civic nationalism is based on common citizenship whereas ethnic nationalism is based on common ethnicity or common ethno-cultural identity. It is however unclear what factors make nations become civic and what factors make them an ethnic type.

A long history of statehood corresponds with the civic type of nationhood. A good example of that is the Polish-Lithuanian Commonwealth which existed towards the end of the 18th century, a multiethnic and multicultural polity with a common sense of citizenship and political rights among the nobility. Civic nations developed in Britain and France. I would argue that of crucial importance in this process is the consolidation of a political nation and its continuity guaranteed by its own statehood. Nations that have lost their statehood, such as Poles or Czechs, become extremely vulnerable and must redefine and strengthen their identity which no longer can be expressed in terms of civic and political principles but in terms of cultural, religious and ethnic components as well as a reference to common national history. This is when national consciousness develops outside or in opposition to the framework of existing states. The interwar period in Central Europe is complicated by the experience of nations that regained their statehood, but still defined themselves in ethnic and cultural terms and referred to history that was lost but was of crucial importance to their memory.[20] In the West the state precedes the nation, whereas in the East, because of discontinuity of statehood, nation precedes the state.

---

20 Debates about "Europe" constituted an integral part of nation-building processes in the 19th century. National elites employed images of "Europe", the "West" and the "East" to construct national consciousness. Historians played key role as nation-builders because they were able to "invent" a nation's tradition, proving its existence from time immemorial and claiming cultural and even political autonomy. Moreover, historians could deliver historical arguments for the "European" character of their nation. Which images of "Europe" did historians implement in their historical narratives and how did they utilize these images as discursive strategies to promote national goals? See e.g. Coakley, J. 'Mobilizing the Past: Nationalist Images of History, Nationalism and Ethnic Politics, 10 (4), 2004, pp. 531–560.

Recent scholarship on nationalist taxonomy has challenged this conceptual dualism[21] by noting that all manifestations of nationalism contain elements of both 'civic' and 'ethnic' types. Stefan Auer concluded that also during the interwar period one could fairly easily find elements of liberal nationalism in the articulation of the national identities of the peoples of Central and Eastern Europe[22]. He suggests that the relative triumph of 'illiberal nationalism' during the period had as much to do with the prevailing intellectual climate than anything intrinsic to the histories or cultures of the Eastern European nations. Along these lines, it is worth keeping in mind that nationality during this period was linked to all sorts of anti-liberal ideas even in Western countries supposedly imbued with civic nationalism[23]. Others argue that the fundamental principles underlying the establishment of nation-states after the Great War closely resembled John Stewart Mill's liberal nationalism. In the spirit of Wilson's Fourteen Points (1918), these principles stated that the new European order should be based on the right to national self-determination[24]. But as Mill was aware already in 1861, there were significant difficulties in implementing the national ideal of a state for each nation, including above all the geographic difficulty. In the Wilsonian era the prevailing belief was that "only large states could be free and progressive, while small ones were doomed to dependence and oppression: The ideal state was nationally

---

[21] See e.g. Brown, D. 'Are there good and bad nationalisms?', Nations and nationalism 5 (2), 1999, pp. 281–302.; Kedourie, E. Nationalism. Oxford: Blackwell, 1993, pp. 136–144; Smith, A. D. The Ethnic Origins of Nations. Oxford: Blackwell, 1986, pp.: 129–152; Nieguth, T. 'Beyond dichotomy: concepts of the nation and the distribution of membership', Nations and nationalism 5 (2), 1999, pp. 155–173.; Kuzio, T. 'The myth of the civic state: a critical survey of Hans Kohn's framework for understanding nationalism', Ethnic and Racial Studies 25 (1), 2002, pp. 20–39; Shulman, S. 'Challenging the Civic/Ethnic and West/East Dichotomies in the Study of Nationalism', Comparative Political Studies 35 (5), 2002, pp. 554–585.

[22] Auer, S. Liberal Nationalism in Central Europe. Taylor & Francis, 2004.

[23] Mentzel, P. C. 'Nationalism, Civil Society, and the Revolution of 1989, Nations and Nationalisms, Vol. 18, No. 4, 2012, p. 628.

[24] Tamir, Y. Liberal nationalism. Princeton: Princeton University Press, 1995.; Vincent, A. Nationalism and Particularity. Cambridge: Cambridge University Press, 2002, p. 142

and culturally homogenous, politically centralized and economically and technologically developed, and militarily powerful, namely, self-sufficient and thus free"[25] hence Poland gained access to the Baltic Sea and Bohemia, and agricultural Slovakia and Ruthenia were combined to create the multinational state of Czechoslovakia.

There is another dimension of the distinction in question that attributes one or the other version of nationalism to the political system. "Civic nationalisms are more likely to be found in more democratic states, so that other mechanisms through which civil and other liberties are protected are established more effectively"[26]. The problem of nationalism may well be associated with the problem of democracy in the interwar period. Recalling John Breuilly's suggestion that 'the language of nationality was central to the task of fusing the principles of territoriality and constitutionalism'[27], it can be suggested that ethnic nationalism may be attributable to the desire for democracy, and if one is concerned with illiberal politics in Central and Eastern Europe it may be more useful to investigate the foundations of liberal and illiberal democracy than to attempt to distinguish between civic and ethnic nationalism[28].

The processes of nation state building and identity formation in Central Europe after 1918 are very complex and escape a simple analytical clarification that the distinction between civic and ethnic nationalism aimed to provide. It does not need to be abandoned altogether, but it cannot be applied to the Central and East European context, almost mechanically, as used to be the case. My aim here was to indicate the complexity of the situation that societies and nations of newly independent states had to face and cope with, including a new sense of belonging, allegiance, identity, engagement or apathy, and

---

25 Ibid.
26 Harris, E. Nationalism: Theories and Cases. Edinburgh: Edinburgh University Press, 2009, p. 33.
27 Breuilly, J. Nationalism and the State. Manchester: Manchester University Press, 1993.
28 Rowley, D. G. 'Giuseppe Mazzini and the democratic logic of nationalism', Nations and Nationalism 18 (1), 2012, pp. 39–56.

being a member of the majority or minority. Civic and ethnic nationalisms, in real stories and perceptions, may well overlap since being a member of an ethnic, dominant nation and patriotic movement do not exclude viewing the state as civic rather than an ethnic/national category, as perhaps Piłsudski's view indicates.

A Heritage of Historic Hungary — Remembrance and Revisionism as an Approach to Hungarian Nation Building in the Inter-war Period

Miklós Zeidler[1]
Hungarian Academy of Sciences

Abstract: The paper examines the influence of historical revisionism and commemoration rituals on the process of Hungarian nation building after the dissolution of the Kingdom of Hungary. Amidst the cultural and political crisis that ensued the fall of the Empire, Hungarians, like other ethnicities that once co-existed in it, had to search for a new, national identity. To establish it, they drew, as the paper argues, on several symbolic systems that referred to an imagined idealistic construction of "Historic Hungary", from then on strongly embedded in Hungarian collective memory.

The year 1896 marked the Millennium of Hungary, i.e. the millenary festivities commemorating the Conquest of the Carpathian Basin by the Hungarian tribes. Besides evoking the vicissitudes of a troubled past, Hungary celebrated its recent political and economic prosperity and a tide of assimilation, which suggested that the integration of national and minority groups was on its way.

A quarter of a century later Historic Hungary—as it was frequently referred to—collapsed as a result of its defeat in World War I, and of the secession of various national minorities. The dissolution of the Kingdom of Hungary was legally sanctioned by the Treaty of Trianon signed, in 1920, by defeated Hungary and by the victorious Allied and Associated Powers.

Such a turn of events shattered the image of "a proud and capable nation in a prosperous country". In Hungarian public speech, however, the "dismemberment" or "mutilation" of Historic Hungary appeared as a plot organized by self-appointed minority leaders, a fatal

---

[1] Email: zeidler.miklos@btk.elte.hu

mistake committed by the peacemakers, and a breach of the laws of nature that had to and would necessarily be rectified. And while Hungary did in fact become integrated into the post-war European order, its main goal from the outset was the revision of the Treaty of Trianon. By evoking the idea of national self-determination as the guiding principle for treaty revision, the Hungarian government could echo the slogans permeating Hungarian public opinion "Everything back!" and "Rump Hungary is no country, heaven is our old Hungary", and call for a complete restitution of the old frontiers.

Therefore, Historic Hungary was not merely a nostalgic memory from the past or an element of Hungarian collective tradition but very much a desired alternative to the present and, ultimately, a political program. Most political parties as well as the major national institutions of education and indoctrination — schools, churches and the military — employed a distinctly revisionist rhetoric which appeared in the Hungarian press as well.

There were three major types in the set of symbols of Hungarian irredentism. The first, and most common, was the vulgarization of Christ's Passion story according to which Hungary had stood before false judges, was handed over to the infidels, taken to Calvary, crucified, debased, abandoned, but coming ever closer to a glorious resurrection.[2] In this nationalistic interpretation of the Passion, several other political actors were also identified. The national minorities who got their "reward" for betraying Historic Hungary took the role of Judas Iscariot who sold Jesus Christ to the Romans for thirty silver pieces or of Roman soldiers who played dice over the last earthly belongings of the Son of God. Patrona Hungariae — a traditional depiction of the Holy Mary as the protector of Hungary — appeared as the Virgin Mother who fed, lost and mourned her Son and finally helped

---

2   This concept of making a parallel between the sufferings of the nation and Christ's passion is very closely related to the tradition of Hungarian Protestantism of the early modern era and included in the verses of the Hungarian national anthem, written in 1823. See Hankiss, E. Hongrie. *Diagnostiques. Essai en pathologie social*. Geneva: Georg, 1990.

his body off the cross. The Great Powers, cowardly and indifferent, were to be seen as Pontius Pilate, who "washed his hands" rather than take the responsibility and be an honest judge of Jesus Christ. And finally, the friends of Hungary were likened to Simon of Cyrene who, on the order of a Roman soldier, relieved Christ from the burden of the cross, or Veronica who gave her kerchief to Christ to wipe the sweat and blood from his face.

Thus, Hungarian revisionist ideas developed into a confessionary movement which identified the dissolution of Historic Hungary with Christ's sufferings, and the road to the revision of the Treaty of Trianon with the Good News of the Gospels. As the official review of the Hungarian Frontier Readjustment League stated, in 1940, "The quest of the Hungarian revisionist movement is to profess Justice for Hungary and to maintain an eternal belief in Justice. It has to profess Justice for Hungary all around the world and to turn it into an ardent religious belief within the country."[3]

In the second set of symbols parallels were drawn to the 1848–49 Revolution and War of Independence in which the Hungarians were united in an exemplary, sublime national independence movement which gained the respect of the whole world and where a large number of outstanding personages stood behind the flag of Hungary, regardless of their nationality.

The third set was based on the actualization of the twin symbols of the conquest and tubsequent heroic protection of the Carpathian Basin by the Hungarians. The conquering hero defends the country against the enemies and then protects the principles of the already Christian country against the godless hordes who rage against her not caring about his own fate and it is this self-sacrifice that makes him eligible for repeated resurrection.[4]

---

3   A magyar revíziós mozgalom és a történelem 1940, p. 2.
4   There was another popular set of symbols based on the contrast of light and darkness, but this is far too characteristic of all conflict situations that it would be mistaken to link it particularly to revisionism. For the whole concept, see Pallos, L. 'Területvédő propaganda Magyarországon 1918–1920', Part 1, Folia Historica, vol. 24, 2005–2006, pp. 33–93. (English summary on pp. 93–95.); Pallos, L. 'Területvédő

It is easy to see that at certain points these symbols meet, complement and even meld into each other. It is even more important that all three symbol systems are eminently suitable for romanticism because all of them were meeting points for extremes where the hero bleeds from the strokes of the evil enemy but does not die and eventually rises to greater glory than ever before.

Commemorating Trianon on certain state holidays and at semi-official meetings started to become a practice from the beginning of the 1920s. The ceremonial occasions were provided by Saint Stephen's day on 20 August, the Commemoration of Heroes on the last Sunday in May (a state holiday from 1926), 4 June (anniversary of the signing of the Trianon Peace Treaty), the middle of November (withdrawal of the Romanian army from Budapest and the entry of the National Army, and the ratification of the Peace Treaty) and 6 December (Regent Miklós Horthy's name day).

The cult of irredentism aimed to occupy public places in varied ways. Newly named public spaces, in the 1920s and 1930s, made passers-by remember Historic Hungary, its detached regions, towns, mountains and rivers, and the heroes of Hungarian revisionism like Count Albert Apponyi, the spokesman of the Hungarian delegation at the Paris Peace Conference in 1920, pro-Hungarian British Press Magnate Viscount Rothermere, and Italian and German dictators Benito Mussolini and Adolf Hitler.

Monuments relating to the revenge policy already began to appear in the beginning of the 1920s. The so-called *Irredentist Statues* symbolising the broken off parts of the country were erected in a central square of Budapest, Szabadság tér, in January 1921. These allegories of *West, North, East* and *South* were dominated by heroic, romantic images and historical symbols. The figure tumbling on the holy crown in the statue entitled *West* was holding the coats of arms of the lost

---

propaganda Magyarországon 1918–1920', Part 2, Folia Historica, vol. 26, 2008–2009, pp. 37–74. (English summary on p. 75.); Zeidler, M. 'A Magyar Revíziós Liga', Századok, vol. 131, no. 2, pp. 303–351. For the theory on "religions of lament," see Canetti, E. *Crowds and Power*. London: Phoenix Press, 2000, pp. 143–145.

counties in his right and a shield with the double cross in his left hand. A turul bird was resting at his feet. On the three-figure composition of *North* a Slovak boy seeking protection was leaning on a crucified Hungaria and a well-built Kuruc soldier was protecting both with his sword. The allegory of *East* depicted chieftain Csaba in a heroic pose as he was liberating the symbolic figure holding Transylvania's coat of arms. On the statue entitled *South* there was a strong-muscled Hungarian man embracing and protecting a Swabian girl, who symbolised the southern region. A wheat sheaf was lying at their feet, symbolising the rich land of Bácska and Bánság counties.

On Saint Stepen's Day in 1928, the Nation's Flag was placed in the middle of the semi-circle formed by the *Irredentist Statues* along with pro-Hungarian quotations from Mussolini and Rothermere, which were unveiled on 20 August 1928. It recalled the conquest, territorial integrity and the glorious and painful events of Hungarian history.

Literature, music and fine arts—high and low alike—produced countless pieces inspired by the bygone greatness of Hungary, by national sorrow and by revisionism. The outstanding achievements of Hungarian scientists, artists and athletes were interpreted as a proof of "national superiority" and a claim for the rectification of the "gross injustices" committed against the nation.

The first Hungarian trans-Atlantic flight stood out from among several events intended to be spectacular, such as stately receptions, wreath-laying and other ceremonies, and the publication of grandiose revisionist albums and their dispatch to influential politicians. Having broken several world records, pilot György Endresz and navigator Sándor Magyar successfully flew across the Atlantic in July 1931. Their aeroplane was called *Justice for Hungary* so that their performance would call the world's attention to Hungary's cause.[5]

---

5   Their story is reported in detail in Magyar, S. *Álmodni mertünk. Harc a levegőért.* Budapest: Műegyetemi Sportrepülő Egyesület, 1941., or Vásárhelyi, M. 1977, *A lord és a korona.* Budapest: Kossuth, 1977.

Besides direct political actions, Hungarian irredentism used the major accomplishments of Hungarian science, art and sports for propaganda aims to prove the capability — if not the superiority — of Hungarian nations. In literature and in art this was difficult because comparisons were hard to make and there were no international competitions. Scientific discoveries and patents, especially Albert Szent-Györgyi's Nobel Prize in 1937, were demonstrated as proofs of Hungarian talent. Sporting victories at world championships, especially at the Olympic Games, provided plenty of "evidence" for the unique qualities of the Hungarians.[6]

In its foreign language propaganda publications, the Hungarian Frontier Readjustment League featured a separate section on sports in which every accomplishment of Hungarian teams and competitors from water polo and soccer through fencing to chess were described in detail to the readers. Similar evidence for Hungarian physical and spiritual excellence was given by Alfréd Hajós, who won two gold medals in swimming at the Athens Olympics and then, at the 1924 Paris Games submitted an architectural plan for the *"Ideal Stadium"* which was selected best in its category.[7] Later triumphs at international competitions, particularly the ten gold medals at the Berlin Games, which put Hungary in third place behind Germany and the United States, raised Hungarian accomplishments to heroic levels, at least in the propaganda publications.

---

6 The demonstration of sporting triumphs were widely considered to be a good way to show the outstanding qualities of a nation. Especially small countries, driven by a persistent desire to compensate for their moderate prestige and little weight in international affairs, were, and still are, keen to resort to this kind of "complex comparison" as a natural "socio-psychological immune reaction" Csepeli, Gy. *National Identity in Contemporary Hungary*, Boulder: Social Science Monographs, 1997, pp. 65–67.

7 Hungary, as a defeated country, could not participate in the 1920 Antwerp Olympic Games which was doubly painful because these games were originally scheduled for Budapest. Therefore, Hajós's victory in Paris, i. e. on "enemy soil," was particularly welcome. In fact, he received only a silver medal — good enough for victory as the first prize was not awarded at all — which was interpreted by Hungarian contemporaries as a sign of hostility of the French, the "authors" of the Treaty of Trianon.

Schools just like Churches also spread the idea of irredentism. The spirit of territorial integrity impregnated all levels of education in the inter-war period and was accompanied by the idea of counter-revolution, with an emphasis on the Christian-national ideal and the idealization of historic Hungary. Educational policy considered the irredentist idea as an important part of not only history teaching but of the whole school education system, and the syllabus transformed the slogans of propaganda into historical arguments, especially in junior classes.[8] As a leading politician of education, Gyula Kornis said on behalf of the National Association of Hungarian Secondary School Teachers in 1921: "All the national subjects (Hungarian language, history, geography and economic studies) in the curriculum of our schools must focus on one axis: on a whole Hungary. We must create *the most effective education of irredentism*".[9]

These educational goals were implemented in schools and textbooks were also written in the same spirit. One of the most popular secondary school textbooks of the period specified four great national catastrophes preceding Trianon: the battles of Augsburg (955), Muhi (1241), Mohács (1526) and the surrender at Világos (1849). "The nation was threatened with final destruction by each, but it experienced a resurrection after all of them."[10] Parallels could be found for the providential remedy of unjust situations in European history, such as the expulsion of the Turks, the rebirth of Poland and, indirectly, even the example of Alsace-Lorraine. The last mentioned served as a pattern for Hungarian textbook publishing in as much as *revanche* was a separate chapter in French school textbooks for forty years before World War I.[11]

---

8   Unger, M. *A történelmi tudat alakulása középiskolai történelemkönyveinkben a századfordulótól a felszabadulásig*. 2nd ed, Budapest: Tankönyvkiadó, 1977, pp. 87–89 and 185.
9   Ibid.
10 Ibid., p. 186.
11 Ibid., pp. 185–186.

The Treaty of Trianon, revision and irredentism were regularly raised in school tests, essays and themes for the matriculation examinations. Nearly one third of written matriculation essays on history (and partly on literature) were likely to have been concerned with the issue, either directly or indirectly, during the Horthy era.[12]

In schools special functions were devoted to various revisionist organisations, which were also supported by fund raising. The programmes of school ceremonies regularly included the most well known irredentist poems. At the beginning and the end of a school day pupils had to recite the *Hungarian Credo*, which won the first prize of a patriotic poetry competition organised by a Hungarian revisionist organisation in 1920.

The little verse — once again — linked religious and political contents by presenting revisionist hopes in the form of a prayer:

> *I believe in one God,*
> *I believe in one Homeland,*
> *I believe in one divine eternal justice,*
> *I believe in the resurrection of Hungary.*
> *Amen.*

Historic Hungary and its dissolution — or rather dismemberment as it was understood — had thus been deeply incised in Hungarian collective memory and served as one of its cornerstones until the end of World War II when another catastrophic defeat and Hungary's subsequent incorporation in the Soviet Bloc swept aside these radical forms of nationalism for almost half a century.

---

12   Jáki, L. (ed.), *Érettségi tételek történelemből, 1851–1949*, OPKM, Budapest, pp. 27–57.

The persons who became myths

From Myths to Reality: the Regionalism of Endre Bajcsy-Zsilinszky (1886-1944)

Ákos Bartha[1]
Hungarian Academy of Sciences

Abstract: The paper examines the ambiguous image of Endre Bajcsy-Zsilinszky in Hungarian history. Due to the fact that his numerous writings have not yet been collected in their entirety and the available document provide diversified ideological narratives, so far the researches only have schematic and--to a large extent--contradictory pictures of him. On the one hand Bajcsy-Zsilinszky was one of the first supporters of the "Hungarian Imperial Idea" and the ideology of racialism, while on the other hand he had a big role in the resistance movement during the German occupation of Hungary during WW2.

"He is in our national history, but – as we all feel – not in the right place yet. Thus he is intrinsically walking up and down, stepping from one group to another"[2]. Despite the huge numbers of papers about Endre Bajcsy-Zsilinszky in the last few decades, this sad situation has not changed substantially. It comes from two main causes. On the one hand Bajcsy-Zsilinszky's enormous quantities of publicistic writings have not been collected yet and on the other different kinds of ideologically narratives can easily and effectively be supported on the basis of his uniquely reach life-work. Researchers can can encounter difficulties, as sources have neither been processed nor collected perfectly and this lack of information leads to schematic — but diversified — pictures.

---

1 E-mail: bartha.akos@btk.mta.hu.
2 Illyés, G. *Zsilinszky 1886–1986*. Budapest: Hazafias Népfront–Bajcsy-Zsilinszky Endre Emlékbizottság, 1986, p. 7.

Life – briefly

Jr. Endre Zsilinszky[3] was born on June 6, 1886, in a town located in South-East Hungary (Szarvas). His middle class, landowner and Lutheran family had Slovak peasant origin on his father's side and Hungarian noblity on his mother's. The first milestone of his political career was the "Áchim-affair" when Endre and his brother (Gábor) killed the well-known peasant politician, András Áchim L. in 1911, leading not only to legal issues but also a black mark on their reputation. Zsilinszky's official carreer was just barely starting in the county bureau, but this judicial process provided rhetorical ammunition for his enemies throughout his life. He belonged to those landowner, state official middle-class ("dzsentri") youth who had fought hard in the Great War and hence later could not accept the disintegration of the historical Hungarian state. This social group found nationalist answers to their questions by assuming betrayals in the hinterland. That was the main reason for which he joined the side of the counter-revolution. Zsilinszky became one of the most talented, high qualified publicist and propagandist of the right-wing racialists in the 1920s. In his opinion, the liberal national theory should be changed by the idea of race and he considered racialism as national self-protection against the "newcomers". He approved the social ostracisation of the Jews and settled for low-key agrarian reform. In 1923–24 he lost his infatuation for the consolidation of Prime Minister István Bethlen and left the governing party, alongside those such as Gyula Gömbös or Tibor Eckhardt. As one of the founding members of the freshly founded racialist party he experienced how an opponent politician could (not) manage in the Horthy system. But when Gömbös and his followers returned to the governing party (1928), Bajcsy-Zsilinszky instead established the National Radical Party (1930). After defeat in the gerrymandered

---

[3] From 1925, when he was awarded with the membership of the Horthy-loyal "Vitéz Order", Zsilinszky used his mother's surname as well ('Endre Bajcsy-Zsilinszky').

election of 1935, the NRP joined with the smallholder party and Bajcsy-Zsilinszky took part in this new challenge and committed to paper his concepts about the lordship and foreign policy. In this period he already attracted attention for the inland ("sváb") and also for the (partly imagined) foreign (imperialist) danger of Germanism and supported radical agrarian reform. On the one hand, he maintained several elements of his racialism, but on the other, he rejected the Jewish Laws. His activity during WWII, and particularly after the occupation of Hungary by Germany on 19th March 1944, is presumably the best-known part of his life, especially the heroic, armed "welcome" to the invaders and his participation in the resistance. He was executed during the right-wing dictatorship lead by the Arrow Cross Party in Sopronkőhida (West Hungary), on Christmas Eve, 1944.

Reception

The first works about Bajcsy-Zsilinszky were impressed by the enormous political changes of 1945 and appreciated the efforts of the antifascist politician before all[4]. With the end of the coalition era (1948), ideological interpretations became more schematic, falling into the dogmatic Marxist canon. These interpretations rated every political factor from the point of view of the class struggle and the communist party. In the Kádár system (1956–1989), a few selected and excised sources, letters[5] and memoirs[6] could be published, and literary works[7], a movie (Magyar rapszódia, 1979) and a biography[8] were also released. Furthermore, historical exploration started as well[9]. Research

---

4 E.g. Lévai, J. *A hősök hőse...! Bajcsy-Zsilinszky Endre, a demokrácia vértanúja.* Budapest: Müller Károly Könyvkiadóváll, 1945.
5 E.g. Tilkovszky, L. (ed.) *Bajcsy-Zsilinszky irataiból.* Békéscsaba: Békés Megyei Tanács Tudományos-Koordinációs Szakbizottsága, 1986.
6 E.g. Talpassy, T. *A reggel még várat magára.* Budapest: Gondolat, 1981.
7 E.g. Illyés, G. *Zsilinszky 1886–1986.* Budapest: Hazafias Népfront-Bajcsy-Zsilinszky Endre Emlékbizottság, 1986, p. 7.
8 Dernői Kocsis, L. *Bajcsy-Zsilinszky.* Budapest: Kossuth, 1966.
9 E.g. Vigh, K. *Bajcsy-Zsilinszky Endre külpolitikai nézeteinek alakulása.* Budapest: Akadémiai, 1979; Tilkovszky, L. (ed.) *Bajcsy-Zsilinszky irataiból.* Békéscsaba: Békés

culminated in the centenary year of 1986[10] but already in the 1970s some new trends emerged. Above all, the emphasis, in line with antifascist political positions, was placed on Bajcsy-Zsilinszky's critical attitude to the Horthy-system. As a part of this interpretation he supposedly undertook "*an enormous development from the tragic Áchim-murdering to his intentional determined martyrdom.*"[11] The break between Gömbös and Bajcsy-Zsilinszky became a key moment in this approach and was defined as a "turn to the left" of the latter. The new ideological construction of "national radicalism" also emerged and was interpreted in a national democratic way[12]. The relations to the smallholder party and to the Hungarian populists were also emphasized in this era. There is no doubt that the correlations detailed above contain useable elements, but they give selective interpretations. This method is not independent of the different (Marxist, populist, right-wing) canons, preconceptions and master narratives. As we know from some newer publications[13], these attempts caused not only changes of emphasis, but deformations on his lifework as well. With regard to the current situation, we have to note that the boom of social studies after 1989 "*has not resulted in the fulfilment and renewal of Bajcsy-Zsilinszky research*"[14]). However, Bajcsy-Zsilinszky's lifework is highly appreciated

---

Megyei Tanács Tudományos-Koordinációs Szakbizottsága, 1986; idem (ed.) *Bajcsy-Zsilinszky. Írások tőle és róla.* Budapest: Kossuth, 1986.

10 E.g. Pintér, I. (ed.) *Bajcsy-Zsilinszky Endre 1886-1986. Tudományos tanácskozás születésének centenáriuma alkalmából.* Budapest: Hazafias Népfront–TIT, 1986; Tóth, L. (ed.) *Bajcsy-Zsilinszky Endre. Emlékfüzet születésének 100. évfordulójára.* Budapest: Hazafias Népfront–Szarvasi Városi Tanács, 1986.

11 Tilkovszky, L. (ed.) *Bajcsy-Zsilinszky irataiból.* Békéscsaba: Békés Megyei Tanács Tudományos-Koordinációs Szakbizottsága, 1986, p. 7.

12 Sebestény, S. 'Bajcsy-Zsilinszky "nemzeti demokrácia" felfogása', *Elmélet és Politika*, 1982/1, pp. 67–73; Vigh, K., *Bajcsy-Zsilinszky Endre. 1886–1944, A küldetéses ember.* Budapest: Szépirodalmi, 1992;   Vigh, K., *Bajcsy-Zsilinszky Endre külpolitikája.* Budapest: Mundus, 2002.

13 E.g. Gyurgyák, J. *Magyar fajvédők.* Budapest: Osiris, 2012; Vonyó, J. 'Zsilinszky és a zsidókérdés' in Vonyó, J. *Jobboldali radikálisok Magyarországon, 1919–1944: tanulmányok, dokumentumok.* Pécs: Kronosz, 2012, pp. 56–71.

14 Kiss, J. *Fajvédelemtől a nemzeti demokráciáig: Bajcsy-Zsilinszky Endre politikai tervei a trianoni Magyarország megújulására (1918–1932)*, PhD thesis, 2007. Available on-

in contemporary Hungary both in terms of public opinion and in the scientific sector. On 13th December 2014, the Upper House of the Hungarian Parliament hosted a conference dedicated to the memory of Bajcsy-Zsilinszky on the occasion of the 70th anniversary of his death, but a PhD thesis[15], a memorial album[16], a public article[17], a novel[18] and a low quality monographic publication[19] have been also published concerning his life, political acts and ideology. The Hungarian Association of Resistance Fighters and Antifascists operates a Memorial Committee for Endre Bajcsy-Zsilinszky.

Regionalism or Imperial Idea

Let it be stated first: Bajcsy-Zsilinszky was one of the last first line representatives of the Hungarian Imperial Idea. "This expansionist ideology emerged and developed in the later decades of the Austro-Hungarian era; its first representatives yearned for greater power and waxed nostalgic about the return to the glory of the Árpád dynasty or the empire of king Matthias Corvinus."[20] However, two important notes have to be taken here. 1. Bajcsy-Zsilinszky mainly focused on the Carpathian Basin (not on the whole Central European region) 2. He tried to combine this expansionism with reform plans. As a key-

---

line: https://dea.lib.unideb.hu/dea/bitstream/handle/2437/79674/ertekezes_magyar.pdf?sequence=7 [accessed: 28 August 2015].
15 Ibid.
16 Kerecsényi, Z. *Az utolsó nyár: Bajcsy-Zsilinszky Endre életének utolsó szakaszairól, valamint magyar antifasiszta ellenállásról*. MEASZ–Bajcsy-Zsilinszky Emlékbizottság, 2013.
17 Murányi, G. 'Bajcsy-Zsilinszky Endre 1935-ös fordulata: tisztességtelen ajánlat', *HVG*, 32 (49), 2010, pp. 40–41.
18 Lőrincz, G. 'Az áruló', *Forrás*, 30 (12), 1998.
19 Nemere, I. *Bajcsy-Zsilinszky Endre magánélete*. Budapest: Anno, 2003.
20 Kerepeszki, R. 'Nationalist Masculinity and Right-Wing Radical Student Movements in Interwar Hungary: The Case of the Turul Association', *Hungarian Studies Review*, 1/2014, pp. 61–88. In details: Romsics, I. 'A magyar birodalmi gondola' in: Romsics, I. *A múltról a mának. Tanulmányok és esszék a magyar történelemről*. Budapest: Osiris, 2002, pp. 121–159. It is notable that Bajcsy-Zsilinszky wrote a book about king Matthias: Bajcsy-Zsilinszky, E. *Mátyás király*. Budapest: Athenaeum, 1939.

player of the Hungarian racialists he was a revisionist who proposed the re-annexation of the territories which had been lost to Hungary after WW1. From his perspective, the reorganization of the Danubian nations was waiting for the new, folk origin Hungarian elite for historical and racial reasons. Hence, racialism, reforms and the imperial idea related and strengthened each other in his continuously altering political thinking. The most important pillar of his foreign policy was Italy (before WW2) a conception which was supported by a deep sympathy for Mussolini and for the fascist movement. Bajcsy-Zsilinszky considered Italy as a counterpoint to the Little Entente and a regional power which could support Hungary to repeal the Treaty of Trianon (1920). In the 1920s, he also looked at the German right wing as an example to follow and refused the Danubian confederation plans which "*would be the selling of the ancient Hungarian heritage for a mess of pottage*".[21]

Between 1928 and 1931, this relation changed and he came to consider Germany as a regional danger and separated the revanchism of Berlin from the revisionism of Budapest. Besides Italy, the second pillar of his foreign policy was surprisingly France since — as per his intentions — Paris should have realized their interest in a powerful Central Europe against Germany. That is the reason why he welcomed the Tardieu Plan in 1932. His defensive[22] partnership aimed to involve Austria as a buffer state against Germany and Poland (a country with which Hungary traditionally had had a good relationship, and common interests and enemies), as well as Czechoslovakia (mostly only in his publicism). For struggling for the independency of the small states in Central Europe he sketched a kind of "vertical axis" containing Warsaw, Budapest, Belgrade and Rome. Moreover, in the program of the NRP he proposed the cooperation of 12 small countries

---

21 (Bajcsi-)Zsilinszky, E. 'Rana Rupta', *Szózat*, 1925.03.22, 1925, pp. 1–2.
22 The grammatical qualifier of "defensive" is a key phrase in this ideology as we could see it concerning his national attitude as well. This approach can be linked to the colonial vision of the "népi" (populist) writers in Hungary. See Romsics, G. *Nép, nemzet, birodalom. A Habsburg Birodalom emlékezete a német, osztrák és magyar történetpolitikai gondolkodásban, 1918–1941*. Budapest: ÚMK, 2010.

with a population of almost 100 million inhabitants. Nevertheless, he emphasized the autotelic, "egocentric" political program of Hungary and he noted that revisionist targets could be completed only if Hungary could join its plans to the conceptions of the powerful European states. From 1937, this "powerful European state" had been found in the United Kingdom. He preferred armed neutrality, trying to keep Hungary out of the new world war.

In 1938 he lost his faith in Mussolini who assisted the Anschluss, letting Germany into the neighborhood of Hungary. In 1939, Poland, a further pillar, was crushed by Germany in cooperation with the Soviet Union. According to the changed situation Bajcsy-Zsilinszky had to find a new partner in the region. He turned to Yugoslavia, whose multiethnic state played a temporary role in the conceptions of the Prime Minister Pál Teleki by this time[23]. Although Bajcsy-Zsilinszky was an oppositionist politician he was involved in official Hungarian foreign policy and participated in the negotiations in Belgrade with Prime Minister Dragiša Cvetković and Foreign Minister Dimitrije Cincar Marković.[24] He also visited the leader of the Croatian Peasant Party, Vladimir Maček who advocated the cooperation of the "peasant peoples" — not only in the Danubian Region but in the whole Central Europe[25]. This idea was quite familiar for Bajcsy-Zsilinszky who had just published a book about the political importance of the Hungarian peasantry[26]. After his visit to Yugoslavia he wrote another important monograph called *"Our place and destiny in Europe"*, where he detailed his regional, geopolitical conceptions from a historical point of view. In his opinion *"every Hungarian era worth as much as its loyalty to the heritage of Árpád and St. István"*[27], a premise which distanced him from

---

23 Ablonczy, B. *Teleki Pál*. Budapest: Osiris, 2005, p. 493.
24 Not much later, on 12 December 1940 Teleki signed the eternal friendship and non-aggression treaty with Yugoslavia.
25 Vigh, K. 'Bajcsy-Zsilinszky Endre szerepe a népi mozgalmakban', *Hitel*, 18 (1), 2005, pp. 80–88.
26 Bajcsy-Zsilinszky, E. *Egyetlen út a magyar paraszt*. Budapest: Kelet Népe, 1938.
27 Bajcsy-Zsilinszky, E. *Helyünk és sorsunk Európában*. Budapest: Gergely, 1941, p. 3.

acceptance of the democratic federation ideas of Oszkár Jászi for example[28]. He repeated his conclusion that the protection of the independence of the Danubian region was a mission for Hungary; although he noted that it should be completed via Hungarian–Southern Slavic cooperation.

As we know, things had accelerated on another track since Hungary had joined the Axis Tripartite Pact in 1940 then assisted the German invasion of Yugoslavia in 1941. Thus, on the one hand another pillar of Bajcsy-Zsilinszky's regional conception had collapsed, on the other he had to be faced with a continually closer German alliance. Although he submitted several memoranda and made brave speeches against this one-sided relationship, these efforts did not have any serious effects on official policy.[29] At the same time, he came to some compromises concerning his revanchism, such as the planned autonomy for Transylvania and Kárpátalja. He would also have accepted the Slovakian state in 1943[30] and autonomy for Bácska and Bánát in 1944[31].

According to Bajcsy-Zsilinszky's published writings, the manuscripts concerning his Slovak–Hungarian dual ancestry did not shape the personal identity of the Hungarian publicist-politician and did not play an important role in his foreign policy. No doubt for that Bajcsy-

---

28   Litván, G. *Jászi Oszkár*. Budapest: Osiris, 2003.
29   He was involved officially once more, when the Kállay government wanted to counteract the international Romanian lobby. For this reason he wrote *"Transsylvania. Past and future"* (Bajcsy-Zsilinszky, E. *Transsylvania. Past and future*. Geneva: Kundig, 1944).
30   Vigh, K. *Bajcsy-Zsilinszky Endre külpolitikája*. Budapest: Mundus, 2002, p. 337.
31   Gyurgyák, J., *Magyar fajvédők*. Budapest: Osiris, 2012, p. 146. Károly Vigh assumed that Bajcsy-Zsilinszky expected a new democratic setup and the spiritualization of the borders in the post-war period, including Hungary and the surrounding countries in a partnership with equal rights, although in a later publication he emphasized the continuous revisionist targets (Vigh, K. *Bajcsy-Zsilinszky Endre külpolitikai nézeteinek alakulása*. Budapest: Akadémiai, 1976; Vigh, K. *Bajcsy-Zsilinszky Endre. 1886–1944, A küldetéses ember*. Budapest: Szépirodalmi, 1992). It seems that to give a detailed and unbiased picture there is no other way than to open up and interpret his entire written heritage of, including hundreds of articles and the numerous relevant exchanges of correspondence.

Zsilinszky's categorical Hungarian identity overwrote his half-Slav origin from the beginning[32] to the end.[33] He refused even his uncle's (Mihály Zsilinszky)[34] dual identity, although he kept an open mind to making offers to the ambient nations (Serbs, Croats, Romans, Slovaks, Czechs, etc.) – under the leadership of Hungary.

Conclusion

The several forms of the transnational partnership between 1918 and 1948 were often based on nationalized principles and served territorial targets. For example, an ethnic revision was supported even by the Hungarian populists who – despite their numerous controversial ideas[35] – struggled for a democratic turn and a peaceful Central Europe[36]. Of course, this attitude was not a Hungarian speciality, alt-

---

32 After the Áchim-affair (1911) he moved to the Upland (Árva County), where the society was dominated by Slovaks. As an administrative trainee Zsilinszky took part gladly in Hungarian official life and he "visited with pleasure the amateur performances of the tót citizens". However, in the latter case he identified himself as a "stranger" (Bajcsy-Zsilinszky, E., 'Egy közigazgatási gyakornok', *Budapesti Hírlap*, 1914.01.25, 1914, pp. 1–2). This approach has been confirmed by the family correspondence as well. Hungarian National Library. Manuscript. 28. fond. 178. and 214. and 217.

33 For a question coming from a Nazi officer (whether he is a Jew or an Aryan) he answered in 1944: "I am Turanian." (Barcs, S. 'A dráma sodrában' in Vigh, K. [ed.] *Kortársak Bajcsy-Zsilinszky Endréről*. Budapest: Magvető, 1984). Turanian theory belongs to the Hungarian imperial and racialist idea.

34 Mihály, Zsilinszky (1838–1925): State secretary, teacher, historian, a member of the Hungarian Academy of Sciences. He operated as a proud Hungarian on one hand, but on the other accepted his Slovak origin and supported the – state-loyal – "tót nationality" in some cases (Kmet, M. 'Híd a magyar-szlovák kulturális kapcsolatokban', *Barátság*, Vol. 16 (2009), No. 3, pp. 6099–6101).

35 Due to the "colonial vision" naturally they had to name the "colonizers" as well. The populist writers considered the Hungarian nobles from historical point of view (within the post-feudal structure of the society), but "newcomers" (Germans and/or Jews) had also been mentioned as a current enemy of the peasantry.

36 Bartha, Á. 'Tojástánc a populizmusok körül: A magyar népi mozgalom fogalmi keretei és regionális dimenziója', *Múltunk*. 59 (4), 2014, pp. 58–105.

hough Hungarian society had been dissatisfied with the Treaty of Trianon, and was traumatized by the new borders.[37] Thinking regionally, we can point also to another example: the early, geopolitically motivated Danubian plan by the Slovak politician Milan Hodža, which, however, can be considered rather an ideological position against Hungary rather than an honest idea for comprehensive regional cooperation. Later, as Prime Minister (1935–1938) Hodža popularized the idea of a huge Central and Eastern European agrarian block[38], which only arose later under the direct danger of the Third Reich. This is similar to Bajcsy-Zsilinszky, who made more and more ideological compromises, but only in the shadow of total collapse.[39]

What is the main message of this historical lesson from a contemporary point of view? Regional cooperation contained (not so) hidden imperial aims as well. The effective empowerment of the East Central European countries was not completed due to national traumas, external expansionism, internal nationalism, and thus to fragmented, tendentious regionalism.

---

37 At the same time, the impact of the Trianon trauma on the Hungarian rural society is questionable. (Bartha, Á., Szilágyi, Zs. 'Történelmi tapasztalat mint mentális valóság. A történelemoktatás és a történetírás néhány kérdése a személyes emlékezet tükrében', *Forrás*, Vol. 43(2011), No. 7–8, pp. 225–242).

38 Kiss, J. 'Szlovákia helye és szerepe Milan Hodža geopolitikai koncepciójában (I-II.)', *Fórum* (2/2004), pp. 83–96. and (3/2004), pp. 85–103.

39 Bajcsy-Zsilinszky made notes on Hodža's famous book "*Federation in Central Europe*" (Hodža, M. *Szövetség Közép-Európában: Gondolatok és visszaemlékezések*. Bratislava: Kalligram, 2004) and cagily welcomed it (Vigh, K., *Bajcsy-Zsilinszky Endre külpolitikája*. Budapest: Mundus, 2002, pp. 118–119, pp. 132–133, p. 236). His review on Hodža's book can be found at the Hungarian National Library (Manuscript. 28. fond. 59).

Štefánik's Death and the Czecho(Slovak) Identity[1]

Michal Kšiňan[2]
Slovak Academy of Sciences

Abstract: The text investigates the image of Milan Rastislav Štefánik as a historical personality of multiple identities, depending on a particular political regime in the states of Central Europe. As the chapter points out, the Slovak conception of Štefánik on one side and the Czechoslovak one on the other differ radically, which mirrors in the interpretations not only of his life, but especially his death. Štefánik's tragic and unexplained death represents an example of "enigmatic" deaths contributing to creating cults of historical heroes, not at all rare in the context of Central Europe.

Milan Rastislav Štefánik is one of the most popular personalities in Slovak history and some say the most popular. His most important contribution was his activity during World War I involving the disintegration of the Austro-Hungarian Empire and the creation of Czechoslovakia. However, his legacy is in fact much more complicated.

The picture of a hero plays an important role in the construction of national identities. Because Štefánik is a national hero, the official presentation of his identity varies depending on the political regimes in Central Europe. Štefánik's identity cannot be understood as something unchangeable and fixed. In Štefánik, we can see a Slovak, a Czechoslovak, a Slav, a Frenchman, or a man of the world. His identity has been subjected to several "metamorphoses" and these identities are not exclusive nor do they exclude each other. As a result, it is not his identities that are in conflict but the way they are presented (Slovak versus Czechoslovak, and also Slovak versus the world view), while others (French, Slovak, Slavic, etc.) can exist in parallel without any problem. This may be due to the conflicts that Slovak identity has faced and still faces between Slovak and Czechoslovak identities and

---

1   This work was supported by the Slovak Research and Development Agency under the contract No. APVV-0628-11 and by project VEGA 2/0135/15.
2   E-Mail: michal.ksinan@savba.sk.

partly between Slovak and the world's identities. That is why these parts of Štefánik's identity are usually presented as contradictory.[3]

These conflicts have also affected the interpretation of another significant event in Štefánik's life. Even today, interpretations of Štefánik's death cause many disputes. The literature on the topic is plentiful and Štefánik's death remains one of the more discussed questions in Slovak historiography. Many historians working on political history disagree with the hypothesis of an assassination commissioned by Edvard Beneš. "*...propaganda of the Slovak People's Party about Štefánik's assassination by Masaryk and Beneš is so groundless and primitive that there is no more point in dealing with it.*"[4] However, as historian Peter Macho reminds us, the interpretations of the reasons for Štefánik's death open a large field for historians working on social history[5]. Taking into account his assumption, this paper will analyze the varying discourses concerning this event. Therefore, the question is no longer how did Štefánik die but what are the uses and misuses of the explanations of his death? Why is it so?

The Slovak dilemma whether to keep the Slovak identity or to give it up in favour of the Czechoslovak identity takes different forms today. Nevertheless, it has influenced discussions in Slovak society for a long time. As for Štefánik's death, there are two common explanations: 1. The assassination was committed by Beneš with the tacit consent of Tomáš G. Masaryk; 2. An accident was caused by bad weather or a shooting by soldiers who confused an Italian flag with a Hungarian one — or another explanation for the crash not supposing a deliberate intention of Beneš and Masaryk to assassinate Štefánik.

---

3   Kšiňan, M. 'Metamorfózy Štefánikovej slovenskosti' in Čaplovič, M., Ferenčuhová, B. and Stanová, M. (eds.) *Milan Rastislav Štefánik v zrkadle prameňov a najnovších poznatkov historiografie*. Bratislava: Vojenský historický ústav, 2010, pp. 97–115.
4   Kováč, D. *Štefánik a Janin. Príbeh priateľstva (Štefánik and Janin. The Story of a Friendship)*. Bratislava: Dilema, 2001.
5   Macho, P. 'Poznámky k výskumu kolektívnych identít v 19. a 20. storočí na Slovensku', *Historický časopis*. 52 (2), 2004, pp. 353–362.

Beneš Ist the Worst (Slovak conception of Štefánik)

The Slovak conception of Štefánik is characterized by three main features:

1. His national identity is Slovak and his Czechoslovakism is only political (he wanted the creation of Czechoslovakia but with two nations: Slovak and Czech[6]);
2. He does not get along with Beneš, the symbol of a Czech "imperialist" policy towards Slovaks; Masaryk is not very supportive either;
3. The peak of these disagreements is the assassination of Štefánik.

Although sociological research would be needed, it seems that the hypothesis of an assassination is the most common one in Slovak society. In fact, 3 books[7] defending this theory were published several times — which is not trivial, if one considers that the Slovak market is made up of only 5 million readers.

According to the Slovak politician and publicist Ferdinand Ďurčanský[8], Štefánik was murdered by the Czechs because he did not agree with their policy towards Slovakia. *"At the time, Czech politicians expected that along with Štefánik's death, the original of the Pittsburgh Agreement would vanish. But it didn't. Štefánik carried the only official copy of the document with him, hence the many surprises and embarrassments."* The Pittsburgh Agreement had been signed by Masaryk and the Slovaks from the *Slovak League* in the United States. It guaranteed autonomy for Slovakia within the frame of the Czechoslovak state but it was never put into force. This agreement, the strongest argument of the

---

6 We use the term nation here in Central European—cultural sense.
7 Čulen, K. *Zločin vo fundamente: Svedectvo o Štefánikovej smrti.* Bratislava: Lúč, 2009; Kautský, E. K. *Kauza Štefánik: legendy, fakty a otázniky okolo vzniku Česko-Slovenskej republiky.* Martin: Matica slovenská, 2004; Novota, M. *Údery pod pás.* Banská Bystrica: M. Novota, 2006.
8 Ďurčanský, F. *Právo Slovákov na samostatnosť vo svetle dokumentov. Biela kniha I.* Buenos Aires: Slovenský oslobodzovací výbor, 1954.

interwar Slovak autonomists, was named the Slovak nation's *Magna Charta* by their leader Andrej Hlinka. The symbolic reading is easy. According to Ďurčanský, the Czechs killed the greatest son of the Slovak nation, the very one who carried the document pledging Slovaks' rights in the new state.

The editor of the autonomist newspaper *Slovák* sent a letter to Radola Gajda[9] asking for information about his investigation into Štefánik's death. The letter was answered not by Gajda, but by a Slovak from Moravia, according to whom Gajda was pressured into silence by powerful people. This Moravian Slovak went on: "*The birth of the Czecho-Slovak Republic in 1918 was accepted by the great powers under the condition that all nationalities would benefit from their own autonomy in the frame of the Republic. The Slovak nation was represented by General M. R. Štefánik who was a signatory [...] and in order for the Czechs to make their own arrangements and prevent Slovakia from being granted autonomy, the only witness had to be liquidated.*"[10]

Konštantín Čulen[11], a Slovak publicist and politician, compared Štefánik's death with Jozef Tiso's, General Ištók's, Matúš Černák's or Vojtěch Tuka's[12] executions. According to him Štefánik's death needs to be called by its real name: a treacherous assassination committed by Beneš. "*Well Slovaks, do you not dig in your heels when Dr. Beneš's collaborators want to move our nation to the point where they can murder, without penance, the brave sons of the Slovak nation? Well, the country where they could do so was the Czechoslovak Republic. Štefánik's death, as well as Tiso's and Černák's, speak to us in an understandable and clear way: No to Czechoslovakia, never again!*"

---

9   Radola Gajda (1892–1948) was a Czech military commander and fascist politician.
10   In Slovák, 4. 5. 1939, p. 4.
11   Čulen, K. *Zločin vo fundamente: Svedectvo o Štefánikovej smrti*. Bratislava: Lúč, 2009.
12   All these four personalities played important role during the 1st Slovak Republic (1939–1945).

TGM noli tangere!!! (Czechoslovak conception of Štefánik)

The Czechoslovak conception of Štefánik is characterized by three features perfectly at odds with the Slovak one:

1. During his stay in Prague, Štefánik became a devout defender of the idea of an ethnic and politically united Czechoslovakia (he therefore wanted the creation of Czechoslovakia as one unique Czechoslovak nation);
2. He had not been in dispute with Beneš and Masaryk or, if so, they were not serious disputes;
3. Štefánik's death was an accident, either provoked by shots fired because the Italian plane was mistaken for a Hungarian one, or by another cause. But what matters most is that neither Beneš nor Masaryk were accountable for it.

These three elements are linked. A dedicated political and ethnic Czechoslovak—as–Štefánik wanted—cannot be in conflict with his Czech collaborators for they share the same goal: creating a centralized Czechoslovakia with the one and only Czechoslovak nation. Thus Beneš and Masaryk had no reason to get rid of him. This Czechoslovak interpretation of Štefánik's death is not limited to showing that his death was an accident but also requires that the first Republic's two "icons", Beneš and Masaryk, show their sincere friendship for Štefánik. The relationships between the members of the Czechoslovak triumvirate are presented as an ideal, and the dissensions are put aside—especially in the case of the ties uniting Štefánik, the Slovak national hero, and Masaryk, one of the greatest Czech heroes. Their relationship is displayed almost as a dogma, according to the idea that: "*We cannot cast any doubt on Masaryk's sincere relation to Štefánik.*"[13] The conflicts between Beneš and Štefánik are often overlooked.

---

13 Kováč, D. 'M. R.Štefánik a dialektika dejín', *Literárny týždenník*, 28 April, 1989, p. 10.

In a book devoted to Štefánik, non-professional Czech historian Miloslav John[14] discusses Štefánik's life, but focusses mostly on his death. "*The Czechoslovak government, the most accused by chauvinistic voices, is above suspicion from a realistic point of view.* [...] *Their* [Štefánik's, Beneš's and Masaryk's] *correspondence shows, without all doubt, that the mutual relationships between the three leaders of the resistance organized abroad were very friendly and civilized. The dispute between Štefánik and Beneš, so stressed by chauvinists, about the sensitive question whether to favour the Italian or French mission was, at first, in conflict but was settled when Štefánik heard that the decision had been made by the Czechoslovak and French governments and that Beneš was only putting it in practise.*"

The daily *Pravda* notified its readers of the commemoration devoted to Štefánik in 1947 where, during the ceremony of commemoration on the 3rd May at the Reduta in Bratislava, a great expert on Štefánik's personality, writer Dr. Ladislav Zvěrina made a speech. He stressed the harmony between the trio of Masaryk, Štefánik and Beneš. According to him, each was singular, but in spite of this all three of them embodied one faith, one spirit, one action[15].

Interwar Czech historian Josef Bartůšek[16] commented on the relationships among the Czechoslovak triumvirate: "*The three of them initiated a close and complete collaboration [in 1915]. Štefánik and Beneš, both being in Paris, could especially complement each other. For more than a year during the war, Beneš lived at home. He knew well the empire's conditions and later, too, had reliable information from the Czech lands. On the other hand, Štefánik had many connections. Together they drafted information notes, speeches, and memorandums, which Štefánik, thanks to his influence, spread among the journalistic and political milieu. He had great plans for the organization and carrying out of our resistance that is why he asked, through Beneš, for Masaryk to come to Paris, so they could consult together.*"

---

14   John, M. *Milan Rastislav Štefánik. Život a smrt národního hrdiny.* Olomouc: Votobia, 2000.
15   In Pravda, 6. 5. 1947, p. 1.
16   Bartůšek, J. *Generál M. R. Štefánik.* Prague: Československá grafická unie, 1938.

Further Interpretations

Štefánik's death was not used only for these two mentioned conceptions although they are the most widespread. His death also became a kind of arm used to attack political opponents.

Communists have used it to attack capitalists and imperialists. This instance is very important in the hypothesis of Ľudovít Holotík[17], a court communist historian. He argued: "*The Czechoslovak soldiers were chauvinistically conditioned by the government to hate the Hungarian Soviet Republic. It could only happen under these conditions that when a foreign plane flew over Bratislava some soldiers could open up with anti-aircraft fire in the belief that it was a Hungarian plane. There is no doubt that this was the reason for firing on the plane carrying Štefánik which crashed near its destination. There is every reason to believe that Štefánik fell victim to the counterrevolutionary psychosis of the Czechoslovak bourgeoisie.*" The Czech historian Václav Král[18] suggested another hypothesis arguing that Štefánik was killed by Italians. According to him, Štefánik was forced to jump or was thrown out of the plane. "*By the way, it would not have been for the first time or the last time when the imperialists settled their accounts in this way.*"

The communist daily *Rudé Právo* reported that witnesses confirmed gun fire at Štefánik's plane as follows: "*Authorities and patriotic newspapers would like to cover up the shooting down of Štefánik.*" *Rudé Právo* continues citing that the principal witness of the fire, Michal Lechta, is presented either as a madman or as a criminal. However, in spite of this, another witness, Mr. Nitsch from Bratislava, confirmed this witness's words. Allegedly, the edition of the newspaper *Nezávislé listy* from the year 1919, also mentioned another testimony about the fire, which was "confiscated". "*Well, a military administration is able to play even more tricks than to hide, for 8 years, serious testimonies about the reasons for the death of the Minister of War. Remember only the invasion of*

---

17 Holotík, Ľ. *Štefánikovská legenda a vznik ČSR*. Bratislava: SAV, 1958.
18 Král, V. *Intervenční válka československé buržoazie proti Maďarské sovětské republice v roce 1919*. Prague: ČSAV, 1954.

the Czechoslovak troops into the territory of the Hungarian Soviet Republic in 1919!"[19]

The hypotheses of V. Král and Ľ. Holotík make use of other arguments but the offender is always the same — the imperialistic enemy. *Rudé Právo* did not identify the offender, only pointed out the unfair practices of the bourgeoisie of the 1st Czechoslovak Republic.

Another group blamed for the murder of Štefánik were the Freemasons. This hypothesis asserts that Beneš is responsible and suggests that Štefánik should be removed because he did not comply with the plans of the Freemasons. J. F. Rudinský[20] suggests a conspiracy of Czech atheists against Slovak Catholics but this national question is not as important as in the Slovak conception of Štefánik. He first described the improper behaviour of Czechs in Slovakia after the year 1918. He also writes that there is much evidence supporting the shooting down of Štefánik's plane and that that step had been decided in Prague. In spite of that, Beneš was not strong enough to organize such a conspiracy at that time. He heard that the motivation for the removal of Štefánik came allegedly from a Freemason's lodge, the same lodge that gave the order for the murder of the successor to the throne, Frank Ferdinand, the reason in both cases was the same: to prevent governance by a Catholic superpower in the Danube area of Europe. "*Milan Štefánik, the son of a protestant pastor, developed good personal contacts with the Vatican during the war. His fiancé was an Italian marquise which generated personal relationships with those involved in Italian politics. Since Štefánik knew very well the slogan-like socialism of Beneš and his working relations to the socialist and Freemason movements, it is very probable that Štefánik tried to use Catholicism as a kind of counterweight. As a result, it was not a problem for Beneš to point an accusing finger at Štefánik: Voilà la bête noire!*"

---

19   Národní archiv (National Archive), Prague, f. MZV-V, Štefánik, generál, 1925–28, Rudé Právo, 24.5.1927.
20   Rudlinský, J. F. *Československý štát a Slovenská republika*. München: Akademischer Verlag Dr. Peter Belej, 1968.

According to another explanation, Štefánik tried to thwart the activities of the Freemasons in Czechoslovakia and that is why he had to die. Peter Podolský[21] refers to "certain sources" that suggest that the Freemasons were also the cause of Štefánik's tragic death. It was ordered by Beneš. He wrote that Štefánik was allegedly disgusted by the destructive activities of the Freemasons and after his return to Czechoslovakia he had intended to have all secret (i. e. Freemasons) societies dissolved.

The religious or national question does not play any role in the explanation made by the Czech author Jan Rys[22]. He suggests that Freemasons are guilty for Štefánik's death and compares it with that of A. Rašín[23] and the Yugoslav king Alexander. All three died a violent death and also all were against bolshevism.

Many Czech enemies of Beneš used the death of Štefánik against Beneš. The Slovak or religious questions do not play any role in these explanations which are based on his unfair practices. According to some dailies, Gajda was authorized by Prime Minister Antonín Švehla to investigate the death of Štefánik. He launched a major investigation and learnt from previously undiscovered documents that Štefánik's death was a conspiracy organized by the Prague Hrad (Castle), mainly by Beneš and Masaryk.

When Beneš and Masaryk found out about the investigation, they immediately suspended it and arranged that the results of the investigation could not be published[24].

---

21 Podolský, P. *Slobodomurárstvo – nešťastie našej doby*. Bratislava: Magnificat, 2007. Available on-line: http://www.magnificat.sk/htm02/sbm2.pdf [accessed: 8 March 2009].
22 Rys, J. *Židozednářství – metla světa*. Prague: Nákladem zednářské korespondence, 1938.
23 Alois Rašín (1867–1923) was a Czech economist and politician. He was shot by the anarchist J. Šoupal.
24 Város, M. *Posledný let generála Štefánika*. Bratislava: Obzor, 1991; Národnie noviny, 17. 2. 1939.

Although the Czech and Slovak uses of Štefánik's death differ, his part in the resistance against the Austro-Hungarian Empire is employed by both as a negative identification mark towards Hungary. Before World War I, Slovaks were living in the Kingdom of Hungary, so Czechoslovakia needed to uproot this state tradition to establish a new one – a Czechoslovak tradition, or, for some Slovaks, an independent (or autonomist) tradition.

The Czechoslovak interpretation goes beyond this, arguing that Štefánik's death was an accident by stressing the sincere friendship of two "icons" of the first Republic, Beneš and Masaryk with Štefánik. In this way, this interpretation can be used as a symbolical proof of the perfect relationship between Czechs and Slovaks. According to the Slovak interpretation, the disagreements of both Beneš and Masaryk with Štefánik led to Štefánik's murder. In contrast, the Slovak interpretation of Štefánik's death served another purpose: it is used as a negative identification mark towards the Czechs, since the Czechs "assassinated" him.

Macho[25] described an image of Štefánik as a hero – combatant which is most often found in the Czechoslovak conception and hero – martyr most often found in the Slovak conception. However, in the Slovak conception the images of combatant and martyr do not exclude one another.

In general, Štefánik's enigmatic and premature death stimulated imaginations and strengthened legends about him. Shortly after he died, the French diplomat Philippe Berthelot wrote: *"His exciting life was devoted to the rebirth of his homeland and ended with a death similar to Icarus so Štefánik's will pass into legend which enriches the glorious history of Bohemia."*[26] In many presentations, the death of Štefánik represents his supreme sacrifice for his nation which, which plays an important

---

25 Macho, P. 'Národný hrdina a politika. Štefánik medzi čechoslovakizmom a autonomizmom', *Človek a spoločnosť* 7 (3), 2004. Available on-line: http://www.saske.sk/cas/archiv/3-2004/index.html [accessed 24 July 2015].
26 Archives du ministère des Affaires Étrangères, Paris, CPC 1914-1940, Z-Europe, Tchécoslovaquie, Vol. 8, Letter from 6. 5. 1919, N° 103.

role in the image of a hero. Ferdinand Písecký[27] in his book characterized Štefánik's death like this: *"Without the catastrophe which occurred near Vajnory, we would not have had a revolutionary hero who was accepted and appreciated by the whole nation. Blessed life, death blessed."* It should be mentioned that in Slovakia, official ceremonies are held on May 4th, the anniversary of his death, not July 21st, when he was born. So it is his death rather than his birth that is commemorated.

A contemporary Slovak writer, Pavol Vilikovský[28], claims that it is not only a tragic and romantic death which matters. There are also circumstances surrounding Štefánik's death which are not sufficiently clarified and explained. This ties together three other important personalities of Slovak history: Ľudovít Štúr[29], Štefánik and Alexander Dubček.[30] *"But what seems to me most important is that all three of them perished under somewhat mysterious circumstances. Štúr shot himself in the leg while hunting and after several days, he succumbed to his injury. While returning to his homeland, Štefánik crashed in a plane which he piloted himself; Dubček died after a two month stay in a Czech hospital as a consequence of a car accident which happened on the road from Bratislava to Prague. The car was an official vehicle driven by his chauffeur. [...] What fertile soil for producing myths and legends!"*

However, it is necessary to say that discussions about "enigmatic" deaths of heroes are not only Slovak or Czechoslovak matters. Here are some other examples from the Central European territory. A search of the remnants and grave of Sándor Petöfi, Hungarian poet and revolutionary who died in 1848 raises an important question for Hungary. According to Réka Albert[31], uncertainty concerning Petöfi's

---

27 Písecký, F. *Generál M. R. Štefánik.* Prague: Svaz národního osvobození, 1929.
28 Vilikovský, P. 'Le panthèon slovaque' in Servant, C. - Boisserie, É. (eds.) *La Slovaquie face à ses héritages.* Paris: L'Harmattan, 2004.
29 Ľudovít Štúr (1815–1856) was a Slovak poet, journalist, politician, linguist and the leader of the Slovak national movement in the 19th century.
30 Alexander Dubček (1921–1992) was a Slovak politician and leader of Czechoslovakia during the Czechoslovak spring (1968–1969).
31 Albert, R. 'Le poirier de Petöfi. Un modèle des cultes littéraires hongrois' in *L'écrivain et ses demeures, Rapport final,* 2003. Available on-line: http://www.culture-

death and the conditions of his remains are the basis for a cult following. "*If Petöfi was or has been found somewhere, it could not have been anywhere: in all the Hungarian localities, under all the regimes and in the slogans of all the Hungarian parties and, last but not least, in all the authentic popular narration a belief in a deep unity of his deeds and his literary works can be seen.*"

Another example is the death of General Władysław Sikorski, the Polish Prime Minister exiled from 1939 to 1943, which stimulates lively discussions in Polish society even now. There are several stories about a plot: some accuse the Russians, because Sikorski required the Red Cross to investigate Katyń. Others accuse the English who were willing, in this way, to improve their relations with Moscow while some even accuse General Władysław Anders, commander-in-chief of the Polish Army in the Middle East, who had had disagreements with Sikorski. These accusations are a reflection of a widespread anti-Russian sentiment in Poland. The Polish Instytut Pamięcy Narodowej (The Institute of National Remembrance) has published new information about these disputes in order to test possible theories about Sikorski's death[32].

The role that premature and enigmatic deaths play in creating the cults of a hero can be demonstrated by a comparison of the Petöfi and Štefánik cases. A comparison of Štefánik's death with the explanations for Władysław Sikorski's death can reveal important problems in creating national identities by analogy with other nations. This creates an opportunity for a comparative research of European societies, with expansion to other societies.

---

communication.gouv.fr/Disciplines-et-secteurs/Patrimoine-ethnologique/Travaux-de-recherche/Rapports-de-recherche/Liste-par-mots-cles/%28offset%29/16 [accessed: 28 April 2014].

32 Gołębiewicz, M. (undated) 'Śledztwo w sprawie katastrofy w Gibraltarze'. Available on-line: http://ipn.gov.pl/wydzial-prasowy/komunikaty/b [accessed: 28 April 2014].

Kamil Krofta and Czechoslovak Identity among Czechs, Slovaks and Germans and Others

Jiří Němec[1]
Masaryk University

Abstract: This paper follows the intellectual trajectory of Kamil Krofta, a prominent historian and politician in mid-war Czechoslovakia. Its focus is primarily in the role of Krofta and his historiographic works in the process of formulation and articulation of Czech and, eventually, Czechoslovak national identity. The article further discusses Krofta's understanding of Czech and Slovak union and his perception of ethnic minorities in Czechoslovakia, predominantly Germans. Finally, the author analyses a key intellectual conflict between Krofta and the philosopher Emanuel Rádl on the Czech-German historical relations and the possibility of Czechoslovakia as a civic nation-state.

On the first anniversary of the creation of the Czechoslovak Republic, the historian Kamil Krofta wrote that 28 October 1918 was a major watershed in *"our"* history, comparable to *"only a few events of the past"*. It was similar to the arrival of *"our"* ancestors in Bohemia, their conversion to Christianity, the fall of the Great Moravian Empire, the death of Jan Hus and the defeat of the Czech gentry at White Mountain, since each of these events apparently *"gives a new direction to our national development, a new content to our national life"*[2]. Three years later, to mark the same occasion, Krofta used the term *"the nation of Hus, Žižka and Comenius"* to describe those whom he meant by "us" in the phrases "our history", "our ancestors", "our development" and "our new free state". This "us" meant Czechs, and Krofta proudly declared himself part of the Czech nation. The three Jans – Hus, Žižka and Comenius – stood at the forefront of its pantheon of national heroes.[3]

---

1 Email: nemec.j@mail.muni.cz
2 Krofta, K. 'Tři úvahy o 28. Říjnu' in Krofta, K. Byli jsme za Rakouska... Úvahy historické a politické. Prague: Orbis, 1936, p. 612.
3 Due to the fact that after Palacký the Czech national pantheon was greatly influenced by his Protestantism, it was not until the end of the 1920s that the first Czech

During the Great War the Czech nation had secured itself its "own" state, providing a happy conclusion to the long historical development which began with the national "awakening" of the 19th century. And because even *"our awakening"* did not come about of its own accord but was the result of the activities of many scholarly "revivalist" enthusiasts, room also had to be found in the national pantheon for other modern national heroes such as Dobrovský, Jungmann, Palacký, Kollár, Čelakovský, Havlíček, Brauner and Rieger. Even their activities *"never cease to fill us with reverence"*, declared Krofta with the requisite pathos of a ceremonial lecture. In an exaggerated manner, he even ventured to call the struggle over the national language and collective memory of the Czechs a purgatory *"which it was necessary for us to go through before we could enter into the longed-for paradise of full political freedom"* in an independent Czech, or rather, Czechoslovak state[4].

Although these sentences may sound almost laughable today, they were not issued by some kind of solitary figure on the margins of the scholarly world. On the contrary, the name of Kamil Krofta had a positive resonance within the professional history community as well as outside of it. As the archivist of the most important Czech archive and a young professor of Austrian history at the only university in Cisleithania where lessons were given in Czech, Krofta was an active populariser and lecturer for the general public and thus became an important player in the struggles to form a Czech historical memory. Moreover, he entered the diplomatic service of the Czechoslovak Republic in 1919, first as an ambassador in Rome, later in Vienna and finally in Berlin, eventually settling down at the ministry of foreign affairs at the end of the 1920s, first as Edvard Beneš's right-hand man and then, after he left to become president of the republic,

---

    saint, St Wenceslas, was fully restored to this pantheon, having been among the most important patrons of Bohemia since the Middle Ages.

4   Krofta, K. (1936) 'Tři úvahy o 28. Říjnu' in Krofta, K. Byli jsme za Rakouska… Úvahy historické a politické. Prague: Orbis, 1936, p. 616–617.

as the minister of foreign affairs (1935–1938)[5]. It can therefore be justifiably claimed that in his history texts and lectures Krofta expressed not only his own personal opinion but also the general opinion of one section of the Czech cultural elites which was closely linked to "Masaryk's" republic. However, it is necessary to add that the pathos of the quotations given above should mostly be attributed to the exalted atmosphere of the early post-war years, and in Krofta's abundant historical journalism it quickly gave way to the much more sober and critical form of expression of a scholar with diplomatic experience. At the same time, Krofta did not shy away from any important subject which was related to Czech history and excited the professional community or general public at that time. He lectured and wrote about Hus, Žižka, the Hussite movement and its intellectual successors, as well as the beginnings of Přemyslid Bohemia and Saint Wenceslas, George of Poděbrady, White Mountain and T. G. Masaryk, the Slovaks or "our" Germans. He always tried to progress beyond mere historical facts and to grasp what historical events and the actions of figures from past historical generations meant for us from the perspective of "state and nation", and at the same time he increasingly inclined towards a conception of the Czech question in accordance with that of President Masaryk, as opposed to the conception of his friend, the conservative historian Josef Pekař.

It is understandable that the Czech intellectual elites welcomed the establishment of an independent Czechoslovakia as the natural culmination of the Czech national politics which had grown up in Habsburg Austria-Hungary in defence of the Czech language and Czech culture and attempted in vain to achieve recognition for the historical right to a Czech state. However, the year 1918 brought with it some important problems of a symbolic nature. These concerned, among other things, the need to find a new way of writing "our" history with regard to the relationship between the nation and the state,

---

5   Dejmek, J. Historik v čele diplomacie. Studie z dějin československé zahraniční politiky v letech 1936–1938. Praha: Karolinum, 1998.

as Krofta's friend Pekař observed in correspondence with him in 1924[6]. Under the old Austria this had apparently been dominated by a narrative of implicit anti-state and anti-Austrian revolt. Now that the independent state actually existed this was no longer appropriate. Much more serious problems from the perspective of writing history—and therefore also from the perspective of forming a significant part of the state identity of the inhabitants—stemmed from the ethnic composition of the new state. First of all, the new state elites perceived and declared the Czechoslovak Republic to be not a civic state but a nation state: it was the state of the Czechoslovak nation. Such a nation, however, had never actually existed here before, because apart from the ideological fellowship of a section of the cultural elites, Czechs and Slovaks had lived separately in distinctly different countries within the Habsburg monarchy and had quite different histories. In order for such a nation to come into being, it was necessary to "imagine" a Czechoslovak national identity in Benedict Anderson's sense of "imagined communities". So, from the time the republic was established, the state officially promoted the doctrine of the unified Czechoslovak nation. Although this nation had been divided into two branches— the Czech and the Slovak—in the distant past, it was essentially still the same nation, albeit with two linguistic dialects, cultures and different histories. At the same time, according to intellectuals of Kamil Krofta's type, Czechs historically had two advantages over Slovaks which gave them more favourable conditions for developing an advanced national culture. Firstly, the Slovaks had been a permanent, integral part of the Hungarian state for a thousand years, so it was rather difficult for them to identify themselves with the existence of some independent historical state of their own. In contrast, the view that the Czech ethnic group, i.e. the Czech part of the Czechoslovak nation, had founded its own "Czech" state with its own ruling dynasty of the Přemyslids was accepted as natural by Czechs in the 19th cen-

---

6   Čechura, J., Čechurová, J. Korespondence Josefa Pekaře a Kamila Krofty. Praha: Karolinum, 1999.

tury. Czech intellectuals were unshakably convinced of its legal continuity, even though it had been suppressed by the ruling Habsburgs, especially in the period following White Mountain, mainly by Joseph II. Secondly, in the last half-century before the creation of Czechoslovakia the Slovaks had been exposed to an uncompromising Hungarian national policy which crushed the development of national communities other than the Hungarian one. In contrast, in relatively tolerant Cisleithania the Czechs were able to develop into a self-confident national community. It therefore seemed self-evident that work on Czechoslovak identity would primarily mean finding a way to incorporate Slovaks, along with their language and culture, into the existing form of Czech identity.[7] We only have to pick up popular Czechoslovak readers or a history book from, say, the first decade of the Czechoslovak Republic — and it needn't be Krofta's Short History of Czechoslovakia from 1931 — to see how the authors envisaged it[8]. The traditional conception of Czech national history, which had evolved canonically from the time of Palacký, was expanded, where historical information was available, by references to a special or analogous development in Slovakia. The adjective "Czech" could then be replaced with "Czechoslovak". Lastly, there were also important references to Czech influences in the history and culture of the Slovaks (though less so the other way round), for example in the Hussite period, and these were combined with evidence of the mutual Czechoslovak or Slavonic nature of Czech and Slovak cultural figures during the national revival. Thus it was expected that in the future a Czechoslovak pantheon would come into existence as a pantheon of Czech heroes enriched by Slovak names. Because the academic study of history in Slovakia was in a state of decline and it was therefore necessary first of all to improve the level of Slovak historical writing, professional

---

7   In fact, a certain model for this already existed before 1918, when some compendiums of Czech literature included chapters about the development of recent Slovak literature.
8   Merhout, C., Němec, B. Československá národní čítanka. Sborník k desátému výročí Republiky československé. Praha: Státní nakladatelství, 1928.

Czech historians attempted to establish a tradition of systematic historical research directly in Slovakia in order to raise the first generation of truly Czechoslovak historians. Kamil Krofta, who was appointed a full professor of Czechoslovak history at the university in Prague in 1919 with Slovakia as his specialization, also contributed to this process himself with a series of occasional lectures and short publications on Slovakian or older Hungarian history[9]. And if he had not gone down the route of diplomacy, it might have been him and not his younger colleague Václav Chaloupecký, the first professor of history at the newly founded Comenius University in Bratislava, who would have been given the task of becoming the semi-official historiographer of the Slovak section of Czechoslovak history[10].

Although some publications by Czech historians elicited critical disagreement from Slovak intellectuals, it would not be right to see this "imagining" of Czechoslovak history as a symbol of cultural imperialism over the Slovaks. It was more a natural process of cultural adaptation in a newly created, relatively ethnically heterogeneous state which responded to a fundamental change in basic political and geopolitical frameworks following the dissolution of Austria-Hungary. In view of the growth of nationalism in the whole of Central Europe from the end of the 19th century, it is not surprising that this process followed on with a natural inevitability from the 19th-century ethnic conception of nation and that it ultimately ended in failure.

---

9   When Krofta was Czechoslovak ambassador in Austria in the first half of the 20th century, he also found time for several courses in Slovak history as a guest professor at Comenius University in Bratislava. The lectures were later published in the form of small popular booklets. Almost half of the two-thousand print run of booklets was then purchased by the Bratislava board of education on a large scale for Slovak schools. (Čechura, Čechurová, 1999, p. 67–68). See Krofta, K. Čtení o ústavních dějinách slovenských, Praha: Nákl. Klubu historického, 1924; Krofta, K. O úkolech slovenské historiografie, Bratislava: Academia, 1925; or Krofta, K. Čechové a Slováci před svým státním sjednocením. Praha: Orbis, 1932.

10 Ducháček, M. Václav Chaloupecký. Hledání československých dějin. Praha: Karolinum, 2015.

However, it was the same source of considerable ethnic heterogeneity within the state which gave rise to a much more serious problem than the Czechoslovak solution to Czech-Slovak relations—also rejected by the Slovaks. However much the new state was presented at home and abroad as a nation state of Czechoslovaks, there was indeed much that was disquieting in the arguments of its critics, especially on the part of German politicians in Bohemia, Moravia and Silesia. They pointed out that large groups of inhabitants numbering up to several million with mother tongues other than Czech or Slovak lived within the borders of the Czechoslovak state, and they spoke of Czechoslovakia with mockery as a multi-nation Austria-Hungary in miniature. It was for this reason that legal protection for the minorities was incorporated into the Czechoslovak constitutional order on the basis of the Paris peace treaties. In addition, the Czechoslovak state—and not only in comparison with the difficult situation of the South Tyrolese Germans in Mussolini's Italy—did not particularly obstruct the political or cultural development of the local Germans, as long as their activities did not turn against the very existence of the state. And so it seemed to the Czech representatives of the republic that the national question in Czechoslovakia had been adequately dealt with. However, the truth is that the political and cultural elites of the German "minority" were never able to come to terms with the Czechoslovak state, with their minority status and with the strictly centralist state organization. This was despite the fact that for many years their democratic section loyally contributed to the government and worked towards improving the position of the German-speaking population through this active cooperation in the development of the republic. Of course, the impact of the global economic crisis, disillusionment with traditional political parties, the rise of fascist ideology and the seductive successes of the revisionist policy of Hitler's national socialism in Germany all had such a detrimental effect on the unstable national situation in Czechoslovakia that in the course of the 1930s the "minority" question became one of the main problems for the very existence of the Czechoslovak state. It was symptomatic that the national concept of the state and the formation of Czechoslovak identity primarily on the basis of Czechoslavism triggered among the German cultural elites in the Czech lands a need to form their own Sudeten German identity, which would ideologically unite the Czech, Moravian and Silesian Germans hitherto fragmented according to which of the historical lands they belonged to.[11] From the outset, "Sudeten-Germanness" as a "national" identity was unequivocally a nationalistic, culturally and ideologically political project[12], which, however, was gradually accepted by a large section of the Germans from the Czech lands (especially the younger generation) at least as an umbrella term. This cultural process was then boosted and politically exploited around the middle of the 1930s by Henlein's fascist Sudetendeutsche Heimatbewegung (later the Sudeten German Party). At the same time, Sudeten German identity did not derive solely from a shared language and common geographical area within one state, delimited by the Sudeten mountain range, but it was also underpinned by a civilizing ethos, derived from the history of medieval colonization, of those who supposedly as people on the border between nations and cultures brought the achievements of a "higher" culture to the land. With the exception of Emperor Charles IV and several church representatives and medieval artists (e.g. Johannes von Tepl, the author of the medieval text Der Ackermann aus Böhmen, or Peter Parler, the second builder of the gothic cathedral of St Vitus) the Sudeten German pantheon was filled

---

11 Influenced by the uniting of the Sudeten Germans, the cultural and political elites of the German-speaking population in Slovakia and Sub-Carpathian Ruthenia began to speak of themselves as "Carpathian Germans" (Karpatendeutschen). The process also had an important political side, which manifested itself fully from the mid-30s.
12 Weger, T. 'Češi a Němci v ČSR 1918–1938 – dějiny a vzpomínání' in Kasper, T., Kasperová, D. Češi, Němci, židé v národnostním Československu. Liberec: Technická univerzita v Liberci, 2006, p. 11–18.

more with the nameless heroes of village founders, enterprising businessmen, craftsmen, burghers and later also industrialists[13]. And yet the greatest heroes of the Czech pantheon, especially Jan Hus and Jan Žižka, were perceived unequivocally by "Sudeten-Germanness" as the originators of supposedly rabidly nationalistic and anti-German Hussitism as symbols of Czech nationalism[14]. To the most radical groupings around Henlein the Czechoslovak Republic even appeared as a hostile state of Hussitism reborn.

Kamil Krofta certainly observed the development of the national situation more attentively than any other intellectual in Czechoslovakia. In 1930 the Czechoslovak Society for the Study of Minority Issues was founded at his initiative, since for the society these particular issues — as Krofta declared in his inaugural speech — "*have a special, absolutely vital significance for us*" and "*the future of our state surely depends to a great extent on the right solution being found to them.*" The society published a quarterly called Národnostní obzor (National Horizon), which provided the reader with detailed information about various aspects of the national question in Europe and about the life of the country's national minorities. In addition, it also published an editorial series of separate publications. Thus a powerful semi-official player entered into the Czechoslovak debate about the nationalities and their coexistence. Here Krofta published, for example, a synthetic interpretation of the country's national development[15] and one of his numerous studies on Germans in Czechoslovakia[16]. Through his historical studies concerning the origin of national plurality in the Czech

---

13   See for example popular history books of Schmidtmyer, A. Der Weg der Sudetendeutschen. Ein Volksbuch. Karlsbad-Drahowitz. Leipzig: Adam Kraft Verlag, 1938.
14   Weger, T. 'Das Hussitenstereotyp in sudetendeutschen völkischen Diskurs' in Dimitrów, E., et al. Deutschlands östliche Nachbarschaften. Frankfurt am Main: Peter Lang, 2009, s. 585–608.
15   Krofta, K Národnostní vývoj zemí československých. Praha, 1934.
16   See Krofta, K. Die Deutschen in Böhmen. Praha: Orbis, 1924; Krofta, K. Die Deutschen in der Tschechoslowakei. Praha: Deutschpolitisches Arbeitsamt, 1928; Krofta, K. Das Deutschtum in der tschechoslowakischen Geschichte. Praha: Orbis, 1935; Krofta, K. Němci v československém státě. Praha: Orbis, 1937; Krofta, K.

lands, Slovakia and Sub-Carpathian Ruthenia, he attempted to define what relationship the various nationalities had and should have had towards the current Czechoslovak state. Krofta came to the conclusion that the Czechoslovak nation, i.e. Czechs and Slovaks, had the right to a special status in Czechoslovakia compared to the Germans, Hungarians and Poles living there. Only Czechs and Slovaks had founded the state, and this independent state of "theirs" was supposedly the only guarantee of Czech and Slovak national existence in the future[17].

So we know that the process of adaptation after the creation of Czechoslovakia proceeded by "imagining" a Czechoslovak national identity made up from ethnic Czechs and Slovaks. Let us, however, pose the question of why, in the liberal and democratic republic which Czechoslovakia wanted to become based on the model of the Anglo-Saxon democracies, it was not the aim to create a civic Czechoslovak nation from all the citizens of the new state irrespective of their ethnic origin. This is by no means as an unhistorical question as it might at first appear. It was indirectly expressed on the tenth anniversary of the republic by the unconventional philosopher Emanuel Rádl in the book "The War between the Czechs and Germans"[18]. Because national identity had traditionally been derived from history as well as language since the 19th century, it was not surprising that in his book Rádl turned on historians with a razor-sharp critique. Why was it that the history written in the Czech lands (at this point Rádl ignored the Slovakian and Sub-Carpathian parts of the state) was apparently *only* that of the Czechs, as was the case with Czech historians, or *only* that of the Germans, as was usually the case with "Sudeten German" historiography?

Would it not be more appropriate to find a historical narrative in which Czechs and German would be the joint heroes and would not

---

Čechy a Německo v dějinném vývoji. Praha: Orbis, 1938; also Dejmek, J. 'Kroftovo chápání sudetoněmecké otázky a její vyústění', Acta universitatis Carolinae. Philosophica et historica 5, 1991, p. 33–49.

17 Krofta, K. Výchova k státnosti, Praha: Masarykův lidovýchovný ústav, 1935, p. 13.
18 Rádl, E. Válka Čechů s Němci. Praha: Melantrich, 1993.

stand in opposition to each other as enemies? Is not this very way of telling Czech history partly to blame for the inhabitants from both language groups defining themselves against each other in a hostile way? And why do Czech and German historians, each apparently cloistered in their own "tribal" nationalism, never pose the question of how it happened that the population of the Czech lands did not unite into a single nation as did the Normans and Anglo-Saxons in Britain, the Gauls and Franks in France or the Swiss nations, "*i.e. why did a unified culture, incorporating both Germanic and Slavonic assimilated elements, not develop here?*"[19]. After all, Rádl asserted out of concern for Czechoslovakia and its democracy, this was the only way in which the country's path towards "cultural progress" could be secured, and in the same breath he urged Czech and Sudeten German historians to step out of the shadow of their nationality.

Krofta felt deeply offended by Rádl's at times truly impromptu and unjust criticism. With reference to the allegedly passive, rather insignificant historical influence of the German population, he defended the conception of Czech history as a history of Czechs, since — as Rádl himself wrote — "*it was and still is Czechs who bear the brunt of the political fortunes of this country*"[20]. But the question about the reasons for the Czechs and Germans not merging into one national community with a single identity intrigued him. Several times he too indirectly considered the possibility of a civic nation, for example when influenced by Meinecke's distinction between state nations and cultural nations, he spoke of state nations in Western Europe or in Hungary prior to 1918. But on the basis of the Hungarian example he deduced that deliberately transforming the nationality of non-Czechoslovak ethnic groups would have necessarily led to cultural violence, which he considered to be utterly inadmissible and immoral. A civic Czechoslovak nation in the Central European context seemed unworkable to him, because in his opinion it did not correspond with the

---

19 Rádl, E. Válka Čechů s Němci, Praha: Melantrich, 1993, p. 59.
20 Krofta, K. 'Rádlova Válka Čechů s Němci', Národnostní obzor 1, 1930, p. 83.

present social reality of clearly demarcated, self-assured national communities. If a moment had arisen at the height of the Middle Ages in the 13th and 14th centuries when, as with the German author of the Zbraslav Chronicle, Petr Žitavský, a common provincial national consciousness was created, it was apparently swept away by the Hussite anti-German wave and was never summoned up again. Krofta understood Rádl's call for a new Czechoslovakian state idea which would not neglect the German inhabitants of the state so much. However, he believed that it was not possible to do otherwise. Just as in historiography it is apparently impossible to abandon the national narrative in the interpretation of the past, it is impossible even in the symbolic politics of the Czechoslovakian state idea to relinquish the preferential position of the Czech, or Czechoslovak nation, because "*it was the Czech nation which twice (the second time together with the Slovaks) created this state through its will and its efforts, and that it is primarily the will and efforts of the Czechoslovak nation which will safeguard its continuation in the present and the future*"[21]. At the same time, however, it was precisely the Czechoslovaks' affectionate relationship towards the state which laid a great responsibility on them to pursue a just minority policy and at the same time to constantly strive for the kind of mutual relationship for future times in which, while preserving the full national identity of both nations, the hostile and antagonistic battle between the Czechs and Germans would be transformed into a "*magnanimous contest between two adversaries who recognize and respect each other.*" However, Krofta did not concede that under such circumstances some state inhabitants would continue to remain lesser citizens of the state than others and that it would also be difficult to find common heroic role models for the future.

So, however much we might have the feeling that in conclusion Rádl — and not Krofta — was more correct in his assessment of the basic principle of a civic nation as opposed to ethnic nationhood with re-

---

21 Krofta, K. 'Rádlova Válka Čechů s Němci', Národnostní obzor 1, 1930, p. 97.

gard to the long-term viability of the Czechoslovak state, it is necessary to point out that Krofta was not the only one who rejected Rádl's idea, which was timeless but at the same time divorced from the historical reality. Rádl was rejected just as vigorously by the German cultural elites of the time working on the "Sudeten German" identity. The nationalist principle governed the order of the organization of society at that time. And it only remains to add that in the end it was the development of German thinking, negatively influenced by the rise of Hitler's Germany with its grand and appealing idea of an empire of all Germans, that became the main obstacle in Krofta's, but also Rádl's struggle for a new "Czechoslovak identity" and "Czechoslovak state".

New States — Old-new elements of nationalism in caricatures (1919-1921)[1]

Ágnes Tamás[2]
University of Debrecen

Abstract: The paper focuses on the problem of representation of nationalist conception through the symbolic device of caricature. It draws on caricatures from popular Hungarian, Austrian and Czech papers from the period between 1919 and 1921. Caricatures of the era frequently thematised the heated topic of dissolution of the Austro-Hungarian Empire and represented nation-specific symbolic systems and stereotypes, associated with other nations and minorities. The paper identifies these stereotypical depictions as well as common tropes and topics (suffering, death, enmity) and undertakes the analysis of their meaning.

A consequence of the peace treaties of Paris following WWI was the collapse of the Austro-Hungarian Monarchy, after which new nation states appeared in the region. The events following WWI — the loss of great power status and of territories — influenced greatly the new nation-building programs of the leading nations of the former Monarchies (Germans and Hungarians) as well as small nations. In Hungary the propaganda for a complete territorial revision appeared already before the signing of the Treaty of Trianon (on June 4, 1920). In Austria the propaganda for Anschluss to Germany appeared, since contemporaries believed that the new small state was unviable. Symbols of national propaganda formed after WWI determined the style of propaganda between the two world wars.

In this paper I analyse caricatures from Hungarian, Austrian and Czech comic papers that were very popular at the time. Comic papers could influence the opinion of civic readers about the topics of revision or "Anschluss" greatly, and new strategies for the nation building

---

1 The research was funded by the Hungarian Scientific Research Fund, OTKA, grant PD 109069.
2 Email: akosbartha@yahoo.com

process can also be observed with the help of caricatures. The analysed period is between the years 1919-1921. 1919 was the first year of peace and in 1921 the Austrian-Hungarian border was redrawn after the Czechoslovak-Hungarian and Austrian-Hungarian armed conflicts. The analysed comic papers are *Borsszem Jankó*, *Mátyás Diák* (Budapest), *Kikeriki!*, *Die Bombe*, *Wiener Caricaturen*, *Der Götz von Berlichingen*, *Figaro* (Vienna), and *Humoristické listy* (Prague).[3]

In the paper I analyse the symbolism of the most important events, the signing of the peace treaties, and the loss and gaining of territories. This analysis of the depiction of the modification of borders and territories provides an opportunity to analyse beliefs about new states and about old and new stereotypes, which can be compared with the results of my previous investigations into nationalities and stereotypes in the monarchies[4].

The signing of the peace treaties

Most of the Hungarian and Austrian comic papers already illustrated the unfairness of the peace treaties in the period before the signing of the treaties, highlighting the motif of force instead of negotiations. The motif of force is represented in the pictures where the Austrian or the Hungarian figure is tied down. The first example of this kind of depictions appeared in *Borsszem Jankó* together with the motif of revenge (ill. 1: BJ, 7 March, 1920, 7).

---

[3] In this paper I will abbreviate the titles of comic papers as follows: *Borsszem Jankó* (BJ), *Mátyás Diák* (MD), *Kikeriki* (K), *Die Bombe* (DB), *Figaro* (F), *Wiener Caricaturen* (WCar.), *Der Götz von Berlichingen* (GB), and *Humoristické listy* (HL). The cited caricatures are examples, each analysed issue contained more caricatures on every topic of the analysis.

[4] Tamás, Á. 'Serbs, Croatians and Romanians from Hungarian and Austrian Perspectives. Analysis of Caricatures from Hungarian and Austrian Comic Papers', in Demski, D., Baraniecka-Olszewska, K. (eds), *Images of the Other in Ethnic Caricatures of Central and Eastern Europe*. Warsaw: Polish Academy of Sciences, 2010, pp. 272-297.

Ill. 1 **"Samson in the treadmill"**
"- Slaveholders, beware! ... Remember Samson from the Bible."

Michal the Hungarian is working as the biblical figure Samson for the Philistines (for US president Woodrow Wilson, Marianne the personification of France, the symbol figure of Yugoslavia, the prime minister of the United Kingdom David Lloyd George, Alexandru Vaida-Voevod, Tomáš Masaryk, and lastly Gabriele D'Annunzio).[5] In the depiction in the caricature, Samson has short hair and is tied down after

---

5   Alexandru Vaida-Voevod (1872–1950), later a Romanian prime minister (first 1919–1920), who campaigned intensively for the winning of Transylvania for Romania. Tomáš Masaryk (1850–1937) Czech politician, the first president of Czechoslovakia. Gabriele D'Annunzio (1863–1938) Italian pilot in WWI, later nationalist politician, who led the Italian free corps in 1919–1920 when they occupied Fiume (today: Rijeka, Croatia). The idea of Yugoslavia arose first in the 19th century, after that among Croatian emigrés in April 1915, but the name of the new state was Kingdom of Serbs, Croats and Slovenes. The official name of the state changed to Yugoslavia in 1929, but the contemporaries used Yugoslavia from the beginning, thus the comic papers called the state Yugoslavia as well-see Pándi, L. *Köztes-Európa, 1756–1997 (kronológia)*. Budapest: Teleki László Alapítvány, 1999, pp. 174, 186, 254.

Delilah has betrayed him, and also has his eyes bored out, as in the Biblical story (BJ, 7 March, 1920, 7, Book of Judges, chapter 16.). In the Old Testament Samson was able to avenge the slavers with God's help, therefore the appetite for revenge appeared before the signing of the peace treaty in the Hungarian comic paper. Another caricature has a less cheerful character, but it is not hopeless: Michal the Hungarian can be observed tied to a column, a Romanian soldier standing next to him. Lloyd George comes up to the Hungarian man and gives him his bride, "Hungarian Peace". She is depicted as an ugly woman and Michal the Hungarian does not want to accept her as his wife. He has no chance to protest, because he is tied up, but later he might have an opportunity: as he puts it, "if my hands were free, I would use them for something else entirely" — but not offering his hand to the woman (ill. 2: MD, 16 May, 1920, 1).

Ill. 2 **"Here comes the bride"**

The word "force" appeared also directly in the title of an Austrian caricature. Lloyd George and the prime minister of France Georges Clemenceau remove the handcuffs from Austria's hands and tell her: "Sign it!" (GB, 24 April, 1919, 1) Austria is half naked, she wears a piece of cloth with the coat of arms of the former Monarchy, and one can see the pain in her face, while the entente politicians wear black hooded coats decorated with skull and crossbones. The scene refers to the vision of the (nation's) death, which is the most often depicted motif in the Austrian comic papers.

In a Hungarian montage caricature one can see a man signing the Treaty of Trianon hiding his eyes with his hand, but he does not look like any of the Hungarian politicians (Alfréd Drasche-Lázár or Ágost Benárd) who signed the peace treaty, his features are not identifiable (ill. 3: BJ, May 30, 1920, 1).

Ill. 3 "Very well... – we'll sign it!..."

In the background one can see a photo of a demonstration, with the demonstrators holding boards with the map of the Hungarian Kingdom and the slogan "No! No! Never!" (BJ, January 25, 1920, 1, BJ, May 30, 1920, 1).[6] In another Hungarian caricature a Hungarian man is depicted with a pen in his hand, an entente soldier holding a gun in his direction and forcing him to sign the peace treaty. The man is not a politician, his name is "Mihály Nagy" and he is depicted wearing Hungarian clothes. In the comic papers countries were traditionally personified by women, nations by men. Hungarians were always called "Mihály Magyar" (Michael the Hungarian). The name of the man in the caricature not wanting to sign the treaty is "Mihály Nagy" and not the traditional name "Mihály Magyar", standing for the average Hungarian person through whom the caricaturist wanted to accentuate that in Hungary no one wanted to accept the peace conditions (MD, November 14, 1920, 1).[7] In the Viennese comic papers the signing of the Treaty of Saint-Germain was also depicted connected with force, but in these caricatures the chancellor, Karl Renner, was recognizable, in contrast with the Hungarian caricatures (GB, September 20, 1919, 3).

In the issues following the signing the caricaturists evaluated the treaties and depicted the (expected) consequences: death and a new war in Europe in the near future. Three witches — one of them looking like a skeleton — christen Austria, the new state, which is depicted as a weak infant, unlikely to survive. In another caricature one can observe the "German-Austrian Dance of Death", where the grim reaper dances over the Austrians, prophesying the destiny of the separate

---

6   Many posters, postcards, ornaments, and objects were adorned with this slogan in Hungary, and it was well known outside of Hungary as well. The meaning of the slogan used the Latin equivalent of Trianon: 'triple no', see Zeidler, M. *A magyar irredenta kultusz a két világháború között*. Budapest: Teleki László Alapítvány, 2002; or Zeidler, M. *A revíziós gondolat*. Bratislava: Kalligram, 2009.
7   "Nagy" is a very common family name like "Smith" in English.

Austrian state (GB, 30 August, 1919, 7, GB, 30 August, 1919, 1).[8] Furthermore, in another depiction Lloyd George cannot enjoy his victory, because the smell of the dead bodies around him—the personifications of Austria, Turkey and Russia—is unbearable. Moreover, in the last example in connection with Death, Austria appears dead in a coffin, and the figure symbolizing the Czech nation, Wenzel covers the coffin. Wenzel wears a French uniform and a French soldier commands him—referring to the leading position of France during the peace negotiations. It is not only Austria's gravestone which is depicted, but also the gravestone of the Peace Treaty of Saint Germaine. On one side of the grave stands Wilson, giving his famous fourteen points to Death (WCar., 15 December, 1920, 1, K, 6 June 1920, 2, F, 25 June, 1919. 8).

The symbols of the loss and gain of territories

The motif of maps was especially suitable as a symbol of the loss or gain of territories. From the many examples found in the magazines I will mention only a few: from the map of the Hungarian Kingdom shaped as tree foliage Austrians are tearing off the region of West Hungary (BJ, August 21, 1921, 2).[9] In another, renitent students—Czechs, Serbs, Italians, and Poles—cut territories off of Austria's map with scissors, or yet in another the politicians of the leading Western powers are preparing to eat the map of Austria in order to decrease the territories of the former Austro-Hungarian Monarchy (ill. 4: K, July 13, 1919, 2) (K, March 23, 1919, 2, K, July 13, 1919, 2).

---

8   The Treaty of Saint Germain forbad the use of "German-Austria" for the naming of the new state, since it could refer to an Anschluss, but one can read this state name often in the comic papers.

9   The green foliage symbolized the hope for a better future. Therefore, the Hungarian Területvédő Liga (Territory Protection League) encouraged everyone to wear a badge with a green foliage, because "the historical Hungarian Kingdom cannot die" in Buzinkay, G. 'A trianoni békeszerződés és a magyar liberális sajtó', *Médiakutató*, Vol. 12. (4), 2011, p. 105.

Ill. 4 **"Dessert in St. Germain"**
"There is no meat on it any more. What should we do with the bones?"

The motif of eating territories is a recurring element in the caricatures. In one caricature, "the pita eaters", Serbs, Romanians and Czechoslovaks, are eating a cake of the shape of the former Hungarian Kingdom, breaking their teeth in the process. In an Austrian caricature, Czechoslovak foreign minister Edvard Beneš and Italian king Victor Emanuel III are feasting, drinking champagne and eating desserts: Beneš the Czech territories of the Monarchy, the Italian king South Tyrol (MD, June 6, 1920, 5, K, February 27, 1921, 2). Gluttony is one of the seven deadly sins; therefore this motif was also appropriate to judge the gaining of territories.

The next motif, the mutilation of a female body symbolizing the country or of a male body symbolizing the nation has long traditions as symbol for the loss of territories. One can observe the total amputation of Hungary in caricatures: the newly formed countries take away severed body parts quickly. The Czech figure runs away with Slovakia, the Romanian with Transylvania, the South Slav with Croatia, and the Austrian with Western Hungary. However the motif of amputation did not appear only in connection with Hungary: the amputated Michael the German, the symbolic figure of the German nation – without an arm, leg and eye – can be seen in the Mirror chamber of Versailles; Georges Clemenceau prepares the statue of the Venus of Milo from Germany, cutting off her arms (Alsace-Lorraine, East Prussia, and Silesia). In an Austrian caricature Michael the Austrian is depicted with one leg and with crutches (K, January 18, 1920, 2, K, April 27, 1919, 8, K, May 18, 1919, 8, WCar., November 20, 1919, 1).[10]

The amputations are linked closely with the depiction of doctor-patient situations, because the doctors — the winners — operate on the defeated countries represented as patients. To illustrate the loss of territories this way was also a common allegory in caricatures after a war defeat. In an Austrian caricature Austria is depicted sitting in the dentist's chair with the dentist, Clemenceau, pulling her teeth in bits and pieces for her sake, but causing great pain to the patient. In a Hungarian depiction, Hungary is lying tied down on an operating table while "the surgeons" are Lloyd George, Clemenceau and Woodrow Wilson. Wilson is warning his colleagues that "Perhaps you have to wait with that operation, sirs. The patient could die." (K, June 8, 1919, 2, MD, January 12, 1919, 1).[11] In another Hungarian comic paper's caricature the doctors are not only preparing for the operation but have already opened the stomach of the tied down patient and removed his internal organs (ill. 5: BJ, December 21, 1919, 1).

---

[10] The statue of the Venus of Milo appeared also in connection with the Hungarian loss of territories: Aristide Briand and David Lloyd George see Hungaria, the woman personifying Hungary, as Venus with bleeding arms, and they state that they made a masterpiece in Trianon (BJ, August 7, 1921, 1).

[11] It is not possible to know for sure if the depiction of Clemenceau as a doctor was connected or not with his original profession as a physician, see Pricker, D. P. *Georges Clemenceau. Politikai életrajz*. Budapest: Gondolat, 1988.

Ill. 5 **"The operation in Neuilly"**
"Michal the Hungarian: Ah, doctor, doctor Clemenceau! ... My intestines!
Clemenceau: I told you already that I do not interfere with your interior affairs."
[In Hungarian a pun on the words 'belem' (my intestines) and 'belügyei' (interior affairs).]

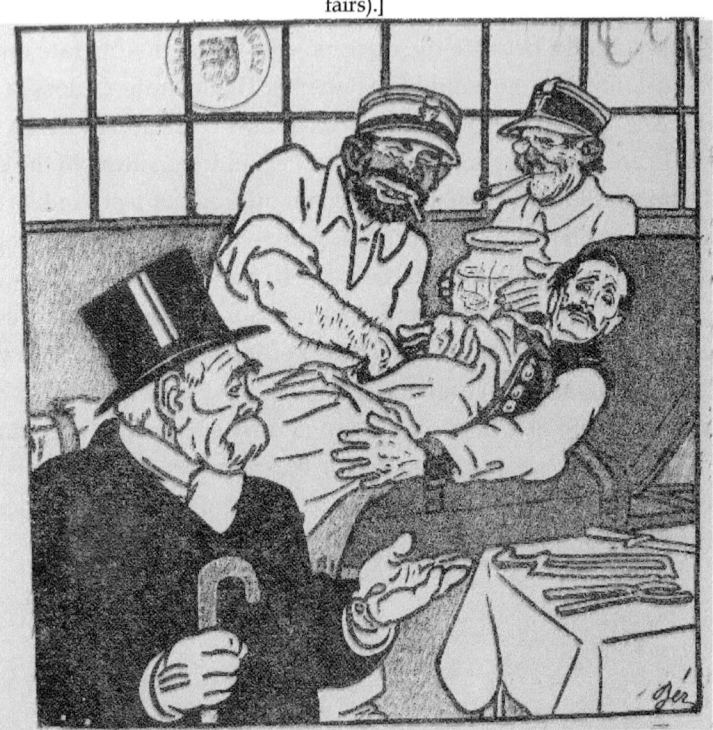

One can observe a similar scene in the Czechoslovak comic paper where Maurice Pellé, the leader of the French military mission in Czechoslovakia and leader of the Czechoslovak army is slashing open the stomach of the person symbolizing Hungary, with towns previously occupied by the Hungarian Red Army (Košice, Prešov, Nové Zámky, and Zvolen) falling out of it (BJ, December 21, 1919, 1, HL, July 18, 1919, 233).

Lastly, one of the common motifs of the Hungarian and Austrian comic papers was the depiction of pain—in a similar way to the suffering of Christ. In the Hungarian comic papers the bitterness appeared first at Christmas 1919, when Michael the Hungarian could not decorate his Christmas tree because its branches (Transylvania, Upper Hungary, Western Hungary, and parts of South Hungary) were torn off, but on a last branch burned a candle with the caption "Hope", and it lit up the whole room. At the end of the year 1921 only suffering was depicted: Michael the Hungarian is lying on the ground, his arms are tied down, and the figures of the new neighbouring states are driving nails marking the new borders into his upper body: one nail into his heart, another over his groin, and one each into both sides of his trunk. One can observe the pain on his face, and the places of the nails suggest that he will not survive. The scene is reminiscent of the sufferings of Christ, which was used in comic papers outside of Hungary as well, where, for instance, Austria can be seen crucified (MD, December 28, 1919, 1, MD, December 4, 1921, 1, DM, November 3, 1921, 1).[12] In the Austrian comic papers the sadness over the forbidden Anschluss was often depicted, too. For example, Clemenceau, again, depicted as a doctor is cutting "the German twins" apart with a saw, but the twins have two heads and one body, therefore the operation is likely to be deadly for both of them (K, December 14, 1919, 8).

Conclusion

The elements demonstrated in the caricatures—the suffering, the vision of a nation's death, the enmity—became a part of the Austrian and Hungarian national identity between the two world wars. The comic papers took an active part in the popularization of this propaganda from the beginning despite the fact their primary function was

---

12   The suffering of Christ appeared in several post cards and posters. The day before the signing of the Treaty of Trianon was Corpus Christi, therefore a parallel seemed obvious to the contemporaries between the suffering of Christ and the destiny of Hungarians and it was made in sermons and in speeches, which could serve as the grounds for latter depictions, see Buzinkay, G. 'A trianoni békeszerződés és a magyar liberális sajtó', *Médiakutató*, Vol. 12. (4), 2011, p. 105. For depiction of pain the suffering of Christ was a common Christian symbol, but the Hungarian caricatures with this motif appeared only after the signing of the Treaty of Trianon. In the Austrian comic papers the crucifying can be observed first at the end of the year 1921.

as entertainment. The Hungarian and Austrian comic papers depicted their new neighbours with sarcastic mockery, and in the Austrian papers anti-Hungarian sentiments can be observed as well. Hungary propagated the idea of territorial integrity; the negative depictions of the former nationalities of the Monarchy lived on in the caricatures, with similar methods of depiction. For decades, the pain and the refusal of the peace treaty, which was judged unfair, made it impossible to analyse the real reasons for what caused the breaking up of the Austro-Hungarian Monarchy.

In the Austrian comic papers anti-Czech feeling lived on like in the period of the Monarchy—with the same motifs in the caricatures, while strong, defensive anti-Hungarianism with anti-revisionism and anti-German feelings were characteristic of the Czechoslovak comic paper. An important feature of the depiction of the self was that it had to be defined through the other group, the enemy—this was found in every comic paper—deepening by the end of the analysed period when every humorous or friendly gesture disappeared from the comic papers. The new elements represented and created a new group identity which was rooted in the past and often had exaggerated aims.

Case studies I

Jozef Tiso: My Enemy—Your Hero?

Jan Rychlík[1]
The Academy of Sciences of the Czech Republic

Abstract: The paper investigates the lengthy and heated debate on the role of Jozef Tiso, the president of the war-time Slovak State, in Slovak history. First, the author presents a brief biography of Tiso, focusing primarily on his ascension to the presidential seat and role in the 1939 splitting of Czechoslovakia, as well as general characteristics of his political conceptions. Further, the author discusses the changing perception of Tiso in after-war Czechoslovakia and his post-mortem rise in prominence in autonomous Slovakia after 1993.

A brief biography of Jozef Tiso, which focuses on his political activities, reads as follows.[2] He was born on 13 October 1887, in Bytča, the Central Váh River region. He studied theology at Vienna University, receiving his doctorate in 1911. He began his career as an assistant priest in various places in Slovakia. During the Great War, in 1914–15, he served as an army chaplain on the eastern front; from 1915 onwards, he taught religion at the Piarist Lyceum in Nitra and was also a spiritual director of the Diocesan Seminary in Nitra. Later he became secretary to the bishop. Before the creation of Czechoslovakia, Tiso was not involved in the Slovak national movement in any way, but he was not against it either. He did, however, become involved in activities of the Slovak People's Party (SĽS) led by the priest Andrej Hlinka. In 1925, seven years after the new state had been born the party was renamed Hlinka's Slovak People's Party (HSĽS). Tiso became the Vice-Chairman and chief ideologist of HSĽS, since, unlike Hlinka, he had a fairly sound education and was proficient in languages. Tiso was first elected a member of the National Assembly in 1925, and succeeded in

---

1   Email: jan.rychlik@ff.cuni.cz.
2   See the entry on Jozef Tiso in Slovenský biografický slovník, vol. 6. Martin: Matica slovenská, 1994, pp. 74–75. For details, see Ďurica, M. S. Jozef Tiso 1887–1947: Životopisný profil (3rd edn). Bratislava: Lúč, 2006.

holding his seat in subsequent general elections in 1929 and 1935. Between 1927 and 1929, he was Minister of Public Health in the right-wing government known as the 'Gentlemen's Coalition'. A dyed-in-the-wool autonomist, or, more accurately, federalist, Tiso was the first to put forth a clear formulation of the Slovaks' right to autonomy within Czechoslovakia.[3] He was a representative of a moderate faction within the HSĽS, and Czech politicians also perceived him as a man with whom an agreement could be reached.

After Hlinka's death on 16 August 1938, Tiso became the leader of the HSĽS and in fact of the Slovak political scene as well. To push through Slovakia autonomy, he successfully used the Munich *diktat* of 30 September 1938, which had resulted in Czechoslovakia's having to cede border areas to Germany and a weakening of the central government. On 6 October 1938, during negotiations in Žilina, he effectively subordinated the leaderships of the other principal political parties in Slovakia and forced the central government in Prague to agree to the declaration of Slovak autonomy. Tiso became Prime Minister of Slovakia's autonomous government. On 13 March 1939, he was invited to Berlin to meet Hitler, who then told him that he had decided to do away with what was remaining of Czechoslovakia and to annex the Bohemian Lands directly to Germany. He strongly recommended to Tiso that Slovakia should detach itself from the Bohemian Lands as fast as possible; if it did not, Germany would lose interest in it. On the next day, the autonomous Slovak parliament declared Slovak independence, and the country became a client state of Germany. On 1 October 1939, Tiso was elected Chairman of the HSĽS and, on 26 October, President of the Slovak Republic. Slovak dependence on Germany was based on a special German-Slovak treaty of protection (*Schutzvertrag*) signed on 23 March 1939. Under Tiso's leadership, Slovakia provided military assistance to Germany in the invasion of Poland and also in the attack on the Soviet Union in 1941. On 13 December 1941,

---

3   Tiso, J. Ideológia Slovenskej ľudovej strany. Prague: Tiskový odbor ÚSČS, 1930.

it also formally declared war on the other states of the anti-Hitler coalition.

The political system created by Tiso cannot be described in unequivocal terms. It was expected to be based on the social teachings of the Roman Catholic Church, combined with ideas of the corporate state as defined by Othmar Spann (1878–1950), an Austrian sociologist and political scientist, whose the teachings greatly influenced Tiso. Spann's idea of a corporate state ultimately did not materialize in Slovakia because Germany was against it. Tiso rejected both Marxism and political liberalism, that is, parliamentary democracy with political parties competing for power.[4] As early as the period of Slovak autonomy within Czechoslovakia, Tiso had managed to establish an authoritarian régime of one party, his HSĽS, in Slovakia. On the other hand, he was no National Social and continued to represent the moderate, conservative faction within HSĽS. With skillful maneuvering, he even succeeded in eliminating the influence of the radical National-Socialist faction led by Vojtech Tuka and Alexander Mach. As a result, the Slovak régime was comparatively moderate with regard to persecution of its opponents (though not towards the Jews); in fact, no politically motivated death sentence was actually passed in Slovakia till the outbreak of the Slovak National Uprising in late August 1944.[5]

Tiso was a dyed-in-the-wool anti-Semite, though his variety of antisemitism was religious rather than ethnic or racial. He himself admitted that while studying in Vienna he had been deeply influenced by the Christian Socialist leader Karl Lueger (1844–1910). At that time, Lueger was the mayor of Vienna, and he made antisemitism the cornerstone of his political programme.[6] Antisemitism was an integral part of Tiso's Slovak nationalism, which constituted the ideological

---

4 For details, see Rychlík, J. 'Ideové základy myšlení Jozefa Tisa a jejich politický dopad', in Bystrický, V., Fano, Š. (eds) Pokus o politický a osobný profil Jozefa Tisu, Bratislava: Slovak Academic Press, 1992, pp. 263–74.

5 For a detailed legal analysis, see Rašla, A. 'Legendy o Tisovi' in Bystrický, V., Fano, Š. (eds), Pokus o politický a osobný profil Jozefa Tisu, pp. 140–43.

6 Šimončič A., Polčín, J. Jozef Tiso, prvý prezident Slovenskej republiky. Bratislava: Zväz slovenských knihkupcov, 1941, pp. 17–18.

foundations of the Slovak State. In his conception, Slovak nationalism reflected the interests of the Slovak nation.[7] But he perceived the nation in purely language-based, ethnic, and religious terms,[8] which basically excluded all minorities, particularly Jews, from the Slovak national community. True, Tiso was not involved in the organization of the deportations of the Jews, but did not speak out against them either. As Prime Minister and later President of the Slovak Republic, he signed several government decrees and legislative acts which curtailed the rights of the Jews in various ways.[9] He also signed a constitutional act (No. 68/1942), on 15 May 1942, which sanctioned the deportation of the Slovak Jews, with few exceptions, to German-occupied Poland.[10] Moreover, in a speech to the public in Holíč, on 15 August 1942, Tiso stated his approval of the deportations and rejected the opinion that they were contrary to Christian ethics.[11] In 1944, he came out openly against the Slovak National Uprising, and acknowledged, and later approved, the call for German military assistance in Slovakia.[12]

---

7   Polakovič, Š. Tisova náuka. Bratislava: Nakladateľstvo HSĽS, 1941, p. 17.
8   For a comparison, see Tiso, J. 'Ideológia', p. 2. For details of Tiso's conception of the nation, see Bakoš, V. 'K Tisovej koncepci národa a nacionalizmu', in Bystrický V., Fano, Š. (eds), Pokus o politický a osobný profil Jozefa Tisu, pp. 275–86.
9   In particular, Act No. 210/1940 passed by the Slovak legislature on 3 September 1940, whereby the government was granted full powers to exclude and debar all Jews from economic and social life in Slovakia for one year. On the basis of the act, the Jews of Slovakia were deprived, by means of various decrees, of all property and political and human rights. It also constituted the basis of the notorious Jewish Code (Act No. 198/1941), promulgated on 9 September1941, which introduced and implemented the Nuremberg race laws in Slovakia. For details, see Kamenec, I. Po stopách tragédie, Bratislava: Archa, 1991, pp. 125–32.
10 It is true that Constitutional Act No. 68 of 1942 of the Slovak Code of Laws sanctioned the deportation of the Jews of Slovakia, but it also exempted some categories of Jews from the deportations, thus paradoxically protecting them. Following the occupation of Slovakia by the Wehrmacht, however, all the deportations of Jews were handled by Germans who disregarded the exemptions. For a detailed analysis of Act No. 68/1942, see ibid., pp. 187–90.
11 Fabricius, M., Hradská, K. (eds), Jozef Tiso: Prejavy a články, vol. 2 (1938–44). Bratislava: Academic Electronic Press, 2007, Doc. 287, pp. 492–93.
12 Ibid., vol. 3 (1944–47), Doc. 1, pp. 7–9.

As President of the Slovak Republic, Tiso remained the last ally of Germany until the bitter end. In April 1945, he left Slovakia, going first to Austria and then to a monastery in Altötting, Bavaria. He was discovered there by US intelligence, arrested, and subsequently extradited to the Czechoslovak authorities. Under the retribution decrees of the Slovak National Council, Tiso was charged, among other things, with active participation in the break-up of Czechoslovakia, the establishment of authoritarian, non-democratic rule, support for the German war effort, participation in the deportations of the Jews, and treason for seeking to suppress the Slovak National Uprising.[13] Following a three-month trial, the National Court in Bratislava sentenced him to death. President Edvard Beneš refused his petition for clemency, since the government had not recommended it. In the early hours of 18 April 1947, Tiso was hanged in the yard of the prison at the Regional Court, Bratislava.

In order properly to understand the discussion that took place around Tiso, it is necessary first to focus both on the principal charges raised against him and on the way Tiso and later his lawyers dealt with them. For the sake of simplicity, let us start with the charge made against him before the National Court, though the criticism aimed at Tiso is not restricted to matters for which he was criminal prosecuted. Even now, criticism of Tiso concerns the points contained in the indictment of 1946. At that time, the first count was Tiso's participation in the break-up of Czechoslovakia in March 1939. Among the other counts were: the non-democratic nature of the Slovak State, participation in the war against the Soviet Union and the other Allies, participation in the deportation and extermination of the Jews, refusal to support, at least passively, the Slovak National Uprising, and siding with Nazi Germany till the end.

The apologetics of Tiso are essentially based on his own defense before the National Court, to which his supporters and followers later

---

13 Decree No. 33/1945 of the Slovak National Council, from the Collection of Decrees of the Slovak National Council, as amended by Decree No. 58/1946 of the Slovak National Council, from the Collection of Decrees of the Slovak National Council.

added further arguments and attempted to support them with some facts. It will thus be enough to look at Tiso's defense in 1947. He refused the charge of having participated in the break-up of Czechoslovakia on the grounds that Slovakia was in danger of being swallowed up by Horthy's Hungary at that time. Tiso's apologists also later argued that every nation was entitled to an independent state, an argument that gradually began to prevail. As to the other counts, namely, the building-up of a totalitarian system, participation in the war on the side of Germany, the deportations of the Jews, and opposing the Slovak National Uprising, Tiso's usual counterarguments included German pressure, which he had been unable to resist, and the 'lesser evil' argument, namely, his efforts to prevent even greater Slovak dependence on Germany, to prevent the assumption of power by the Slovak National Socialists around Vojtech Tuka and Alexander Mach, and simply the necessity to defend the interests of the Slovak nation under all circumstances. Tiso dismissed the accusation that he had participated in the genocide of the Jews by claiming that he had known nothing about their tragic fate. His supporters later especially emphasized his role in the creation of the Slovak State, explaining its non-democratic character by the war raging around it, claiming that Slovakia's participation in the war was merely a token gesture, and that Tiso had only agreed to the deportation of the Jews to forced labour camps but had known nothing about their actual fate. They also explained Tiso's opposition to the Slovak National Uprising by the fact that it had been aimed against the Slovak State.

Czech post-war society naturally perceived Tiso's participation in the break-up of Czechoslovakia in March 1939 as his greatest crime. But it was not seen as a crime by most Slovaks. Actually, few people realized the difference between Czech and Slovak perceptions of Tiso's role in the declaration of Slovak independence. It is surely no coincidence that Anton Rašla, the military prosecutor in Tiso's trial, suggested constructing the indictment on Tiso's participation in crimes against humanity rather than on his role in the break-up of Czechoslovakia. Rašla probably realized that the prosecution's arguments would be weak in this particular area and that Tiso might be made a martyr of Slovak independence. But Rašla's proposals were not accepted.[14]

This explanation clearly indicates that, from the Czech post-war perspective, there was hardly any difference between Tiso and Sudeten German leaders such as Konrad Henlein or Karl Hermann Frank who had also caused the break-up of the Czechoslovak Republic. Czech society would undoubtedly have found Tiso and the Slovak State much easier to accept had the Czechs not lost their own state at the same time.[15] Indeed, the events of 14 March 1939 are inseparable from those that took taking place on the next day, 15 March 1939, when Bohemia and Moravia were occupied as a German Protectorate and the Bohemian Lands were annexed to the Reich. Despite what many Slovaks erroneously believed, the Protectorate was not a Czech state, but merely an autonomous region of the Third Reich. The way Tiso was perceived amongst Czechs was therefore far more negative than how Emil Hácha, President of the Protectorate, had consented to the occupation of the Bohemian Lands in Berlin, on the night of 15 March 1939. As a matter of fact, Hácha himself had not contributed to collapse of the Second Republic, and saw the Protectorate as a temporary solution, which would again be superseded by something else with Czechoslovak or at least Czech independence when the favorable time came. On the other hand, Tiso continued flatly to reject the restoration of Czechoslovakia in any form, though he knew from Jozef Kirschbaum, a Slovak envoy in Switzerland, that the Allies did not

---

14 Smolec, J., Sokol, L., Vasiľková, Ľ. (eds), Proces s dr. J. Tisom: Spomienky obžalobcu Antona Rašlu a obhajcu Ernesta Žabkayho. Bratislava: Tatrapress, 1990, pp. 33-34. Rašla mentions that one of the attorneys, Ľudovít Rigan, was of the same opinion.
15 For details, see Rychlík, J. 'Vznik Slovenského štátu a česká společnosť' in Bystrický, V., Michela, M., Schvarc, M. (eds), Rozbitie alebo rozpad? Historické reflexie zániku Česko-Slovenska. Bratislava: Veda, 2010, pp. 392-405; idem, 'Situace v Protektorátu Čechy a Morava v roce 1939 a na počátku roku 1940 ve zprávách Generálního konzulátu Slovenské republiky v Praze', Český časopis historický vol. 109 (4), 2011, pp. 716-38.

envisage an independent Slovakia after the war.[16] Moreover, many Czechs had been confronted with the anti-Czech policy of the Tiso régime in 1938 and 1939, especially with the expulsion of Czechs from Slovakia. Because of the anti-Czech measures of the Slovak government, Czech society, with good reason, perceived the Tiso régime as anti-Czech[17] and Tiso as their enemy.

Most Czech political parties had similar attitudes towards Tiso. Both the Communists and the Social Democrats, on the left, and the National Socials, then the most right-wing Czech political party, demanded Tiso's death. Only the Czechoslovak People's Party was more moderate; being a clerical party, it did not consider it suitable to execute a Roman Catholic priest. The view of the Czech agrarians, whose party had not been permitted to reform after the war, leaving most to join either the Czechoslovak People's Party or the National Social Party, was similar. Ladislav Feierabend, a pre-war Agrarian Party politician, who had joined the post-war National Socials, wrote: 'Josef Tiso, President of the Slovak State, also received the death sentence, and rightly so, but I did not think the carrying out of the sentence was actually sensible in his case.'[18] The National Socials as a whole had no doubt about the punishment for Tiso, and the same is true of the Communists. Prokop Drtina, the National Social Minister of Justice, refused to recommend that Tiso's petition for clemency be granted. He first asked the government to return Tiso's petition to the Presidium of the Slovak National Council, which was supposed to provide an unequivocal opinion. When the Communists had scuttled his request, he refused to support the petition.[19]

---

16 Kirschbaum, J., M. My Last Diplomatic Report to the President of Slovakia. Furdek: Jednota, 1972, p. 85.
17 Rychlík, J. 'K otázke postavenia českého obyvateľstva na Slovensku v rokoch 1938–1945', Historický časopis vol. 37 (3), 1989, pp. 405–10.
18 Feierabend, L., K. Politické vzpomínky, vol. 3. Brno: Atlantis, 1996, p. 348.
19 In his memoirs, Drtina wrote: 'We, the four National Social Ministers, thus stood or voted against the clemency. I did not receive the proposal to grant clemency, which I had made quite clear to Lettrich and Nichols was a condition of my approval, so I did not feel bound by anything. On the other hand, the treason of the Czechoslovak state at the time it had been facing an increased threat by someone

In Slovakia, the perception of Tiso greatly depended on one's attitude to the Slovak State and its régime. The state as such might have been fairly acceptable for most Slovaks, but the same was not true of the régime. The 'Ľuďák' (HSĽS) regime was unacceptable both to the Communists and to democrats of various political orientations. The Communists considered the Ľuďák regime a fascist dictatorship promoting the interests of the Slovak bourgeoisie and saw Tiso as its leading figure. What the Communists therefore disliked most about the Slovak State was its bourgeois and fascist nature.[20] In the eyes of the various democrats, the Ľuďák regime represented the rejection of democratic principles, parliamentary government, and civil liberties. Both the Communists and the Democrats had a highly negative perception of the fact that Tiso had hitched his wagon to Nazi Germany and stayed on its side till the end. On the other hand, it is obvious that Tiso was a hero for Slovak Nationalists striving for an independent state; in their eyes, the declaration of Slovak independence was a morally justified, politically correct act. The fact that the Slovak nation had obtained its first independent state in history, albeit fully dependent

---

who had been a member of the Czechoslovak Parliament and even a minister of the government several times was unquestionable, and Tiso had been committing it continuously and repeatedly since Hitler's assumption of power [sic] and since the establishment of Henlein's and Karmazin's Nazi Party of Czechoslovak Germans. He had been supporting them politically, and maintained contacts with Henlein even before Munich. Later, he had betrayed even Hácha, by declaring the secession of Slovakia, even against the will of Hlinka's heir and successor Karol Sidor. He had maintained his Nazi [sic] dictatorship in Slovakia till the end of the war. He had declared war on the United States and sent Slovak soldiers together with the Wehrmacht against Soviet Russia. When the Slovak National Uprising broke out, his speeches had helped suppress it, as had his broadcast speeches and his arrival in the captured city of Banská Bystrica at the side of an SS General. Is there anyone who has committed greater crimes or greater treason against Czechoslovakia than this Catholic priest?! No. The death sentence was fitting, and so was its execution. It was not possible for us ministers of the Czech-minded National Social Party to go any farther than we had in the matter of Jozef Tiso. And it was not possible to expect more from us than we had done.' Drtina, P. Československo můj osud, 2 vols. Prague: Melantrich, 1991, 1992, vol. 2 pp. 303–304.

20 Sirácky, A. Klerofašistická ideológia ľudáctva. Bratislava: Slovak Academy of Sciences, 1955.

on Germany and with a highly questionable régime, was of such paramount importance to the Slovak Nationalists that they regarded any of its imperfections as completely irrelevant.[21]

Between 1946 and 1947, the attitude of the Communist Party of Slovakia (CPS) towards Tiso matched that of the Czech Communists. On the question of capital punishment for Tiso, they had the same opinion as the Social Democrats and National Socials. When talking about the attitude of the Slovak Communists, I am referring especially to the Party leadership, since the opinion of many rank-and-file members was demonstrably different.[22] The implacable attitude of the CPS was, however, based on political calculation more than anything else; in the spring of 1946, the Democratic Party (DP) leadership entered into an agreement with Roman Catholic politicians, concerning support in the coming general elections. The subsequent victory of the Democratic Party was largely thanks to Roman Catholic voters (most of whom had previously voted HSĽS). The Communists believed the deal, later to known as the 'April Agreement', had contained a secret promise by the Democratic Party to prevent the sentencing of Tiso or at least the carrying out of the sentence. The Communists were thus convinced that if Tiso were executed, the Catholic voters would abandon the Democratic Party. In fact, they did not care about Tiso at all. The existence of the secret agreement has never been proved and is in fact very doubtful.[23] Although one of the parties that had actively par-

---

21 Vnuk, F. 'Ľudová strana v slovenskej politike', Alamanach Slováka v Amerike, 1968, pp. 44–45.
22 Ursíny, J. Z môjho života. Martin: Ústav T. G. Masaryka and Matica slovenská, 2000, p. 122.
23 It is unreasonable to assume that the Democratic Party would have committed itself to prevent the sentencing of Tiso, for it simply could not have kept such a commitment. Ján Ursíny, one of the masterminds of the 'April Agreement' on behalf of the Democratic Party, does not mention such a commitment at all in his memoirs. Pavol Čarnogurský, who took part in the negotiations on behalf of the Roman Catholics, claims that the Democratic Party had indeed undertaken to strive for a lenient sentence or clemency, but admits that there is no written document to this effect. See Čarnogurský, P. Svedok čias. Bratislava: USPO Peter Smolík, 1997, pp. 198–99.

ticipated in the struggle for the restoration of Czechoslovakia, and certainly not harboring any sympathies toward Tiso, the Democratic Party indeed had a negative attitude to the carrying out of the death sentence; up until the last moment, its representatives kept trying to obtain a pardon for Tiso. Indeed, they were worried, and rightly so, that the execution would harm the relations between Czechs and Slovaks, as well as relations between Catholics and Protestants; they were also worried that only the Communists would ultimately benefit from it politically.[24]

True, the Slovak public (and not just Catholics) disagreed with Tiso's execution, but most took it in stride.[25] Tiso of course continued to be perceived positively by Catholic Slovaks. And what the Protestant Slovaks had been most worried about actually happened — namely, Tiso did indeed become a martyr for many Catholic Slovaks. Many Slovaks also believed that Tiso had been executed by the Czechs. President Edvard Beneš, who had never been too popular in Slovakia, was especially blamed for Tiso's death. In popular legend, it was

---

24 Jozef Lettrich, Chairman of the Democratic Party and one of the leaders of the Slovak National Council during the uprising, who himself had been persecuted by the Tiso régime, wrote: 'Even before the trial started, the Communists had repeatedly made it known that Tiso had to be executed. The Democrats were against the execution, both for state reasons and political (Czechoslovak) reasons, as well as for purely Slovak reasons. They were rightfully afraid of possible deterioration in relations between Czechs and Slovaks if a representative of Slovak radical nationalism was executed, as well as of confessional relations in Slovak society, if a Roman Catholic priest were executed. In addition, psychological reasons and a sense of justice also spoke against the execution. It would have been unwise to give radical political circles an opportunity to make a martyr out of a politically guilty person. Despite all his actions during the totalitarian Slovak State, Tiso did represent a moderate faction and it would have been unfair to disregard this.' Lettrich, J. Dejiny novodobého Slovenska. Bratislava: Archa, 1993, p. 191. The book was originally published in English by Praeger in New York, in 1955, and in London, a year later, in both cases as A History of Modern Slovakia.
25 For reactions to Tiso's execution, see Vnuk, F. Dokumenty o postavení katolíckej církvi na Slovensku v rokoch 1945–1948. Martin: Matica slovenská, 1998, Doc. VI/7, pp. 118–19, Doc. VI/8, p. 119, Doc. VI/15, p. 128, Doc. VI/16, pp. 128–29; Rychlík, J. Češi a Slováci ve 20. století: Česko-slovenské vztahy 1945–1992. Bratislava: Academic Electronic Press, 1998, pp. 95–96.

called an act of revenge on Beneš's part. Together with the Czech leaders' having alleged ordered the shooting down of the airplane in which Milan Rastislav Štefánik was returning home in 1919 and the legend that Beneš had swapped the Spiš and Orava regions for the Těšín and Ostrava coal mines in 1920, Tiso's execution thus became a permanent part of Slovak anti-Czech stereotypes and legends, regardless of the fact that Tiso had been tried by a Slovak court and under Slovak laws on retribution, which had been enacted by the Slovak National Council. Needless to say, the Slovak laws — much more draconic than the Czech retribution decrees — simply did not provide for any other sentence for Tiso but thirty years in prison or capital punishment.[26] In the Catholic community, the portrait of Tiso as a good-natured priest who had saved the Slovak nation from the Hungarian and German occupation and ensured Slovak well-being during the Second World War has been passed down from generation to generation and, though a bit faded, has partly survived to the present day. The passing on of such 'true information' has assumed a form well known to folklorists.[27] The popular tradition sees Tiso as someone with only positive qualities; contrary to historical fact, he has been given credit where credit was not due (for example, for allegedly having saved Slovak Jews), while negative attributes are ascribed only to his opponents. In other words: a popular hero always appears as the people (the masses) want him to appear, and he does the deeds the people want him to do, so that he fits their notion of a good ruler.[28]

---

26 Concerning the petition for clemency, the Slovak Roman Catholic community failed to consider the fact that it was the Presidium of the Slovak National Council that should have been 'given credit' for the rejection of the plea. Its members refused to make any statement concerning the plea and passed it on, without any comment, to the government in Prague. President Beneš undoubtedly made a political mistake by not granting the clemency but one must bear in mind that the right to grant clemency is a privilege of the head of the state, rather than a privilege of the convicted person to claim.
27 Rychlíková, M., Rychlík, J. 'Problémy výzkumu transmise lidové kultury', Národopisný věstník československý, vol. 2 (1985), no. 44, pp. 85–93.
28 Rychlík, J. 'National Consciousness and Social Justice in Historical Folklore', in Hoerder, D., Rößler, H. (eds), The Roots of the Transplanted, vol. 2. Boulder: East European Monographs, 1994, pp. 43–53.

Interestingly enough, most Slovaks, including Slovak Roman Catholics, also welcomed the Slovak National Uprising, completely forgetting that Tiso had openly come out against it. On the other hand, Slovak Protestants always distanced themselves from Tiso and had a reserved attitude to his régime, in which they had been treated as second-class citizens. But even they considered the death sentence wrong and a political mistake.

Naturally, the Tiso cult could not develop in Slovakia under the Communist régime and officially approved historians saw Tiso in a purely negative light. Even the year 1968, when the mass media raised various historical questions as part of the Slovak efforts for a Czecho-Slovak federation, brought no major change in the assessment of Tiso. He simply did not fit the bill, since the struggle for the federation was based on the legacy of the Slovak National Uprising, which he had openly come out against. Perhaps the only exception was an article by Ladislav Hoffmann, 'Katolícka cirkev a tragédia slovenských Židov' (The Catholic Church and the Tragedy of the Slovak Jews), published in *Kultúrny život*, a liberal weekly.[29] The onset of the process to re-establish hardline Communism (called 'normalization'), beginning within a year of the Soviet-led military intervention, of course put a stop to all attempts to rehabilitate Tiso.

Amongst Slovak exiles, especially in the United States and Canada, the Tiso cult began developing shortly after the end of the Second World War. Its primary propagators were local compatriot organizations, such as the Slovak League of America (SLA) and the Canadian Slovak League (CSL), particularly in their publications. There was also a personal connection of sorts; quite a few public figures of the Ľuďák régime had emigrated to the United States or Canada, and some of

---

29 Hoffmann, L. 'Katolícka cirkev a tragédia slovenských Židov', Kultúrny život, 7 June 1968, p. 6. Ladislav Hoffmann and his brother, Gabriel, were Jews but had converted to Roman Catholicism long before the Slovak State was established. Tiso granted them an exemption from the anti-Jewish legislation. Out of gratitude, they defended Tiso and his anti-Jewish policy. See Hoffmann, G., Hoffmann, L. Katolícka cirkev a tragédia slovenských židov v dokumentoch. Partizánske: G-print, 1994.

them became important representatives of the compatriot associations and communities. For example, Jozef Paučo, former Editor-in-Chief of *Slovák* (the leading daily of the HSĽS), became the Editor-in-Chief of *Slovák v Amerike*, a Slovak-language daily in the United States. And Slovak compatriot institutions were places for the activities of people such as Konstantin Čulen, a journalist turned historian, and the historian František Hrušovský. In the United States as early as in 1947, Čulen published a panegyrical biography of Tiso, whose title translates as 'Our Second Head of State after Svätopluk', which he dedicated to 'the undying memory of the victims of the "National Court" and the "People's Courts", which were established all over Slovakia because of the malice of the religious intolerance of our [Protestant] brethren and at the will of the greatest enemies of the Slovak nation, Beneš and the Czechs.'[30] Paučo was also the first to publish Tiso's final statement before the National Court.[31] In 1953, he published a book entitled *Tisov odkaz* (Tiso's legacy), in which he presents Tiso as a martyr revered by the entire Slovak nation.[32] A long chapter in his memoirs, published in 1967, is also dedicated to Tiso.[33] In 1972, to mark the twenty-fifth anniversary of Tiso's execution, the *Slovakia* miscellany, of which Paučo was Editor-in-Chief at that time, published several panegyrical articles about Tiso; the most prominent among them was by Jozef Mi-

---

30 Čulen, K. Po Svatoplukovi druhá naša hlava: Život Dr. Jozefa Tisu. Middletown, PA.: Prvá katolícka slovenská jednota, 1947, p. 1.
31 Paučo, J. (ed.), Dr. Jozef Tiso o sebe. Passaic, NJ: Slovenský katolícky Sokol, 1952, pp. 353–55. This version of the final statement was based on a transcript made by one of the observers in the courtroom, and is thus neither complete nor accurate. A complete version of Tiso's final statement based on the stenographic record was published only in 2010. See Fabricius, M., Hradská, K. (eds), Jozef Tiso, vol. 3, pp. 101–217.
32 'Dr. Jozef Tiso had entered a hiding place in the heart of the entire Slovak nation long before his execution, long before he became the head of the independent state of the Slovaks, long before anyone would have thought there would be villains who would murder our righteous and noble ruler [sic].' Paučo, J. Tisov odkaz. Middletown, PA: [Jednota], 1953, p. 71.
33 Paučo, J. Tak sme sa poznali: Predstavitelia Slovenskej republiky v spomienkach. Middletown, PA.: Jednota Press, 1967, pp. 221–78.

loslav Kirschbaum, ex-Secretary General of the HSĽS and later the Slovak chargé d'affaires in Bern.[34] The Tiso cult was also spreading among Slovak exiles in Argentina, the country chosen by Slovak émigrés who had failed to obtain US or Canadian entry visas. For example, Štefan Polakovič, one of the principal ideologist and thinkers of the Ľuďák régime, who had published a collection of Tiso's articles and speeches in Slovakia during the war, was active in Argentina until his death.[35] During the Cold War, the Ľuďák émigrés were of course emphasizing the anti-Communist character of their régime, and even using it to justify the participation of the Slovak army in the campaign against the USSR during the Second World War.[36] Last but not least, Tiso was popularized in the 1960s and 1970s mainly by František Vnuk and Milan Stanislav Ďurica, exile historians of the younger generation. In 1957, for example, Ďurica took up the highly sensitive question of Tiso's responsibility for the deportations of the Jews in 1942. Regardless of the historical facts, he describes Tiso almost as the saviour of the Slovak Jews, who had allegedly been making presidential exemptions on a mass scale.[37] The declaration of war on the United

---

34 Kirschbaum, J. M. 'Dr. Joseph Tiso: The Prelate-Politician who Died on the Gallows for His People', Slovakia vol. 22 (1972), no. 45, pp. 5-20.
35 Polakovič, Š. Z Tisovho boja. Bratislava: Vydavateľstvo HSĽS, 1941.
36 Paučo, J. Slováci a komunizmus. Middletown, PA: Jednota Press, 1957, pp. 107-11.
37 Ďurica, M. S. 'Dr. Joseph Tiso and the Jewish Problem in Slovakia', Slovakia, 3-4 (1957), pp. 1-22 (2nd edn, Padua: Stamperia Dell' Universita, 1964); published in Slovak as 'Dr. Jozef Tiso a problém Židov na Slovensku', Jednota nos. 34-36 (1957). Ďurica also published his thesis on Tiso as the saviour of the Slovak Jews in other languages – see, for example La República Eslovaca y la tragedia de los judios europeos. Buenos Aires: Dorrego, 1975. The argument to the effect that Tiso saved several thousand Slovak Jews by his presidential exemptions is a standard argument used by Tiso apologists; as a rule, these arguments have been adopted, lock, stock, and barrel, from Ďurica's work. What Ďurica says, however, is untrue. The President of the Slovak Republic did indeed, under Article 255 of the 'Jewish Code' (anti-Jewish regulations), have a right to grant an exemption from all or some of the provisions of the Jewish Code. A holder of a so-called 'full exemption' was not de iure considered a Jew, which meant that he and his family were exempted from deportation. Available documentation in the Slovak National Archive indicates that President Tiso granted about 900 exemptions, most of them to Jews who had been christened for some time and to Jews living with a non-Jewish spouse. But

States and the United Kingdom on 13 December 1945, a very unpleasant fact for the Ľudák exiles, was downplayed by Ľudák publicists by pointing out that the declaration of war had not been the decision of the Slovak parliament and that there had not been any actual fighting. They also often argued that the United States and the United Kingdom had never paid attention to the declaration of war.[38] And they explained that Tiso had come out against the Slovak National Uprising because of its Communist character. As a matter of fact, some Slovak exiles — contrary to most Slovaks at home — believed that the Slovak National Uprising had been an 'incredible, unimaginable conspiracy' against the Slovak Republic.[39] By contrast, for Slovaks who emigrated after 1968 Tiso was no authority and they did not identify with his legacy. These people realized that if an independent Slovak state was ever to be restored; it would have to be on completely new foundations.

Attempts by the Ľudák exiles to rehabilitate Tiso in American political circles were not warmly received abroad. During the Cold War, the United States was supporting the Council of Free Czechoslovakia, which consisted both of Czech and of Slovak Czechoslovak-oriented politicians in exile. Although they too were all dyed-in-the-wool anti-Communists, these politicians refused to cooperate at all with the Ľudák exiles associated with the Slovak National Council Abroad and the Slovak Liberation Committee. Tiso was a *persona non grata* for the Council of Free Czechoslovakia and remained one; in this respect, the exile politicians differed little from their Communist counterparts in Prague. Unlike their predecessors, who had left the country because of the Communist takeover in February 1948, the Czech émigrées who

---

the deportations did not apply to christened Jews and mixed-marriage Jews anyway. As a matter of fact, so-called 'ministerial exemptions', granted by cabinet ministers, were much more important and helped to save a substantial number of Slovak Jews.

38   The problem consisted in the fact that the United States and the United Kingdom did not officially recognize the Slovak Republic in 1941, which was why they were legally unable to react to the declaration of war in any way.

39   Vnuk, F. Neuveriteľné sprisahanie. Middletown, PA: Jednota, 1964.

had left the country after the Soviet-led intervention of August 1968 and witnessed the birth of the Czechoslovak federation were much more favorably disposed to the idea of an independent Slovakia, but still refused any possibility of Tiso's rehabilitation.[40]

Tiso and the Ľuďák régime remained unacceptable to Czech dissidents in the 1970s and 1980s. The situation in Slovakia was rather different, since the prime movers of the opposition in Slovakia were Roman Catholic dissidents. Slovak Catholics found it difficult to come to terms with the fact that a Catholic priest, the head of the first-ever Slovak national state, could have committed such ignoble acts. In purely human and psychological terms, their attitude is understandable. But, since many Catholic activists, such as František Mikloško and Ján Čarnogurský, realized that championing Tiso would have discredited the opposition, they preferred a prudent, wait-and-see approach. The attitude of Čarnogurský, a leading representative of the Catholic opposition, is a case in point. He studied law at Charles University, Prague, and later, in Bratislava, where he successfully defended his doctoral dissertation on the Slovak anti-Jewish laws. In October 1988, he signed a declaration by opposition intellectuals expressing sorrow over the deportations of the Jews of Slovakia in 1942.[41] Yet when asked his opinion of Tiso by the Czech samizdat magazine *Alternativa*, he replied: 'I am not an historian and my knowledge of the history of the Slovak State is not that good. I studied a part of its legislation once, but that was some time ago. Nor do I have a clear-cut opinion about Tiso. I only know recollections of Tiso, and opinions about him, which I come across in Slovakia. And these are rather positive.'[42] But for the general Slovak opposition, Tiso was as taboo as he was for the Czechs. In the light of the overall political situation and the efforts to create a united opposition, Tiso was not an example to

---

40   Ibid., pp. 121–22.
41   Čarnogurský, J. Videné od Dunaja. Bratislava: Kalligram, 1997, Doc. 3, pp. 122–24.
42   Ibid., p. 112.

follow even for the Catholic dissidents. After all, his vision of a conservative Slovakia was no longer attractive for Slovaks in the 1970s and 1980s.

Despite their negative attitude towards Tiso and the wartime Slovak State, most members of the Czech opposition felt that even Tiso's advocates in Slovakia should have a right to voice their opinions, and should not be persecuted by the state authorities for that. This attitude was clearly manifested in the case of Ivan Polanský, a Slovak printer, who published a samizdat magazine called *Historický zborník* (Historical Journal) in Slovakia. The first issue, which came out in 1986, was concerned with Tiso. Polanský's arguments in favor of Tiso's rehabilitation were not his own. They were completely adopted from Ľuďák exile literature. Polanský showed *Historický zborník* to the secretly consecrated bishop Ján Chryzostom Korec, who probably agreed with its content, but realized that it was politically unsuitable. Korec therefore recommended Polanský to suspend his activities. Although Polanský promised to do so, he still prepared another issue, this time dedicated to Hlinka. The police confiscated all the copies and Polanský was arrested on 5 November 1987, and charged with promoting Fascism. Naturally, his articles defending and glorifying Tiso could hardly be expected to meet with a positive reaction in the Bohemian Lands. Nevertheless, the Czech opposition stood behind Polanský and signatories of the Charter 77 human rights document recognized his right to free expression. In November 1987, the Committee for the Defense of Unjustly Prosecuted (VONS) stated that Polanský's arrest was an attack against civil and religious activities. On 12 October 1988, a Committee of Solidarity with Ivan Polanský (Výbor solidarity s Ivanem Polanským), which included several dozen Czech journalists and samizdat publishers, was founded. It also included a four-strong 'information service', consisting of one Slovak (Ján Čarnogurský) and three Czechs (Václav Benda, Jiří Gruntorád, and Heřman Chromý). The Archbishop of Prague, Cardinal František Tomášek, also came out in support of Polanský; in his letter to Polanský's wife Ida, he expressed his appreciation of Polanský's contribution to the publication of Roman Catholic literature. The Democratic Initiative, a group of Czech right-wing liberals who naturally felt no personal or political sympathy for Tiso, also rushed to Polanský's defense, sending a protest against his arrest to the Federal Prime Minister, Lubomír Štrougal, on 9 September 1988. The overt support was partly successful; Polanský was eventually sentenced only for subversion, not for promoting Fascism, and was released on parole in the autumn of 1988 as part of an amnesty declared by President Gustáv Husák to mark the seventieth anniversary of the founding of Czechoslovakia.[43] Later, Čarnogurský expressed his great appreciation for the support of the Czech opposition:

> The State Security Forces were really after Ivan Polanský in 1987. They arrested him and accused him of supporting and promoting Fascism. Rallying international support for Polanský would have been extremely difficult because of the nature of the charges. After all, who would come out in support of a Fascist? At that time, Polanský was greatly helped by the Charter 77 initiative, which confirmed to people abroad that Polanský was not a Fascist, but simply an opponent of Communism.[44]

The fall of the Communist regimes in Europe prompted a reassessment of the roles of politicians and other individuals whom Communist historians had criticized or even condemned in one way or another. But the process often led only to a mechanical about-face rather than to a search for a balanced, objective view of them. The new opinion was therefore as distorted as the old one. Thus, for example, Poland witnessed the uncritical defense of Jozef Piłsudski and his Sanation régime, Hungary rehabilitated Miklós Horthy, there were attempts to rehabilitate Ion Antonescu in Romania, and Boris III was rehabilitated in Bulgaria. In the multi-national states of Eastern Europe, various nationalist politicians and movements were partly reha-

---

43   Rychlík, J. Rozpad Československa: Česko-slovenské vztahy 1989-1992. Bratislava: Academic Electronic Press, 2002, p. 47.
44   Čarnogurský, P. Videné od Dunaja, p. 319.

bilitated regardless of their questionable character. In Croatia, for example, there were attempts to rehabilitate the Ustaša movement and its leader, Ante Pavelić. This process also took place in Czechoslovakia. Amongst the Czechs, indiscriminate idealizations of the first Czechoslovak Republic and the defense of President Hácha appeared, although the latter was of a marginal importance. In Slovakia, some political circles started uncritically extolling the wartime Slovak State and inevitably Tiso as well. Arguing that 'people have to be told the truth', although the truth did not actually matter at all, some Ľuďák exiles returned to Slovakia and began openly to foster the Tiso cult there. Some of their works previously published in exile were now republished in Slovakia. Since 1990, many movements were born which more or less openly demanded full independence for Slovakia. Of them, the Slovak National Party (SNS) is the most prominent, but there were also strong secessionist tendencies in Čarnogurský's Christian Democratic Movement and later also in Vladimír Mečiar's Movement for a Democratic Slovakia (HZDS). Although these political forces did not espouse Tiso and the wartime Slovak State, emphasizing instead that a future independent Slovakia would have to be democratic, there certainly were the supporters of the former Slovak State and admirers of Tiso among their members. Yet, at that time, Tiso became a subject of political clashes, both between Slovaks and Czechs and among Slovaks themselves.

On 8 July 1990, a plaque commemorating Tiso was ceremonially unveiled on the wall of a former teachers' training college in Bánovce nad Bebravou.[45] The plaque was officially blessed by Bishop Ján Chryszostom Korec. The official explanation for the choice of location of the plaque was that Tiso, as the former parish priest[46] in Bánovce between the wars, had been responsible for establishing of the college.

---

45 Jablonický, J. Glosy o historiografii SNP. Bratislava: NVP International, 1994, p. 143.
46 Tiso travelled to Bánovce nad Bebravou to say Mass every Sunday, regardless of his being a member of parliament or being a minister, and he continued to do so even as Prime Minister and later President of the Slovak State.

It was clear from the very start, however, that this was an attempt to make Tiso's trial in 1947 a 'cause of all Slovaks' and to achieve at least his political rehabilitation, if not his exoneration under the law.[47] No one could have reasonably doubted that the plaque to Tiso was just a step towards this objective.

The affair immediately sparked big debates. The opinion begun to be expressed in the Czech mass media, that Czechs could not live in a state, in one half of which, someone who had participated in dismantling the first Czechoslovak Republic was now recognized as an official hero, adding that if Tiso were to become a symbol of the Slovak struggle for self-determination, Czechs would be better off dissociating themselves from Slovakia as fast as possible. Tiso was causing a deep rift in Slovak society again. As early as in 1990, a book was published about Tiso's trial, written by Anton Rašla, the military prosecutor in the trial, and Ernest Žabkay, the counsel for the defense.[48] In the book and in his subsequent public appearances, Rašla, who had been imprisoned during the 1950s, expressed his view that the charges had been correct and justified and he rejected any efforts to cast doubt on the trial.[49] Naturally, the dispute also had a domestic-policy dimension in Slovakia. Tiso was as unacceptable to liberals in the Public against Violence (VPN) party, left-wingers, and Hungarian parties in Slovakia as he was for Czechs. The Presidium of the Slovak National Council condemned the unveiling of the plaque.[50] The governing Christian Democratic Movement (KDH) found itself in a predicament.

---

47 Tiso's 'legal rehabilitation' (exoneration) was difficult to consider for two reasons: first, there was no appeal available against verdicts of the National Court; second, even it had been available, Tiso would have had to be re-tried for the same acts as in 1946–47, which means he would probably have been found guilty again. The term 'rehabilitation' means that the court concludes that the defendant did not actually commit the acts of which he was accused, or that the law had been applied incorrectly. None of the above options was true of the 1946–47 trial. The 'Neo-ľudáks' calling for Tiso's rehabilitation in fact demanded the invalidity of the trial and its verdict, or declaring both the trial and the verdict null and void.
48 Smolec, J., Sokol, L., Vasiľková, Ľ. (eds), Proces s dr. J. Tisom.
49 Rašla reconfirms his opinion again in his memoirs. See Rašla, A. Zastupoval som československý štát: Vyznanie. Prešov: Privatpress, 1999.
50 Slovenský denník, 18 July 1990, pp. 1–2.

In its statement of 14 July 1990, it ultimately approved the unveiling of the plaque, while voicing reservations about Tiso at the same time.[51] Only three days later, however, the Protestant wing of the Christian Democratic Movement condemned the unveiling and declared any such events leading to Tiso's rehabilitation unacceptable to the Slovak Protestants.[52] Tibor Böhm, the federal Attorney General with close ties to the KDH, was given the task of examining whether the unveiling of the plaque did not constitute the criminal act of promoting Fascism. His analysis was ultimately in Tiso's favor, resulting in another wave of disagreement and Böhm's ultimately deciding to resign. On 24 July, President Václav Havel removed Böhm at his own request and appointed Ivan Gašparovič in his place.[53] Jozef Šrámek, formerly Deputy Director of the Czechoslovak section of Radio Free Europe and Vice-President of the Slovak World Congress, came out in Tiso's defense in the *Slovenský denník* (The Slovak Daily).[54] By giving Šrámek an opportunity to voice his opinions in its newspaper, the Christian Democratic Movement implied that it identified with these views.

The Tiso plaque was ultimately removed from the wall of the former college and placed in a repository.[55] For a while, public interest ebbed. On 13 October 1990, a small-scale event commemorating the 103rd anniversary of Tiso's birth was held in Bánovce nad Bebravou, where speakers demanded that the plaque be reinstalled, but it went

---

51   Ibid., 16 July 1990, p. 1.
52   Ibid., 27 July1990, p. 4.
53   Ibid., 25 July 1990, p. 1.
54   Ibid., p. 5.
55   An organization little known to the public and calling itself 'Slovakia' protested against the removal of the plaque. Its president sent Prime Ministr Vladimír Mečiar an open letter demanding Tiso's rehabilitation. The opening sentences of the letter are characteristic: 'Dear Prime Minister Mečiar, on 8 July 1990, a plaque commemorating Dr Jozef Tiso was unveiled on the building of the former teachers' training college in Bánovce nad Bebravou. Czechs, Jews, anti-Fascists and similar anti-Slovak elements unleashed a furious campaign against the plaque and its unveiling in Slovakia ....' The letter was signed by Milan Kres, President of the Committee of Slovakia, and Jozef Bernhauser, editor of the Zvesti magazine. The letter was published in Slovenské ozveny 1 (1990), pp. 1 and 7.

largely unnoticed.⁵⁶ In the minds of the public, the plaque question was soon replaced by the old question of Tiso's responsibility for the deportations of Jews and the nature of the Slovak state. In Slovakia the historians Ďurica and Vnuk, returning from exile, started giving voice to the old, long-disproved arguments that Tiso not only was in no way responsible for the deportations, but had even saved tens of thousands of Jews by his presidential exemptions. Former Ľuďáks who had never fled the country had made similar statements shortly after the Changes beginning in mid-November 1989. Together with the exile historians, they succeeded in winning several followers amongst young Catholic intellectuals (including Róbert Letz, Peter Mulík, and Anna Magdolénová) and extreme nationalist historians, some of whom had been Communists before the Changes (including Ján Bobák). It must be added, however, that their views met with little support amongst historians and other intellectuals. Even some intellectuals sympathizing with the Slovak National Party (SNS) had reservations about them; thus, for example, in a discussion with Čarnogurský, the historian Anton Hrnko publicly rejected attempts to justify Tiso's policy towards the Jews.⁵⁷ The exiles stepped in once again and began circulating leaflets explaining their 'truth' about Tiso all over Slovakia.⁵⁸ At the same time, the exile historians and journalists were calling for a 'Slovak view of history'; in their opinion, anyone criticizing Tiso or the Slovak State was speaking against Slovak interests.⁵⁹

---

56   Čas, 15 October 1990, p. 2.
57   In his memoirs, Hrnko later recalled: 'I asked him not to defend the undefendable. Though the so-called solution of the Jewish question in Slovakia could be explained, it could not be defended, because a crime remains a crime, even though it might not have been initially intended.' Hrnko, A. 'Nežný prevrat, alebo revolúcia?', Slovenské pohľady 11, 1999, p. 66.
58   Echo 12 (1991), p. 3 — a copy of the 'Poučenie' leaflet.
59   Rychlík, J. 'František Vnuk a tzv. slovenský pohľad na dejiny', Kultúrny život 25 (36), 1991, p. 4.

In the autumn of 1991, a new Tiso plaque was unveiled on the house in which he was born in Bytča. The international press took notice of the event as well. The whole affair was unpleasant for the KDU-led government; but the chairman of the Slovak National Council, František Mikloško, made no direct comment on this at a press conference in Bratislava on 16 October 1991; he only 'recommended' that Czech historians focus on the Jewish deportations from the Protectorate rather than on the deportations of Jews from Slovakia.[60] Čarnogurský's attitude towards the affair was also fuzzy; he said that the man responsible for the anti-Jewish laws was Vojtech Tuka, whom no one was mentioning, whereas Tiso's alleged responsibility was being brought up all the time. As for President Havel, the affair was obviously unpleasant for him and he publicly condemned the plaque.[61] But, compared to the unveiling of the plaque in Bánovce, the event in Bytča aroused much less attention and fewer emotions.

The question of Tiso's attitude toward Jews had a special sequel in the spring of 1992. During his visit to the United States, on 28 March 1992, Bishop Ján Chryzostom Korec, who had been appointed Cardinal in the meantime, repeated the old story about Jewish rabbis' having visited Tiso in 1942 and requesting him to retain his post. The well-known (but completely false[62]) legend was also repeated by Mikloško in an interview for the *Rudé právo* daily. Two events took place while an international conference on the deportations of Jews from Slovakia was held in Banská Bystrica on 25–27 March 1992. It was attended by

---

60 Český deník, 18 October 1991, p. 3.
61 International Herald Tribune, 4 December 1991, p. 5.
62 As correctly pointed out by Yeshayahu Jelinek, it would have been unthinkable for orthodox rabbis to visit Tiso without telling Slovakia's Chief Rabbi Armin Frieder, and he does not mention any plea to Tiso to remain the President in his diaries. No rabbis visited Tiso. On the other hand, Frieder handed over a letter of rabbis asking Tiso to keep Jews in Slovakia for the sake of humanity on 8 March 1942. Tiso did not respond, just like in the case of a previous letter/memorandum of Jewish congregations with a similar content dated 5 March 1942. See Hubenák, L. (ed.), Riešenie židovskej otázky na Slovensku 1939–1945. Dokumenty II. Bratislava: Slovenské národné múzeum, Historické múzeum, Oddelenie židovskej kultúry, 1994, Doc. 156, pp. 31–33; Frieder, E. Z denníku mladého rabína. Bratislava: SNM, Oddelenie židovskej kultúry, 1993, pp. 50–51.

Yeshayahu A. Jelinek, a Slovak-born Israeli historian, who openly rejected such statements as fabrications, and proposed to establish an international commission of historians to examine the question.[63] But the commission was never established, particularly because the Tiso apologists had no interest in it.[64]

Tiso the man was something of a ball and chain for the Christian Democratic Movement (KDU). Its leading representatives tried to take a neutral stance; on the one hand, they realized that Tiso was indefensible; on the other hand, they could not afford to reject him publicly.[65] The Christian Democratic Movement was at the same time under pressure from the exiles, who were demanding the 'truth' about Tiso — in other words, calling for his political rehabilitation. The KDU-led government decided to pass the hot potato to the historians. Between 5 and 7 May 1992, a major international conference, 'An Attempt at a Political and Personal Profile of Jozef Tiso', was held at the Training and Conference Centre of the Slovak National Council in Častá-Papierničky. It was attended by local and exile historians and journalists, including Jozef M. Kirschbaum, ex-Secretary General of the HSĽS, as well as Czech and foreign historians. Though many different opinions were voiced there, the conference must have been a disappointment to the Ľuďák exiles, for it did not result in Tiso's rehabilitation. Most of the local Slovak historians rejected the Ľuďák interpretation.[66]

The discussion about Tiso continued of course, even after the demise of Czechoslovakia. In the summer of 1993, the Bishop of Košice, Alojz Tkáč, said that the Czechs should apologize for putting Tiso to

---

63   Rudé právo, 31 March 1992, p. 2; for materials from the conference, see Tóth, D. (ed.), Tragédia slovenských Židov. Banská Bystrica: Múzeum SNP, 1992.
64   Vnuk in particular reacted negatively, rejecting Jelinek's proposal as one that cast doubt on Korec's veracity, albeit without producing any proof thereof.
65   Pavol Čarnogurský gave an interview for the Rudé právo daily on 25 January 1992, in which he defended Tiso and the Slovak 'Ľuďák' régime. Reactions to the interview were largely negative. See Rudé právo, 1 February 1992, p. 16.
66   For the conference papers, see Bystrický, V., Fano, Š. (eds), 'Pokus o politický a osobný profil Jozefa Tisu'.

death. His words prompted various reactions, especially in Slovakia, but went unnoticed in the Czech Republic. The Czech Ambassador to Slovakia, Filip Šedivý, refused to comment, claiming that the bishop had expressed a personal opinion, and the Czech government had no wish to react to it. The longer the Czech Republic exists, the deeper Tiso falls into oblivion amongst the Czechs.

From the perspective of the second decade of the twenty-first century, Tiso is definitely not a figure who would divide Czechs and Slovaks. Young Czechs hardly know his name, and older ones simply do not care. Tiso is definitely not a hero for any Czech, but nor is he still an enemy or a traitor in the eyes of most Czechs. By contrast, Tiso has always divided, and still divides, Slovak society; a very small proportion of Slovaks sees him as a hero and a martyr,[67] who laid down his life for Slovak independence; others perceive him as an unsuccessful politician who brought Slovakia under the yoke of Nazi Germany, including all the consequences of that. Today's Slovak political élite do not promote the legacy of Tiso and his régime. A modern democratic country, the Slovak Republic of today perceives itself as a successor not to Tiso's wartime Slovak State, but to democratic Czechoslovakia, just as the Czech Republic looks back positively to that period. If there is anyone or anything that Tiso still divides today, it is Slovak society, nothing and no one else.

---

67 Some Tiso apologists even pushed to have him canonized, but this was publicly rejected by the Slovak Jewish community and many Slovak intellectuals.

Jozef Tiso, Patriot or Traitor? A Slovak Debate That Has Been Carried on from the Second World War to the Present Day

Milan Zemko
Slovak Academy of Sciences

Abstract: This paper focuses on Jozef Tiso, the controversial priest-president of the wartime Slovak Republic. It scrutinizes the heated debate on Tiso's role in Slovak history that tends to oscillate between two irreconcilable poles. For some, Tiso was a patriot who managed to save and protect the nation amidst the Second World War, while for others he had been a traitor participating in the dissolution of Czechoslovakia and mass murder of Slovak Jewry. Finally, the paper examines also current surveys of public attitudes on Tiso and Slovak states to see how Tiso is being perceived today, after 70 years of controversy.

Opinions about controversial historical figures tend to get polarized when discussed by neighbouring nations and countries.[1] Yet when it comes to the president of the war-time Slovak Republic, Jozef Tiso (1887–1947), a profound and irreconcilable debate has been taking place within Slovak society. Originally a Roman Catholic priest, teacher, and author of religious and educational works, Tiso[2] took an active part in political life from late 1918 to spring 1945, that is, practically throughout the period of inter-war Czechoslovakia and under the first Slovak Republic (or Slovak State, 1939–45). Tiso's political activity went through several stages. In the 1920s and the first half of the 1930s, he was among the more conciliatory politicians in Hlinka's Slovak People's Party, ready to work with the government parties. In 1926, Tiso played an important role in political deliberations on the

---

1   This article was written as part of the 'History of Slovakia in the History of Europe' research project of the Centre of Excellence at the Slovak Academy of Sciences.
2   See Kamenec, I. *Tragédia politika, kňaza a človeka: Dr. Jozef Tiso 1887–1947*. Bratislava: Archa, 1998, pp. 17–31.

creation of the coalition of centre and right wing parties and from 1927 to 1929 he served in the government as Minister of Health and Physical Education. In 1935, he did his best to ensure that the People's Party deputies and senators would vote for Edvard Beneš as the Czechoslovak president.[3] As a conservative Roman Catholic, Tiso was critical of Nazism and Fascism.[4] In the second half of the 1930s, however, he sided with other People's Party members in moving away from democratic principles towards the authoritarian political ideas that were then gaining ground in most countries of Europe.[5] He saw Slovak political autonomy as possible within the framework of the Czechoslovak State,[6] but from May 1938 onwards, as the international position of Czechoslovakia was quickly deteriorating, he explored the possibilities of Slovak autonomy within Hungary (which Slovakia had been joined with for centuries before independence in late October 1918) in the event that the Czechoslovak Republic should cease to exist.[7]

For decades, the greatest debate has been about Tiso's political activity in autonomous Slovakia within the so-called second Czecho-

---

3   Ďurica, M. S. *Jozef Tiso 1887–1947: Životopisný profil*. Bratislava: Lúč, 2006, p. 199, and Kamenec, *Tragédia politika, kňaza a* človeka, pp. 53–54.
4   At the 1934 congress of the Slovak People's Party, Tiso said: 'From the Roman Catholic point of view, the State is an instrument of human life. Catholicism therefore keeps the State from upheaval, but there can be no word about Hitler's totalitarianism, and cannot allow the State to decide all matters and interfere in everything. Hitlerism and Mussolini's Fascism must realize that God is a higher power than man and that the Church is more than the State.' Tiso, J. *Prejavy a články*, vol. I, (1913–38), ed. by Miroslav Fabricius and Ladislav Suško, Bratislava: Historický ústav SAV and AEP, 2002, p. 438.
5   At the September 1936 congress of the People's Party, after the outbreak of civil war in Spain, Tiso expressed the right of the People's Party to be the only representative of the Slovak nation in the spirit of the slogan 'one nation, one party, one leader'. Tiso, *Prejavy a články*, p. 508.
6   For example, in the parliamentary debate about the bill on State defense, on 29 April 1936, he argued that autonomous programme of the Slovak People's Party 'is the most respectable basis of the stability of the State and the Republic'. And, in February 1938, he declared in parliament: 'Yes, the Slovak nation as an ethnically autonomous, politically sovereign, nation wants to live in its own state, the Czechoslovak Republic [...]'. Ibid., pp. 490 and 541.
7   See Deák, L. *Slovensko v politike Maďarska v rokoch 1938–1939*. Bratislava: Veda, 1990, p. 51.

Slovak Republic, that is, from the signing of the Munich Agreement, or the acceptance of Slovak political autonomy by the central government in Prague on 6 October 1938, to the Czecho-Slovak crisis in March 1939 and, consequently, throughout the period of the Slovak State (or the Slovak Republic), from its emergence on 14 March 1939 to the beginning of April 1945, when President Tiso fled Slovak territory together with the Slovak government and other state officials.

First, I will consider the critical opinions about Tiso's political activity from autumn 1938 to the dissolution of the Slovak Republic in April 1945. Such opinions were formed and published as early as during the Slovak State, where Tiso was its supreme representative, in the underground press, in radio broadcasts from London and Moscow, and, from September to October 1944 during the Slovak National Uprising and in the underground press.[8]

After the war, ex-President Tiso was of course already facing press criticism in the restored Czechoslovakia, but it was sporadic criticism of him, while the political régime of the dissolved state he had headed and its transformation to a vassal state of the Third Reich, were in general criticized much more. Still, in these sporadic newspaper articles the terminology there already appears which ended up in the formal accusations against him.[9]

---

[8] The criticism was, however, aimed at the political régime, the State, and, less often, directly at Tiso, who maintained his authority and had the sympathy of a considerable part of the Slovak public. Criticism of Tiso was expressed in broadcasts from London, especially from 1942 onwards, for example., by Vladimír Clementis, a Communist deputy of the Czechoslovak National Assembly in the 1930s, who together with other politicians characterized him, for example, as a Judas, Hitler's servant, a traitor, a corrupter, and an accessory to crimes,. See Clementis, V. *Odkazy z Londýna*. Bratislava: Obroda, 1947, pp. 36, 41, 42, 54, 59, and 159. During the Slovak National Uprising, although the daily of the Democratic Party, *Čas*, as well as that of the Communist daily, *Pravda*, and *Nové slovo*, a weekly, paid only marginal attention to Tiso, it was usually by describing him as a traitor, and so forth. See *Čas*, 17 Sept 1944 and 12 Oct. 1944; *Pravda*, 27 Sept. 1944, and 6 Oct. 1944; *Nové slovo*, 10 Aug. 1944.

[9] Jozef Lettrich, Chairman of the Democratic Party, declared at the first session of the Slovak National Council in Bratislava on 15 May 1945 that all collaborators and traitors of the Slovak Uprising would be punished and the main culprits sentenced to death. He also referred to Tiso, in *Čas*, 17 May 1945. In the same daily, a

The highly accusatory words, which also marked the indictment of Tiso before the National Court, were heard in speeches by the Czechoslovak President Edvard Beneš, in BBC broadcasts from his London exile. In the early years of the war, Beneš actually ignored the Slovak State in his speeches, or mentioned it and its representatives only marginally. But on the eve of the fourth anniversary of the establishment of the Slovak State, on 13 March 1943, in a special speech to the Slovaks, Beneš spoke about the 'treacherous establishment of the so-called Slovak State', which had been the work of Tiso and all those who had come and gone with him. Allegedly with the Sudeten German leader Henlein, behind Prague's back, Tiso had agreed to the betrayal even before the Munich Pact. He had broken his word and also betrayed his oaths as a member of the Czechoslovak National Assembly and as a priest, while collaborating with Hitler and sending Slovak men to fight on the Eastern Front, ultimately putting the restoration of an intact Slovakia in jeopardy.[10] After his return to the restored Czechoslovakia from his London exile by way of Moscow, on 9 May 1945, Beneš gave a speech at a public meeting in Bratislava, in which he emphasized that 'from 1938 onwards, the treason had been planned in Slovakia. The People's Party intentionally and consistently abandoned the Republic [...]. After the Munich Pact, [the leaders of the People's Party] intentionally prepared for a carving up of the State in March 1939 [...].' Beneš pointed to the collaboration of People's Party politicians with the Germans, which continued to the bitter end, and he called on the Slovaks 'consistently, mercilessly, hastily, and resolutely to do away with the collaborators once and for all'.[11]

---

week later, Tiso was characterized as an unworthy priest and bad Slovak who had sold out his nation and discredited it. *Čas*, 24 May 1945, and in connection with the transfer of the imprisoned Tiso and other politicians from Prague to Bratislava, *Čas* reported on 'Slovak traitors led by the former president, Dr Jozef Tiso', *Čas*, 31 Oct. 1945.

10 See Beneš, E. *Šest let exilu a druhé světové války: Řeči, projevy a dokumenty z r. 1938-1945*. Prague: Družstevní práce, 1946, pp. 196-202.

11 *Čas*, 12 May 1945.

The first major book after the war really to criticize the 'treacherous activity' of Tiso and his party was by an interwar Slovak Social Democrat leader, Ivan Dérer, particularly in the part dealing with the breakdown of unity in interwar Czechoslovakia. The book, which was actually written in 1943, describes the role of the People's Party and its leader, Tiso, in the break-up of interwar Czechoslovakia.[12] But the book completely fails to ascribe any political or moral responsibility for the Munich capitulation (the basic power-politics prerequisite for the end of the Czechoslovak State) to the politicians led by Beneš, or indeed to himself as Minister of Justice until 22 September 1938.

The core of the criticism and condemnation of Tiso's political activity is contained in his indictment before the National Court and the subsequent confirmation of the death sentence delivered by the Court. I will briefly describe the reasoning for the death sentence, which has up to the present day served as a basis for the critical interpretations and rejection of Tiso's political activities.

First of all, I would begin with a brief description of the basic features of the special court named in Decree[13] No. 33/1945 by the Slovak National Council, of 15 May 1945, whereby it was set up as the People's Court but has generally been known as the 'Court of Retribution'. Anton Rašla, the then prosecutor acting before the National Court, the supreme judiciary body, characterized the People's Court as 'revolutionary';[14] it was not a regular court for the two simple reasons that its principles included political criteria for assessing the acts of the accused, and in regular criminal law the unacceptable principle of retroactivity had been introduced, and it was impossible to appeal the judgement.

---

12 See Dérer, I. *Slovenský vývoj a luďácká zrada: Fakta, vzpomínky a úvahy.* Prague: Kvasnička a Hampl, 1946, pp. 309-31.

13 In contrast to the laws which were passed by the National Assembly in Prague for the entire state, the Slovak National Council in Bratislava, after the war, passed, decrees with legal force in Slovakia.

14 *Proces s dr. J. Tisom: Spomienky obžalobcu Antona Rašlu a obhajcu Ernesta Žabkayho.* Bratislava: Tatrapress, 1990, p. 30.

The prosecutor brought the charges against Tiso under Decree No. 33 in all three defined categories of crime—high treason, collaboration with the Nazis, and betrayal of the Slovak National Uprising.[15] In the decree, war crimes were not explicitly mentioned, and Tiso was therefore not tried and sentenced as a war criminal.

According to the judgement, Tiso had sought the break-up of the Republic, the elimination of its democratic system, and the introduction of a Fascist régime. By his direct negotiations with Hitler, and in other ways, he had contributed to the establishment of the Slovak State under German protection. He provided considerable support to the military, political, and economic interests of Hitler's Germany and Horthy's Hungary, to the detriment of the war efforts of the Allies, including the USSR, and causing damage to the Slovak nation, including democratic and anti-Fascist organizations and groups in Slovakia. He had impeded the struggle of the Slovak nation against traitors and invaders, for freedom and the restoration of Czechoslovakia, and had specially hampered preparations for the Slovak National Uprising and Slovak military participation in it. He had taken an active part in the efforts of the Fascist invaders and traitors at home to suppress the Uprising and to hinder the struggle of the partisan fighters. He had commanded, organized, and ardently prosecuted democratic and ant-Fascist individuals and organizations, committing wrongful acts against other people because of their race, nationality, religion or political adherence, or because of their anti-Fascist beliefs. In this sense, according to the sentence, Tiso had repeatedly committed the criminal acts of high treason, collaboration, and the betrayal of the Uprising, for which he was condemned to die on the gallows.

Tiso's responsibility for the persecution and deportation of the Jewish population of Slovakia, which is frequently debated today, ap-

---

15 See the Decree No. 33 of the Slovak National Council, of 15 May 1945, Article 2, sections (a) to (d), and Article 4, sections (a), (b), and (c).

pears in the fourth, and final, list of charges, that is, it was not emphasized separately.[16] On the contrary, the emphasis was on Tiso's high treason, his acts to destroy the democratic system, his collaboration with the Third Reich, and his betrayal of the Uprising.[17]

Soon after the sentencing and execution of Tiso, President Beneš, in his wartime memoirs, again emphasized that Tiso and his companions had, during the German occupation, committed an 'intentional, villainous, betrayal, shamefully plunging a dagger in the back of his own nation'.[18]

In such an interpretation of his criminal responsibility throughout the following decades — from the end of war in May 1945 onwards and, particularly after the Communist takeover in February 1948 — the Slovak Communists, the Czechoslovak-oriented non-Communists, and, of course, the Czech Communists and non-Communists, shared an identical or at least highly similar view of Tiso.

During the Communist régime, criticism of Tiso and other People's Party representatives for having eliminated democracy in 1938 sounded odd, since the Communists themselves had eliminated it again in 1948.[19] The reasons why Tiso was given the death sentence, particularly for having 'betrayed the Uprising', did not sound persuasive either, since it is almost impossible for anyone to betray anything one has never participated in or has previously considered wrong and unacceptable, and therefore never had such intentions or took part in such activities before 'the betrayal'. And such was Tiso's attitude to the Uprising from its very beginning, seeing it as an attempt to destroy the State he headed. A critical assessment of Tiso's wartime activity is

---

16 Part D, the conclusion of the decision of 15 April 1947, which is also concerned with the Jews of Slovakia, includes the brief general statement that 'he did wrong to others for their racial, national, religious and political beliefs and anti-Fascist convictions'. See *Proces s dr. J. Tisom*, p. 234.
17 For more on Tiso's trial, see *Proces s dr. J. Tisom*, pp. 223-33.
18 Beneš, E. *Paměti: Od Mnichova k nové válce a k novému vítězství*. Prague: Orbis, 1947, p. 89.
19 Under the Communist régime, M. Kropilák (ed.) *Dejiny Slovenska V (1918–1945)*. Bratislava: Veda, 1985, pp. 264-83, 354-90.

also given in a brief biography of him published after 1989 by the historian Ivan Kamenec,[20] who maintains an impartial and analytical approach to Tiso's activity and its consequences for Slovakia and for Tiso himself.

The People's Court was therefore clearly of a political nature and its decisions and arguments behind the decisions (by means of various forms of propaganda) from the beginning met with tacit disapproval among some members of the Slovak public and with open disagreement and sharp criticism among Slovak exiles, former representatives, and adherents of the wartime Slovak Republic, using arguments of their own.

The first substantial book devoted to Tiso's political activities and his trial was the biography by Konštantín Čulen, published in two volumes in the USA in 1947 and 1948. The second volume is devoted to the circumstances under which the trial took place.[21] In the first volume, Čulen, a former deputy of the parliament of the Slovak Republic and a consistent advocate of an independent Slovakia, wrote an apologetic, even hagiographical, biography of the executed President Tiso. In the second volume, he takes issue with political aspects of the trial, the biases of the prosecution, particularly of the President of the Court, Igor Daxner, the intentional limitations of the defence, and circumstances of the refusal to grant Tiso a pardon and then of his execution. After this publication, or in conjunction with it, further testimonies were published in exile on the life and work of Tiso, whom the Slovak émigrés from immediately after the war considered a martyr and the embodiment of short-lived Slovak independence.[22]

---

20 Kamenec, I. *Tragédia politika, kňaza a človeka: Dr. Jozef Tiso 1887–1947*. Bratislava: Archa, 1998.
21 Čulen, K. *Po Svätoplukovi druhá naša hlava: Život Dr. Jozefa Tisu*, 2nd edn (1947). Partizánske: Garmond, 1992.
22 For a short bibliography of non-Slovak works, published by Tiso's secretary, see Murín, K. *Spomienky a svedectvo*. Hamilton, Ont.: Zahraničná Matica slovenská, 1987; 2nd edn. Radošina: Priatelia prezidenta Tisu v cudzine a na Slovensku, 1991, pp. 338–61.

A certain generalizing approach to Tiso was formulated by a prominent ideologist of the wartime Slovak régime who went into exile, Štefan Polakovič. According to him, 'Dr Tiso, as the President of the Republic, embodied and represented to the world the fundamental sovereignty of the Slovak nation, which was elevated in relation to all the nations and recommended to the United Nations by Pope John Paul II in his speech at UNESCO, Geneva, in 1980. Tiso was a living symbol of the nation. This was what we, the entire nation, felt, and this emotion was also manifested by the nation in the Slovak Republic, spontaneously, without orders [...].'[23] Yet, as Polakovič himself admitted, 'not everything was as it should have been'. There were the 'labyrinths' of that period to blame. 'All the traps ensuing from the geopolitical position of the nation, from the constant intrigues of the neighbour to the south [Horthy's Hungary], but, most of all, from pressures of all kinds and all the power of the Reich [...].'[24] Consequently, Polakovič sees the causes of all the shortcomings or faults of the régime and Tiso's policy as the result of external factors.

The hitherto most comprehensive view of Tiso's life and political work is the book by the former exile historian, Milan S. Ďurica, entitled *Jozef Tiso 1887–1947: Životopisný profil* (A Bibliographic Profile), published in Bratislava, in 2006. It is actually an apology which takes issue with critical views of Tiso, and argues that Tiso's decisions and actions, especially in the years 1938–45, were in principle just. In its basic attitudes, Ďurica's book is in accord with Čulen's. In Ďurica's, Tiso appears as a Slovak patriot, the protector of Slovak interests, the father of the first independent Slovak State, which faced certain limitations owing to its geopolitical position in the sphere of influence of Hitler's Reich.[25]

---

23 Quoted in Polakovič, Š 'Úvodné slovo', ibid., pp. 8–9.
24 Ibid.
25 Milan S. Ďurica also published a brochure entitled *Dr. Jozef Tiso v hodnotení Hitlerových diplomatov a tajných agentov*. Lakewood, OH: Slovenský výskumný ústav v Amerike, 2000), in which he presents opinions critical of German diplomats and secret agents on the activity and attitudes of President Tiso towards Germany during the war.

The emergence of Slovak autonomy in Czechoslovakia after the Munich Agreement is understood by Ďurica as the culmination of years of People's Party efforts to achieve autonomy within Czechoslovakia, an impossibility as long as the central government in Prague was strong and stable, that is, until the Munich Agreement. The responsibility for Munich and the Czechoslovak catastrophe should not, he argues, be borne by Tiso and the People's Party, but, as the National Court also found, by the Western powers that had backed the establishment of Czechoslovakia in 1918 and, twenty years later, sacrificed it to the Reich in support of their short-sighted interests. Czechoslovakia also paid the price for its erroneous policy, led primarily by Beneš, who abandoned the dismembered State after Munich, and then, together with other politicians, fled the country.[26]

The origin of the Slovak State in the dramatic days of March 1939 was also, according to Ďurica, an expression of the Slovak nation's desire to achieve full independence and, under the circumstances in which the State was established, a result of Hitler's aggressive policy, which aimed to destroy even the rump Czecho-Slovakia. The central government in Prague had also made a mistake when it allowed itself to become involved in political adventure by organizing a military coup against Tiso's autonomous government in March 1939, thus causing turmoil, fed in particularly by the ethnic Germans in Bratislava. This enabled Hitler to intervene by blackmailing Tiso into summoning the Slovak Parliament that declared an independent Slovak State on 14 March 1939.[27] At the same time, the author adds, the trend towards an autonomous Slovakia had already begun, and it would have happened under other circumstances, some other time, because, to quote Tiso, 'it was necessitated by the rigorous logic of the natural development of the Slovak nation'.[28] Ďurica argues that the correctness of the 14 March 1939 decision stems from Tiso's words to the National Court: 'I am still persuaded that we acted well; otherwise we

---

26 See Ďurica, *Jozef Tiso 1887–1947*, p. 203.
27 Ibid., p. 216–33.
28 Ibid., p. 233.

would not have saved the nation'.[29] This act of salvation allegedly consisted first of all in preserving the territorial integrity of Slovakia from the ambitions of its more powerful neighbours.

In Ďurica's opinion, Slovak vassalage to the Third Reich was accepted by Tiso and supported only in an inevitable measure with the intention to prevent the existence of the Slovak State from being jeopardized. After all, even much older and bigger European countries had strived to be on as good terms with the Reich as possible. Slovakia and its president were forced to follow them. The so-called 'radicals' headed by Prime Minister Vojtech Tuka and Minister of the Interior Alexander Mach, were active collaborators, while the German diplomats, or secret agents, had several times pointed out insufficient interconnection of Slovakia (and Tiso himself) and the interests of Germany.[30]

In the spirit of other Tiso defenders, Ďurica also absolves Tiso of the responsibility for Slovak involvement in the war against the Soviet Union and the Western Allies; for that, he argues, Prime Minister Tuka should bear full responsibility. Tuka declared war on both the USSR and the USA without the approval of the President or the Parliament. According to Ďurica, in this matter, too, Tiso appears to have been a victim of pro-Nazi radicals.[31] Tiso reportedly did not want a German victory, because he feared that as much as he did the Red Army's advance.[32] As a Roman Catholic priest, he saw the way out as being in the hands of God, and forebodings about himself.

Lastly, even for the deportations of the Jews of Slovakia to German-occupied Poland, Ďurica sees the main reason in Nazi German policy and even in Nazi deception when the Nazis agreed to admit

---

29   Ibid., pp. 233–34.
30   See Ibid., the chapter 'Tiso a Nemci', pp. 302–37.
31   See Ibid., the chapter 'Tiso a Vláda Slovenskej republiky', pp. 262–301.
32   Ibid, p. 331.

Jews as a workforce instead of Slovak workers, to be exploited on formerly Polish territory.[33] Since, according to Ďurica, no Slovak politician could at the beginning of the deportations in March 1942 have known about the Nazi decision on the 'Final Solution to the Jewish question', taken in Wannsee in January 1942, or the mass killing of the Jews, the Slovaks had not deliberately sent the Jews to their deaths.[34] Moreover, the Slovak government completely stopped the deportations in October 1942 when the German authorities denied their request to inspect the camps where the Slovak Jews were supposed to work. On the matter of anti-Jewish policy, Ďurica tries to absolve Tiso of the responsibility because as president he had granted exemptions which, according to Ďurica, saved about thirty thousand Slovak Jews, a number that critical historians consider extremely exaggerated.

The very brief depiction of the attitudes expressed by Tiso's critics and defenders, which we have seen so far, signifies their unfading but still uneven impact, including polarization, in Slovakia today, where there are more critics than adherents of President Tiso among historians and the general public. This is also true of attitude towards the wartime state that Tiso was the head of.

By far more people in the Slovak Republic today undoubtedly sympathize with the anti-Fascist resistance and the Slovak National Uprising than those whose sympathies lie with the wartime Slovak Republic and its representatives. This has been demonstrated by public opinion surveys since 1990, which document the development of these opinions in results published from 1990 to 2011. The surveys were carried out by several agencies using various methods. And though they cannot therefore be automatically compared, the basic trend in the development of public opinion on the wartime resistance

---

[33] For the Jewish question and Tiso's attitude to it, see the chapter 'Tiso a Židia', ibid., pp. 356–411.

[34] A similar opinion was also expressed in the early 1990s by Anton Rašla, the prosecutor at the Tiso trial: 'At the time of the decision on the deportation of the Jews, neither Tiso nor anyone else could be accused of having already known that the Jews would go to their deaths.' *Proces s dr. J. Tisom*, p. 33.

movement and the Uprising, as well as on the wartime Slovak Republic, is in principle similar in all the survey results.

Already in the 1990 opinion poll, which asked respondents about milestones in Slovak history, 21.5 per cent of the Slovaks asked, that means most of the respondents who had an opinion, expressed their pride in the anti-Fascist resistance, while the proportion of those who were proud of the Slovak State was only 5 per cent.[35] The survey covered a wide spectrum of historical events, which also meant a wide dispersion of responses. Moreover, since it was conducted shortly after the change of régime, one could reasonably expect that a great part of the public would have been informed of the conditions in Slovakia during the war, especially by means of official, Communist propaganda, which rejected almost everything from the wartime republic and was in favour only of the resistance fighters, especially the Communist ones.

A 1994 book by Martin Bútora and Zora Bútorová, published in 1994, presents a 1993 survey, taken after the split of Czechoslovakia into two new sovereign states. Eighty per cent of the respondents agreed with the statement 'The Slovak National Uprising was a demonstration of the rejection of Fascism and we should therefore be proud of it'. Only10 per cent inclined to the view that the Uprising had been an insurrection against their insurgents' own state and should therefore be assessed negatively. At the same time, about 20 per cent of the respondents admitted that the new Slovak Republic might also be linked to the legacy of the wartime Republic, the main representative of which was Tiso. The authors of the publication explain the discrepancy in these attitudes by the fact that some respondents were more critical of Nazism than of the wartime Slovak Republic.[36]

---

35   *Aktuálne problémy Česko-Slovenska: Správa zo sociologického prieskumu.* Bratislava: Centrum pre výskum spoločenských problémov, November 1990, p. 18.
36   See Bútora, M., Bútorová, Z. (eds) *Slovensko rok po: Cesty a križovatky nového štátu očami jeho obyvateľov.* Prague: SLON, 1994.

In another publication with long-term assessments of leading twentieth-century politicians in Czechoslovak history, the negative assessment of the most important representative of wartime Slovakia, Tiso, predominates in all replies from 1991 to 1999, even though there are fewer divergences than before. The negative assessments dropped from 47 per cent, in 1991, to 32.4 per cent, in 1999, and the positive ones also decreased from 28.1 per cent, in 1991, to 20.7 per cent, in 1999. The proportion of undecided respondents also increased.[37] In a publication on political opinions and values in Slovakia on the threshold of the twenty-first century, in a section on Slovak perceptions of historical figures in the 1990s, a comparison of the results from 1993, 1997, and 1999 shows a predominantly negative attitude to Tiso (42, 40, and 32 per cent) as compared to a positive one (25, 18, and 21 per cent), while the proportion of respondents with a balanced assessment increased slightly (from 18 to 17 and then 19 per cent) and the proportion of those undecided about Tiso substantially increased (from 15 to 25 and then 28 per cent).[38]

There are also assessments of twentieth-century historical periods and events presented in the book from a survey carried out in October 1997. The respondents judged the Slovak National Uprising as follows: very positively and largely positively: 59 per cent; equally positively and negatively: 17 per cent; very negatively and largely negatively: 5 per cent; and undecided: 19 per cent. The assessments of Tiso's Slovak Republic were very positive and largely positive: 27 per cent; equally positive and negative: 18 per cent; very negative and largely negative: 24 per cent; and undecided: 31 per cent.[39]

A large sociological survey carried out in November 2003 was published the following year. It asked adult Slovaks about collective identities in Slovakia today. The survey also included historical events

---

37 Krivý, V. *Politické orientácie na Slovensku a skupinové profily.* Bratislava: Inštitút pre verejné otázky, 2000, p. 73.
38 Gyarfášová, O., Krivý, V., Velšic, M. (eds) *Krajina v pohybe: Správa o politických názoroch a hodnotách ľudí na Slovensku.* Bratislava: Inštitút pre verejné otázky, 2001, p. 255.
39 Ibid., p. 260.

and their leading actors. From a list of 25 historical events, the respondents were asked to choose three events they considered the most positive and three they considered the most negative. Among the most positive events was the Slovak National Uprising, with 28 per cent of the respondents, ranking it in third place (after the creation of Czechoslovakia in 1918 and of the Slovak Republic in 1993), while 10.3 per cent of the respondents chose the declaration of Tiso's Slovak Republic in 1939, ranking it seventh. Among the listed events, the one given the most negative assessment was the Uprising, with 0.6 per cent of the respondents choosing it, thus ranking it second to last (just ahead of the creation of Czechoslovakia in 1918), while the creation of the Slovak Republic in 1939 was estimated negatively by 2.7 per cent of respondents, but the confiscation of the property of the Slovak Jews was cited by 12.7 per cent of the respondents and the deportations of the Slovak Jews was cited by 47.8 per cent of the respondents. Respondents, however, saw the last two events that are named here as closely connected with the existence and policy of wartime Slovakia.[40] In the same survey, the head of that state, Tiso, was appreciated at most by 2.3 per cent of the respondents; whereas 14.2 per cent of the respondents found him to be the most objectionable.[41]

In connection with the seventieth anniversary of the establishment of the Slovak Republic, in 2009, the daily *Hospodárske noviny* (Business and Economic News)[42] reported the results of a public opinion survey carried out by the Focus Agency. The survey found that opinions on the Slovak Republic led by Tiso were equally divided — 34 per cent of the respondents evaluated this State very positively or rather positively; 32 per cent very negatively or rather negatively, and 34 per cent had no strong view. A certain increase in the proportion of respondents who sympathize with the wartime Slovak Republic was

---

40 Krivý, V. *Kolektívne identity na súčasnom Slovensku: Pramenná publikácia dát zo sociologického výskumu*. Bratislava: SAV, 2004, pp. 24–25.
41 Ibid., pp. 21–22.
42 'Tisov režim: Nevieme povedať jasné nie', *Hospodárske noviny*, 13–15 Mar. 2009, pp. 18–19.

explained by the director of Focus, Ivan Dianiška, by the fact that in the meantime several textbooks had been published in Slovakia (though he could have mentioned other books as well), which evaluate the Slovak State positively, and a similar view had been spread by some high-ranking Roman Catholic clerics. At the same time, however, most Slovaks, as many as 83 per cent of the respondents, were now proud of the Slovak National Uprising. That means that not only those who would be against the wartime Slovak Republic and, possibly, the undecided, but also some of the respondents who sympathize with it, assess the Uprising positively. The head of the agency explained this by the fact that such an opinion may have developed amongst the public by the years of Communist mass propaganda praising the Uprising and also by the fact that the importance of the Uprising for Slovakia was not doubted by any post-war Slovak régime.

In the most recent public opinion survey on the topic of historical figures, which was held in the countries of the Visegrád Four, in 2011, Tiso received a positive rating from 14 per cent of the Slovak respondents; 28 per cent of the respondents evaluated him neither positively nor negatively; 41 per cent assessed him negatively, and 17 per cent gave no answer at all.[43] This survey also reveals the predominantly critical reserve of the Slovak public towards the president of wartime Slovakia, as well as a certain increase in the proportion of those who rate him positively.

These results of opinion polls carried out in the last decade of the twentieth century and the first decade of the twenty-first century, though of different natures, indicate a certain increase in the positive assessment of the historical importance of the Slovak Republic headed by Tiso. The positive evaluation of the Slovak National Uprising, which rejects this republic and the policies of its leaders, is clearly

---

43 See *Do We Know Each Other?*, a public opinion survey about historical memory in the V4 countries. Oľga Gyárfášová, Institute of Public Affairs, Bratislava, prepared for the international academic conference 'My Hero, Your Enemy: Listening to Understand', Prague, 1–3 December 2011.

higher despite the efforts of advocates of the wartime Slovak Republic, at home and abroad, to change Slovak public opinion on this State and its representatives, particularly President Tiso.

In the dispute over the wartime Slovak State and its representatives, opinions have also been formed not only about interwar Czechoslovakia and the entire post-war period in the restored Czechoslovakia, but also, indeed especially, about the ideological and historical roots of the new Slovak Republic, which came into being on 1 January 1993. One of the reasons for the relatively sharp polarization in views about Tiso, his state, and his political régime is the fact that even after almost seventy years this topic is not only a special focus of historical research and one of the layers of historical memory of Slovak society, but is also a live political question.

Welcoming the Admiral on a White Horse: The Depictions of the Horthy Regime in Slovak Historical Culture[1]

Miroslav Michela[2]
Charles University, Prague

Abstract: This article examines the reasons for the existence of the specific Slovak discourse related to the Horthy regime and the principles of its functioning, as well as its manifestation in Slovak historical culture, especially in one of its parts, historiography. I endeavours to answer the question of why the history of Slovak-Hungarian relations in the nineteenth and twentieth centuries is often represented as a permanent conflict. The author embarks on the thesis that narratives about the past of society form a significant identifying (identity-forming) category and that they participate in creating borders between 'us' and 'them'. Concurrently, they are a significant source of symbolic capital and power, while several institutions are responsible for their production.

The Slovak mass media have recently been full of news about the commemoration of Count János Esterházy (1901-1957), a noted politician of the Hungarian minority in Czechoslovakia, who died in Mírov prison, Moravia. Since the early 1990s, discussions about Esterházy have provoked a lot of emotion among the general public and among scholars.[3] Many people ardently joined in the debate at this time, and the topic was even discussed amongst the most senior politicians in both Slovakia and Hungary. The Slovak president, Ivan Gašparovič, claimed that Esterházy had been a sympathizer with Hitler and fascism. Influential Hungarian politicians, by contrast, called him an exemplary humanist and a hero, a martyr who should be exonerated. This highly publicized case mobilized politicians, the general public,

---

1 This research was supported by the Slovak Research and Development Agency grant No. APVV-0628-11.
2 E-mail: Miroslav.Michela@ff.cuni.cz.
3 Malfatti, A. (ed.) *Esterházy János emlékkönyv*. Budapest: Századvég. Pol. Isk. Alapítvány, 2001; Deák, L. *Politický profil Jánoša Esterházyho*. Bratislava: Kubko Goral, 1995.

233

and historians and it stirred up the already uneasy Slovak-Hungarian relations. Violence occurred during the unveiling of a bust of Esterházy in Košice, when the artist Peter Kalmus tried to wrap it in toilet paper. According to him, this was his protest against the unveiling of a bust of an antisemite. Another participant in the demonstration against the unveiling, said: 'Esterházy welcomed Horthy's fascist troops when they invaded this country and he supported efforts directed against Slovak statehood, and today, in the sovereign Slovak Republic, we are unveiling his bust. That is outrageous.'[4] Later that night, someone damaged the statue by pouring red paint on it. This incident was also reported during a plenary session of the European Parliament.[5] Another point should be mentioned in this respect. In my home-town of Komárno two memorials were ceremonially installed in the summer of 2011 praising Esterházy—a commemorative plaque and a statue. They were the gestures of two associations connected to two different political platforms jostling in the public sphere to win the support of the locals. Honouring Esterházy and emphasizing his humanism and the deeds he did for Hungarians was common to both sides in the struggle, regardless of the fact that they were manifesting this separately. On the other hand, in the Slovak national discourses one notices the vigorous and unified avoidance of such interpretations of the past and Esterházy's political activities. Different views are manifested also by the proclamations of several Slovak and Hungarian historians.[6]

This conflict is not, however, only about interpreting the activities of a single historical figure. It is the outcome of the representation

---

4 See Ogurčáková, J. 'Odhaľovanie Esterházyho busty v Košiciach sa skončilo bitkou'. Available on-line: http://kosice.korzar.sme.sk/c/5806387/odhalovanie-esterhazyho-busty-v-kosiciach-sa-skoncilo-bitkou.html [accessed 7 October 2012].
5 See HVG.hu: 'A külügy elítélte a kassai Esterházy-szobor megrongálását.' Available on-line: http://hvg.hu/vilag/20110328_eliteltek_esterhazy_szobor [accessed 7 October 2012].
6 See the documentary film *Üldözöttek védelmében*. Available on-line: http://www.youtube.com/watch?v=8WmoH4ckmS4, or, alternatively, the Declaration of the History Institute of the Slovak Academy of Sciences: http://www.history.sav.sk/esterhazy.htm [accessed 10 October 2012].

of the past thematized in the dichotomy of national narratives, Slovak and Hungarian, while an important role is played by the cross-border 'Hungarian-Hungarian relations'. Another important role in this changing complex of questions is played by the depictions of the Treaty of Trianon (1920) and predominantly the meta-narrative of Slovak–Hungarian relations as a bundle of founding narratives of national history—national myths.[7] In this context, Miklós Horthy represents a highly emblematic, symbolic figure.[8] His famous triumphant marches on a white horse to Budapest in 1919 and then, after the First Vienna Award to Košice in 1938, have been represented in Slovak discourse as a symbol of social and national oppression, as the return of the intolerant spirit of the pre-1918 Kingdom of Hungary to present-day Europe.[9]

The argument that history is (re)produced as different 'Slovak' and 'Hungarian' narratives is not new. It is spread among the general public as well as in the debates of intellectuals. It is actually trivial in the context of functioning national ideologies and nationalism.[10] But the fact that these arguments are still more or less strictly followed simply maintains and legitimizes the long-term state of intellectual backwardness conserved by parallel interpretations of history. The

---

[7] For more on the use of the term 'myth' and on modern national mythologies in Slovak-Hungarian relations, see Schöpflin, G. *Nations, Identity, Power.* London: Hurst, 2002, pp. 79–98; Krekovič, E., Mannová, E., Krekovičová, E. (eds.) *Mýty naše slovenské.* Bratislava: AEP, 2005; Findor, A. '(De)constructing Slovak National Mythology', *Sociológia* 2 (2002), pp. 195–208.

[8] In Hungary, polemics about Horthy and the nature of his rule have been discussed for decades. See Zeidler, M. (ed.) *Trianon: Nemzet és emlékezet.* Budapest: Osiris, 2003, pp. 709–819. The latest debate erupted in 2012 after the installation of several statues, while in academic circles debates on antisemitism started. For more on this, see www.galamus.hu.

[9] See, for example, the results of the research on the depictions of the disintegration of the Kingdom of Hungary and the so-called 'Trianon complex': Michela, M., Csaba, Z. (eds.) *Magyarország felbomlása és a trianoni békeszerződés a magyar és szlovák kolektív emlékezetben 1918–2010, LIMES: Tudományos szemle* 4 (2010) and 1 (2011).

[10] See Vörös, L. *Analytická historiografia versus národné dejiny: "Národ" ako sociálna reprezentácia.* Pisa: Edizioni Plus and Pisa University Press, 2010.

outcome is that a 'Slovak historian' is expected to defend 'Slovak interests', that is, the Slovak national narrative, and the same is expected on the 'Hungarian side'. This results in an unproductive recycling of nationalist history. László Vörös has emphasized a strong connection between so-called 'traditional historiography' and nationalism, and argued that "the primary aim of traditional historiographies is to produce identity-forming narratives'. He has emphasized that traditional historical epistemology and methodology actually do not allow different writing about history.[11] The social role of historians is therefore often limited to the guarding of national canons or, occasionally, to modifying them.

In this article, I will discuss the reasons for the existence of this discourse and the principles of its functioning, as well as its manifestation in Slovak historical culture, especially in one of its parts, historiography. I will endeavour to answer the question of why the history of Slovak–Hungarian relations in the nineteenth and twentieth centuries is often represented as a permanent conflict. In my argument, I start from the thesis that narratives about the past of society form a significant identifying (identity-forming) category and that they participate in creating borders between 'us' and 'them'. Concurrently, they are a significant source of symbolic capital and power, while several institutions are responsible for their production. That means that knowledge of history is not produced 'naturally', by itself, but that it is largely intellectuals, politicians, and social actors who influence these processes by various types of media. The construction of identities/identifications is, apart from some individual dispositions, also connected with some cultural and social frames. A significant role in these processes is played by the State, which has a great impact on the creation and spreading of cultural representations.[12]

---

11   Ibid., p. 2.
12   Sperber defines cultural representations as ideas about the world, which are held by multiple individuals. Sperber, D. 'Anthropology and Psychology: Towards an Epidemiology of Representations', *Man*, New Series, vol. 20 (Mar., 1985), no. 1, pp. 82–85.

History, memory, and cultural trauma

Zdeněk Beneš characterizes the concept of historical culture as a collection of all historical knowledge or thinking about history, which is characteristic of a particular society. It is primarily a social and cultural phenomenon, which contains communicated, used, and, therefore, interpreted information on history.[13] This broad category of discourses contains various forms of relations between society and historical narratives, including knowledge and attitudes created and reproduced at different levels, ranging from the family to rigorously analytical writing by scholars. In this respect, Miroslav Hroch has identified six sources of historical consciousness as one of the counterparts to historical culture — namely, the results of historiography and its popularization in the mass media; school education; journalism in the broad sense; artistic interpretation of the past; mobility — travelling; and the informal passing on of information within the family and other groups.[14] The Slovak historian Ľubomír Lipták proposed three important areas where history is (re)produced.[15] The first area — the official one — is presented by a political régime and its agents. It represents an institutionally created and reproduced historical canon legitimizing ruling values and the preferred ideological orientation and social practices. It is present in public spaces, at the celebration of state holidays and selected historical events, in laws, and in school curricula. A state uses certain economic, controlling, and repressive mechanisms to stay alive. Pierre Bourdieu writes in this sense about symbolic capital and symbolic violence which is manifested, for example, by the school system and mandatory state education, through which the state implements common forms and categories of thinking, social

---

13 For more on this, see Beneš, Z. *Historický text a historická kultura*. Prague: Karolinum, 1995; Le Goff, J. *Paměť a dějiny*. Praha: Argo, 2007; Rüsen, J. 'Was ist Geschichtskultur?,' in Füssmann, K. (ed.) *Historische Faszination: Geschichtskultur heute*, Cologne: Böhlau, 1994, pp. 3–26.
14 Hroch, M. 'Historické vědomí a potíže s jeho výzkumem dříve i nyní', in Šubrt, J. (ed.) *Historické vědomí jako předmět badatelského zájmu: teorie a výzkum*. Kolín: Nezávislé centrum pro studium politiky, 2010, p. 33.
15 Lipták, L *Storočie dlhšie ako sto rokov*. Bratislava: Kalligram, 2011, p. 191.

frames of understanding, and structures of knowledge among the citizens. It is actually a state-controlled type of knowledge.[16] Nowadays, this has been altered by the Internet. Of course, it is also historians who participate in the production of contemporary historical canons. Their professional interest is to interpret the past. The second area, in Lipták's view, is therefore represented by a scholarly discourse, which is officially not obliged to be subordinated to the dominant canon (though it often is). In this case, Pierre Nora writes about memory and history as about two opposites. He claims that carriers of memory are living groups, and thus the content of memory is subject to change. Memory is selective and influenced by emotions. It hallows the memories which are, on the other hand, ruined by historical criticism. In the meanwhile, writing about history is perceived as an intellectual activity that requires an analytical and critical approach and tries to avoid self-censorship and overly intensive emotional ties to the researched subject.[17] The third area suggested by Lipták is the personal one. It is a reflection of social relations that exist around an individual, which are created by different personal dispositions and experiences. This area often stands in opposition to the preceding two, but is also part of them. Tzvetan Todorov has pointed out different strategies of narratives produced by witnesses, historians, and those who are remembering. He claimed our knowledge is complicated by historiography, but is considerably simplified in the process of remembering.[18] These areas of constructing narratives about the past do not exist in isolation. They represent coexisting, but also competing, forms of historical discourses, where an important role is played by institutions and social agents. Therefore, as Peter Burke argues, it is our task to answer the questions: Who wishes to remember what and whom?

---

16   Bourdieu, P. *Teorie jednání*. Prague: Karolinum, 1998, pp. 87–94, a Czech translation of *Raisons pratiques: Sur la théorie de l'action* Paris: Seuil, 1994.
17   Nora, P. 'Between Memory and History: Les Lieux de Mémoire', *Representations*, No. 26, Special Issue: Memory and Counter-Memory (Spring, 1989), pp. 8–9; idem: *Emlékezet és történelem között*. Budapest: Napvilág Kiadó, 2008, pp. 14–15.
18   Todorov, T. *Mémoire du mal, tentation du bien*. Paris: Robert Laffont, 2000.

Whose version of the past is recorded and stored? Who wishes to forget what and why?[19]

Narratives about the past are often based on 'victories' and 'defeats'. Research on historical culture that is based on the narratives about victims, suffering, and trauma, currently represents a relatively important trend in social studies.[20] Apart from the existence of several schools focused mainly on researching psychological, historical, social, and cultural contexts, scholars largely agree with the view that processing this problem and coming to terms with it is determined by particular situations and conditions, the institutional and media context of the topic, and the social actors — meaning everything that creates, confirms, and revises the topicality and meaning of particular events for a particular group of people.

The depiction of Slovak–Hungarian relations is also characterized by narratives with an impact on the identity of people. I will mention only the two most influential narratives which are closely connected with the topic of my article: the narratives of Magyarization and Trianon. There may be many possible triggers of collective trauma, including a particularly surprising and sudden turning point in events influencing substantial social and cultural changes, such as wars, revolutions, coups d'état, economic crises, and natural disasters. Their development, however, depends on the social and cultural contexts in which a concrete event has taken place and the meanings are reproduced. Trauma need not always follow from this. Jeffrey Alexander et al. interpret cultural trauma as an event which enters- collective memory by means of narration. In this connection, he considers a new way of constructing identities based on representations of the

---

19   Burke, P. 'A történelem mint társadalmi emlékezet', *Regio* 1 (2001), pp. 3–21.
20   See Alexander, J., Eyerman, R., Breese, E. *Narrating Trauma: On the Impact of Collective Suffering*. Herndon: Paradigm, 2011. For the central European context, see, Stegmann, N. (ed.) *Die Weltkriege als symbolische Bezugspunkte: Polen, die Tschechoslowakei und Deutschland nach dem Ersten und Zweiten Weltkrieg*. Praha: MÚA, 2009; Franzen, K. E., Schulze Wessel, M. (eds.) *Opfernarrative: Konkurrenzen und Deutungskämpfe in Deutschland und im östlichen Europa nach dem Zweiten Weltkrieg*. Munich: Oldenbourg, 2012.

past.[21] He emphasizes that culture represents an already formed narrative form that contains a social life. Culture both forms individuals and is formed by them. It is therefore important to focus on the contents and ways of creating the cultural representations expressed in narrative practices, and to show the impact of these approaches on the (re)constructions of identifications in society.

The admiral on a white horse

Just as Horthy is regarded as a symbol of one period (depicted in the Slovak discourse mainly negatively) in the history of Hungary, Esterházy can be denoted in these discussions as an emblematic figure representing several existential dilemmas of the Hungarian minority in Slovakia. This symbolic position undoubtedly has a strong impact on discussions about his work and political career.[22] It is obvious, however, that public discussions on this personality entail a strong politicization, which dominates the topic. These discussions are usually not based on analytical argumentation, which should, in my opinion, be the main agenda of historians. Rather, they are based more on efforts to gain dominance and impose one's own version of the historical narrative on the public. There is a difference between the aim and the meaning of academic and political approaches to history, and there is a difference in asking questions and making arguments. Both approaches, however, with their own methods and meanings, are legitimate.

But I would not like to promote an incorrect argument based on an often repeated and overly simplified scheme juxtaposing politicians as manipulators and historians as indisputably objective. Regardless of the fact that there is a significant difference here in opin-

---

21   See Alexander, J., et al. *Cultural Trauma and Collective Identity*. Berkeley: University of California Press, 2004.
22   Thanks to the support of the Visegrad Fund, an international project was started in 2012, whose aim is to research the activity of this politician based on primary historical sources, which will be available also to the general public.

ions between 'Slovak' and 'Hungarian' historians. Apart from our professional specializations, we are also part of certain social and cultural structures that influence our thoughts and actions. Individual and cultural representations of the past are significant and constitutive elements of our societies. Based on them, we form the society in which we live, while being formed by it.

It is actually the construction of 'imagined communities' that is closely connected with the image of the Other. In the Slovak discourse, there has long been a trend of frequently ascribing a 'counter-image' to Hungarians. Since the nineteenth century, Slovak ethno-nationalists have been projecting themselves and Slovak history in juxtaposition to the dominant Hungarian state ideology and this approach has been maintained up to the present day. These different cultural representations have been canonized in official state policies and national culture policies, mainly regarding the interpretations of the Great Moravia/Cyril and Methodius and St Stephen traditions, despite the fact that, in Hobsbawm's words, they are 'invented traditions', which achieved their present forms mainly in the nineteenth century, are connected to the early Middle Ages, and are constantly projected into the distant past.

From the institutional point of view, a very important role in this sense was played by the establishment of the first Czechoslovak Republic, often interpreted as the end of 'national subjugation'. The outcome was that in the new state, a new official master narrative and historical canon were established. In regard to the Paris Peace Conference, 1919, a contemporary synthesis of the history of Hungary claims:

> The peace conference finally brought to fruition the long-term efforts of the non-Hungarian nations to achieve their political and national freedom; it eliminated long-term injustice, and it liberated the non-Hungarians from the embrace of the state that thoughtlessly served only one minority nationality and the selfish needs of the Hungarian privileged classes, and its internal composition made it a relic in modern Europe.[23]

---

23 Macůrek, J. *Dějiny Maďarů a Uherského státu*. Prague: Melantrich, 1934, p. 289.

The Czech sociologist Emanuel Chalupný wrote in regard to inter-ethnic relations: 'The Magyar and the Slovak character go together like fire and water'.[24] As Peter Haslinger puts it, it was mainly a negative image of the Hungarians and Hungarian history that was one of the constituting elements of identity construction in the politics of the Czechoslovak state.[25] The continuous emphasizing of the 'oriental character of the Hungarians' was connected to the image of their barbarity and the idea of Slav cultural superiority and civilizing mission. A depiction of the past was established, which would interpret it as national slavery and suppression.[26] The narrative about the historical presence of 'Hungarians' in the region was depicted by the metaphor of a wedge in a Slavic settlement, which led to the 'tearing [apart] of the brotherly Czechoslovak nation', the eastern part of which Saint Stephen included in the Kingdom of Hungary.[27]

The Great Moravian tradition was represented in the sense of the historical legitimacy of the 'restored' Czechoslovak state, and also in present-day Slovakia it is one of the most important traditions that the State made into a national holiday. On the other hand, the cult of Saint Stephen was depicted by most of the Czech and Slovak elites as a symbol of an outdated and irrecoverable past, violent subordination, and their oppression as a nation. Saint Stephen was also presented in interwar Czechoslovakia as a symbol of the revisionist politics of Horthy's Hungary.

---

24   According to Haslinger, P. 'The Nation, the Enemy, and Imagined Territories: Slovak and Hungarian Elements in the Emergence of a Czechoslovak National Narrative during and after WWI', in Wingfield, N. (ed.) *Creating the Other: The Causes and Dynamics of Nationalism, Ethnic Enmity, and Racism in Eastern Europe*. Oxford and New York: Berghahn, 2001.
25   Ibid.
26   See Deák, L. (ed.) *Súčasníci o Trianone*. Bratislava: Kubko Goral, 1996.
27   For more, see Michela, M. 'Functions of the Myth of "National Oppression" in Slovak Master Marrative, 1918–1945', in Szarka, L. (ed.) *A Multiethnic Region and Nation-State in East-Central Europe: Studies in the History of Upper Hungary and Slovakia from the 1600s to the Present*. Boulder: Social Science Monographs, 2011, pp. 253–68.

Political declarations against the Horthy regime were often connected in Czechoslovakia with an anti-revisionist attitude, for example, at the time of the attempts at restoration by Charles Habsburg in 1921. Politicians closely linked their arguments for defending peace, democracy, and stability in the region with strong criticism of the ruling Hungarian elites.[28] Similar arguments were also presented during the campaign against the pro-Hungarian newspaper publisher Lord Rothermere (whom the Czechoslovaks believed had been deceived by Budapest) in 1927:

> They were not working for national interests, or for the blossoming of the Hungarian state, but for the development of their own privileges and glory. They sought the restoration of those old rules when it was easy to live in Hungary, where all you needed was to have a bit more significant name and to beat your chest to show your nationalism [...] they sought their rule and power and [the rule of] several hundred chosen from the upper classes. Hungarians in vain promoted the fading image of their noble predestination.[29]

The anti-revisionist movement in Czechoslovakia was very active also in the 1930s. There were campaigns denouncing revisionism and also the Horthy regime. Horthy and contemporary Hungarian governments were seen as the key players in the revisionist movement. The situation in Hungary at that time, characterized by a highly developed irredentist cult and revisionist discourse that was often openly promoted by the most influential politicians, only provided evidence of this attitude. In the Czechoslovak public discourse, Hungary was often criticized also, for example, for its intolerant policies towards the minorities, its nationalist conservatism, undemocratic ways, and exaggerated aristocratic practices.

Czechoslovakia and Hungary presented themselves in this period by means of heavily confrontational politics. One of the results

---

28 PSP ČR. *Minutes from the meeting of the NS RČS, on 26 October 1921*. Available online: www.psp.cz [accessed 7 October 2012].

29 *Slovensko proti revízii Trianonskej smluvy*, Bratislava: Slovenská odbočka čsl. národnej rady, 1929, p. 45.

was that in Czechoslovakia any identification with Hungarian national traditions or the Hungarian state was suppressed the Czechoslovak authorities as an anti-state activity. (Suffice it to mention the annual celebrations of the anniversary of the 1848-49 Revolution on 15 March or Saint Stephen's Day on 20 August).[30] It is fair to say that Czechoslovak citizens of Hungarian nationality in Slovakia became hostages of two state nationalisms. The outcome was that some people—mainly of a liberal or socialist orientation—strongly criticized the Horthy regime, while others—mainly conservatives—emphasized their dissatisfaction with the current situation in Czechoslovakia and focused on maintaining ties with Budapest.

A significant role in creating the image of the Horthy regime was played by the First Vienna Award (1938), which was perceived in Slovakia as a huge injustice and part of the 'Munich betrayal' of the Republic, which resulted in the tearing away of part of the 'national territory'. (Slovakia was already depicted by Slovaks as the land between the Tatra mountains and the river Danube.) Meanwhile, Czechoslovak, as well as Slovak, propaganda from 1938 to 1945 was, like the Hungarian, revisionist.[31] Besides, the Ľudák regime was heading towards a totalitarian system much more dynamically than Horthy's already not particularly democratic Hungary, as was shown, for example, in its use of political antisemitism. The disintegration of Czechoslovakia and its ceding of territories to Hungary have long been represented as a great injustice towards the Slovaks. Lipták, in his synthetic work, from the late 1960s, highlighted the disastrous consequences of these events:

> Anyone harbouring illusions was soon taught a hard lesson by the occupation regime that nothing would change regarding the old denationalizing aristocratic policies, including the suppression of national and democratic rights, so well known to the Slovaks from before 1918. And, even more, these were strengthened

---

30 Simon, A. 'Maďarská komunita, štátna moc a 15. marec v období prvej Československej republiky', in Macho, P. et al., *Revolúcia 1848/49 a historická pamäť*. Bratislava: Historický ústav SAV, 2012, pp. 95-107.

31 Janek, I. 'A Magyarországgal szembeni szlovák propaganda és revíziós elképzelések 1939-1941 között', *Limes* 1 (2010), pp. 25-40.

by the brutality of the Horthy dictatorship. The raging occupying army and the local chauvinists who immediately took the opportunity to take revenge for 'twenty years of injustice' in democratic Czechoslovakia made tens of thousands of people fleeing north [from occupied south Slovakia], without their property, often at night, grateful to escape with their lives. Amongst the Slovak public, the fate of the occupied part of Slovakia opened old wounds that had been almost healed by time and by a rather well-organized coexistence of both nations in the southern border region. The fate of the Ukrainians and the Slovaks in Hungary provoked an acute sense of national emergency.[32]

A parallel between the Hungarian gendarmes firing into the crowd in Černová, in 1907, and in Šurany, in 1938, also mentioned by Lipták, represents an important cornerstone of Slovak history retold as historical trauma.

Later, after the Second World War, collaboration with the Horthy regime became one of the strongest arguments in the process of the ethnic cleansing and homogenization of Slovakia. Other arguments included those about the past, which were used to promote a current solution. Contemporary politicians demanded a strict cleansing of society, and Hungarians were blamed for being content with no longer being part of democratic Czechoslovakia and joining fascist, feudal Hungary, as well as for being the main ally of Germany, actively participating in the denationalizing of Slovak towns and villages.[33]

A few years later, when the position of the Communists grew stronger in both Czechoslovakia and Hungary, an interesting phenomenon occurred. Czechoslovak historical argumentation was largely identical with the interpretations in the Hungarian historiography of the 1950s and 1960s — namely, that Horthy represented the interests of the aristocracy and the upper-middle classes and thus also represented a common enemy who was hiding the suppression and exploitation under his chauvinistic slogans. It is fair to say that in general the history of Hungary from 1919 to 1944 was largely neglected by scholars in the Communist era; indeed, only a couple of works

---

32 Lipták, L. *Slovensko v dvadsiatom storočí*. Bratislava: Kaligram, 2011, p. 148.
33 Zvara, J. *Maďarská menšina na Slovensku po roku 1945*. Bratislava: Epocha, 1969, p. 51.

were written on the topic, even though a Czechoslovak-Hungarian historians' committee was established in 1960.³⁴ Among the authors I would mention are Juraj Fabián, Juraj Purgat, Marta Romportlová, Juraj Kramer, and Martina Vietor. Information on Horthy's Hungary was limited mainly to customary class-based ideological formulae and information on the nationalist and non-democratic character of the country. These points of view were influenced by the works of Hungarians including Endre Kovács, György Ránki, Magda Ádám, and Lóránt Tilkovszky. One such point of view appears in a work by probably the most influential Slovak scholar researching this topic, Ladislav Deák, who, citing the work of Ránki and drawing on Hungarian diplomatic sources, — pointed out that 'Horthy's Hungary was one of the first states to understand the impact that Hitler's coming to power had for the future political development of Europe and the achievement of Hungarian revisionist aims.'³⁵

Contrary to the hitherto promoted ethnocentric model of the interpretation of relations, a new argument was disseminated. It claimed that minorities could be a mediator (using the bridge metaphor), and that the 'national question in the strict sense, as an antagonistic relationship between the members of the two nations, had been settled in the southern districts.' This was based on the Marxist-Leninist thesis that the end of antagonistic classes also meant the end of antagonism between majority and minority nations.³⁶ As it later turned out, this state of affairs, based on a shared ideology and the necessity to cooperate in the Soviet bloc, was ever fully established.

(Re)producing national fears in democratic dress

The discussions about the past which began after the Changes of 1989 were commonly known as the 'return of history', characterized by a reassessment of the past, together with a rise in nationalism in east-

---

[34] See also Matula, V. (ed.) *25 rokov československo-maďarskej historickej komisie*. Bratislava: Veda, 1985.
[35] Deák, L. *Zápas o strednú Európu 1933–1938*. Bratislava: Veda, 1986, p. 44.
[36] Ibid., p. 215.

central Europe.³⁷ Nationalism could provide the missing social cohesion, and it once again became an important legitimizing attribute in contemporary discussions, which was very much evident in the process of the deconstruction and reconstruction of the history of the region. But, as is persuasively argued by Rogers Brubaker, nationalism in the post-socialist countries is popular mainly because of the high level of its institutionalization before 1989.³⁸ Under the Communist regime, ethnic/national themes were merged with the dominant theory of class struggle, which appeared, for example, in narratives about the plebeian origin of the Slovaks, and in the metaphor about a 'thousand-year-old bee', which presented the image of the Slovaks as the anonymous movers of history.³⁹ Some ordinary, ideologically ambivalent citizens, in a seeming paradox, also depicted the 'nation' again as the key category. These people based their ideology on competing traditions motivated, for example by religion, which are captured in competing historical narratives. In the twentieth century, the ethnic principle in (re)constructing group identifications was continually being recast in different forms by the State as well as by various social agents. Consequently, in spite of a number of political ruptures, it is fair to see in the twentieth century a kind of continuity in the reproduction of

---

37 Rupnik, J. *Jiná Evropa*. Prague: Prostor, 1992, pp. 317–18, originally published in English as *The Other Europe: The Other Europe: The Rise and Fall of Communism in East-Central Europe*, New York: Pantheon, 1989; Johnson, O. V. 'Begetting & Remembering: Creating a Slovak Collective Memory in the Post-Communist World', in Kopeček, M. (ed.) *Past in the Making: Historical Revisionism in Central Europe after 1989*. Budapest and New York: CEU Press, 2008, pp. 129–143.

38 Brubaker, R. 'Nationhood and the National Question in the Soviet Union and Post-Soviet Eurasia: An Institutionalist Account', *Theory and Society* 23 (1994), pp. 47–78; Ferencová, M. 'Od ľudu k národu: Vytváranie národnej kultúry v etnografickej produkcii v socialistickom Československu a Maďarsku', *Etnologické rozpravy* 2 (2006), pp. 104–133.

39 For more on the representation of Slovak national history as plebeian, see Mináč, V. *Dúchanie do pahrieb*. Bratislava: Smena, 1970; Káša, P. 'Román Tisícročná včela ako slovenský obraz "fin de siècle"', *Acta Universitatis Palackianae Olomucensis* 5 (2007), pp. 155–160.

cultural depictions constituting national master narratives in the banality of nationalism, as Michael Billig pertinently notes.[40]

An important factor influencing this boom was the opportunity to focus more freely on topics that until recently had been avoided or were unmentionable. There was also an interest in strengthening the collective (Slovak) and state identity (the establishment of the Slovak Republic), and also in dealing with personal and family histories, illustrated by a popular saying: if you know where you come from, then you know who you are. This process was manifested by a great boom in writing about history, both by professional historians and others, where the leitmotif was often the 'digging up' of new truths or filling in the blank spots' in the mosaic of 'our' history.[41] There was an increased interest in the perception of history as a unique narrative of the history of the Slovaks and their current territory, while the Czechoslovak aspect, until recently emphasized, was pushed to the side or exchanged for a reinvented Hungarian past. And arguments that were popular from 1918 to 1945 once again became valid.

The new situation also brought greater diversification and polarization among historians, manifested in conflicts related to the character of 'national history' which were characterized by debates on terminology and content and corresponding, to a certain extent, to the situation in Slovak political life.

After 1989, several works on the Horthy regime and revisionist politics were published. Among their authors were Ladislav Deák,

---

[40] Billig analyses nationalism as a type of discourse which strengthens, through everyday practices, the feeling of solidarity. The reality of the nation is constantly represented and confirmed by a number of social categories, classifications, and practices, while being materialized in the form of concrete symbols. Billig developed his argumentation using the examples of money, flags, and sporting events. He has shown that it is the 'hidden character' of modern nationalism which makes it such a strong ideology. The fact that it remains non-problematic and is not researched makes it a strong basis of political movements. He has also pointed out the utilitarian usage of the term patriotism (for example, 'our' correct patriotism and 'their' wrong nationalism). Billig, M. *Banal Nationalism*. London, Thousand Oaks, and New Delhi: Sage, 1995.

[41] See Krekovičová, E. 'Identity a mýty novej štátnosti na Slovensku: Náčrt slovenskej mytológie na prelome tisícročia', *Slovenský národopis* 2 (2002), pp. 147–170.

Marian Hronský, and Dagmar Čierna-Lantayová, who were at that time already established professional historians of the topic. The approaches were based on a mixture of the kinds of argument established in the first Czechoslovak Republic and the Communist period. Sometimes there was a stronger presence of ethno-nationalist argumentation, which partly overlaid the class-based arguments that had until recently been strictly maintained.

An important role in this process was played by émigré historians, who now joined the debates in Slovak historiography. Consequently, an ultra-nationalist argument praising and defending the tradition of the Slovak State, a Nazi-satellite from 1939 to 1945, was established in the public discourse. Topics from the period 1938 to 1945 became very popular amongst both the general public and historians after the collapse of the Communist regime. The second relevant period in this context is the time of the establishment of the Czechoslovak Republic. Both of these topics are also connected with the depictions of Horthy and his regime; the former is characterized by its interpretation forming a negative, even traumatic depiction of Slovak-Hungarian relations in the public discourse. Here one should mention the effective functioning social and cultural guidelines that are adopted by people in the courses of their lives and influence their perceptions, opinions, and actions. It cannot be different in the homogenous institutionalized system of education, where schools often offer only the 'valid' (national) truths. In this sense, many shortcomings have been highlighted in several instructive analyses of the arguments used in history textbooks.[42]

---

42 For recent works, see Findor, A. *Začiatky národných dejín*. Bratislava: Kalligram, 2011; Otčenášová, S. *Schválená minulosť: Kolektívna identita v československých a slovenských učebniciach dejepisu*. Košice: FF UPJŠ, 2010; Pekar, M. 'Maďari a maďarská menšina na Slovensku v slovenských učebniciach dejepisu po roku 1989', in Šutaj, Š., et al. *Maďarská menšina na Slovensku po roku 1989*. Prešov: Universum, 2008, pp. 184–99; Sallai, G., Szarka, L. 'Önkép és kontextus: Magyarország és a magyarság történelme a szlovák történetírásban a 20. század végén', *Regio* 2 (2000), pp. 71–107; Vajda, B. 'Magyarságkép a csehszlovákiai történelem tankönyvekben 1950–1993', in Hornyák, Á, Vitári, Z. (eds.) *A magyarságkép a közép-európai tankönyvekben a 20. században*. Pécs: Pécsi

Even today, the Vienna Award is depicted in the Slovak national narrative as an act of injustice against the nation, as the occupation of the south of Slovakia and the re-institution of 'subjugation' under Hungarian rule for part of the Slovak population. By contrast, in the Hungarian discourse, it is represented as an act of justice, an attempt at a fairer approach to the ethnic question, which is still a relevant political question.[43] Although there is a new social environment today, characterized by a plurality of opinions, and that more is said about Horthy and his regime, while incorporating different points of view, there has been no marked change in the established representation, which has actually existed continuously since 1918. This is also illustrated, for example, by the following words: 'The Hungarian nobility, Hungarian authorities, and the Magyarones continued to hold power in the country. They organized mass activities to undermine the new state.'[44] It is fair to conclude that a unified and continual image has been repeatedly (re)produced by different social agents. Securing and maintaining its legitimization still provides symbolic as well as political capital. Most often it is the aristocratic character of the regime that is mentioned in this context. This allows for a traumatic linking of the narrative about Magyarization, emphasizing the differences in the cultural and emotional dispositions of the 'Slovaks' and the 'Hungarians'. Another important part of the narrative is the focus on the revisionist activities of the contemporary elites, a topic intensively employed in politics from 1918 to the present. A good example of this phenomenon is the figure of Esterházy, with which this article opened.

Tudományegyetem, 2009, pp. 259–82; Kollai, I. 'A szlovák középiskolai történelemtankönyvek összehasonlító jellegű bemutatása', in Hornyák, Á., Vitári, Z. (eds.) *A magyarságkép a közép-európai tankönyvekben a 20. században*, Pécs: Pécsi Tudományegyetem, 2009, pp. 283–319.

43 See also Pekár, M. 'Neznalosť a konfrontácia: Dve podoby pozostatkov kontroverzných slovensko-maďarských vzťahov 1939–1945', in Šutaj, Š. (ed.) *Národ a národnosti na Slovensku v transformujúcej sa spoločnosti – vzťahy a konflikty*. Prešov: Universum, 2005, pp. 127–31; Michela, M. 'Okupácia, či návrat?', *História: revue o dejinách spoločnosti*, 6 (2007), pp. 42–43.

44 Ferko, M., Marsina, R., Deák, L. *Starý národ – mladý štát*. Bratislava: Litera, 1994, p. 92.

The key to understanding the relative stability of the image of the Horthy regime and of the regent himself in the Slovak discourse is the thesis that Slovaks were granted freedom after 1918. This factor is also present in Deák's argument:

> The Hungarian authorities did not wish to give up their rule over this region. In 1918–20, the Slovak politicians rejected the autonomy offered by Budapest, as it not only came too late, but after bad experiences with Hungary, Hungarian promises did not have any value for Slovaks. This meant that by the establishment of the Czechoslovak state, the Slovaks ended forever the chapter of their Hungarian past.[45]

All activity that has aimed to change the status quo and restore Hungarian rule is perceived as an attack on the national community and its independence. In this context, it is also reasonable to understand the Slovak critical reactions to recent attempts at restoring or rehabilitating the Horthy cult in Hungary. As has often been shown, in Slovakia little is actually known about Horthy and his era, but his adoration leads Slovaks to feel they are endangered.

---

45   Ibid., p. 92

Changing Images of Miklós Horthy

Ignác Romsics[1]
Eötvös Loránd University

Abstract: The paper undertakes a survey of conflicting opinions on Miklós Horthy, the Regent of Hungary from 1920 to 1944. Starting with the 1920s, when Horthy first entered Hungarian politics, the paper follows his political career, examining salient interpretations that arose with changing internal and external political affairs. Furthermore, the paper scrutinizes the transformation of the Regent's image during the Socialist era as well as after the revolution 1989 and his changing appeal to the public.

Miklós Horthy, Regent of Hungary from 1920 to 1944, has been a subject of heated debates ever since he entered the counterrevolutionary government in Szeged in 1919, and started organizing the National Army as part of the efforts to overthrow the Hungarian Soviet Republic. From the initial reactions to his activity, the early 1920s saw three distinct images of Horthy emerge: the savior of the country, the murderer with blood on his hands, and the traitor to the throne, who stripped the Habsburgs of their title and right to the crown of Hungary.

Horthy's image as a savior was largely received in groups of the propertied classes and certain elite groups, the strata of society whose assets had been nationalized in the Hungarian Soviet Republic, which lasted from 21 March to 1 August 1919. In addition, he also had a fair number of supporters from the lower middle classes, notably citizens who had come into conflict, for one reason or another, with Communist rule. For them, the propaganda materials which interpreted the Soviet of 1919 as a national catastrophe equal to the defeat of the medieval Hungarian kingdom at the hands of the Mongols in 1241 and by Ottoman arms in 1526, seemed real and acceptable. Horthy himself was likened to the greatest figures of Hungarian history, in particular to Árpád, who led the conquest of the Carpathian basin,

---

1   Email: romsicsi@vnet.hu.

Saint Stephen, founder of the medieval Christian kingdom of Hungary, and Béla IV, re-builder of the country after the Mongol invasion. Further parallels included János and Mátyás Hunyadi, who distinguished themselves in the Ottoman wars, and leaders of anti-Habsburg independence movements such as Ferenc Rákóczi II and Lajos Kossuth. There can be little doubt that Horthy himself sought to reinforce his image as savior. He depicted himself as a leader above party politics and taking his inspiration from the national idea and Christian morality, most famously so in his speech of 16 November 1919, on his entry to the capital. This image was also conveyed by various kinds of printed matter, most famously the poster that shows strong arms holding the wheel of a ship on a stormy red sea. (In a green field with bold white print, the poster says merely 'Horthy!')[2]

In parallel to the conscious image-building around Horthy as the savior of the country, images promoted by his opposition, both democratic-progressive and Communist, crystallized around the theme of the savage murderer. This pattern of representation was rooted in the memory of the 1919–20 reprisals which targeted both revolutionaries and Jewish citizens who were not involved in the revolution. The 'White Terror' cost the lives of many people: even moderate estimates put the number of victims at more than 1,000. No document has ever been produced to show Horthy as having issued a direct order to commit the atrocities, especially executions. Yet it cannot reasonably be doubted that he had been aware of the murders and showed a great degree of leniency towards the perpetrators — officers of his very own National Army. It was therefore hardly surprising that political opponents capitalized on his involvement in the criminal acts of the counterrevolutionary period, even if the precise extent of his personal responsibility for these crimes was unclear.

This veritable counter-cult, constructed in opposition to the cult of the nation's savior, was first promoted by left-wing Budapest dailies. Articles with titles like 'The Horrible Crimes of the Horthy Boys',

---

2   Pilch, J. *Horthy Miklós*. Budapest: Athenaeum, 1928, pp. 241–86, 358–92.

'The Prison-guard of the White Terrorists of Siófok', 'The Persecution of Jews in Transdanubia', Prison Hell', and 'The Bloodbath of Kecskemét' barely required one to read the article in order to get the intended message. Space for such criticism, however, became very limited after Horthy's election to the office of Regent in March 1920. Afterwards, the counter-cult lived on primarily in periodicals and memoirs published abroad by exiled leaders of the 1918–19 revolutions. According to the Social Democrat and one-time People's Commissar for War, Vilmos Böhm,

> the rampage of Horthy's warbands will forever rank among the darkest pages of Hungarian history. The number of murdered people was in the hundreds. [...] Shooting unarmed citizens, hanging, castration, dismemberment, blinding, rape, the murder of children—these were the military actions of the 'glorious' Transdanubian campaign.

In a reversal of received pro-Horthy imagery, Böhm summed up the activities of the National Army neither as the saving of the country, nor as the founding of the realm, but as a second Ottoman invasion.[3]

Oszkár Jászi, a one-time minister of Mihály Károlyi's October government, also concentrated his criticism of Horthy and his regime on the war crimes committed by his troops. The Horthy dictatorship, he argued, may have raised Christianity to state doctrine, but since his rise to power Hungarian public life has been 'symbolized by the gallows and torture'.[4]

Elite groups loyal to the Habsburgs, including parts of the aristocratic and bourgeois upper classes, the Roman Catholic high clergy and some officer groups, as well as segments of the middle classes, held a similarly negative image of Horthy—although for quite different reasons. Their dismay sprang from Horthy's checking Charles's attempts to return to the throne in 1921, followed by the formal dethronement of the Habsburgs on 6 November. When Horthy had been

---

3   Böhm, V. *Két forradalom tüzében*. Munich: Verlaf für Kulturpolitik. 1923, pp. 477–79.
4   Jászi, O. *Magyar kálvária – magyar föltámadás*. Budapest: Magyar Hírlap Könyvek, 1989, pp. 152–61.

elected Regent (or, more accurately, Royal Governor), these pro-Habsburg groups viewed the situation as temporary, to be replaced by the 'legal' rule of the crowned king upon his expected return. Once the Treaty of Trianon had been signed on 4 June and then ratified in November 1920, many felt that the time for restoration had come. In Charles's two attempts to retake the throne, Horthy did in fact declare him the legitimate ruler of Hungary. At the same time, however, he insisted that the international environment did not permit an immediate restoration. In March 1921, he used words alone to convince Charles to leave the country, but in October he used armed force to expel the king. Following the failure of Charles's second attempt, Horthy also conceded to the dethronement act and to the short-term imprisonment of a few leading royalists.

The Regent's behavior in 1921 was never forgiven by the royalist camp. In such circles, he was routinely referred to as an upstart and a worthless man whose word meant nothing. Socially this entailed that some sections of the traditional elite sought to avoid contact with Horthy. They found numerous ways to express their contempt for him and their devotion to Charles, to his wife, and, after the king's death in 1922, to his son Otto. These groups, however, lacked the means to launch a propaganda campaign against the Regent, and their influence on public opinion decreased year by year.

As we have seen, it was hard in the early 1920s to predict which of the competing images of Horthy would emerge as the dominant one. Once the consolidation of the new regime got underway after 1921, this matter was settled within a few years. Though the negative images shaped by the leftists and the progressives, as well as that of the royalists, did persist, they rapidly lost their relevance for the greater part of society. The strong military man who had saved the country was the image projected by the whole state apparatus and was increasingly accepted. This was especially true amongst younger Hungarians who had little personal experience of the past era and relied largely on information gained during their schooling. Their vision of the events of 1919–21 was based mostly on the official interpretation.

The peak of the Horthy cult, however, came much later, in 1938-43. In these six years, according to the catalogue of the Hungarian National Library, 28 Hungarian and foreign-language volumes dedicated to Horthy appeared in print. This is especially significant in light of the output of the preceding 18 years: from 1920 to 1937 only 17 such books had been published. The series of books of the late 1930s began with the biography by the journalist Baroness Lily Doblhoff. The 300-page work, timed to coincide with the Regent's 70th birthday, was the first to provide a detailed account of Horthy's family and his childhood, his service in the Austro-Hungarian navy and at court, as well as the years of the World War and the events that followed. Though Doblhoff does address the alleged 'overreactions' of the National Army in her book, she merely states that 'a civil war was underway in the country, and these private acts of vengeance are inseparable from civil wars.' Also, she intimates that random acts of violence were necessary to re-establish order and the rule of law. Concerning the other chief accusation directed against Horthy, Doblhoff leaves no doubt as to her belief that Horthy made the right choice in resisting Charles's attempts to retake the throne. She concedes that 'both parties were led by their patriotism', but only Horthy had a realistic perception of the situation.[5]

In the same year, a huge genealogical synthesis, almost 600-pages strong, was also published. It attempted to prove that the Horthy family had been raised to the nobility long before the seventeenth century (as it had been thought), linking the Regent's ancestry to the 'world of the free Seklers' and also succeeding in positing him as a descendant of the House of Árpád.[6] This perfectly unfounded statement was aimed at providing an ancestry for Horthy that matched the already accepted greatness of his deeds, an undertaking which may

---

5 Doblhoff, L. *Horthy Miklós*. Budapest: Athenaeum,1939, pp. 243–44, 283–84, 290, 321.
6 Sándor, J. *Vitéz nagybányai Horthy Miklós, Magyarország kormányzója és népe az Árpádházi királyok vérében*. Budapest: Szerző, 1938, pp. 5–13.

have been motivated by the desire to furnish the Regent with an appropriate lineage for the founding of a dynasty by making his position hereditary.

1940 saw another anniversary, that of Horthy's election to the regency in 1920. Of the numerous publications from this period, one multi-authored volume richly illustrated with photographs stands out. It was edited and introduced by Ferenc Herczeg, the foremost conservative writer of the day. He conjured up highly ritualized memories of the turbulent years 1918-19, when 'the flood of corruption had infected the souls.' The memory of this most unhappy period was contrasted with the march into Budapest on 16 November 1919, which he likened to the return of the Hun army of Prince Csaba, Attila's youngest son, descending from the heavens to rescue the Seklers—a story captured in a popular ancient folk myth known to most Hungarians. 'When Prince Csaba and his horsemen rode down from the Milky Way,' Herczeg writes, 'they came to help the orphaned country.' Herczeg goes on to describe the rebuilding of the country in similar terms: 'As it had been after the Mongols and after the Ottomans, the miraculous regenerative powers of Saint Stephen's realm triumphed in the end'. In the present, he saw the Regent as the very core of the 'central power around which the thousand-year-old machinery of the state revolves'. In fact, he uses the metaphor of a 'diamond axis' to describe Horthy's role in the machinery.

> The working man sees in him the greatest guardian of law and order. The patriot has placed his hopes in him as the fulfillment of the nation's desires. Every soldier in the army remains loyal to him unto death. Even the faithless have no choice but to have faith in him; even the inconstant have to find constancy in his person. Without him, the masses of Hungarians can imagine neither their present nor their future.[7]

Beyond the two anniversaries, a further cause of the Horthy cult reaching its peak in the later 1930s and early 1940s was the partial success of Hungarian revisionism. The reoccupation of southern Slovakia

---

7   *Horthy Miklós*. Budapest: Singer es Wolfner, 1939, pp. 7–11.

and Northern Transylvania following the two Vienna Awards, in 1938 and 1940, were both commemorated in feature-length documentary films, while the newspapers published ecstatic reports on the return of historically significant townships. The central figure in all of the reports was Miklós Horthy. On a white horse, reminiscent of the one he rode in 1919, Horthy often chose to lead the parade of Hungarian troops into the city; at other times he looked on from a reviewing stand as the troops paraded by. In the process of reoccupation, he delivered scores of short speeches and listened to many, many more from speakers often in tears. Accordingly, Horthy the savior of the nation received a further epithet, that of the 'enlarger of the country'.

Attested by scores of historical examples, living persons who became subjects of a cult tend increasingly to believe they truly are great and endowed with exceptional abilities. Well-known examples include twentieth-century dictators such as Hitler, Mussolini, and Stalin. Horthy, for one, never developed ambitions like the former three — he was too much the nineteenth-century traditionalist and conservative for that. But he did undertake to expand his powers, and did develop an ambition to prepare the ground for a family succession upon his eventual demise. The founding of a dynasty was also suggested by members of his personal network. Such plans met with most opposition, as one might expect, from royalists attached to the Habsburgs — a small platform but not without considerable influence. Similarly, the extreme right rejected such plans, though for different reasons: they found the Regent and his family too embedded in the conservative tradition of anglophilia. The end result of these opposing preferences was the election of Horthy's elder son to the post of vice-regent in February 1942. Just how significant a step this would become in the carrying out of Horthy's plans we shall never know, since the fighter pilot István Horthy died shortly thereafter in a plane crash on the Russian front. His death, however, led to renewed debates about succession. It was proposed, that the two-year-old son of the late vice-regent should be either crowned or made vice-regent, cementing the power of the Horthy family over Hungarian politics. Very important groups of the social and political elite, however, opposed all such designs. Royalists and conservatives pushed to have the whole matter swept aside. Ideally, they envisioned offering the crown to Otto of Austria after the war, or, alternatively, to a member of Italy's royal dynasty. They inclined, only as a third option, to consider the Regent and his family on the throne.[8]

Hungary's place in the Soviet orbit after the Second World War made all dynastic plans illusory. Horthy had resigned his post under German pressure on 16 October 1944, and handed over power to the leader of the Hungarian extreme right, Ferenc Szálasi. The German authorities had interned him in Bavaria, where, even after the war, he continued to live until 1949. He moved from there to Portugal as a permanent exile until his death in February 1957.

While Horthy was living the quiet life of a political exile without any concrete ambitions for the future, opinions about his role had undergone a total change at home. With Soviet support, the very forces that had branded him a murderer in 1919 and 1920 came to power in 1944–45. They had led the resistance to the canonical image promoted by the political system in the interwar period. The Regent's role in the Second World War only provided them with more ammunition in their quest against Horthy. Social groups under the influence of their education prior to 1945 did not abandon their attachment to the figure of the Regent, a phenomenon that propelled the new holders of power to engage in a vigorous, systematic effort to construct a counter-cult. In the counter-language of the new régime, the Horthy era became the nadir of Hungarian history, a position which entailed stripping the Regent's memory of any positive features and accomplishments.

The first purportedly Marxist synthesis of Hungarian history, titled the *History of the Hungarian People* and published in 1951 (a book that doubled as a textbook for secondary schools, as well), presented the narrative of the counter-cult in its definitive version. Accordingly,

---

8   Szinai, M., Szűcs, L. (eds), *Horthy Miklós titkos iratai*. Budapest: Kossuth, 1972, pp. 327–37; Lehman, H. G. *Der Reichsverweser-Stellvertreter*, Mainz: Hase 81 Koehler, 1975, pp. 48–49, 55, 92.

the National Army of 1919 was a 'band of mass murderers', which had emerged from the 'reactionary officers, kulaks and the scum of society' that Austria-Hungary had left behind. Its leader Miklós Horthy, a "one-time lackey to the Habsburgs", responsible for "putting down the rebellion of navy men at Cattaro", spoke only a "broken Hungarian", and was known for "his hatred of workers and his animosity towards the Soviets". In this reading, responsibility for the 'terrible deeds committed during the White Terror' was borne collectively by Horthy, his clique, and entente-imperialism. The political system he shaped was described as 'fascist from its inception', and his role in it as that of a 'bloody military dictator', responsible, among other things, for the attack on Yugoslavia in 1941, the invasion of the Soviet Union, accepting the German occupation without having put up a fight, the deportation of the provincial Jewish population, the failure of the attempt to break with the Axis in October 1944, and for having legitimized the seizure of power by Szálasi and his Arrow Cross men.[9]

The re-professionalization of Hungarian historiography that had unfolded after 1956 failed to offer a more nuanced interpretation of Horthy's person in the short run. György Ránki, a prominent figure in this process, perpetuated the schematic image in his synthesis of the interwar period, published in 1964. A relatively more balanced assessment of Horthy and his era did not appear until the mid-1970s. The eighth volume of a multi-volume synthesis of Hungarian history of the interwar period was published in 1976. This account omitted most of the previously customary accusations and overstatements. A short portrait of Horthy was also included in the book authored by Zsuzsa L. Nagy. She argues that Horthy rose to prominence in 1919 because he was a well-known soldier, who impressed the officers in Szeged with his 'determined countenance'. His election to the Regency was, Nagy went on to explain, determined by the relative power relationships in about 1920, including the support, domestically, of officer

---

9   Heckenast, G., Incze, M., Karácsonyi, B., Lukács, L., Spira, Gy. *A magyar nép története*, Budapest: Művelt Nép, 1953, pp. 552–58, 638.

groups and, internationally, of Great Britain.' According to her, Horthy managed to hold on to power for a quarter of a century primarily because 'as Regent [...] he distanced himself from extreme rightist officers [...] and adopted the general views and interests of the ruling class.' Other authors argue convincingly in their chapters that Horthy did in fact expressly consent to the disarming of rampaging officer detachments, that Charles's attempts to reclaim the Hungarian throne were doomed to fail and Horthy very much had the support of the entente powers in standing up to Charles. Even his role in the Second World War receives a more nuanced treatment here. Gyula Juhász, for instance, mentions in the same volume that Hungarian participation in the war against Yugoslavia was not based upon a decision made by Horthy but followed the agreement of the Supreme Defence Council and in accordance with a proposal by Prime Minister Pál Teleki. He also notes the Regent's opposition to, and outrage over, the German occupation of March 1944, which he eventually accepted, allegedly, only after heated debates and much soul-searching. Finally, he notes that after coming out of the passivity with which he had tolerated the deportation of Hungarian Jews from the provinces, Horthy intervened and 'all but stopped the deportations' in early July 1944, saving the Jews of Budapest.[10]

This professionalization of historiography has had a beneficial effect on textbook images of Horthy as well. Here, however, the shift to a more nuanced interpretation was slower and more fragmented. The new history textbook for Hungarian grammar schools, published in 1982, still had the old topoi about him. It was highlighted that Horthy had been the one to 'put down the Cattaro navy rebellion, wading in blood'. And once again the textbook claimed that Horthy had been forced to relearn Hungarian in 1919, because 'during his years of service in the joint Imperial and Royal forces he had all but forgotten his mother tongue.'[11] On the same note, it has to be mentioned that while

---

10 Ránki, G. (ed.) *Magyarország története 1918–1919, 1919–1945.* Budapest: Akadémiai, 1976, pp. 305, 415–16, 431, 434, 1040, 1152–53, 1162, 1188.
11 Szirtes Jóvérné, Á. *Történelem IV.* Budapest: Tankönyvkiadó, 1982, p. 84.

historians increasingly held the view that the Horthy regime had been neither a fascist system of government nor a clear-cut dictatorship, the secretary for ideology of the Central Committee of the Hungarian Socialist Workers' Party warned, as late as 1986, that 'the fascist character of the Horthy regime', as well as 'the sometimes hidden, sometimes overt dictatorship' were indisputable facts, which yield, taken together, 'a reactionary politics [...] for which there can be no excuse and which does not deserve sympathetic interpretation'.[12]

The change of system in 1989 and 1990 brought about, among other things, a rapid and thorough loss of legitimacy for the old historical and political canon. The newly gained freedom in the interpretation of the national past, including the recent past, made a series of reassessments unavoidable. The wave of revisionist history reached the memory of Horthy with the Hungarian-language publication, in 1990, of Péter Gosztonyi's 1973 German-language biography of the Regent. Including post-1945 Hungarian historiography, Gosztonyi was right to emphasize that during the regency, a conservative establishment had ruled the country and 'corruption and abuse of power' were alien to Horthy's thinking. Among other things, 'he did not consider his place in the state and the establishment — as circumscribed by legislation — a means to enrich himself'. He also emphasized 'the numerous signs' of Horthy's dislike of Hitler. While he was 'an accomplice' in the deportation of Hungarian Jews from the provinces in spring 1944, he did 'order further deportations halted' in the wake of domestic and international protest. One may even argue that there is truth to observations such as the one explaining the White Terror as a 'reaction to the terror perpetrated by the Hungarian Soviet Republic'. On the other hand, Gosztonyi's claim that the source of the White Terror 'was not the National Army' is very difficult to support — unlike its opposite, for which historical evidence abounds. Other arguments, for instance, that the reprisals were not initiated or ordered by Horthy personally, do little more than avoid the question of his responsibility.

---

12   Berecz, J. 'Gondolatok a nemzet és a munkásmozgalom történetéről', *Társadalmi Szemle* 6, 1986, pp. 3–13.

It should therefore also be evident by now that talking about 'Horthy's lack of personal ambitions of power' also requires some stretch of the imagination. Similarly, the view that 'the Regent was respected and trusted by the greater part of society' is based on selective evidence. In sum, Gosztonyi's legitimate attempt to counter the negative image of Horthy which is present in much Hungarian journalism and writing on history included some evasion of problematic points. This ultimately undermined his endeavour. Willingly or unwillingly, the book idealizes the image of Horthy.[13]

In the continuing historical and political discourse about the role of Horthy and the necessary reassessment of his actions, his reburial in 1993 marks a clear and predictable juncture. The many books, articles, and interviews which were published in this period reflect the right-of-centre political parties' efforts to rehabilitate Horthy the man and his politics. One richly illustrated publication aimed to cleanse his image 'of the layers of lies' smeared on it 'by the propaganda and the establishment history of the regime that sought to banish him'.[14]

Of all the opinions heard in 1993, the most important were probably those in the long interview given by Prime Minister József Antall. Attesting to the relatively rapid consolidation of the 'rehabilitating' discourse about Horthy, Antall echoed much the same opinions that Gosztonyi had expressed in his book. Accordingly, he referred to the White Terror as a reaction to Bolshevik acts of cruelty, which was neither instigated nor tolerated, but halted, at least in part, by Horthy. There was no alternative to his taking the office of Regent, since, according to Antall, 'the republic of the October revolution [...] was simply unfit to continue'. The restoration plans entertained by Charles IV were equally unrealistic. In such a situation, the Prime Minister concluded, 'the regency of Miklós Horthy became the only option that

---

13 Gosztonyi, P. *A kormányzó, Horthy Miklós*. Budapest: Téka, 1990, pp. 30, 149, 161–64.
14 Pusztaszeri, L. 'Egy élet Magyarországért' in Vuray G. (ed.) *Vitéz nagybányai Horthy Miklós élete képekben*. Budapest: Faktor, 1993.

promised stability for the country in both domestic and foreign policy.' He also added that the Regent 'never trespassed against the principles of constitutionalism and the order of the constitutional monarchy'. Moreover, he 'was strongly opposed to both Bolshevism and Nazism'. While many of these claims are debatable, Antall also made some remarks that can only be described as thoroughly unfounded. He argued, for instance, that 'Horthy's antisemitism simply did not exist after the First World War' and that Horthy had opposed Hungarian entry into the war in 1941. Antall made sure to emphasize Hungarian moral culpability for the deportations of the Jews after the German occupation of 1944. But he seemed to exclude Horthy from the circle of culprits, arguing that as soon as he 'secured for himself the smallest room for manoeuvre [...] he saved the Jews of Budapest'. Concluding his narrative of Horthy, Antall labeled him a 'Hungarian patriot', and voiced his conviction that it was the task of politicians 'to accord him his rightful place in national history and the mind of the people'.[15] The final sentence of the Prime Minister's interview clearly expresses the desire on the part of resurgent Hungarian conservatism and right-of-centre thinking in general to break in all respects with the legacy of the Communist past, from 1949 to 1989, and, in doing so, simultaneously to reach back to the interwar years, integrating its memory and its leaders into the historical canon of national identity.

With his rediscovery in about 1993, Horthy became part of a debate on identity politics, one that has not subsided for 15 years. During this time, Thomas Sakmyster's biography of Horthy, originally published in 1994, appeared in Hungarian translation as well. The professional political biography spanning the years from 1919 to 1944 paints a portrait of Horthy which is in keeping with that of official Hungarian historiography in the 1970s and 1980s.[16] Gábor Bencsik's large journalistic analysis of Horthy, another book from 2001, reiterated many of the same opinions about Horthy. The author avoided both

---

15   'Interjú Horthy temetéséről Antall József miniszterelnökkel', *HIR-LAP melléklete*, Sept. 1993, pp. 1–8.
16   Sakmyster, *T. Admirális fehér lovon*. Budapest: Helikon, 2001.

the revisionism of Communist authors and the apologist twists employed by sympathizers. If anywhere, Bencsik was perhaps a little too appreciative in his evaluation of Horthy's actions as commander-in-chief, yet in other aspects he retained a fortunate balance in his narrative.[17]

The interest in these books was, however, dwarfed by the success of the memoirs of Countess Ilona Edelsheim Gyulai, the widow of Vice-Regent István Horthy. The first volume of the memoirs was published in 2000, with the second, and final, volume following in 2007. As she made clear in the introduction, her aim was to present 'the truth' to Horthy's 'descendants' and the general public, so that they 'need not ponder what grains of truth there may be in the sea of Nazi and Communist slanders published over the years'. Of the episodes in Horthy's life which are routinely addressed by historical narratives, the memoirs barely address the pivotal years 1918-19. Practically the only key statement about this period concerns a parallel the author draws between the turbulent period after the Great War and the change of régime in 1989. In this, she holds Horthy's actions up as an example for of our generation: 'He brought new energy into the scheme of things — something someone called a blood transfusion. Such energies are needed today as well.'

Taking up the detailed course of events after 1930, the only really controversial time the Countess discussed in detail was 1944. She chose, however, to focus only on one, admittedly crucial, series of events: the tragedy of Jewish Hungarians. Her publication makes it clear that in her view, Horthy bears little responsibility for the fate of the Jews living in the provinces. Her second key statement is that Horthy's decision to halt the deportations to Auschwitz, thereby saving the lives of many Budapest Jews, was made not under foreign and domestic pressures, but in response to having received the so-called 'Auschwitz Protocols' (the Vrba-Wetzler report) on 3 July 1944. The gist of this argument is that once the Regent found out that Jews were

---

17 Bencsik, G. *Horthy Miklós: A kormányzó és kora*. Budapest: Magyar Mercurius, 2001.

being exterminated rather than being taken to labour camps, he took action to try and prevent this.[18]

These extremely successful memoirs do not, however, represent the last chapter in the continuing story of symbolic politics and memorialization of Horthy. Just as the second volume of the Edelsheim memoirs hit the streets in spring 2007, a new Horthy documentary, directed by Gábor Koltay, opened in a few cinemas. Of all the attempts to revive the cult of Horthy which was characteristic of the interwar period, this film stands out as the most obvious example of glorification. As several critics were quick to point out, the documentary is not merely apologetic, but 'makes false statements that go beyond mere apology'.[19]

The most recent chapter of identity politics involving Horthy concerns various plans to secure representation for his figure in public spaces. The apropos for these propositions was provided by the fiftieth anniversary of the Regent's death in February 2007. One such initiative was launched by the president of the fringe party Movement for a Better Hungary, Gábor Vona, who, as he put it, saw the time was right to rehabilitate the Regent, 'who is represented in public opinion, politics, and the teaching of history in equally negative colours'. This could be remedied, he suggested, by removing the statue of Mihály Károlyi, leader of the October 1918 revolution from Kossuth Square, by the Parliament building, and erecting one of Horthy in its place.[20]

A civic initiative and private individuals proposed a similar commemoration of Horthy in Szeged at virtually the same time. In acknowledgment of the Regent's deeds, this would have entailed erecting his statue in the city square, next to those of István Széchenyi and Ferenc Deák, two nineteenth-century moderate progressives. The socialist mayor of the town reacted dismissively (as might be expected),

---

18   Edelsheim Gyulai, I. *Becsület és kötelesség*, vol. 1. Budapest: Európa, 2006, pp. 257–64, Vol. 2. Budapest: Európa, 2007, p. 449.
19   Ungváry, K. 'A Kormányzó 139 éves', *Népszabadság*, 12 February 2007
20   Online: www.hirextra.hu/hirek/article.php?menu-id=1962

stating that as long as he was 'the mayor of Szeged, neither János Kádár, nor Miklós Horthy will receive a statue.'[21] The debate that flared up in Szeged reflects the trauma of Hungarian collective memory and the lines of division which run through this memory.

At the same time, if a summary of the current situation is to be made, it has to be stated first and foremost that the persistent attempts since 1989 to reinstate the cult of Horthy in some form have failed to convince most Hungarians. According to Median, a leading polling agency, Miklós Horthy ranked third on the list of the most negatively viewed twentieth-century public figures in 1999. He scored 20 per cent on the cumulative index, preceded by Mátyás Rákosi (52 per cent) and Ferenc Szálasi (35 per cent), while János Kádár came in fourth with 12 per cent. When interviewed, barely more than five per cent of the representative sample placed Horthy among the three most positively viewed historical personalities of the century.[22] Opinions may have shifted slightly since 1999, but a fundamental change is unlikely to have taken place. This seems to be confirmed by the non-representative survey of Hungary's largest popular historical periodical, *Rubicon*. According to *Rubicon* readers, Rákosi and Szálasi are the least savoury figures in Hungarian history, while Horthy ranked fifth on the negative list – due to János Kádár and Béla Kun taking third and fourth place, respectively. Horthy failed, however, to make it into the top ten of most positively viewed historical figures.[23] All this suggests that it is only a small, if vocal, minority that think of Horthy as a great patriot and statesman, while their numbers are far exceeded by those who hold a highly negative opinion of the man.

---

21   Kő, A. 'Horthy Miklós szobra Szegeden?', *Magyar Nemzet*, 18 June 2007
22   Romsics, I. 'Történelem és emlékezet', *Heti Világgazdaság*, 10 July 1999, pp. 66–69.
23   'Szavaztak az olvasók', *Rubicon* 10, 2006, pp. 4–5.

Edvard Beneš and His Image: 'Hero or Villain'?

Kristina Kaiserová[1]
Jan Evangelista Purkyně University in Ústí nad Labem

After his mentor Tomáš Garrigue Masaryk, Edvard Beneš (1884–1948) is indisputably the most important politician of the newly established Czechoslovak Republic.[2] That is why, leaving aside the Slovak question, which is another matter altogether, the national minorities of the country see him in a negative light. Since Beneš had pushed for a Czechoslovak state within the historical borders of the Bohemian Lands and Slovakia, according to military and economic strategies that had to do with Poland, and even more with Hungary, Hungarian historians today view him very critically.

László Gulyás, who since the late 1980s has researched Beneš and questioned his role in central Europe, views him negatively in almost every respect. From the Hungarian angle, Gulyás is critical because of Beneš's role in dismantling historical Hungary, redrawing the borders under the Treaty of Trianon, the treatment of the Hungarian minority that found themselves in the new Czechoslovak state, and their resettlement after the Second World War. Gulyás states that Beneš would top the list of politicians who were successful in anti-Hungarian policies.

Another work, published almost at the same time as the Gulyás book, has a title that translates as 'Who was Edvard Beneš really?'[3] Its author, Magda Ádám, has long been researching the history of the diplomacy of central Europe in the first half of the twentieth century. In

---

1 E-mail: kaiserova@albis-int.cz.
2 For his inspiring assistance, I am very grateful to Petr Králíček, Mgr., and, for her providing me with material on Hungarian historiography, I thank PhDr. Eva Irmanová, Ph.D.
3 Ádám, M. *Ki volt valójában Edvard Beneš?* Budapest: Gondolat Kiadó, 2009.

her pursuit of a clear picture of Beneš's role in the events, the conclusion that she reaches about the initial stage of his career has provided a model for many other scholars' assessments. She claims:

> Beneš's role in the dismantling of the Monarchy has in many respects been overemphasized. His opponents made him responsible for destroying the Monarchy and 'Balkanizing' the region; his supporters have given him all the credit for the creation of an independent Czechoslovakia. This reflects only part of the reality. Though he undeniably influenced developments, Beneš was still mostly powerless against the Great Powers. He was successful only when there was a consensus of his opinion with them. In their decision-making about the Monarchy, the decisive role was played only by power and strategic interests.

Most attention has been paid to the period 1938–1948. Especially in the last twenty years, a number of works have been published by Czechs, which relate to Beneš directly or indirectly.[4] Some of them of course remain overly subjective, despite good intentions to achieve objectivity.[5]

Polish, German, and Austrian historians have also done a good deal of work on Beneš, often presenting their research at conferences.[6] A certain 'risk' in the perception of his character arises in works that seek to compare him with Tomáš G. Masaryk. Such is the case of Ferdinand Seibt, who, to put it simply, compared the depth of Masaryk's

---

4 Especially Zeman, Z. *Edvard Beneš – politický životopis*. Prague: Mladá fronta, 2009, and Dejmek, J. *Edvard Beneš: Politická biografie českého demokrata*. Prague: Karolinum, 2006 and 2008.
5 For a good discussion about displacement, see Kopeček, M., Kunštát, M. 'Tzv. Sudetoněmecká otázka v české akademické debatě po roce 1989', *Český a slovenský zahraniční časopis*, No. 9, 2006. Available on-line: http://www.cs-magazin.com/index.php?a=a2006091039 [accessed 11 June 2012].
6 Suppan, A., Vyslonzil, E. (eds.) *Edvard Beneš und die tschechoslowakische Außenpolitik 1918–1948*. Frankfurt am Main: Peter Lang, 2002. An interesting approach is taken in 'Edvard Beneš, Němci a Německo', mostly a publishing project of the Masaryk Institute and the Archive of the Czech Academy of Sciences, which is also accompanied by a series of lectures from international experts. Fundamental literature on the topic of 1938 and the war years are Brandes, D. *Exil v Londýně 1939–1943: Velká Británie a její spojenci Československo, Polsko a Jugoslávie mezi Mnichovem a Teheránem*. Prague: Karolinum 2003; idem, *Sudetští Němci v krizovém roce 1938*. Prague: Argo, 2011; idem, *Cesta k vyhnání 1938–1945: Plány a rozhodnutí o 'transferu Němců' z Československa a z Polska*. Brno: Prostor, 2002.

thinking with Beneš's view of the world, which Seibt finds rather one-dimensional.[7] The current state of comparative research on Beneš should now be clearer from the papers given at the conference 'Different Images: Perceptions of Edvard Beneš in Czech and European Contexts', held at the Goethe-Institute, Prague, in autumn 2011.[8]

Leaving the upper levels of history, which seem to be dominated by endeavours to assess Beneš in the wider European context, we are faced with a mosaic of opinion.

Back in the late 1980s, even before the Changes beginning in mid-November 1989, some topics that had been suppressed by the régime now cautiously returned to public discussion. Among them were the founders of the Czechoslovak Republic. On the fiftieth anniversary of the Munich Agreement, historians' attention was, naturally, to a considerable extent focused on Beneš. For example, an issue of the weekly *Hlas revoluce* (Voice of the revolution), published by the Union of Antifascist Fighters, was largely devoted to the topic, even though most of the contributions were concerned more with military aspects of the Munich crisis. A series of articles in that periodical entitled 'Fate and Chance', however, included one written in an admiring, colloquial tone, the recollections of a man who had been in Great Britain as an airman during the war. He had, among other things, met there with a Czech emigrant tailor called Hojtaš. Hojtaš told him how Beneš had once come incognito to have a uniform sewn for him as Commander-in-Chief of the Czechoslovak Armed Forces the night the German bombing of Prague was expected.[9]

Immediately after the Changes, the Edvard Beneš Society was established in Prague. It declared itself the successor of the Edvard Beneš Institute for Political and Social Studies (Ústav dr. E. Beneše pro

---

7   Seibt, F. *Německo a Češi: Dějiny jednoho sousedství uprostřed Evropy*. Prague: Academia 1996.
8   'Unterschiedliche Bilder: Wahrnehmungen Edvard Benešs in tschechischen und europäischen Kontexten', the Masaryk Institute and the Archive of the Czech Academy of Sciences, Prague, and the Collegium Carolinum, Munich, with the support of the Goethe-Institut, Prague, 13th–14th October 2011.
9   Tikovský, V. 'Osudy a náhody', *Hlas revoluce* 3, 1987.

Politické a Sociální Studium), which operated in London from 1950 to 1964, run by Jaromír Smutný, the head of the President's Office under Beneš. The new Society, associated primarily with the historian Věra Olivová,[10] has largely been a defender of Beneš and his work, sometimes verging on adoration.

At the other pole, the demonization of Beneš in expatriate circles continues unabated. This negative image did not, however, emerge only after the Second World War; it was already abundantly present in the interwar period and flourished during the German occupation.[11] A clear summary of this image has recently been provided by Eva Hahn and Hans Henning Hahn.[12] The Hahns also refer to works from which we can deduce that Beneš's diplomatic potential during the Second World War was even more limited than was previously argued, being most successful of course when Beneš and Great Britain had the same political interests regarding policy towards Germany.[13] The Hahns then discuss the degree of Beneš's influence on achieving the expulsion of the ethnic Germans from liberated Czechoslovakia, taking issue with the historian Detlef Brandes, who sees this in a much wider European framework.[14] Drawn caricatures have probably provided the best glosses on the development of this perspective.[15] A First Republic satire depicts Beneš as an ambitious dwarf, who had to be in

---

10   See also Olivová, V. *Dějiny první republiky*. Prague: Karolinum, 2000. Here she takes issue in particular with Klimek's view of Beneš in Klimek, A. *Velké dějiny zemí Koruny české* XIII *(1918–1929)*. Prague and Litomyšl: Paseka, 2000.

11   Weger, T. *'Volkstumskampf' ohne Ende? Sudetendeutsche Organisationen, 1945–1955*. Frankfurt am Main: Peter Lang, 2008, p. 124.

12   See the chapter 'Edvard Beneš: "Das schwarze Biest" als Ursache,' in Hahn, E., Hahn, H. *Die Vertreibung im deutschen Erinnern: Legenden, Mythos, Geschichten*. Paderborn: Ferdinand Schöningh, 2010, pp. 97–98.

13   They refer to Brown, M. D. *Dealing with Democrats: The British Foreign Office and the Czechoslovak Émigrés in Great Britain, 1939 to 1945*. Frankfurt am Main: Peter Lang, 2006.

14   Hahn, E., Hahn, H. *Die Vertreibung im deutschen Erinnern: Legenden, Mythos, Geschichten*. Paderborn: Ferdinand Schöningh, 2010, pp. 102–11. This work takes issue with Brandes, *Cesta k vyhnání 1938–1945: Plány a rozhodnutí o 'transferu Němců' z Československa a z Polska*. Brno: Prostor, 2002.

15   I am grateful to Petr Kralíček, who has been systematically researching the topic of political caricature.

every Czechoslovak government, though he usually could not attend cabinet meetings, because he was always travelling from one international conference to another. Beneš's main motivation was (not only according to humorists) to become president after Masaryk. And in late 1935 Beneš did indeed succeeded Masaryk.

The sympathetic Czechoslovak mass media quickly dubbed him the 'President-Builder', the successor to Masaryk the 'President-Liberator'. Caricatures of President Beneš then disappeared from the press until he resigned in October 1938, just after the Munich Agreement. Except for the extreme right, which began to promote the slogan 'Not Beneš's Republic!', the mass media of the 'Second Republic' (the brief interlude between the Munich Agreement and the German occupation) tended to keep tactfully silent about Beneš. He was, however, recalled by the Germans of Bohemia and Moravia, especially on the Independence Day, 28th October 1938, when they commented on him with malicious glee.

In keeping with Nazis propaganda, however, even the Czech press had to comment on Beneš's resistance work in London, which Czechs in the Protectorate learnt of by clandestinely listening to broadcasts of the Czech Service of the BBC. The Nazi-controlled Czech commentary presents the well-known figure of the ambitious little man, again busy travelling, this time, however, not as Minister of Foreign Affairs, but as a failed émigré. After the assassination of the Deputy Reich Protector Reinhard Heydrich in June 1942, the propaganda hardened. Beneš the political provocateur, who was written off as a nobody, now became Public Enemy No. 1 of the Czech nation, the President of Lies, and a British agent, whose sole task was to sow discord and wreak havoc in an otherwise thriving Protectorate. At a mass demonstration of Czechs on the Old Town Square, Prague, which publicly condemned the assassination of Heydrich, Beneš was verbally ostracized from the nation.[16] Though he was thus officially pilloried, many Czechs privately sympathized with Beneš and acknowledged his leadership in the resistance to German occupation. His role after the war was, and very often still is, narrowed down to the issuing from London of the many Decrees of the President of the Republic (commonly known as the Beneš Decrees). Beneš is thus seen as the architect of the expulsion of the ethnic Germans. In the Bohemian Lands, the appellation 'Beneš Decrees' was initially used mainly by opponents of Beneš's post-war policy. They were a symbol of events in the immediate post-war period, particularly negative events. In roughly the last ten years, however, almost all the mass media (including most of the serious periodicals and broadcasts) have come to use the term 'the Beneš Decrees' as a quick, convenient, and emotionally charged label, in arguments supporting as well as criticizing the expulsion.

One of the peaks of political instrumentalization was the activities, often linked, of politicians and associations of deportees, before the accession of the Czech Republic to the European Union. The expulsion of the German population as an act of injustice was again symbolized by the Presidential Decrees, which were perceived in the Czech Republic as an obstacle to EU accession. Jan Kuklík Jr., an historian and lawyer, rightly called absurd the arguments of some Members of the European Parliament, who assessed Czech preparedness for EU membership partly by comparing the compatibility of legislation during Beneš's time in office, in 1945–1946, and current European law.[17]

---

16 'The symbolic execution of Mr. Beneš on the Old Town Square, Prague, on 2 June 1942, will remain an historic date for the country of Bohemia and Moravia and the Czech nation', *České slovo*, No. 151, 4 June 1942, p. 2.

17 Kuklík, J. *Mýty a realita tak zvaných Benešových dekretů*. Prague: Linde, 2002. See also, Domnitz, C. *Zápas o Benešovy dekrety před vstupem do Evropské unie: Diskuse v Evropském parlamentu a v Poslanecké sněmovně Parlamentu ČR v letech 2002–2003*. Prague: Dokořán, 2007.

The Czech public mostly reacted to this with an uncritical defence of Czechoslovak post-war developments as a whole. Concerning Beneš, this culminated in the drafting, debating, and passing of a curious act of legislation in 2004, honouring the memory of his service to the state (Zákon ze dne 13. dubna 2004 o zásluhách Edvarda Beneše; č. 292/2004 Sb.), which was inspired by the 1930 legislation about Masaryk. The 2004 Act was passed to declare a commitment, at home and abroad, to defend the post-war expulsions and to prevent any outside interference. The figure of Beneš, the second Czechoslovak president, thus came simply to personify the permanency of the post-war measures and was also intended as a defence against German expellees from Czechoslovakia calling Beneš a liar and a war criminal. The act has, however, not solved this; on the contrary, it has created new problems. Political commentary is ever present — it accompanies not only various Beneš anniversaries, most recently the sixtieth anniversary of his death, but will also surely appear again in connection with electoral campaigns and other politically charged events.

How has Beneš's image been used and added to in the mass media? The adoration of Beneš has never attained the same heights as that of the 'President-Liberator' Masaryk nor even of his own adoration as 'President-Builder' from pre-war Czechoslovakia, an example of which, is the 1936 essay by the respected literary critic F. X. Šalda, 'The New President'.[18]

Indeed, not just German expellees, but ethnic Czechs too have, more recently, added to the image of Beneš as a despicable man. For example, the Web commentary of an expatriate, Ross (Rostislav) Hedviček, who judges Beneš mostly in terms of his relations with the Soviet Union, regularly labelling him a Soviet agent. Hedviček is probably also the author of a contribution to the discussion on the website

---

18 For a quintessential example of Beneš adoration, see Šalda, F. X. *Nový prezident: Značka E. B.* Prague: Společnost F.X. Šaldy, 1993; reprinted from *Šaldův zápisník* 8 (193536), No. 4 and 5, pp. 91–95. It was repeatedly used anonymously as the preface to *Dr. Edvard Beneš ve fotografii: Historie velkého života*, Prague: Orbis, 1936. It was reprinted by Orbis but with newer photographs, in September 1946.

of Jaroslav Čapek (who represented František Oldřich Kinský in his property claims under Czech restitution legislation), which depicts Beneš as almost worse than Stalin.[19] It is a sad state of affairs when the vocabulary of contemporary journalists uses much of the same vocabulary as the Nazi press, describing Beneš as an 'embezzler', 'an agent of foreign powers', and so forth. The serious newspapers of course do not use the satirical image of the ambitious dwarf that was present in the 1920s or the image of 'the failed statesman', which was prevalent after the Munich Agreement.[20]

An example of how these ideas and modes of expression have survived fairly consistently in the press is the rhetoric of the German and Austrian leaders of the expellee organizations (for example, the *Landsmanschaft*) as published in the *Sudetendeutsche Zeitung* and the *Sudetenpost*, the latter of which is the somewhat more sophisticated of the two. The well-known 'documentary novel' by Sidonia Dedina (Sidonie Dědinová, b. 1935), *Edvard Beneš–der Liquidator: Dämon des Genozids an den Sudetendeutschen, Totengräber der tschechoslowakischen*

---

[19] Available on-line: http://www.atllanka.net/index.php and http://www.knize-kinsky.cz [accessed 13 August 2012]. The quintessence of Beneš's "pro-Soviet criminality" is almost surreal in contrast with his memoirs, in which he considers his journey to the Soviet Union to be the logical culmination of the politics and travels of his great Czech predecessors from 1848, 1867, the beginning of the twentieth century, and of course of Masaryk before and after the First World War. Beneš, E. *Paměti: Od Mnichova k nové válce a k novému vítězství*. Prague: Orbis, 1948, p. 355; see also *Memoirs of Dr. Eduard Benes: From Munich to New War and New Victory*, transl. G. Lias, London and Boston: George Allen and Unwin and Houghton Mifflin, 1954.

[20] Of interest in this regard are the publications of the neo-Communist 'Club of the Czech Borderlands', which are not always aware of the authors' orientation. Thus, for instance, they publish an essay such as the conservative Roman Joch's 'Edvard Beneš se zasloužil o stát...', Available on-line: http://www.kcprymar ov.estranky.cz/clanky/vyznamne-osobnosti/roman-joch-do-diskuse_-edvard-benes-se-zaslouzil-o-stat-___.html [accessed 13 August 2010]. Beneš 'contributed to the state twice: once, to the Greater German Reich in 1938 and once to the Soviet Union in 1948 [...]'.

Demokratie *(published in Czech as Edvard Beneš — likvidátor),* [21] also employs this vocabulary. This is well advertised by the lurid dust-jacket, with a slyly smiling Stalin on the back and a grim Beneš on the front cover, both watching Soviet and Czechoslovak troops marching together.

This attitude to Beneš also yields some surprises. After the Changes of late 1989, instead of being known by its original name, Beneš Bridge (proposed by the German Social Democrat mayor of Ústí nad Labem, Leopold Pölzl, during its construction, in 1934-36,), the second most important bridge in Ústí nad Labem, is now nicknamed by the expellees the 'Bridge of the 31 July 1945 Massacre'. Bronze plates with a German inscription, 'Präsident Dr. E. Beneš Brücke 1936'[22], were placed on the bridge. In connection with the lynching of German civilians in July 1945, the view 'from the other side' is understandable, especially since the bridge became a kind of symbol of all the anti-German excesses immediately after the war.

The fact that Beneš was popular among the left-wing of Ústí nad Labem is illustrated by his portrait painted for the town hall in 1937 by the Jewish painter Ernest Neuschul. As an exile in London, Neuschul created another notable painting, in 1943, of Beneš in front of ruins, with the Kremlin on the left, and the Tower of London on the right.[23]

There is also a memorial culture around Beneš. Its centre is surely Beneš's house in Sezimovo Ústí, south Bohemia. The house, which Beneš's widow, Hana (1885-1975), left to the Museum of the Hussite Revolution in Tábor, has been renovated several times (most recently in the 2006-09). Since the mid-1970s it has been the property of the

---

21 Dedina, S. *Edvard Beneš — der Liquidator: Dämon des Genozids an den Sudetendeutschen, Totengräber der tschechoslowakischen Demokratie: zeitgeschichtlicher Roman.* Eichendorf: Eichendorf Verlag, 2000; idem. *Edvard Beneš — likvidátor: dokumentární román.* Prague: Annonce, 2003.
22 Kaiserová, K., Kaiser, V. (eds.) *Dějiny města Ústí nad Labem.* Ústí nad Labem: Město Ústí nad Labem, 1995, p. 168.
23 Ibid., pp. 195-196.

Czech Cabinet Office (Úřad předsednictva vlády), and only the gardens and the Beneš grave can be visited by the public. As the Sezimovo Ústí website aptly puts it, it is a 'national disgrace' that although the President's wife bequeathed the house as the future museum of her husband's legacy, her will has been ignored for decades. In 2000, the Czech Government decided to carry out some of Hana Benešová's wishes, and established the Edvard Beneš Museum at the house in Sezimovo Ústí. On public holidays and anniversaries of the birth and the death of Edvard Beneš, two restored rooms — the bedroom and the study — are opened to the public.[24] The Hussite Museum in Tábor manages the newly established memorial, which includes an exhibition. Other forms of memorial culture are statues and monuments of Beneš. Some are also controversial for the former Czechoslovak citizens of German ethnicity.

The Beneš statue in front of the Czernin Palais (the Ministry of Foreign Affairs), Prague, was an initiative of the Edvard Beneš Society, with the support of the Czechoslovak Legionnaires Association (Československá obec legionářská), RAF airmen, and freedom fighters. Sculpted by Karel Dvořák, the original was in the Pantheon of the National Museum from 1948 to 1951. At the behest of the Czechoslovak Legionnaires Association, a copy was erected in Brno in April 2010. What is particularly interesting is not the unsurprising protests of former Czechoslovak citizens of German ethnicity, but why they make replicas of original sculptures and do not announce a tender for new work. Is it really just a matter of funding?

Novelists too have been unable to ignore the second Czechoslovak president. Beneš inspired Jan Křesadlo (1926–1995) in his trilogy *Fuga Trium* (Fugue for a trio; 1992). One of the characters (an exile politician called Beňodzor) resembles Beneš, of whom Křesadlo is highly critical, and ridicules him throughout the novel and is ironic about his work.[25]

---

24   Information on-line: http://www.sezimovo-usti.cz/_turista/ben_vila.php [accessed 11 June 2012].
25   Křesadlo, J. *Fuga trium*, Brno: Host, 1992.

The notable penetration of Beneš's character into literature can also be seen in a novel by Ota Filip (b. 1930), *Sousedé a ti ostatní* (Neighbors and the rest; 2003). A neighbour of the hero of the novel, which is set in Murnau, Bavaria, is a Sudeten German from the town of Nýrsko, west Bohemia. An insidious poisoner of local animals, he is writing a scholarly work about Beneš's guilt. After 800 pages full of sadness and anger, he reaches the conclusion that the Sudeten Germans were better off under Beneš than under Hitler. He confides his secrete to the hero, a Czech immigrant. In an attempt perhaps to add a tragicomic touch, the hero dies almost immediately of heart failure after drinking cheap Czech rum.[26]

And lastly, in a book-length historical essay, *Beneš jako Rakušan* (Beneš as an Austrian), the dissident writer and later Czech diplomat Jiří Gruša (1938–2011) presents Beneš as a technocrat who fatally overestimated his strengths. Half his success, according to Gruša, was thanks to Masaryk, and when Masaryk died, little remained. The moment democracy failed, at least in his own eyes, Beneš's wanted to substitute himself for it.[27] This work tends to hark back to the left-wing dissident literary historian and critic Václav Černý (1905-1987) and to subsequent reflections, but they would go beyond the scope of this article.

And so I will conclude with a slightly different view. In 'The Greatest Czech', a survey conducted by Czech Television in 2005, viewers were asked to send in their opinion of who the most important Czech figures were of the past and the present. Beneš ranked 22nd, between the shoe-factory owner Tomáš Baťa and the scientist Otto Wichterle. In another contest for the top ten 'negative heroes' of Czech history, Beneš was not amongst the 'winners', but the contest reflected the mood in society even more. The undisputed villain, Klement Gottwald (1896-1953), came in first, but was followed by Stanislav Gross (1969-2015), a banal contemporary politician, and then by President Václav Klaus (b. 1941), who, as is generally known, otherwise regularly reaps positive

---

26 Filip, O. *Sousedé*, Brno: Host, 2003.
27 Gruša, J. *Beneš jako Rakušan*, Brno: Barrister & Principal, 2011.

points in popularity polls. The Czech TV viewers' assessments of the tense year of 'decrees and discussion', 2005, suggests that society sees the past as being rather complicated. On the one hand, Beneš's holding 22nd place in history as a whole is certainly not so bad; on the other hand, if public opinion were to reflect the political passions about the decrees, Beneš would surely occupy a far more prominent place in the poll.[28]

---

28 Available on-line: http://www.ceskatelevize.cz/specialy/nejvetsicech/oprojektu_top100 [accessed 11 June 2012].

Freemason, Coward, Russophile, Schemer: Edvard Beneš in the Eyes of the Poles, 1918–45[1]

Piotr M. Majewski[2]
University of Warsaw

Abstract: The texts examines the perceptions of Edvard Beneš in the eyes of Poles between 1918–1945. The meaning of Polish politicians and diplomats at that time was generally negative, especially due to his alleged links to Freemasonry, his handling of the Czech-Polish territorial dispute and sympathy to the policies of the Soviet Union. Drawing on the analysis of historical sources, media, as well as opinions of other historians, the author claims that for many Poles Beneš naturally personified all the negative qualities attributed to Czechoslovakia at that time.

Edvard Beneš[3] was one of the best-known and most easily recognized Czech (Czechoslovak) politicians in Poland, both in the interwar period and during the Second World War. His name surfaces again and again in documents, diaries, memoirs and the press, very often in the context of events that were of central importance to Poland, such as the Paris Peace Conference, the Munich Pact, and the beginnings of the Sovietization of central Europe.

In Jerzy Tomaszewski's noteworthy essay about Polish diplomats' opinions of Beneš in 1918–39, Beneš appears in a negative light already in the first years of Poland's independence. Contributing to

---

[1] This article is published here in English with the kind permission of the Collegium Carolinum, Munich, which already published it in German: Majewski, P. M. 'Freimaurer, Feigling, Russophiler, Intrigant. Edvard Beneš in den Augen den Polen 1918–1945', in *Edvard Beneš: Vorbild und Feindbild: politische, historiographische und mediale Deutungen.* Göttingen: Vandehoeck & Ruprecht, 2013, pp. 71–91.
[2] E-mail: pm_majewski@wp.pl.
[3] The practice of writing his name in Polish transcription was established already then. This explains why most of the authors quoted here spell it 'Benesz', while I consistently use the Czech spelling, perhaps giving the impression of inconsistency. Also, Polish sources and older historical writing distort his Christian name into 'Eduard'.

this perception were his alleged links to Freemasonry (which the National Democrats were especially anxious about) and, most importantly, the decisions he made, or at least endorsed, as Czechoslovakia's foreign minister, which were unfavourable to Poland. They included the territorial dispute in 1919-1920 over Teschen Silesia (Śląsk Cieszyński, Těšínsko), won by Czechoslovakia; Prague's ambiguous stand on the Polish-Bolshevik war; the Czechs' intransigence on the potential adjustment of the border near Jaworzyna Spiska (Tatranská Javorina); Prague's distancing itself from Poland to avoid spoiling its relations with Germany; and the two countries' different views on the resolutions of the Locarno Conference.[4]

To many Polish politicians and diplomats, Beneš appeared as Poland's adversary. This was largely a correct perception, since Polish and Czechoslovak national interests differed in many respects and the Czechoslovak foreign minister often talked brusquely with his Polish partners. Among those who came away with this impression was Deputy Minister of Foreign Affairs Władysław Skrzyński, who talked to Beneš during the Paris Conference in April 1919:

> [Beneš] mentioned the compensations in Upper Silesia, but without letting on whether they would be economic or territorial [...] and also threatened [...]. He also emphasized the Russophilia of the whole Czech nation, which has been pressuring the government to enter into an alliance with Russia, said openly that in any Polish-Russian conflict, which he anticipates, the Czech nation will stand by Russia, unless a closer rapprochement with Poland is found.[5]

The Peasant Party politician Stanisław Thugutt noted Beneš's views in 1924 about Czech sympathies for Russia as being similar in spirit but definitely less confrontational.[6] The Poles interpreted such opinions, which in fact were often probably not well thought-out or driven by

---

4   Tomaszewski, J. 'Edvard Beneš w opiniach polskich dyplomatów', *Mówią wieki* 4-5, 1997, p. 46.
5   Paderewski, I., Janowska, H. (eds.) *Archiwum Polityczne Ignacego Paderewskiego*, Vol. II: *1919-1921*. Wrocław: Zakład Narodowy im. Ossolińskich, 1973-1974, pp. 122-23.
6   Account by Rataj, M. *Pamiętniki 1918-1927*. Warsaw, 1965, p. 212.

tactical concerns, as official representations of Czechoslovak foreign policy. This strengthened their suspicion that all Czechs were Pan-Slavs, which endangered Poland's interests.[7] They then developed the belief in Beneš's own Russophilia, even when in discussions with other Polish politicians he showed much more distance to Russia, for example, stressing that he would not like to share a border with her.[8]

Polish politicians' opinions of Beneš varied, depending on their political and, one suspects, personal sympathies. Interestingly, memoirs by several National Democrats show some generosity, or at least a lack of prejudice, towards him. Their leader, Roman Dmowski, mentions Beneš twice, recalling cooperation with Czech and Slovak politicians during the First World War and describing his own speech to the Council of Ten about the future of Cieszyn Silesia. In both cases, the accounts are factual and unemotional, even though in the latter Beneš was Dmowski's direct competitor.[9]

Stanisław Kozicki, a close ally of Dmowski's and secretary of the Polish delegation to the Paris Peace Conference of 1919, gives Beneš even higher marks as he writes about meeting him in London during the First World War and later about his performance as head of the Czechoslovak diplomatic corps:

> Of small stature, slender and inconspicuous, this young man did not at first come across as an eminent personality. Yet a few discussions about politics sufficed to let one know that one was dealing with a politician who was, if I may say so, a

---

[7] Ignacy Jan Paderewski wrote in a report for Foreign Minister Eustachy Sapieha: 'The Czechs would like to be influential in Russia, and continue to think deep down about sharing a border with Russia and are quietly lending support to the Galician Ukrainians. They would like to represent the League in the East, but we are standing in their way. This is why they are attempting to weaken our influence and our importance. This is why they are our adversaries' natural allies'. Paderewski, I., Janowska, H. (eds.) *Archiwum Polityczne Ignacego Paderewskiego*, Vol. II: *1919–1921*. Wrocław: Zakład Narodowy im. Ossolińskich, 1973–1974, p. 596.

[8] Rataj, M. *Pamiętniki 1918–1927*. Warsaw: LSW, 2011, p. 237.

[9] Dmowski, R. *Polityka polska i odbudowanie państwa*. Warsaw: Nakładem Spółki Wydawniczej Niklewicz, 1926, pp. 211, 395–96.

purebred politician, who not only grasped the course of events but also had a deep understanding of European politics.[10]

Beneš played a historic role in the period of rebuilding the Czech state. During the war he worked wisely and selflessly in France and England, he steadfastly defended Czech interests during the conference and behaved properly towards us, but was unrelenting on the question of Cieszyn Silesia. He had political intelligence and was extremely agile in diplomacy, which helped him at the conference and afterwards allowed him to maintain a strong position and to play a major role in the life of the League of Nations.[11]

As can be seen from these remarks, Kozicki not only appreciated Beneš's diplomatic skills, but also accepted his right to defend his country's national interest as he defined it. Interestingly, this opinion was not burdened by Beneš's membership in a Masonic order, even though, like many National Democrats, Kozicki suspected that the Czechs had won France's assistance on Cieszyn Silesia with the Freemasons' help.[12]

The National Democrats' reserve vis-à-vis Beneš was due to their geopolitical concepts, according to which Slav Czechoslovakia was to be Poland's natural ally in resisting pressure from Germany. Thus, an escalation of disputes between the two was not in either country's interest, but calming them down was. It was from this perspective that they judged Beneš's actions, viewing him foremost as their partner in anti-German policies. It is in this context that the prominent National Democratic politician Stanisław Grabski remembered Beneš appreciatively as he spoke of the behind-the-scenes support Beneš had given Poland on the question of dividing Upper Silesia in 1921:

> He completely agreed with me that Germany, which has not known the catastrophe of war on her own territory, whenever she has the slightest hope of winning, will sooner or later strike at Czechoslovakia and Poland in retaliation. Therefore, anything that makes Poland stronger vis-à-vis Germany lies in Czechoslovakia's

---

10 Kozicki, S. *Pamiętnik 1876–1939*. Słupsk: Wydawnictwo Naukowe Akademii Pomorskiej, 2009, p. 355.
11 Ibid., p. 414.
12 'I have always thought that Masaryk, Beneš, and other Czech politicians of that era belonged to lodges'. Ibid., p. 425. See also p. 444.

interest. This whole conversation took place in an atmosphere of true friendship.[13]

But certainly not all National Democratic politicians and sympathizers gave Beneš this much credit of trust. The writer Antoni Potocki, who had known him in Paris during the First World War when Beneš was working to achieve Czechoslovak sovereignty, in September 1939, during the German siege of Warsaw described the president of Czechoslovakia as a 'ruffian', whose 'ideal was always to isolate Poland, and have Germany, Czechoslovakia, and Russia in the centre of Europe'. He predicted that Beneš would 'surprise us more than once', which proved to be true.[14]

One can sense animosity towards Beneš also among some of the Poles who had a positive view of the Czechs and wanted to draw closer to Czechoslovakia. Zygmunt Lasocki, an envoy to Prague (1924-1927), remained distrustful of Beneš, believing that he did 'not want to talk with Poland or to have anything at all to do with her'.[15] Recalling his visit to Prague in November 1921, Konstanty Skirmunt, the minister of foreign affairs in 1921-1922, emphasized the differences between Beneš and the president of Czechoslovakia: 'Masaryk gave the impression of being a true statesman. He was serious, restrained and elegant; he had nothing of the parvenu or of the bourgeois, that is, the characteristics that Benesz had in addition to his intelligence and dexterity'.[16] Skirmunt stops there, so we unfortunately do not know what it was precisely that bothered him about Beneš's behaviour. We can only guess that, with his noble roots and life in the landowning class, Skirmunt viewed his Czechoslovak colleague, who was born to a peasant family and shaped by the world of the petite

---

13 Grabski, S. *Pamiętniki*, Vol. 2. Warsaw: Czytelnik, 1989, pp. 191–92.
14 Irzykowski, K. *Dzienniki*, Vol. 2: *1916–1944*. Cracow: Wydawnictwo Literackie, 2001, p. 347.
15 Zbyszewski, W. A. *Gawędy o ludziach i czasach przedwojennych*. Warsaw: Czytelnik, 2000, pp. 152–53, 157.
16 Skirmunt, K. *Moje wspomnienia 1866–1945*. Rzeszów: Wydaw.Wyższej Szkoły Pedagog., 1997, p. 121.

bourgeoisie, with a dose of superiority, and was likely not alone in holding these views.

Nevertheless, Beneš's intelligence and professionalism were widely appreciated. The Marshal of the Sejm, Peasant Party deputy Maciej Rataj, observing him in 1925 noted: 'He is very unobtrusive but intelligent, bright, goes so far with self-assurance that he is conceited, but to some extent he has the right to be that way'.[17] Taking into account Warsaw's and Prague's contradictory interests and the conviction that the Czechoslovak minister did not have much sympathy for Poland, it is easy to imagine that these characteristics made the Poles fearful of him rather than making him likeable. As early as the 1920s, the public perceived Beneš as a crafty and treacherous politician, an image to which his successes no doubt contributed as much as the history of Polish-Czechoslovak relations in 1919–1920. The satirical journal *Mucha* commented on Minister Skirmunt's visit to Prague in a fictitious toast raised by Beneš and in mocking pseudo-Czech (*czeszczyzna*), the Poles' favourite form of jokes about their southern neighbours:

> How I loves them Poles, what a silly nation they is, even though the Czechs cuts them up with scythes, here they comes back to Canossa. As the proverb says: the Czech is a musician or a thief, let that be your reward [...]. I speaks for the Czech nation, so we can be friends, let me forgives you for all our crimes: oppressing the Polish in Cieszyn and at that terrible time you was fighting Moscow, we stopped firing, and all our intriguing, so low and I forgive so you will loves me. You, gracious Sir, Skirmunt, no spitting on our wickedness, because when we can we will happily plunge the knife into yours. We Czechs are naturally well-behaved, let me raise the glass to your harm and our profit. Long live Czechoslovakia![18]

---

17 Rataj, M. *Pamiętniki 1918–1927*. Warsaw: LSW, 2011.
18 'Ja sem milujem Polaki, to hlupi naród je taki, choć Czech ich krajal jak kosy, przyszli tu znów do Kanosy. Prislowie pak stare dowodi, że Czech je muzykant lub zlodij; niech to wam budie zapłatą. [...] W imieniu czeskiego narodu ja wam wybaczam na zgodu, te wszystkie zbrodnie w tej chwili, cośmy wam tylko zrobili: gnębienie polskości w Tieszynie i w trudnej dla was hodinie, gdystie szli z Moskwą na boje, te zatrzymane naboje i nasze intrygi, podlosti dla waszej wybaczam milosti. Wy, milostpanie Skirmuntie, na nasze podlosti nie pluńtie, bo

The same magazine published a poem recapping the Czechoslovak foreign minister's visit to Warsaw in mid-April 1925, an instant of temporarily improved relations between the two countries during negotiations leading up to the signing of the Rhine Pact (the basic document of the Locarno Treaties):

> Here comes Benesz with his pleasant and odd mission,
> Benesz carrying the olive branch [...].
> For he knows the crux of his visit:
> The Czech cannot resist the German without the Pole.
> So he's coming! Let him come to this marriage of friendship,
> The Poles are always keen to have harmony between neighbours [...].
> But a single thought is rattling in my head:
> Whether all that the Pole is eager for
> Is in our common interest,
> Whether Benesz will adhere to the friendship pact?[19]

The belief in the Czechoslovak foreign minister's treacherousness, so widespread in Poland, also stemmed from his unique way of talking, which many of his contemporaries interpreted — rightly or wrongly — as devious and dishonest. (It was the reverse of his diplomatic smoothness). Wacław Alfred Zbyszewski, a correspondent for the conservative *Czas* daily, many years later wrote about his interview with Beneš:

> Behind the desk sat an ugly little man, whom I already knew by sight from Geneva [...]. We spoke for over an hour. I admired Benesz's skills, there is no denying it. One could have thought from the conversation that no bilateral Polish-Czech problems existed, that we have only the League of Nations in common because that was what Benesz carried on about, devoting all his statements to it [...]. He made an unpleasant impression on me, that of an earthworm or an amphibian, which is always slipping away. His smile was mocking, false, unpleasant and permanently dishonest. He was like the other side's attorney, trying to

---

jak se okazja nadarzy, chętnie w was wbijem nóż wraży. Czechy są grzeczne z natury, wznosim pak kielich do góry, wam krzywda, nam korzyść — to racja, na zdar więc Czechosłowacja!' *Mucha*, No. 47, 18 November 1921, p. 2.
19 *Mucha*, No. 15, 10 April 1925, p. 5.

make you look like a fool. Our whole conversation made a negative impression on me.[20]

Blaming Beneš for the entirety of Czechoslovakia's foreign policy, especially for its less-than-good relations with Poland, became established, widespread, and more pronounced after Józef Piłsudski's coup d'état in May 1926, and even more so after Józef Beck became Poland's foreign minister in 1932. Then, the list of reproaches against Beneš came to include his alleged pro-Sovietism (after Czechoslovakia signed a treaty with the USSR in May 1935), Prague's support for the Ukrainian insurrectionists in Poland, its toleration of the anti-Polish activities of the Communist movement on its territory, and the persecution of the Polish minority in the part of Cieszyn Silesia annexed by Czechoslovakia in 1919.

But the main source of this new wave of disfavour towards Beneš, characteristic of the whole Polish group of 'colonels', was Piłsudski's views: he considered Czechoslovakia a *Saisonstaat* (a state for only one season) whose policies were hostile to Poland, and he simply looked down on the Czechs. He was unrestrained in expressing this also to representatives of third countries, including Nazi Germany. For instance, in Warsaw, in January 1935, in conversations with Hermann Goering, as Minister Beck later recalled, 'Marshal Piłsudski did not hide his belief that the Poles neither respect nor like the Czechs'.[21] To Polish diplomats, Piłsudski spoke about the Czechoslovak foreign minister as 'that ass Benesz'.[22]

By some accounts, there was also Piłsudski's mistrust of people close to the Freemasons, among whom he counted Beneš. Unlike for the National Democrats, in his case this had no ideological roots but

---

20 Zbyszewski, W. A. Gawędy o ludziach i czasach przedwojennych. Warsaw: Czytelnik, 2000, pp. 155–57. Zbyszewski's opinion was certainly influenced by his extremely negative attitude towards Russia, since he considered Beneš a Russophile.
21 Beck, J. *Ostatni raport*. Warsaw: Państwowy Instytut Wydawniczy, 1987, p. 50.
22 Wysocki, A. *Tajemnice dyplomatycznego sejfu*. Warsaw: Książka i Wiedza, 1988, p. 138.

could be attributed to an obsessive drive to free Poland's foreign policy from the influence of any international organization, even though the effect of these biases was naturally the same.[23]

Beck fully accepted Piłsudski's geopolitical and personal views.[24] He also shared his prejudices. Paweł Starzeński, Beck's personal secretary in 1937-1939, recalls his superior's words:

> Our policies and the official Czech ones are diametrically opposed. They continuously get in my way. There was a moment, when the Marshal was still living, when it looked like we would be able to agree with them, I was on the verge of going to Prague, but Benesz ducked out. He has no courage, is afraid of committing to us. He is a slight, big-headed man. Towards the end of the war the Czechs treated us in a revolting way, more than once. The Marshal promised a delegation of Poles from Zaolzie [the Polish name for the part of Cieszyn Silesia incorporated into Czechoslovakia], who had come to see him in the Belvedere Palace, that they would return to Poland. This promise must be kept, all the more so now that he is no longer with us [...]. Two questions: Czechoslovakia and Lithuania, Lithuania and Czechoslovakia [...]. The Marshal has left us these two matters to resolve.[25]

The lost chance for reconciliation discussed in this quotation is Beck's proposal made in spring 1933 for a joint Polish-Czechoslovak statement against the Quadripartite Agreement, which Beneš dropped. This was probably one of the reasons for the personal insult that Beck thenceforth cultivated for his Czechoslovak counterpart, which revealed itself in attributing to him lowly motivations and character flaws, such as cowardice, conceit and pettiness. Yet it is certain that Beck's and Piłsudski's ill feelings towards Beneš did not stem solely from the disappointment that there was no diplomatic understanding between Poland and Czechoslovakia, but coincided with their general

---

23 Gawroński, J. *Moja misja w Wiedniu 1932-1938*. Warsaw: PWN, 1965, pp. 14-15.
24 In conversation with the Swedish foreign minister, Rickard Sandler, in May 1938, Beck said: 'Ultimately, the creature made by the peace treaties which is called Czechoslovakia has always seemed artificial to us and not in agreement with the principle of the freedom of nations, because the Czechs, who are actually a national minority in their country, have conducted brutal police actions towards the other nations, despite the alleged democracy of the official name of their regime.' Beck 1987, p. 143.
25 Starzeński, P. *Trzy lata z Beckiem*. Warsaw: PAX, 1991, p. 53.

antipathy towards the Czechs. This was very clear in the contrast with the equally emotional but opposite attitude towards the Hungarians. To quote Starzeński again:

> Talking about the Czechs, and meaning Beck, it is impossible to overlook the Hungarians, towards whom he deeply felt our traditional friendship. There was an aspect in it that he had inherited from the Marshal, who had told Beck: 'Don't ever forget our Hungarians, even though there is nothing we can do for them right now'. Beck inserted much personal feeling into this part of foreign policy, and a comparison of the characteristics of Hungarians and Czech could only incline the hot-tempered Beck towards the Hungarians. The person of Benesz, whom Beck completely distrusted, stood powerfully in the way. The friendships and antipathies of people at the helm play a role in the foreign policy of a given country. Not only Poland's. Beck's and Benesz's mutual animosities are comparable to those that existed between Eden and Mussolini, with their influence on Great Britain's policy towards Italy.[26]

Beneš appears many times in Beck's *Ostatni raport* (Last report), which was written during his wartime internment in Romania. In it, Beck defends his earlier policies, but always presents Beneš in a negative light. He describes him in exceptionally malicious terms, in contrast to the way he generally writes about politicians, including the leaders of the Third Reich — unemotionally. This appears not in Beck's radically subjective perspective on Polish-Czechoslovak controversies, but in his choice of words, which disqualify Beneš in the reader's eyes. In commenting on Beneš's plans for a concert of powers in 1933, Beck writes: 'in contrast to our position, Prague was already prostrating itself before the Quadripartite Agreement and, as may have been expected, it has avoided adopting a more courageous position [...]. Dr Beneš and Mr Titulescu rushed with "servile" declarations vis-à-vis Paul-Boncour's politics, avoiding a clear stand on the pact, despite their initial reservations'.[27]

Beck writes about his one-on-one conversation with Beneš in Geneva in January 1934 with somewhat more balance when he reproaches him for mistreating the Poles in Cieszyn Silesia and for

---

26   Ibid.
27   Beck, J. *Ostatni raport*. Warsaw: Państwowy Instytut Wydawniczy, 1987, p. 55.

Czechoslovakia's backing of the anti-Polish actions both of the Ukrainian irredentists and of the Communists, although even this description is not totally devoid of sarcasm: 'Dr Benesz avoided [then] all concrete discussion by making only murky statements. When different questions arose, he excused them solely with the Czechoslovak regime's alleged liberalism, but this did not hold water, since we know all too well that liberalism is only a sign to the outside, while in practice Czechoslovakia is a classic police state'.[28]

Next, Beck parodies Beneš's role in the negotiations leading up to the acceptance of the USSR into the League of Nations: 'Mr Benesz, forever helpful, ran up and down, doubly enthusiastic, pulling the Romanians behind him'.[29] Describing Czechoslovakia's announcement of partial mobilization on 22nd May 1938, he comments with disdain: 'Mr. Benesz also mobilized and marched in a way that did not convince anyone that he was intending to fight'.[30]

Beck's exceptional pleasure in implying Beneš's lack of courage, his servility towards the Great Powers, and his unidealistic pragmatism ('I am a realist: economic questions determine everything'[31]) comport with the widespread Polish stereotype of the Czech as a Švejkian coward, yet a commonsensical, unidealistic, and calculating upstart, happy to conform to those who were stronger than him'.[32]

---

28   Ibid., pp. 63–64.
29   Ibid., p. 78.
30   Ibid., p. 145.
31   Ibid., p. 64.
32   The negative influence of this stereotype on Czech-Polish relations was already noticed in the interwar period. Karol Bader, Poland's chargé d'affaires in Prague in 1923–1924, writes in a brochure critical of Beck's politics published in 1938 (prior to the Munich crisis): 'It has always been very difficult to overcome the differences between the Polish and the Czech temperaments. This has psychologically got in the way of and overshadowed the most important questions. There is almost no point in discussing its causes. Enough has been said in writing, serious and trashy, about why the Czech nation lacks the chivalrous demeanour, which for the high-born and lowly on this side of the border is a true source of joy in life and makes for the only adornment in death. Generalizing and simplifying by sketching out national types is a sort of psychological crutch that easily becomes caricature. Thus, the Pole's reflection in the Czech curved mirror gives the Czechs an image of a Don Quixote and, in return, for us the Czech is a Sancho Panza

Top Foreign Ministry officials and Polish diplomats accredited to Prague shared Piłsudski's and Beck's prejudices against Beneš, the Czechs and Czechoslovakia. The deputy director of the Political-Economic Department of the ministry and head of its Eastern Department, Tadeusz Kobylański, considered the president of Czechoslovakia a 'high priest of freemasonry', whose influence he could observe everywhere. The director of Beck's cabinet, Michał Łubieński, shared this view, and furthermore saw Beneš as a Pan-Slavist and a politician striving to subordinate his country to Russia.[33] Deputy Minister of Foreign Affairs Jan Szembek also exhibited a palpable aversion to Beneš.[34]

Marian Chodacki, who in 1935–1936 served as the chargé d'affaires in the Polish embassy in Prague, revealed his anti-Czech stereotypes even more. He remarked in a conversation with Szembek on 31st January 1936:

> Czechoslovakia is a superb police state [...]. As for the qualities of the Czech nation, one must admit that it is a very odd one. Lacking any idealism or faith in its own strength, it stands out with its extreme materialism. One cannot sense in it any state patriotism whatsoever, and in this it resembles pre-war Austria, whose advantage over contemporary Czechoslovakia was that it had a dynasty [...]. This lack of faith in itself—the fundamental trait in the Czech character—is the starting point for Beneš's politics, which lie in seeking support in external factors, in foreign power (the Soviets), in the desperate holding on to Geneva, and in undying loyalty to all types of international organizations.[35]

Kazimierz Papée, Poland's ambassador in Prague in the years of the escalation and culmination of the Sudeten crisis, had the same tendency to make negative generalizations about Beneš and the Czechs.

---

    reincarnated as Švejk, a soldier with the outrageously pedestrian soul of a civvy'. Bader, K. *Stosunki polsko-czeskie*. Warsaw, 1938, pp. 19–20.

33 Gawroński, J. *Moja misja w Wiedniu 1932–1938*. Warsaw: PWN, 1965, p. 15; Komarnicki, T. (ed.) *Diariusz i teki Jana Szembeka (1935–1945)*, Vol. I. London: Polish Research Center, 1964, pp. 288–289.

34 Ibid., p. 354.

35 Komarnicki, T. (ed.) *Diariusz i teki Jana Szembeka (1935–1945)*, Vol. II, London: Polish Research Center, 1965, pp. 62–63.

He believed that the Czechs were only pretending to want good relations with Poland, 'while the things they say about us to diplomats are always perfidious'. He blamed Beneš for systematically ignoring him, never trying even to talk with him, and blamed him for escalating the conflict with the German minority'.[36]

The tone of the telegrams and reports from Prague was the same. In the second half of the 1930s, they were almost never well-disposed to Czechoslovakia, and attributed the worst intentions or at least the flawed motivations of its decisions to its foreign minister (later president). This is clearly visible in the year of the crisis, 1938, when, after Czechoslovakia's 23rd September declaration of universal mobilization, Papée reported:

> A growing number of sources are confirming that yesterday's mobilization is a huge provocative manoeuvre by Beneš, calculated to bring out a premature reaction mostly from Hungary or Poland and thereby to gain a more favourable platform to expand the conflict and to go for broke. Beneš's game is clearly a move to preserve his personal position by unscrupulously joining Moscow's efforts to set Europe on fire.[37]

The language of this commentary, most likely borrowed from the German propaganda of the day, clearly shows the degree to which Poland's diplomats were blinded by their hatred of the Czechoslovak president. It appears even to surpass opportunism, something Tomaszewski emphasizes, which would dictate reporting from Prague precisely what Beck wanted to hear about Beneš.[38]

Moreover, even those diplomats who were more critical of Beck's policies, such as Jan Gawroński, Poland's ambassador in Vienna in

---

36 'Czech public opinion has a negative attitude towards making any sort of concessions to the Germans. Benesz and the government basically want to do nothing', Papée said in a conversation with Szembek on 4 July 1938. Komarnicki, T. (ed.) *Diariusz i teki Jana Szembeka (1935-1945), Vol. IV*, London: Polish Research Center, 1972, pp. 205-206.
37 Kornat, M. (ed.) *Polskie Dokumenty Dyplomatyczne, 1938*. Warsaw: PISM 2007, doc. 288, coded radiogram of 24 September 1938, p. 566.
38 Tomaszewski, J. 'Edvard Beneš w opiniach polskich dyplomatów', *Mówią wieki* 4-5, 1997, p. 48.

1933–38, much later spoke of Beneš with a visible ill feeling, exactly like Beck's attributing to him ties to 'various international centres' and 'being infected with compulsive conformism'.[39]

The pro-Piłsudski press propagated a negative portrayal of the Czechoslovak president. Beginning in about 1935, *Mucha*, a satirical journal, published increasingly unsophisticated jokes about the Czechs and Beneš personally, reaching a high point in the autumn of 1938. It eagerly stressed his membership in Freemasonry, using this to dig at the National Democrats whose papers, in the opinion of pro-government circles, continued to be excessively reserved. A typical example of such writing was a poem by one Władysław Buchner entitled 'Plenipotentiary of the "Great East"':

> Benesz scores huge victories
> On the Sarmatian side,
> The ultramontane papers sing my praises,
> The National Democrats bow low.
> Such is the power of the 'Great East',
> Its refined and inexplicable power:
> To make out of the Polish nation
> A throne for the plenipotentiary's Masonic lodges.[40]

Another approach movement's mockery of Beneš in the press, and drawing on the traditional National Democratic repertoire, consisted in little poems appearing fairly regularly in *Mucha*. They were stylized as letters to the editor, allegedly sent from Czechoslovakia by one Jojne Fisz, a Jew using ungrammatical Polish, in those days commonly and vulgarly called *żydłaczenie*. The Czechoslovak president, who appears in them as a great friend of the author's, is brimming with grotesque megalomania, arrogance, and revulsion towards Poland.[41] It is difficult to know whether his closeness to Jojne Fisz was intended to suggest that Beneš was a Jew or only that he surrounded himself with Jews. But considering the frequency of antisemitic jokes in *Mucha* in

---

39   Gawroński, J. Moja misja w Wiedniu 1932–1938. Warsaw: PWN, 1965, p. 15. This statement refers to the attitude to the Quadripartite Agreement.
40   Buchner, W. 'Prokurent "Wielkiego Wschodu"', *Mucha*, No. 25, 1 June 1937, p. 2.
41   See, for example, *Mucha*, No. 5, 4 December 1936, p. 4.

the interwar years, either way it was intended to ridicule and disgrace the president of Czechoslovakia.

But the most important traits attributed to Beneš in these satirical attacks were cowardice and deception, usually followed by similar generalizations about the whole Czech nation. Buchner, who clearly developed this as a specialty, wrote, on 30 September 1938, the day the government of Czechoslovakia accepted the Munich diktat:

> O, Benesz, my great Benesz,
> How the world's beams creaked,
> When you, your grandness in mind,
> Threatened someone in the Little Entente.
> But there were some, mostly in Warsaw,
> And I was among them,
> Who spread rumours across the world,
> That the Czech is an athlete, a sportsman, but made of cotton wool,
> That when history's tiniest lightning strikes,
> This whole silly construction will collapse.[42]

'The silly construction' is, of course, Czechoslovakia. Very many other insults for Beneš and the Czechs appeared that year. The next issue of *Mucha* (together with another poem by Buchner about the Czechoslovak president's ties to the Freemasons) ran a drawing entitled "Niezaszczytna narodowość" (A dishonourable nationality) depicting a young man with his arm around a dreamy girl hugging him, as she says: 'O, darling, it's so wonderful that you're not a Czech!'[43] The nastiest was a caricature on the front page of the 21st October issue, representing Beneš fleeing from a collapsing building with 'ČSR' written on it, with the caption: 'When the ship starts sinking, the rats flee' and at the bottom, 'Ex-President Benesz — To gallop off, while I'm still alive, to where my money is hidden in a hive'.[44]

It is difficult to know now exactly to what extent other Polish politicians, let alone the public, shared this view promoted by Sanacja's propaganda. The national democratic rightwing's initially

---

42   Buchner, Wł. 'Czechy a Polska', *Mucha*, No. 40, 30th September 1938, p. 2.
43   *Mucha*, No. 41, 7 October 1938, p. 2.
44   *Mucha* No. 43, 21 October 1938, p. 1.

friendly distance that it kept from the president of Czechoslovakia was transformed into dislike in the early 1930s. The literary weekly *Prosto z Mostu* (a supplement to the *ABC* daily), associated with the National-Radical Camp despite the fact that it was often in conflict with the governing coalition, did not hide its liking for Beck's imperial politics. It took advantage of the occasion to attribute to Beneš the responsibility for the resolution of the Cieszyn question in 1920 on terms unfavourable to Poland, and in the wake of the Munich Conference commented with blatantly malicious glee that the internal disintegration of Czechoslovakia 'is expressed primarily in the complete collapse of President Benesz's domestic authority, since the Czechs have finally realized that he is to blame for their catastrophes and defeats'.[45]

The opposition Polish Socialist Party, Labour Party, and Peasant Party politicians were much better disposed towards Beneš, if only because Czechoslovakia had granted political asylum to many of them. Thus, it is impossible to find any anti-Beneš bias in Wincenty Witos's diaries from his years of exile in Czechoslovakia (1933-1939). Despite the fact that his interlocutors from the Czech Agrarian Party repeatedly criticized their foreign minister and then president, Witos evidently avoided talking about him, not reacting to the tirades aimed at him. Witos even left his notes from personal meetings with Beneš in January and February 1935 without comment.[46] It seems that the only words of criticism he permitted himself were about Beneš's co-responsibility for the Munich catastrophe.[47]

Witos's restraint in expressing his opinions about Beneš was likely due to the caution he needed to maintain in exile, as well as his loyalty towards the Czechoslovak government, which had granted him asylum. It can also be attributed to Witos's distinctive peasant perspective on Czechoslovakia and the Czechs. On 22nd September

---

45 *Prosto z Mostu*, No. 43, 2 October 1938, p. 1.
46 Witos, W. *Dzieła wybrane, t. 3: Moja tułaczka w Czechosłowacji*. Warsaw: LSW, 1995, pp. 22, 36, 58, 63-64, 206, 260.
47 'Even at this moment of catastrophe, to which he has contributed most of all, he has not managed to rid himself of the slogans he has been repeating for so many years'. Ibid., p. 299.

1937 he described a peasant youth congress in his diary: 'In the afternoon, President Beneš arrived in the stadium where the young people were performing. They were so informal with one another, and there was no harm in it. There was not an ounce of lordliness or pretension in it'.[48] It may be that what appeared to the Polish diplomat and landowner Skirmunt to be Beneš's *arrivisme* and petit-bourgeois characteristics, was to this peasant politician plainly down-to-earth.

Beneš's image improved only slightly when the September 1939 catastrophe led to the creation of a Polish government-in-exile, dominated by politicians who had been in opposition to the pre-war governing Piłsudskiites. As the leader of an allied nation, Beneš tried to be a useful partner in political talks and even negotiations about a post-war Polish-Czechoslovak confederation (which, as we know, ended in failure), but he continued to be distrusted.

This distrust is visible in documents about a discussion of Beneš, which took place on 17 August 1940 during a government in exile meeting devoted to recognizing the Czechoslovak government. Generał Kazimierz Sosnkowski, a moderate Piłsudskiite, argued that 'a powerful Czechoslovakia shields our flank, and yet we must not forget that Benesz remains Poland's enemy, and in talking about a confederation with Poland he sets the condition that Poland stay within strictly ethnographic borders'. Backing him was Minister Stanisław Kot (Peasant Party), well-known for his anti-Sanacja views, who reminded the meeting that 'Benesz was never keen to talk with us', and that he had 'welcomed the Soviet armies' entry into Poland, and wanted to send Moscow congratulations for occupying Vilna [in 1939]. Also, please do not forget that Benesz is despised by some in Czechoslovakia itself'. National Democrat Marian Seyda emphasized Beneš's earlier sins vis-à-vis Poland: 'In all his activity, Benesz chose the road of intrigues. Already in Versailles, we met with the case of Cieszyn being preordained by the French thanks to Benesz's intrigues. Benesz

---

48   Ibid, pp. 63–64.

wants to share a border with Russia'. General Józef Haller, who represented the Labour Party, was a little more restrained when he argued: 'Benesz opposes a Great Poland, but he does head the government today, and may therefore be a partner for Poland'. Abstaining from criticism of the Czechoslovak president were President Władysław Raczkiewicz, Foreign Minister August Zaleski, and Ministers Henryk Strasburger (independent) and Jan Stańczyk (Polish Socialist Party). Prime Minister and Commander-in-Chief General Władysław Sikorski tried to summarize this debate with a Judgement of Solomon, ruling that 'the government will not repeat the mistakes of Beck's policies', but he also declared some support for Slovak aspirations and enigmatically informed the gathering: 'Benesz's ideas include a union with the Soviets, which would also include Poland'.[49]

This exchange of views shows that, during the war, differences in perspectives on Beneš did not follow political divisions, but it was his opponents who set the tone of the discussions. Just as before September 1939, so too during the war matters on which, objectively speaking, the Polish and Czechoslovak national interests clashed had a negative influence on his image. They included a stalemate on the question of Zaolzie, which was caused by both sides' fears lest territorial concessions in this area be used against them as a precedent for changing other borders, different visions of a potential confederation, and different ideas about relations with the Soviet Union, due largely to the Kremlin's different approaches towards Poland and Czechoslovakia.

The Polish politicians' statements reveal negative generalizations, which can be summarized in statements such as 'In all his activity, Benesz chose the road of intrigues' and 'Benesz remains Poland's enemy'. Yet because these generalizations were so widespread, as they

---

49 Rojek, W. (ed.) *Dokumenty Rządu RP na obczyźnie: Suplementy do tomów I–VIII protokołów posiedzeń Rady Ministrów Rzeczypospolitej Polskiej, październik 1939–sierpień 1945*. Cracow: Oficyna Wydaw.-Drukarska Secesja, 2010, doc. 41C, minutes of 17 August 1940, pp. 51–68.

had been before the war, it is reasonable to suppose that what solidified these views was the way in which Beneš discussed things, his famous Sophistic performances. Even those interlocutors who were not biased against him got the impression that he was purposely complicating discussions and avoiding the concrete. 'He was like an eel, and oiled to boot', the Socialist Adam Pragier, who as a political émigré had received help from Beneš in 1933, noted after their discussion about plans for a confederation.[50] The National Democrat Stanisław Grabski had a similar impression of negotiations with Beneš.[51]

Very few of the political figures of that period were capable of the insight that the responsibility for the impasse in the confederation negotiations lay not only with Beneš but also with the Poles. Those who could see it included Polish Ambassador in London Edward Raczyński, who understood the nonsense of the anti-Beneš intrigues being conducted so passionately by some Polish politicians (including Minister Kot), and called for greater tolerance in relations with the Czechoslovak exiles: 'In weighing the two sides' faults, I tend to burden the Polish side with the greater responsibility. For it is a fact that Benesz from time to time seeks an opportunity to discuss our goals unofficially and in depth, which we evade'.[52] A little later, Raczyński presents an even further-reaching diagnosis, in which he critiques the damage done by demonizing the president of Czechoslovakia:

> The paradox lies in the fact that, in my view, our politicians have an exaggerated suspicion of Benesz's unwillingness to be linked with us and rightly suspect that in any case he would seek a loose association with Poland, and at the same time do not want to show this man, whom they see as 'cunning and unreliable', a concrete Polish plan, instead giving him an opportunity to pull us into his game.[53]

---

50 Pragier, A. *Czas przeszły dokonany*. London: Bolesław Świderski, 1966, pp. 624–25.
51 Grabski, S. *Pamiętniki*, Vol. 2. Warsaw: Czytelnik, 1989, pp. 401–03, 428–29.
52 Raczyński, E. *W sojuszniczym Londynie: Dziennik ambasadora Edwarda Raczyńskiego 1939–1945*. London: Niezależna Oficyna Wydawnicza "Nowa", 1997, p. 107.
53 Ibid, p. 115.

In the opinion of a majority of Poles, one of the main reasons for Beneš's inconsistency on the question of a confederation was his Russophilia, which they usually attributed to all Czechs. Amongst them were even politicians and diplomats who viewed him favourably, such as Raczyński and Kajetan Morawski, Poland's ambassador to the Czechoslovak government-in-exile. Morawski attributed Beneš's stand to his disillusionment with the West, which he had experienced in 1938, and he suspected him not of ill will towards the Poles but merely of a political calculation, different from the Polish one, which in the end proved wrong:

> It would be wrong to suppose that Benesz, with all his sympathy for Russia, even Soviet Russia, was closing his eyes to the danger of Communism [...]. A clear change in Benesz's attitude and behaviour began to surface only when he became the object of Soviet diplomatic pressure, but also realized how far London and Washington defer to their eastern ally. If the world were to be divided into spheres of influence, then he, an old Russophile, who had been betrayed in Munich by Chamberlain, never wanted to land in the eastern sphere with the label of an Anglo-American client.[54]

Morawski sketches out a very interesting portrait of the Czechoslovak statesman, focusing on the differences between his character and mentality and that of the Polish politicians, which stem from being shaped by completely different historical and cultural environments (in those days, people would likely say: from the differences in the Czech and the Polish national characters):

> His reactions, both personal and political, were always almost diametrically opposed to ours. Tactics dominated strategy, which he left to those who were mightier than him. He became influential because he never imposed either his person or his views, never wanted to be either 'head boy' or arbiter; but there was no seemingly remote matter that he would refuse to mediate. Every time he served as mediator, he took a modest five per cent fee for his nation and his country. Not much because they were not important. He paid with big mistakes and big disasters for the fact that he was thought to be right and successful on so many small questions. It would be difficult to imagine a man who seemed less predestined to play the role of protagonist in a historical tragedy. And yet his fate

---

54 Morawski, K. *Tamten brzeg: Wspomnienia i szkice*. Warsaw: Editions Spotkania, 1996, p. 172.

was tragic. There is the heroism of Kmicic or Wołodyjowski [the brave heroes of nineteenth-century Polish novels], and next to it is the heroism of the brave soldier Švejk. And is this unchivalrous tragedy any less devastating?[55]

It would seem that even in this generally sympathetic description of Beneš there was a bite, a moderated form of the pejorative, anti-Czech stereotypes operating in the interwar period, such as subservience to the mighty or self-interest. Morawski by no means accused Beneš of cowardice, but there were many Poles during the war who did. An example would be Jerzy Kurcyusz, a pre-1939 adherent of the National-Radical Camp, who wrote in his memoirs of wartime emigration: 'in contrast to Benesz himself, the Czechs stood out with good training and courage, especially in the air force'. He also cites the contemptuous opinion of a Turkish diplomat: 'Benesz wants to create a state by talking, just as the Poles want to do it with an honest effort'.[56]

The Polish charges that Beneš was a Russophile became more frequent after he visited Moscow in December 1943 to sign the Czechoslovak-Soviet Treaty. From the point of view of the Polish government-in-exile, at that instant Beneš became the Kremlin's client. His opinions about the positive changes in Soviet politics irritated the Poles, as did his acceptance at face value of slogans about Slav solidarity, which the USSR mouthed cynically.

Even those Polish politicians and diplomats who wished Beneš well expressed their dislike for his new strategy. Poland's envoy in Teheran, Karol Bader, whose acquaintance with Beneš dated to the

---

55 Ibid., p. 171. Morawski goes on to discuss (p. 173) the differences in the Polish and Czech mentalities: 'One cannot close one's eyes to this difference. It was and continues to be visible in many customs. How often has Polish society declined a real profit in favour of shining with a noble deed, how often have the Czechs refused an empty gesture to attain a concrete profit? The Czechs are masters of propaganda, while we usually muster cockiness and contemptuous silence. The world press has written more about Lidice than about the Warsaw Uprising. The Polish emigration's support has been the poetry of Adam Mickiewicz [...], and the Czechs' Bata balances'.
56 Kurcyusz, J. Na przedpolu Jałty: Wspomnienia z tajnej służby w dyplomacji. Katowice: Societas Scientiis Favendis Silesiae Superioris-Instytut Górnośląski, 1995, pp. 371-372.

early 1920s, wrote in a letter to Foreign Minister Tadeusz Romer on 3 January 1944 that he reproached him for 'verbosity, exuberance of ideas, and clichés', as well as recklessness and a 'fantastic suppleness of dialectics', despite which he was unable to explain his toleration of the dictatorial system in the USSR. Bader nonetheless thought that Beneš truly believed in Stalin's good intentions towards both Czechoslovakia and Poland. He blamed it on the typical tendency to be seduced by abstract concepts and the naivety of intellectuals. But he did not believe that Beneš consciously aimed to turn Czechoslovakia into a Communist state.[57]

The Poles were deeply divided on the latter question. Ambassador Morawski thought similarly, whereas, for example, Pragier leaned towards the view that Beneš had opted for a deal with the Kremlin in order to secure his own political interests ('he was convinced that the sooner he managed to enter the Communist apparatus, which already existed in Czechoslovakia, the more of a say he would have domestically').[58] Colonel Antoni Szymański, resident in the Polish Military Office in Cairo during this period, described Beneš as a Soviet agent of influence. The Polish historian Marek Kazimierz Kamiński later adopted and expanded this view to cover the whole context of the Second World War.[59]

The Poles' disenchantment with Beneš in that era is easy to understand when one takes into account the fact that his policy of cooperating with Stalin worsened the already difficult situation of the Polish government-in-exile, caused by the severing of Polish-Soviet diplomatic relations in April 1943 and by Poland's ensuing isolation

---

57   Quoted after Kamiński, M. K. *Edvard Beneš we współpracy z Kremlem: Polityka zagraniczna władz czechosłowackich na emigracji 1943-1945*. Warsaw: Neriton, 2009, pp. 105-06.
58   Pragier, A. *Czas przeszły dokonany*. London: Bolesław Świderski, 1966, pp. 872-873.
59   Kamiński, M. K. *Edvard Beneš we współpracy z Kremlem: Polityka zagraniczna władz czechosłowackich na emigracji 1943-1945*. Warsaw: Neriton, 2009, p. 107; idem. 'Czy Edvard Beneš mógł być dla Polski wiarygodnym partnerem?', *Arcana*, 4/1997, pp. 126-131.

and marginalization in the Allied camp. But it is important to remember that charges that Czechoslovakia was servile to the Kremlin naturally fit excellently into the already negative cliché of Beneš, which the Poles used to criticize him before the war. It looked to the Poles like the Czechoslovak president continued to be a 'toady', this time not to France and Great Britain, but to the Soviet Union. This seemed to have the effect of strengthening Beneš's image of being hostile to Poland, disloyal, and duplicitous.

This analysis of the Poles' attitudes towards Edvard Beneš is preliminary, and greater detail and elaboration will certainly be added in the future, especially with the Polish politicians' and diplomats' positions vis-à-vis the Czechoslovak president in 1945–48. But it seems that we can now reasonably advance the hypothesis that the Poles' image of Beneš was generally negative, surprisingly cohesively and lastingly so: it survived the September 1939 catastrophe of the Polish Second Republic unaltered, and was then adapted to completely new circumstances during the war. In this image, we must treat seriously the role played by the contradiction of Poland's and Czechoslovakia's interests, as well as Beneš's actions and political style. Yet the negative opinions of him correspond so closely to the dominant Polish negative stereotype of the Czechs that this is an example of a co-dependence of the two phenomena. Beneš, who became a symbol of Czechoslovakia internationally, to many Poles naturally personified all the negative qualities attributed to his nation. People interpreted his actions through the prism of these stereotypes, in turn strengthening them. A feedback loop explains the cohesiveness and persistence of Edvard Beneš's 'dark' image in Poland.

Case Studies II

'A Wasted Year':
Władysław Gomułka and 1956

Paulina Codogni[1]
Collegium Civitas

Abstract: This paper tries to find an answer for the question if the political upheavals which occurred in Poland in 1956 resulted in a change in the Communist system or, on the contrary, consolidated it. It examines the role of the First secretary of the Polish United Workers' Party Władysław Gomułka during the whole political crisis. By carefully analysing the events of 1956 and involvement of various institutional and societal actors, the author comes to conclusion that the course as well as the consequences of October strengthened and authenticated the national legitimacy of the Polish Communists but on the other hand, 1956 bequeathed a mission in a state under a Communist regime.

Without a doubt, the year 1956 became one of the most significant moments in the post-war history of central and Eastern Europe, a region mostly behind the Iron Curtain. The first serious political crisis of the Communist system since the end of the Second World War took place in Poland at that time. According to most scholars, its scope could be compared only to the events of 1980–81, when the Solidarity movement was created and remained active for the next 16 months. Despite the often drastic course subsequently taken by the crisis—in March 1968, December 1970, and June 1976, none of these resulted in such a serious strain on the foundations of the system and of the whole Communist régime.

The title of this article on the most significant Polish events of 1956 refers directly to a fundamental case. It presents us with the question whether it was a wasted year. In other words — was 1956 a turning point or a continuation? Or, to formulate the question more precisely, did the events that took place in that year result in a change in the Communist system or, on the contrary, did they consolidate it?

---

1 E-mail: paulina.codogni@collegium.edu.pl.

The year 1956 in Poland consisted of a highly dynamic sequence of events. At the beginning of the year, in February, the first shock came—Nikita Khrushchev openly declared something that almost everyone had long been whispering about—namely, that Joseph Stalin was a criminal. Khrushchev presented Stalin as someone who changed the direction of the political vision of Vladimir Lenin after the October Revolution. Khrushchev cleverly absolved himself of all the crimes committed by the generalissimo, underlining that they had resulted from the particular traits of Stalin's character.

In March, the authorities of the Polish Communist Party (officially, the Polish United Workers' Party) decided to make Khrushchev's 'Secret Speech' public. This decision was unprecedented. Poland became the first country in the Communist bloc where the leaders took such a step.[2] The three weeks when Khrushchev's report was read and discussed during Party meetings throughout Poland changed the political atmosphere irrevocably. Widespread shock and disgust caused by the facts revealed in the report were visible during numerous speeches given at Party meetings. The reactions of people who had just listened to the report were extreme—from fainting and outbursts of sobbing to absolute silence.

Participants of the meetings started posing questions about Władysław Gomułka (1905-1982), also known as, 'Wiesław', who was a proponent of the so-called 'Polish way to socialism'. For that reason, Gomułka was expelled from the Party and was imprisoned. He was released in December 1954, but this information was not revealed at the time. The participants of the meetings emphasized that if the Khrushchev report condemned Stalin's crimes and Gomułka had already dared to oppose his policy a few years before, this basically meant that the former Polish Communist leader had been right. In a sense, it was a paradoxical situation. As Paweł Machcewicz has aptly noted: 'Without being directly involved in the game, Gomułka became

---

2   This decision was taken in March after the death of Bolesław Bierut, the first secretary of the Polish United Workers' Party, who was considered one of Stalin's most loyal disciples.

a true participant in it. He became the political personification of the political alternative that hung over Polish political life'.[3]

The atmosphere of common discussion, which arose after the Khrushchev report was revealed, moved very fast from Party meetings at various levels, right down to the factory floor. Workers started openly demanding changes in the economic policy of the State. People started discussing things about which not long before they had been afraid even to think about. They stopped being afraid. The workers' revolt in Poznań which erupted at the end of June 1956 was evidence of that. And it was just the beginning of a really hot summer in Polish politics. The immediate causes of the Poznań revolt were social and economic. Workers marched in the streets to protest against the poor organization of work, which had resulted in lower wages, as well as against scandalously bad working conditions and the huge waste of raw materials.[4] Some of the slogans, however, were openly anti-Soviet and anti-régime.

Though the revolt was suppressed practically the same day it broke out, the Party leadership had to face the fact that they could no longer ignore the voice of the public and that a revolt could break out again at any moment. Despite the authorities' efforts, it was impossible to prevent information about the revolt and its bloody end from spreading. It was visible on the walls in many Polish towns, where anonymous authors had scribbled graffiti expressing their admiration for the brave citizens of Poznań. Legends of their courage began circulating throughout Poland.

The Poznań revolt created a tense atmosphere in factories all over the country. As soon as workers started demanding better working conditions, directors of the state enterprises usually reacted by offering immediate pay rises. The economic slogans were often accompanied by demands for the restoration of civil freedoms and independence from the Soviet Union. The dependence on the Soviet Union,

---

[3] Machcewicz, P. *Polski rok 1956*. Warsaw: Oficyna Wydawnicza-Mowia Wieki, 1993, p. 18.
[4] See Jankowiak, S. *Wielkopolska w okresie stalinizmu 1948–1956*. Poznań, 1995.

especially that resulting in Soviet economic exploitation, was identified as the main cause of Polish poverty.[5]

The June revolt in Poznań and its aftershocks forced the Communist authorities to understand that maintaining total control over society was simply no longer possible and that changes in the political and economic systems were necessary.

At that moment, it appeared that the only one person able to gain the confidence of the Polish people was Władysław Gomułka. Till 1948 he had been the head of the Polish Workers' Party (which in 1948 was united with the Polish Socialist Party). As an advocate of the Polish road to socialism, however, he fell out of favour with Joseph Stalin and was subsequently expelled from the Party and imprisoned. After the Khrushchev report was revealed and criticism of Stalin's methods became common, the accusations against Gomułka became one of his own main political cards. In May 1956, Party representatives started negotiating with him and he was soon readmitted to the Party.

Beginning in the spring of 1956, two factions in the Party started competing for Gomułka's support. One of them, the so-called 'Puławianie' (the Puławska group), was considered the more reformist wing of the Party and the second, the 'Natolińczycy', were seen as the more conservative. Each hoped that after regaining power, which from month to month became increasingly possible, Gomułka would decide to carry out their vision of change.[6]

Eventually, in October 1956, Gomułka again became First Secretary of the Party. But his comeback took place in dramatic circumstances, when the Soviet leaders had decided to ascertain the situation in Warsaw themselves. Khrushchev and his closest comrades became quite worried that they might lose control over the situation. At the same time, the Soviet troops stationed in Poland were given the order

---

5   Jankowiak, S. 'Poznański Czerwiec 1956—Kon', in Szymoniczek, J., Król, E. C. (eds.), *Rok 1956 w Polsce i jego rezonans w Europie*. Warsaw: Instytut Studiów Politycznych PAN, 2009, p. 11.

6   Soon after regaining the position of Party leader, he removed from power some representatives of both fractions. None of the groups managed to persuade him otherwise. Gomułka was determined to follow his own political vision.

to start advancing towards the Polish capital. It was the only time since the end of the Second World War when the possibility of Soviet intervention in Poland became not only a real possibility, but also actually began. The troops stopped less than 100 kilometres away from Warsaw awaiting further orders.

Gomułka managed to persuade Khrushchev that he could control the situation and that the Soviet leaders need not be afraid of losing control over Poland. Khrushchev agreed that from now on the Polish ministry of Defence would be ruled by a Polish minister, not a Soviet one as had hitherto been the case. That was one of the rare occasions when the Soviet rulers agreed to reach a compromise.

In October, the Party leaders were also forced to confront an uncontrolled mobilization of the masses. It was the first such experience for the Polish Communist leaders. Till that time, they had never experienced such strong pressure from mass demonstrations, marches, and rallies. Since the end of the Second World War, Polish society had been much more passive than before the war, and that made governing comparatively easy for the authorities. The Polish October opened up discussion of topics that had never publicly been even mentioned before: economic and political dependence on the Soviet Union, the presence of the so-called Soviet advisers, the Katyń massacre, the Home Army, the security forces, and the privileges of the Communist authorities.

Because of this atmosphere, without precedent in Communist Poland, comprising a mixture of demands, anxiety, and tension, but also mobilization of the public and hope for change, this month went down in Polish history as the Polish October.[7] The biggest rally took

---

7   For more information about social activity in Poland during 1956, see Codogni, P. *Rok 1956*. Warsaw: *Prószyński i Spółka*, 2006; idem, 'Aktywność społeczna w Polsce w 1956 roku: Obszary i kulminacje', in Szymoniczek, J., Król, E. C. (eds.) *Rok 1956 w Polsce i jego rezonans w Europie*. Warsaw: Instytut Studiów Politycznych PAN, pp. 174–190; idem, 'Gesellschaftliche Aktivitäten in Polen im Jahre 1956: Bereiche und Höhepunkte', in Szymonicek, J., Król, E.C. *Das Jahr 1956 in Polen Und Seine Resonanz in Europa*. Warsaw: Instytut Studiów Politycznych PAN, 2010; idem, 'La

place in Warsaw on 24 October, when Gomułka was enthusiastically greeted by 300,000 people, but his reply was brief and resolute: 'No more rallying or demonstrating'. From the moment he regained power and the support of the masses, Gomułka endeavoured to stop the wave of public activity, which had in fact begun to worry him.

As the new First Secretary of the Polish Party, Gomułka skilfully dealt with the expectations of society, touching upon most of crucial problems. He publicly stated, for example, the need to negotiate new rules in the relationship with the Soviet Union, to bring about deep changes in the Polish economy, and to implement of new agricultural policy. He also stated that the workers of Poznań who had revolted in June had had the right to do so. This declaration was of huge symbolical importance. At the same time, however, Gomułka clearly emphasized that there was a limit to these changes. To cool down the atmosphere that had been created especially by students and other young people, he stated: 'From our young people and especially the ones receiving higher education, we have a right to demand that they zealously search for ways to improve our present situation in the framework of the declaration made by our Party today. We can forgive a lot. But life does not forgive anyone steps taken in haste.'[8] These words can reasonably be considered the first but still cautious indication that the Party planned to retain the monopoly on setting the limits of change. In the meantime, the wave of public demonstrations subsided, but the atmosphere during the demonstrations in November and December was heated by the news of the Hungarian Uprising.

The atmosphere of the Polish October was characterized by a shared feeling of trust in the new first secretary. The support that he gained was demonstrated in numerous letters and donations sent to

---

différenciation du communism: Le cas de la Pologne', in Mink, G., Lazar, M., Sielski, M. (eds.) *1956, une date europeenne*. Paris: Noir sur blanc, 2010, pp. 217–223.

8 Gomułka, W. 'Droga demokratyzacji jest jedyną drogą prowadzącą do zbudowania najlepszego w naszych warunkach modelu socjalizmu. Przemówienie Władysława Gomułki wygłoszone na VIII. Plenum KC PZPR', *Trybuna Ludu*, 21st October 1956, p. 3.

the Central Committee. The participants in the demonstrations declared their willingness to make production commitments as well as to transfer part of their wages to the State. Some farmers declared that they would surpass their obligatory supplies without extra payment. The scale of Gomułka's popularity was also visible in the reactions of society after the news spread that he was planning to visit Moscow in November. The citizens of Cracow who signed their letter to the first secretary as 'true friends' wrote: 'We are very concerned by the news about your visit to Moscow and for that reason we dare to send you an ardent appeal to abandon, please, any thought of going there, if at all possible. If, however, you must go, because of the importance of diplomatic relations, we beg you to take your own private cook, food, and doctor with you.'[9]

A question that needs to be posed is what was behind the great social support for Gomułka? To answer this properly, it might be helpful to provide a brief description of the man. Without a doubt, his idea of a modern, well-functioning state was in keeping with the rules of the totalitarian system.[10] What made Gomułka's idea about the State different from the idea of totalitarian rule was his understanding of national ideology. He was certain that Communist ideology should be connected with patriotic ideas. He believed that society would support Communist ideology, as soon as it truly understood it.[11] Gomułka's general idea of the collectivization of private farms was also different from that of his predecessors. He supposed that collectivization should be a long-term process that would be voluntarily accepted. He was sure that the rate of the process depended only on demonstrating to farmers that the profitability of the collective economy is

---

9   Machcewicz, P. *Polski rok 1956*. Warsaw: Oficyna Wydawnicza-Mowia Wieki, 1993, p. 184.
10   Madajczyk, P. 'Gomułka—dwie odmienności od linii stalinowskiej', in Szymoniczek, J., Król, E. C. (eds.) *Rok 1956 w Polsce i jego rezonans w Europie*. Warsaw: Instytut Studiów Politycznych PAN, 2009, p. 57.
11   Ibid., p. 58.

much better than that of the system of individual farms.[12] He therefore believed that the Communist Party could gain wide social support, and consequently he did not consider terror a necessary instrument to achieve the stability of the system. In his opinion, violence and terror were justified during the struggle for power, but it was not necessary permanently to search for enemies of the system or continuously to fight with them using terror. For Gomułka, terror was a justifiable instrument in the struggle for power, and in times of crisis, but not permanently, not as a basic element of the system. At that time, Gomułka had great political intuition.

In June, during the revolt in Poznań, the public considered the Polish Communists to be puppets and servants of Soviet interests. Symbolically, they were excluded from the national community. In October, they became a part of the nation, and in a sense opposed Soviet domination. As Machcewicz has convincingly argued, anti-Soviet sentiments were the main feature unifying society at that time; they were much stronger than anti-Communist and anti-system ideas.

The wave of enthusiasm about Gomułka was connected not only with the fact that he had become the new number one in the Party but also, much more important, he had suddenly become the leader of the nation, and managed to oppose the Soviet rulers. At that time, he was considered the true leader of national resistance to the Soviet Union. This led to the legitimization of Communist power in Poland, which had previously had only a revolutionary character. In October, the Party was legitimated by the slogans of the national sovereignty of Poland and of partner relations with the Soviet Union.

The symbolic end of the Polish October came with the general elections in January 1957 and the closure of the *Po prostu* (Plain talk) weekly, which was considered a centre of revisionism in October 1957. In that month, during the 10th plenary meeting of the Party, Gomułka warned against going too far with changes, in a very figurative comparison:

---

12   Jarosz, D. *Polityka władz komunistycznych w Polsce w latach 1948–1956 a chłopi*. Warsaw: DiG, 1998.

> As at any other construction site, the construction of socialism requires strong leadership. What would happen if the main builders, architects, engineers, each as he wished and according to his own estimations, began changing the plan and designs that had already been made and approved? What if each gave his own instructions to the workers, technicians, and foremen working on this building? In real life, this is simply not possible. The builders of houses and factories are all practical, rigorous people. [...] They are pretty aware that the construction would collapse if each one of them started to build on his own. And in the ranks of our Party there are 'sages' who think that this is the way to build socialism in Poland.[13]

These words were obviously directed both against revisionists who demanded changes and against the part of society which sympathized with them. Gomułka was a dogmatist and an autocrat, who paradoxically became afraid of such huge support expressed by the masses. He also feared the reaction of Moscow, especially after the Soviet military intervention in Hungary.

To decide whether 1956 was a wasted year or not, one must consider the consequences of the events we have been discussing. Some of them were short lived, but others survived, leaving permanent traces in the way the Communist system operated. The most lasting were the changes in agriculture. In 1956, 85 % of the existing collective farms ceased to exist. The authorities practically abandoned the idea of creating collective farms. Compared with other Eastern-bloc states this was a distinctly Polish feature. Throughout the years of the Communist régime, privately owned farms survived in Poland. This did not mean of course that the agricultural policies of the Party were rational. Individual farmers had to face many obstacles, including the low prices that the State set for their produce.

After the Polish October, changes occurred also in two pillars of the Communist system—terror and propaganda. After 1956, the brutality of the régime decreased. Though the authorities did not abandon using terror, its scale decreased and the methods were not so hard. In the 1960s and 1970s terror was more selective than before. After

---

13 Gomułka, W. 'Sytuacja w partii i w kraju. Referat tow. Władysława Gomułki na X Plenum KC PZPR', *Trybuna Ludu*, 26th October 1957, p. 3.

October, the authorities abandoned the wide-scale repression of the Polish people. The pressure on the form and substance of the arts and sciences was also diminished and some autonomy of artistic circles as well as contact with Western culture was accepted.

The Communist authorities also changed their policy towards the Roman Catholic Church. The anti-Church offensive began again in 1958, but thanks to the mass religious practices of the Polish people as well as the cautious politics of the bishops, the Church managed to defend itself and even to strengthen its position. The Church supported groups in society such as clubs of Catholic intellectuals and the Catholic University in Lublin.

In the area of economic policy, however, any changes were stopped quite soon. Any attempts at reform of the planning system or creating a modern system of workers' councils misfired. In 1959, the return to intensive industrialization became visible.

The Polish October did not bring about any changes in the structure of power, the Party, or State. The State continued to dominate in the social division of labour, and the State ownership of the means of production continued to be the basis of the economic system. The centralism of the Party continued. There was no freedom of speech or any chance to hold free elections.

It needs to be emphasized that the strengthening of the position of the Communist authorities was connected with the uprising in Hungary and its bloody suppression by the Soviet troops.[14] The Polish authorities used it in their propaganda as a bugbear — an example that such bloodshed could happen whenever society dares to revolt. Already in November and December, the Communist authorities cleverly used the Hungarian tragedy and the news coming from that country to stifle the spirit of revolt in the Polish people. Memories of the experiences of the Second World War, especially of the Warsaw

---

14 Another stabilizing factor that stopped the Poles from revolting was the consciousness that the other countries of the Eastern bloc were in much worse circumstances.

Uprising, meant that the fate of Hungary served as an effective warning to the Poles.

An additional element that helped to buttress Communist power was connected with the problem of defining the Polish-German border. This factor restrained the aspirations of Polish people and kept Poland dependent on the Soviet Union.[15]

The most important factor limiting the social activity in late 1956, however, resulted from Gomułka's having managed to win genuine trust, something unparalleled in Polish history in the era of Communist rule.

What must not escape our attention is Polish consciousness. The years of war and occupation, the change of state borders, the resettlements connected with it, and the mass migrations of young farmers to towns all greatly changed the consciousness and aspirations of Polish society. This inevitably influenced its political horizons.[16] Young people who made successful careers constituted a huge social group which was unwilling to revolt. This group was simply wary of any deep changes, particularly of the prospect of a return to the pre-war order.

The events of 1956 also resulted in some changes connected with social attitudes. These changes were permanent but not positive. The October events made the Party attractive for many people, who considered it an organization that was now truly Polish. They were sure that Party membership would allow them to play a positive role in society. Some intellectuals saw Marxism as the correct lens through which to understand history, politics, science, and the arts. As Communist ideology became less hard-line, the social resistance to it abated too. More and more people considered the relative stability and liberty to be achievements that should not be jeopardized by setting impossible tasks. As Piotr Madajczyk has rightly noted:

---

15   Friszke, A. 'Polski październik 1956 r. z perspektywy pięćdziesięciolecia', in Rowiński, J. (ed.) *Polski Październik 1956 w polityce światowej*. Warsaw: PISM, 2006, p. 315.
16   Ibid, p. 316.

Gomułka achieved success also in creating attitudes which in the coming years would be registered by scientists as learned helplessness, a limitation of individual initiative as well as domination of bureaucratic restrictions. The attitude that was directed to the collective featured a lack of tolerance to different behaviours and ideas. With time, the authorities became the victims of their own politics, as they created expectations that could not be met by the inefficient economy. When the economic situation required a reduction in the standard of living, the legitimacy of the authorities collapsed.[17]

It is time now to return to the questions that were posed at the beginning of this essay: Was 1956 a breakthrough or a continuation? Did it influence changes in the Communist system or, on the contrary, did it fix it? Unfortunately, the answer is that the Polish experiences of 1956 were not unequivocal. These questions have no reasonable answers.

On the one hand, the course as well as the consequences of October strengthened and authenticated the national legitimacy of the Polish Communists. They removed the odium of being alien to the nation, which till 1956 had been very strongly felt. It is in fact reasonable to say that after the political crisis of 1956 the system gained stronger foundations. As Andrzej Paczkowski has written: 'After getting rid of the most visible "mistakes and distortions" it became something obvious and common: just as the river Vistula flows from south to north, and after winter comes the spring, Poland was socialist'.[18]

On the other hand, 1956 bequeathed a mission in a state under a Communist régime: freedom of speech and opinion, freedom of association in clubs and other social organizations, and in workers councils were possible and acceptable. It also established a tradition of discussion about the shape of economic reform in order positively to influence economic efficiency. As we have seen, the post-October political debate revealed topics that had not been publicly discussed before, for example, history and the achievements of the Home Army, and the presence of Soviet advisers.

---

17   Madajczyk, P. 'Gomułka—dwie odmienności od linii stalinowskiej', in Szymoniczek, J., Król, E. C. (eds.) *Rok 1956 w Polsce i jego rezonans w Europie*. Warsaw: Instytut Studiów Politycznych PAN, 2009, p. 70.
18   Paczkowski, A. *Pół wieku dziejów Polski 1939–1989*. Warsaw: Wydawnictwo Naukowe PWN, 1995, p. 318.

For many years to come, the traditions and experiences of October influenced the thinking of circles critical of the system, by becoming an important point of reference which allowed them to consider the horizons of possible change. The influence of October 1956 on the thinking of Poles continued even though it became obvious that after October the authorities were no longer willing to listen to any criticism. The only thing that they could accept was unconditional subordination.

The Polish people were robbed of part of the achievement of that brief time, but 1956 gave them a moment's respite. For that reason, 1956 should be included amongst the most important experiences of the Polish nation on the path to the change in political system that finally took place in 1989. The Polish people believed Gomułka's assertion that there was such a phenomenon as humane socialism, something that could be called the Polish way to socialism. They were deceived. This great experience can, and should, be considered the most important gain of 1956 in Poland. It was its one and only lesson.

Imre Nagy — Hero or Victim?

Zoltán Ripp[1]
Institute of Political History, Budapest

Abstract: The text examines the role of Imre Nagy in the Hungarian political history, the events of 1956 and the perceptions of his personality in the Kádár era and then after the fall of the communist regime. The author embarks upon a comparative perspective, taking a look at the situation in 1956 in Hungary and Poland and the role of Imre Nagy in comparison to Władysław Gomułka. There were four main factors connected to Nagy and influencing the course of the events of 1956 in Hungary: the international situation and the Soviet preference for stability in their satellites, the emergence of alternatives in the Hungarian Socialist Workers' Party, moral crisis of the communist regime and finally the widespread popular discontent amongst all the main strata of society.

In the course of the peaceful transition from the Communist régime to a parliamentary, free-market democracy in Hungary the greatest mass demonstration was held during the June 1989 ceremonial re-burial of Imre Nagy (1896–1958) and his other executed comrades, just a few days before the beginning of the round-table talks.[2] It seemed likely back then that Imre Nagy, who had never denied his Communist identity even on the gallows, would be the foremost representative of the 1956 revolution, and contrary to the Kádár era, when he was treated as a traitor, he would become a national hero.

Nevertheless, the downplaying of Nagy's importance began immediately in 1990, when the first freely elected parliament passed its first legislation about the historic importance of 1956, but Nagy's name was expunged from the bill. In the process of creating the new canon of the 1956 events, the Christian Conservative parties wanted to find somebody other than Nagy to praise as a national hero of 1956. Since there were no important politicians to take his place in the national memory, street fighters and victims of the reprisals became the heroes

---

[1] E-mail: rippz@t-online.hu.
[2] On the re-burial of Imre Nagy, see György, P. *Néma hagyomány*, Budapest: Magvető, 2000, p. 347.

of 1956 who merited celebration.[3] The Right did not want Imre Nagy, a Communist, to be a commonly acceptable national politician, yet they did not want to acknowledge that the post-Communist Left would celebrate him as one of their own. János Rainer's excellent Nagy biography[4] seems to have been published in vain, since it has had far less effect on public opinion than the political divisions have. The negation of the left-wing traditions of 1956 has been continuously increasing, and more and more people want to see Nagy purely as a victim of the well-known internal struggles amongst Communists, that is, as a politician who is respected for having continued to act morally, but as someone who nevertheless could not be seen as a symbol of 1956.

In any case, the question is perhaps rather antonymic: how could a Communist, Imre Nagy, be a national hero symbolizing the anti-Communist revolution of 1956? An answer is offered in Márta Mészáros's film about Nagy, *A temetetlen halott* (The Unburied Dead), made in 2004. It, however, aroused the greatest indignation among Nagy's descendants and his co-defendants. The director was accused of falsifying history by allegedly presenting a fictionalized account as a true documentary, and deceitfully depicting Nagy's co-defendants. Furthermore, she falsified Nagy's final statement at the end of the trial: in the movie he renounces his Communist identity. This is because Mészáros's film is a 'passion play', a story of a moral hero who stands by the failed revolution in the face of Communist inhumanity, but she has discarded the real drama of Nagy's fate. She has erased the story of Nagy, the reformer who remains totally faithful to the Party, maintains his Communist identity, takes the side of the people in revolt, and seeks to achieve the democratic aims of the revolution.

---

3   Ripp, Z. 'Az ötvenhatos hagyományok és a politika', *Mozgó Világ*, vol. 29 (2003), no. 8, pp. 15–26.
4   Rainer, J. M. *Nagy Imre: Politikai életrajz*, vol. 1 *(1896–1953)*; vol. 2 *(1953–1958)*. Budapest: 1956-os Intézet, 1996–99, p. 553; p. 452.

To understand the Nagy phenomenon it is helpful to analyze the Polish and Hungarian events of 1956 comparatively, though the essence would be visible not in the similarities, parallels, and mutual influences, but in the disparities.[5] The differences would elucidate that while a revolution and fight for freedom took place in Hungary, the Communists of Poland were able to avoid a greater evil after the Poznań riots.

The first consideration is that as prime minister, Nagy had already led an attempt at de-Stalinization even before the 20th Congress of the CPSU. Although it is true that in June 1953 he became the leading figure of the government on orders from Moscow, and with a programme accepted there, he not only adopted it, but also intended to move further in the process he had just begun. He was popular because he had to struggle for changes against the will of Mátyás Rákosi (1892-1971), the General Secretary of the Party, and this struggle did not remain hidden from the public. A considerable number of intellectual reformers in the Party supported him;[6] they later played an important role in the intellectual preparation of the revolution, and took part in the efforts to convince him in October 1956 to try and implement the demands of the revolutionaries.

This early de-Stalinization period of his life might have turned Nagy into the 'Hungarian Gomułka' if the reforms had not been so obstructed, that is, if the commitment to the extent and intensity of the changes had not been so limited. A different situation began in early

---

[5] For the relationships between the Polish and Hungarian events of 1956, see Tischler, J. *Rewolucja Węgierska 1956 w polskich dokumentach*. Warsaw: Instytut Studiów Politycznych Polskiej Akademii Nauk, 1995, p. 206; idem, 'Wladyslaw Gomulka und Imre Nagy (Der Verhältnis zwieschen beiden Staatsmännern im Lichte ausgewählter Dokumente und Erinnerungen 1956-1958)', in Hahn, H., Olschowsky, H. (eds.) *Das Jahr 1956 in Ostmitteleuropa*. Berlin: Akademie Verlag, 1996, pp. 146-61; idem, 'Poland and Hungary in 1956', in Congdon, L., Király, B. K., Nagy, K. (eds.) *1956: The Hungarian Revolution and War for Independence*. New York: Atlantic Research and Publications, 2006, pp. 95-127.

[6] Litván, G. 'A Nagy Imre-csoport kialakulása és tevékenysége', *Társadalmi Szemle*, vol. 47(1992), no. 6, pp. 89-95.

1955 when the Rákosi group triumphantly returned to power, and relieved Nagy first of his post and then of his Party membership.

When, out of power, Nagy articulated his criticism of Hungarian Stalinism and emphasized the necessity of a reform programme, he refused the self-criticism demanded by Moscow and stood by his views on the authentic national road to socialism and the need for equality in the relationship with the Soviet Union. In these ways he sought to avoid a social explosion. He was hardly full of revolutionary fervour. He sought a dénouement under the leadership of the Communist s who had broken with the Stalinist past, based on a wider 'policy of alliance'.

Revolutions do not erupt when the oppression is at its worst but when the conditions are sufficiently ripe. If popular discontent with the unbearable situation had been enough for a revolution, then it is hard to explain why exactly Hungary was the right place and October 1956 was the right time, since there had already been uprisings in Berlin in 1953 and in Poznań in summer 1956, but they did not turn into revolution.

The ripening of the conditions for the Hungarian revolution consisted in at least four basic elements; all of them are connected with Nagy. The first element was international events. The 20th Congress of the CPSU helped to generate a situation in Hungary that was slightly different than in other Eastern bloc countries. In a way, the Congress provided justification after the fact for Nagy's policies of 1953–54, and also compromised the re-Stalinization efforts of Rákosi. Nevertheless, the Soviet leaders sought stability in the region, and wanted to base it on reliable cadres. They did not reckon with János Kádár (1912–1989) to be the head of the Party instead of Rákosi, although Kádár's political character was closer to Gomułka's than Nagy's. Even less did the Soviet leaders intend to rehabilitate Nagy.

Khrushchev wanted reconciliation with Tito in a way that would not strengthen 'national Communism' in the countries of the bloc, and would not encourage independence from Moscow.[7] The inauguration of co-existence, the promise of a policy of détente, was coupled with the hope that strong dependence on the Soviet bloc would be slightly modified — a hope also encouraged by the Soviet and Yugoslav declarations. In his writings Nagy urged that the 'Bandung Principles' (1955) of the Non-Aligned Movement should be adapted to the relations of the Socialist countries with each other.[8]

Nevertheless, Moscow's anxiety was growing because of the tendency of 'national communism', particularly in the light of the Polish and Hungarian developments. The Soviet leaders wanted to re-establish stability in the client states, whose leaders had been overwhelmed by the 20th Congress, and did not welcome any reforms that posed a threat to their own power. The Soviets sought both a cautious policy of de-Stalinization and to stabilize their power. Fearing a Poznań-like uprising in Hungary, they substituted for Rákosi the hardliner Ernő Gerő (1898-1980), who was loyal to Moscow; although they hoped that he would be able to manage the double task, this decision only deepened the crisis.[9]

The second factor was the emergence of alternatives inside the Party, with regard to both the programme and the leadership. Hopes reappeared in the spring of 1956, but now, unlike in 1953, they took the form of new demands made to new political leaders. The public wanted fundamental changes and also guarantees that the changes would last. Only the Communist reformers around Nagy, however, were able to present alternatives to the programme and the leadership, since no other political power was allowed to emerge. Conversely, the

---

7   For Yugoslav factor and the 1956 revolution, see Ripp, Z. 'Hungary's Part in the Soviet-Yugoslav Conflict, 1956-58', *Contemporary European History*, vol. 7 (1998), no. 2, pp. 197-225.
8   For Nagy's writings from 1955-56, see Nagy, I. *"A magyar nép védelmében": Vitairatok és beszédek 1955-1956*. Paris: Magyar Füzetek, 1984, p. 265.
9   For the international relations of the Hungarian revolution, see Békés, C. *Az 1956-os forradalom a világpolitikában*. Budapest: 1956-os Intézet, 2006, p. 391; idem (ed.) *Evolúció és revolúció: Magyarország és a nemzetközi politika 1956-ban*. Budapest: 1956-os Intézet and Gondolat, 2007, p. 404.

opposition inside the Party increasingly gained publicity. It was clear that there was important social support behind the gradually shaping programme. Most likely, the majority was far even from the reformist wing of the Communist Party, but the only realistic possibility was to support Nagy.

The third factor forming the conditions of revolution was the moral crisis. The denunciation of the crimes of the terrorist dictatorship was an element in the struggle against the Rákosi group, together with the introspection of the intellectuals of the internal-Party opposition and the need for exoneration. Denunciations had begun even before the 20th Congress. In his writings, Nagy condemned the Rákosi group for having built a 'Bonapartist dictatorship', and, though he did not want a pluralist democracy, he espoused a movement of renewal, and serving the people was no mere slogan for him. In the autumn of 1956, radical demands, in parallel with those of the public, were increasingly heard even amongst the people in power; these voices called for the dismissal of the compromised leaders and deemed the leadership of Nagy and Kádár a possible way out of the moral crisis. If this had actually happened in time, it would have resulted in a Gomułka-like solution. But the conditions inside the Hungarian Party made it impossible. Nagy was re-admitted to the Party only in mid-October.

The fourth and most important factor was the widespread popular discontent amongst all the main strata of society, which was intensified by the abuses committed by those in power. In addition to this people were beginning to hope in the possibility of change. Discontent was expressed by the youth, who wanted Nagy to take power. His popularity was more than mere anticipatory trust; it was an appreciation of his former presidency as well.

The political struggles before 23 October did not really prepare or trigger the revolution. Rather, they gave it potential. The changes in Poland merely provided the final impulse to the uprising. That the demonstration of solidarity became an uprising and the uprising turned into a revolution and then a struggle for national liberation came as a shock to Nagy as well.

In the process, he always remained in the centre, but in truly diverse situations. On the day of the demonstration, hopes for change were invested in him, and he was asked to lead the country. But he was considered an enemy when he accepted the office of prime minister yet accepted the Soviet intervention. After the turning point on 28 October, as he established a coalition government and was seen to be the one accomplishing the democratic and national demands, Nagy increasingly came to be accepted as the leader of the revolution. By condemning the second Soviet invasion and the Kádár government, he accepted a fate that made him a national hero. By being imprisoned, he became the symbolic figure of the resistance that was active till the end of the year, and he came to be esteemed as the legitimate leader of Hungary.[10]

For a proper assessment of Nagy's role in 1956, one fundamental characteristic of the Hungarian revolution has to be borne in mind — namely, the interdependence of the armed struggles and the political contests. Considering this context makes it possible to understand the revolution as an organic movement, despite all its diversity and contradictions. It allows one to assess the political contests and the armed struggles more accurately as elements of a strictly interlinked chain of events. Furthermore, on this basis one can understand how the massive role played by Communists in an anti-Stalinist popular movement became possible. The axiom I propose is twofold: (1) without the armed uprising and the subsequent nationwide revolutionary movement, the Communist Party, even with the emergence of the reformers, would have been unable to meet the initial, minimal demands of the revolution; (2) without the political struggle inside the Communist Party (with the Kremlin's Budapest emissaries, Mikoyan and Suslov), and without the subsequent turnaround, the revolution would never

---

10 Even the worker's councils, the main source of resistance, demanded the reconstitution of the Nagy government.

have reached its successful phase of initial institutionalization.[11] The relationships between them seem obvious, though in fact the debates about the revolution and Nagy are centred on the various interpretations of these two factors.

The question arises of whether there was a real chance to solve the crisis in the 'moderate' Polish way? The Kremlin was well aware of the situation in Hungary, but its attention was focused on Poland, strategically more important. There were great differences between the situations in the two countries. Unlike the attitude of the rest of the Polish leadership towards Gomułka, the majority of the Party leadership in Hungary was not behind Nagy. They were not even considering putting pressure on Khrushchev to appoint him leader of the Party. In Warsaw, the lesson of Poznań was well understood. The Hungarian leadership, on the contrary, immediately judged the events in Budapest to be a counter-revolutionary rebellion, and, in agreement with Moscow, they decided at once to ask the Soviets to intervene with armed force.[12] The Polish did not demand the withdrawal of the Soviet troops — apparently because of the geopolitical situation of their country. Following the peaceful settlement of the Polish conflict, the Soviet leadership obviously deemed even a single precedent of backing-down to be one too many. In Hungary they may have seen the risks of intervention as being smaller, and hoped for a successful repetition of the instant suppression of the 1953 Berlin uprising.

The moment the Soviets intervened militarily, the chances for a Gomułka-type solution vanished. In Warsaw, the Communist Party leadership appeared to be a source of resistance against the imposed Soviet model. Gomułka gained support as a Communist, but he also demonstrated that he had a democratic and national side. In Budapest,

---

11 For events in the Party leadership, see Ripp, Z. 'A pártvezetés végnapjai', in Horváth, J., Ripp, Z. (eds.) *Ötvenhat októbere és a hatalom*. Budapest: Napvilág, 1997, pp. 169–314.
12 For the military history of 1956, see Horváth, M. *1956 hadikrónikája*. Budapest: Akadémiai Kiadó, 2003, p. 482.

the Party leadership was uncertain, yet it used force immediately and thus demonstrated it was not with the nation in the face of a popular movement built on a national basis against Soviet intervention. Nagy made a mistake when he accepted the presidency during the intervention without insisting on the immediate dismissal of the Stalinists. He had to pay the price to regain his credibility — and this also helped him to accept the revolutionary demands. Instant repression of the uprising became impossible not only because the Soviet leadership failed in their hopes of bringing about the repetition of the Berlin example. The revolution had expanded to the whole country, with rebels' taking control of villages and workplaces as well. The struggle within the Communist Party also complicated a solution based on arms alone.

The Hungarian Party leadership depended on the Soviet Union in a twofold way. On the one hand, it could maintain its power only by the use of outside force; on the other, it had to secure Moscow's agreement to make substantial concessions to channel the uprising. The leadership of the Soviet Communist Party based its decisions on information from its Budapest emissaries, Mikoyan and Suslov, the KGB chairman Serov, and Ambassador Andropov.[13]

Inside the Hungarian Communist Party, debates arose between the Nagy group, who tended towards concessions and urged a 'political solution', and hardliners, who demanded a 'military solution'. Nagy was being swept along by events, and gradually realized that there was no intermediate solution: either the popular movement had to be suppressed thoroughly or its main demands had to be met. The fact that Kádár had also taken the side of Nagy was important in convincing the Soviets to change their view.

---

13 For documents of the Soviet decisions, see Szereda, V., Sztikalin, A. (eds.) *Hiányzó lapok 1956 történetéből*. Budapest: Móra, 1993, p. 326; Gál, É., Hegedűs, A. B., Litván, G., Rainer, J. M. (eds.) *A "Jelcin-dosszié": Szovjet dokumentumok 1956-ról*. Budapest: Századvég – 1956-os Intézet, 1993, p. 242; Szereda, V., Rainer, J. M. *Döntés a Kremlben, 1956*. Budapest: 1956-os Intézet, 1996, p. 256.

Even Tito and Gomułka supported the turning-point of 28 October. They changed their minds when it became clear that the Communist régime itself had become unsustainable. They looked to Nagy to consolidate the situation, but it became clear that the only possible way to consolidate was to accept the revolutionary demands. In the light of the acceptance of pluralist parliamentary democracy, free elections, and the Soviet government declaration on 30 October, the hope of national independence seemed to promise victory for the revolution.

The further violence from outside, the second Soviet attack, compelled Nagy's coalition government to institutionalize the achievements of the revolution. If we start from the point that the Soviet leadership found these demands intolerable, the victory of the revolution itself meant its defeat. Some contemporary experts, like Charles Gati, blame Nagy first for his delay and second for his excesses; the ignoring of the Soviet standpoints, they state, and the absence of Gomułka-like moderation led to the defeat of achievements that were still sustainable.[14]

Nagy in fact fell into a trap: if he was unable to prove that under his leadership there would be fast consolidation, the Soviets would intervene; but to consolidate, he had to overstep the bounds that were still acceptable to Moscow.

The key point was the declaration of neutrality by the Nagy government, which accomplished the main requirement of domestic consolidation. It aimed to create a new situation in global politics by means of a re-assessment of the international status of Hungary. Hence it avowedly placed the fate of the Hungarian revolution into the hands of the great powers. Nevertheless, that fate was already in their hands. The act simply made it even more obvious. It did not provoke intervention; on the contrary, it wanted to stop it and to seize the last faint opportunity. The western powers did not react, because if

---

14 Gati, C. *Vesztett illúziók: Moszkva, Washington, Budapest és az 1956-os forradalom*. Budapest: Osiris, 2006, p. 254.

they had they would have had to admit that the status quo was unchangeable and that the American doctrine of liberation was deceitful.

Moscow well understood that not the modification of the Communist system, but its fall was on the agenda. The Communist leaders of East Germany, Czechoslovakia, Romania, and Bulgaria welcomed further armed intervention in Hungary with relief. Gomułka and Tito were not against it either, since events had already gone beyond the limits of their tolerance.

The revolution made Nagy understand that it was a mistake to identify the reform programme of June with the will of the majority of the people. From the point of view of his own principles, he judged the acceptance of bourgeois democracy as a step back, but he found it more important that the legitimacy of power should be created by achieving the democratic aims and national independence, according to the will of the majority of the people. He did not abandon Communist doctrine as a whole, but he did break with one of its basic tenets, the dictatorship of the proletariat. In this sense, he was a forerunner of Eurocommunism.

On 4 November, Nagy had a choice between betraying the people — the Kádár way — and martyrdom. His resistance to the second Soviet intervention constituted an irreversible statement: being the legitimate prime minister of Hungary, he refused the suppression of national independence and the legitimation of the reconstruction of the despotic regime; hence he refused to acknowledge the puppet-government of Kádár.

In his notes written in captivity in Romania, Nagy tried to provide theoretical support to break with Stalinism. Based as they were, however, on Marxist-Leninist principles legitimating Communism, these notes are not without contradictions.[15] Similarly to many other Communists, he contrasted the promises of the humanist utopia with the Stalinist reality. Moral indignation led him to criticize the system,

---

15   Nagy, I., Vida, I. (ed.) *Snagovi jegyzetek: Gondolatok, emlékezések 1956–1957*, ed. Budapest: Gondolat, 2006, p. 447.

but he never stepped beyond the point where he would give up Marxist theory and his Communist political identity.

To the Communists who sentenced him, however, Nagy could only be a traitor to Communism, an initiator and leader of the counter-revolution. Nobody, not even Gomułka, could deviate from the international campaign against revisionism and Titoism without risking excommunication from Moscow. Because of his own domestic position, it would have been better for Gomułka if Nagy had not been executed, but after some hesitation he was forced to accept it. In Hungary Gomułka was increasingly seen to be just like the other Communist leaders.

Nagy continued to be denounced as a traitor in the official version of 1956 during the Kádár era. He and Rákosi had to be condemned, each as a representative of an extreme. Nevertheless, the State's aim increasingly was to forget him, and also to suppress any sympathy for him.[16] Nagy's memory was cultivated by his former followers in exile and, from the 1980s onwards, also by the opposition publishing in samizdat, whose main effort was to refute the slander about him. His leftism was therefore evident, nothing disturbing; moreover, it was an element of the Kádárian slander. As we have seen, the downplaying of Nagy's positive role began in 1990. In 2006, on the 50th anniversary of the revolution, when Budapest was again disturbed by street violence that had not been seen for decades, there were hardly any events or articles commemorating him except some academic articles. The political struggles to create a new 1956 canon are, however, are harmful to history as an academic discipline as well.[17] Nowadays, during the 55th anniversary, the laying of wreathes at the foot of Nagy's monument has gone unnoticed, as if he had been sentenced to oblivion as he had been in the Kádár era. The statue was probably not going to be removed from Kossuth Square near the Parliament. But just

---

16 On the memory-policy of the Communists, see Ripp, Z. '1956 emlékezete és az MSZMP', *Múltunk*, vol. 47 (2002), no. 1, pp. 146–71.
17 Now, after two decades of work, the future of the 1956 Institute, which among its other research cultivates the Imre Nagy tradition as well, has become rather doubtful.

because it is not right on the square, it is not affected by the decision that the square must again look as it did before 1944. With the introduction of the new constitution of Hungary, the Imre Nagy Prize will cease to exist. He is no longer a national hero, just a victim of Communism at its most extreme.

Alexander Dubček, the Best-known Slovak Politician

Stanislav Sikora[1]
Slovak Academy of Sciences, Institute of History

Abstract: The aim of this article is to introduce the life and personality of Alexander Dubček, the best-known (Czecho)Slovak Politician. Both of his parents having lived in the USA, later moved back to Uhrovec, to the house where both where both Ľudovit Štúr and 106 years later Alexander Dubček were born. The latter became a communist official. After childhood in the and half of his studies in the UCCP, he pursued a career as a politician, being an exceptionally active and powerful figure during both the early and latter days of the Prague Spring and inn the end becoming the Chairman of the Federal assembly of the CSSR.

> 'A prophet is not without honour save in his own country, and in his own house.'
> Matt. 13: 57

Dreams and reality

Alexander Dubček (1921–1992) belonged to the part of Slovak society which was dissatisfied with the dismal social and political conditions after the end of the *'thousand-year'* Hungarian empire and was looking for work and a better life abroad. In 1912, at the age of twenty, his father, Štefan, was sent to the USA. His mother, Pavlína Kobydová, had been sent there at the age of thirteen, just two years before. The two met in Chicago, where they lived, and that is also where they wed. Devoted to the dream of a better tomorrow, they welcomed the founding of the first Czechoslovak Republic. And even though they were not suffering from poverty, they decided, as true patriots, to return to Slovakia in 1921. As Alexander Dubček much later recalled, he was already in his mother's womb on the journey to Slovakia, so only a few months separated him from a chance to be born in the America.[2] Štefan and Pavlína Dubček came back to the village of Uhrovec in

---

1 Email: stanislav.sikora@savba.sk
2 Dubček, A. *Nádej zomiera posledná*. Bratislava: Nová Práca, 1993, p. 13.

northwest Slovakia, and, by remarkable coincidence, Dubček was born in the same house where, 106 years earlier, Ľudovít Štúr (1815–1856), the most important figure of the Slovak National Revival in the nineteenth century, which influenced the whole of Slovak history, the true father of the nation, was born.

In the circumstances of the economic depression after the war, however, even the Dubčeks came to regret their homecoming. The reality was markedly different from the dream. Largely because of the bad economic and social conditions in Czechoslovakia at the time, as well conflicts in the international labor movement in the early twentieth century, even the Uhrovec chapter of the Social Democratic Party joined the Third Communist International, the Comintern; it became the local cell of the Communist Party of Czechoslovakia (CPCz). Its chairman was Štefan Dubček. But that is not all. His romantic, revolutionary and adventurous spirit changed the course of events for the Dubček once again. As a part of the Interhelpo cooperative, he and his family left to build Communism in the Soviet Union in late 1925.

Naturally, the reality here was also utterly different from the dream.[3] Especially in the first part of his sojourn in Pishpek (renamed Frunze in 1926, today Bishkek), the capital of Kyrgyzstan, where the expedition encountered shocking backwardness. Their mission was to create bearable living conditions. Later, in 1933, the family moved to the city of Gorky (today, Nizhny Novgorod), where Štefan Dubček was employed in a car factory. He could now put his knowledge of English to good use, since many American engineers and technicians also worked in Gorky.

When Alexander Dubček moved to the Soviet Union he was only of three and half years old. Stalin's methods of terror made an impression on his astute, child's and, later, adolescent mind. Even if he had not fully understood what was happening at the time, Dubček often recalled the persecution of a Kyrgyz farmer during forced collectivization, and later, in Gorky, recalled the purges and show trials in the

---

3   Dubček, A. *Nádej zomiera posledná*. Bratislava: Nová Práca, 1993, p. 17–23.

second half of 1930, when former heroes were branded as traitors and enemies of the people, and were sentenced to death or deportation to the gulags of Siberia. Back then, the resistance to Stalin's totalitarian socialism, which had nothing in common with the people's striving for freedom, work, and a respectable life, was engrained into his subconscious.

The Dubček family returned to Czechoslovakia in autumn 1938, shortly after the signing of the Munich Agreement. The leadership of the Soviet Union had decided that in the event of war, which was brewing, it would be good to have a *'clean slate'* Dubček's father, even if he was a convinced Communist, had decided to return home. He did not want to risk his or his family's future in the conditions of Soviet society, which was characterized by constant suspicion and endless terror.[4] After the now nominally independent Slovak State (de facto a satellite of Nazi Germany) banned the Czechoslovak Communist Party, Štefan Dubček joined in the underground activities of the Slovak Communist Party (CPS), which was created at that time. His young son, Alexander, also helped him, for example, by distributing handbills and various documents. In 1939, Alexander Dubček joined the CPS, quite naturally, in accord with his beliefs and family tradition. He therefore did not join at the height of its power, when the Communist Party was able to offer the rewards, but when the Slovak State was being established and membership of the Communist Party was punishable by persecution, jail, and, during Second World War, even by death. In the same year, he found a job at the Škoda factory in Dubnica nad Váhom, where he was trained as a mechanic.

When, in late August 1944, the Slovak National Uprising erupted, Alexander Dubček, in his family's tradition of fighting for a better world, became directly involved. He was even twice injured while fighting for a new, socially more equitable Czechoslovak Republic in which Slovaks and Czechs would live as equals. In February 1948, the dream of every Czechoslovak Communist seemed to come

---

4   Dubček, A. *Nádej zomiera posledná*. Bratislava: Nová Práca, 1993, p. 36.

true: establishing the power of the working class, which would build a new, more equal and just society. Back then, hardly anyone could have told that the ruthless Stalinist régime at the peak of its expansion would immediately be *'transplanted'* into Czechoslovakia.

Beginning as a professional politician

After the re-establishment of the Czechoslovak Republic in May 1945, Dubček found a job as technician in a yeast factory in Trenčín, Slovakia. Since he had demonstrated his skills, the management was counting on him to become the deputy director. Nevertheless, the Slovak Communists that had known him from his previous underground activities in the resistance, and appreciated his natural communications skills and interest in the public affairs, had different plans for him. In 1949, after some hesitation, he became a member of the Trenčín District Committee of the Slovak Communist Party,[5] and for a time also worked as the first secretary of this body. [6] His hesitation stemmed from the fact that Communist functionaries in Czechoslovakia, at least at the district level, earned far less than the best workers, for example, of a small industrial enterprise. Perhaps Marx's words during the Paris Commune (1871), that the working-class politician should not earn more than a factory worker, were still respected back then. In 1951, Dubček became a deputy of the Czechoslovak National Assembly.

In October 1951, Dubček moved to the Central Committee of the Slovak Communist Party secretariat in Bratislava, and in January 1953 he became the secretary and soon the first secretary of the Regional Committee of the Slovak Communist Party in Banská Bystrica. That was a relatively important Party post. He was one of the working-class cadres who were taking over different posts in the Communist Party,

---

[5] In late September 1948, the hitherto relatively independent Slovak Communist Party was changed into the territorial organization of the Czechoslovak Communist Party in Slovakia.

[6] Laluha, I. *Alexander Dubček, politik a jeho doba*. Bratislava: Nová Práca, 2000, p. 18–20.

full of the enthusiasm of the era. At the time, however, when the Party proceeded from political activity to direct control of every aspect of social life and was also replacing competent government and economic bodies, a lot depended on whether a Party functionary was just trying to impose his personal decisions to subordinate section or if he was open to other's arguments and was able to surround himself with a group of experts. Dubček belonged to the second type of leading Party worker. He remained modest and caring, and actually even managed to play football with boys from the street during his free time. Ivan Laluha (b. 1932), a Slovak politician, historian, and political scientist, remembers Dubček in this respect also. The boys allegedly remarked: '*He is such a normal man.*'[7] For someone of his rank, that was great acknowledgement.

Moscow sojourn

Alexander Dubček, however, did not remain in Banská Bystrica. In late 1954, he was informed that he would be sent to study at the University of Politics attached to the Central Committee of Communist Party of Soviet Union (CC CPSU) in Moscow, although at that time he was already in his sixth semester of law at Comenius University, Bratislava, where he studied externally from 1955 to 1958. But the most important thing is that was in Moscow when Nikita Khrushchev, at the 20th Congress of the CPSU in late February 1956, revealed Stalin's tyranny, lawlessness, mass terror, and his ordering of the deaths of hundreds of thousands of innocent people. Then, unlike in his childhood and youth, when his aversion to Stalin's tyranny was more emotional, Dubček could now consider the matter rationally. Like other Communists after him (including Mikhail Gorbachev, Zdeněk Mlynář, Ota Šik, Josef Smrkovský, and Čestmír Císař), Dubček later claimed that even though Khrushchev's criticism of the '*cult of personality*' at the 20th Congress had not been thorough and

---

[7] Laluha, I. *Alexander Dubček, politik a jeho doba*. Bratislava: Nová Práca, 2000, p. 21.

systematic, it was the turning point in his and others' perceptions of the Soviet or, rather, Stalinist model of Socialism.[8]

The Slovak 'Early Spring'

Slovak historians tend to call the years 1963-67 the *'Early Spring'*, in view of the fact that the *'Prague'* or the *'Czechoslovak Spring'* of 1968 did not arise in a *'vacuum'*, and that an important source of this democratization and liberalization was also developments in Slovakia in this period.[9] It was led by Dubček as General Secretary of the CC CPS, after 1958-60, when he was leading secretary of the Regional Committee of the Slovak Communist Party in Bratislava, and 1960-62, when he was the CC CPCz Secretary for Industry in Prague. It should be emphasized that he was elected to this post in April 1963 against the will of the then all-powerful first secretary of the CC CPCz, Antonín Novotný (1904-1975), because while Dubček was CC CPCz Secretary for Industry, he and Novotný had some misunderstanding, even an argument, over their different perceptions of the political situation in Slovakia and over how to solve its economic problems.

Consequently, Dubček and his followers in the Presidium and the Plenum of the CC CPS happened to be caught between two millstones in 1963-67. One of them, acting from *'above'*, was the dogmatic conservative leadership of the CPCz, led by Novotný and the other one, acting from *'below'* — were the Slovak Communists in revolt, working in the arts, science, and the mass media, mainly in Bratislava, who even by that time may be reasonably considered reform Communists. They were seeking to eliminate the deformations in socialism caused by the so-called *'cult of personality'*, meaning the Communist rulers' criminal disregard for the law and the hellish conditions that resulted in the years the régime was establishing itself in Czechoslovakia, 1948-54. Naturally, Dubček and his followers had skillfully to

---

8   Dubček, A. *Nádej zomiera posledná*. Bratislava: Nová Práca, 1993, p. 80-81.
9   Londák, M., Londáková, E., Sikora, S. *Predjarie: Politický, ekonomický a kultúrny život na Slovensku v rokoch 1960-1967*. Bratislava: Veda, 2002.

navigate between these two poles, because they had to be Prague's reliable *'governors'* in Slovakia and at the same time prominent representatives of the *'revival process'*, as the partial liberalization of the Communist régime in Slovakia was called in the period known as the *'Early Spring'*.

These were the constants of power that Dubček had to respect if he wanted gradually to push through his continuously evolving ideas of a fair socialist society. A good soldier, after all, does everything he can simply not to get killed at the beginning of the war. And the effect of the jailing of the Minister of the Interior, Rudolf Barák (1915-1995), for having *'rebelled'* against Novotný, was still felt. That's why, in the Slovak efforts to achieve national emancipation, Dubček was not yet pushing the idea of a federation of Slovaks and Czechs, which had not been enshrined in the 1960 Constitution of the Czechoslovak Socialist Republic (CSSR), but he was trying considerably to strengthen the Slovak national institutions within the limits of the asymmetrical model characterized by the co-existence of statewide Czechoslovak and autonomous Slovak institutions.[10]

At the same time, Dubček sought to achieve a new style of Party work, different from the administrative power-politics style that was made notorious by his predecessors Karol Bacílek and Viliam Široký and had become characteristic of the Novotný leadership of the CPCz. He emphasized patient explanation, persuasion, and opening up communication between the highest bodies of the Party and its rank-and-file members, *'even though sometimes it takes much longer, than we plan.'*[11] In the relationship between the CPCz and the other parts of the political system, Dubček advocated the idea that the Party was not supposed to give orders to society, but was to set tasks and create space for social engagement and activity. In that case, all other parts of the political system were not to be continuously monitored by the Party, but should have worked with considerable autonomy, and the uniting

---

10   Londák, M., Londáková, E., Sikora, S. *Predjarie: Politický, ekonomický a kultúrny život na Slovensku v rokoch 1960-1967.* Bratislava: Veda, 2002, p. 73-94.
11   Slovenský národný archiv, *ÚV KSS – tajomníci, A. Dubček,* c. no. 2380.

factor should have been the CPCz general line (based on expert analysis of the needs of society) blended into the government programme and the legal system. It is clear, that this method of applying the '*leading role of the Communist Party*' would have shift the Party's apparatus, the cornerstone of the totalitarian régime, into background — after all, it was the one concerned with the continuous monitoring of the whole society.[12]

The Slovak mass media were at that time much freer than those in the Czech part of the country. *Kultúrny život* (Cultural life), the weekly newspaper of the Association of Slovak Writers, for example, is among the best Slovak journalism ever.[13]

Of course, we must not overestimate Dubček's efforts in this period. They never went beyond Lenin's understanding of the role of the Communist Party in Soviet-type socialism. But, compared to the previous state of affairs in this field, they were unquestionably beneficial.

Dubček's political ideas and practical steps led to a growing conflict between him and Novotný. Novotný was always trying to have Dubček removed from the post of First Secretary of the CC CPS, and to replace him with the servile Michal Chudík (1914-2005). Sometimes he used '*heavy artillery*' too: the State Security forces were '*working on him*' in an attempt to prove that Dubček and his wife had collaborated with the Germans during the Second World War while working in the arms factory in Dubnica nad Váhom.[14] The regional secretaries of the CPCz in Slovakia, mainly the regional secretary of Banská Bystrica, Rudolf Cvik, encouraged by Novotný, often acted against Dubček. Between Christmas 1967 and New Year's Eve 1968, when his future was highly uncertain, Novotný even attempted to take over by military

---

12 Londák, M., Londáková, E., Sikora, S. *Predjarie: Politický, ekonomický a kultúrny život na Slovensku v rokoch 1960-1967*. Bratislava: Veda, 2002, p. 119.
13 Fabian, J. 'Analýza masových oznamovacích prostriedkov (1967-1970)' in *Slovenská spoločnosť v krízových rokoch 1967-1970*. Bratislava: Politologický cabinet SAV, 1999, p. 132-135.
14 Pešek, J. *Nástroj represie a politickej kontroly: Štátna bezpečnosť na Slovensku 1953-1970*. Bratislava: Veda, 2000, p. 79.

force, but failed. In the end, when everyone had forsaken him, he resigned from the office of first secretary of the CC CPCz in early 1968. Dubček was unanimously elected in his place.

The Czechoslovak Spring of 1968

When considering Dubček as the new first secretary of the CC CPCz, the most important function in Czechoslovakia at the time, it is still relevant to ask what kind of politician he actually was. Was he really naive, indecisive, hesitant, easy to influence, as his enemies have claimed? He certainly was not naive, as anyone who knows at least a bit about the rules in the CPCz and especially its most powerful part, its *apparat*, would confirm. Here, many different groups were mercilessly struggling for power, and anyone who did not know how to navigate in the '*crowd*' would immediately be crushed. Dubček, in the course of almost 19 years, made great progress from being the district secretary of the District Committee of the CPCz in Trenčín to being the first secretary of the CC CPCz, including work in the *apparat* of the CC CPCz and the CC CPS. It was mainly the conservatives and dogmatists who considered him indecisive and hesitant, for they rejected discussion, always having a clear answer for everything right away. The same people also considered him easy to influence, for he surrounded himself with experts and listened to their advice.

Although Dubček was not a political adventurer, he never let slip an opportunity. But that does not mean that he never made a mistake or never wrongly estimated a situation. One of his biggest mistakes (similarly to his followers in the Party leadership) was that after the CC CPC session in January, he hesitated to approve the Action programme of the CPCz, even though it was completed in mid-February 1968. On the other hand, he also approved the resumption of publishing *Literární listy* (Literature gazette), which had been stopped in summer 1967 because of the IV Congress of the Czechoslovak Writers' Union—an act which was at the time generally understood as the lifting of censorship.[15] The work of the mass media at that time is now considered the best result of the 1968 democratization process. If politics is indeed the '*art of the possible*' and a successful politician should avoid mistakes that may lead to his failure, then the tumultuous democratization in the Czechoslovak mass media at this time appears in a very different light. It was a phenomenon that was mostly criticized by Czechoslovakia's Warsaw Pact allies, especially the Soviet Union, as a tool of '*counter-revolution*'. On the other hand, it was the key to enlivening the Czechoslovak democratization process to such a point that when, in early April 1968, the Action Programme of the CPCz was approved, it could no longer really influence political developments in the country: civil society, particularly in Bohemia and Moravia, was far ahead of the Action Programme.[16]

Dubček is often reproached for not rushing into making immediate personnel changes in the leading positions in the Party or the State, especially by hastily convening a '*cadre*' conference of the CPCz, which might have stopped the Soviet-led military intervention by the Warsaw Pact troops in August 1968. It is now known that the Soviet Union wanted to change the Czechoslovak political course before the Extraordinary 14th Congress of the CPCz because the democratization process was meant to have been confirmed there and the conservatives would definitively have been removed from the leadership. But Dubček was true to his principles: he was trying to achieve pluralism and a true exchange of views in the CPCz, which would have led to consensus based on a realistic assessment of the facts. That's why he wanted the 14th Congress of the CPCz to be thoroughly prepared well in advance and to achieve, not only fundamental cadre changes, but also firm confirmation of the democratization course of Party policy.

---

15   Sikora, S. *Rok 1968 a politický vývoj na Slovensku*. Bratislava: Pro Historia, 2008, p. 50–51.
16   Sikora, S. *Rok 1968 a politický vývoj na Slovensku*. Bratislava: Pro Historia, 2008, p. 65.

Dubček's approach most certainly stemmed from his firm conviction that the Soviet Union and the other Warsaw Pact states definitely would not intervene militarily in Czechoslovakia. This attitude of his seems incomprehensible to us nowadays, especially when we have at our disposal the record of his conversation with the general secretary of the CC CPSU, Leonid Brezhnev, from 13 August 1968. For example: 'Brezhnev to Dubček: "*But surely you understand that this arrangement, this way of fulfilling the obligations undertaken at Čierna nad Tisou, will create a completely new situation which we, too, hadn't reckoned with, and this obviously will compel us to reevaluate the whole situation and resort to new, independent measures.*" Dubček to Brezhnev: "*Comrade Brezhnev, you should resort to all measures that your CC Politburo believes are appropriate.*" Brezhnev to Dubček: "*Do not you see, Sasha, that we undoubtedly will be adopting the measures we believe are appropriate?*" Dubček: "*We are able to resolve all these matters on our own, but if you believe it's necessary for you to adopt certain measures then by all means go ahead.*"'[17]

It is fair to assume that in this highly tense situation between the CSSR and its Warsaw Pact allies, these threats of Brezhnev's, totally undiplomatic, can be understood in only one way—namely, the time for military intervention had come. An important Czech historian and an expert on this topic, Jan Pauer, has argued that Dubček obviously understand neither the scope of Brezhnev's words nor his own.[18] From the words that Dubček repeated several times in this conversation, expressing that he was about to announce his resignation at the upcoming Party conference, it is fair to deduce that he realized the severity of the situation, but was no longer able to resist the Soviet and other Warsaw Pact allies' pressure and had already given up. But what if he noticed the threats, yet did not take them seriously? Or was

---

17 Navrátil, J., Vondrová, J. (eds.) *Mezinárodní souvislosti československé krize*, Prague and Brno: ÚSD and Doplněk, 1995, 1996, 1997, and 2011, p. 176, 178.

18 Pauer, J. *Praha 1968: Vpád Varšavské smlouvy, pozadí – plánování – provedení*. Prague: Argo, 2004, p. 171.

he trying to gain the time he so badly needed in order to accomplish the preparations for the Party congress?

Rearguard actions

After the occupation of Czechoslovakia by armies of the Warsaw Pact, the space in which the reformist leaders of the Party could employ their power and resist external pressures was dramatically reduced. Nevertheless, the leadership attempted *'rearguard actions'* that aimed, in the new circumstances, to salvage as many of the post-January democratic achievements as possible. According to Dubček: *"Our situation was not entirely hopeless. There were a number of ways we could continue to resist, but everything depended upon unity within our ranks – at the top and between us and the Czech and Slovak peoples."*.[19] But the Soviet leadership successfully undermined the fragile unity of the reform forces, and the importance of the so-called realists (including Gustáv Husák, Ludvík Svoboda, and Lubomír Štrougal) increased. The realists were willing to meet the Soviet requirements. In terms of deepening the normalization process, the key role was played by the CC CPCz session of 14–17 November 1968, during which two organizational measures with far-reaching consequences were approved. The first was the creation of the Executive Committee of the Presidium of the CC CPCz (a presidium within the presidium of the CC CPCz). Only two of its eight members—Dubček and Smrkovský—were former proponents of reform. The second was the creation of a Bureau of the CC CPC for the Direction of Party Work in the Bohemian Lands, led by the realist Štrougal. This really weakened Dubček's position and curbed his powers.

The unity of the Czechs and the Slovaks was thus markedly weakened during the politically fabricated struggle in late 1968 over who would become Chairman of the Federal Assembly of the CSSR. Husák made efforts to help the Soviets to eliminate one of the *'men of January'*, Smrkovský, from high politics. He thus demanded a Slovak to become the chairman of the Federal Assembly. Consequently, the

---

19 Dubček, A. *Nádej zomiera posledná*. Bratislava: Nová Práca, 1993, p. 220.

four highest functions in the newly federalized CSSR would be held by two Czechs and two Slovaks. Until then, power would be held by three Czechs (President Ludvík Svoboda, Chairman of the National Assembly Josef Smrkovský, and Premier Oldřich Černík) and one Slovak (the first secretary of the CC CPCz, Dubček). Even if Husák claimed that this was not about Smrkovský, but only about a fair and equal sharing of posts between the two nations, everyone knew that another aim was behind this maneuver. Nevertheless, the move caused discord among pro-reform Czechs and Slovaks.[20]

From the beginning of 1969, the power of the reform Communists quickly decreased. Neither the desperate act of the student Jan Palach, who set himself on fire in January 1969 to protest against the continuing *'normalization'* of political and public life, nor the great demonstration against the occupation, which began in late March 1969 after the Czechoslovak team defeated the Soviet team in the World Ice Hockey Championships in Stockholm helped the cause of reform. After great pressure from Soviet politicians, conservative Czechoslovak politicians and the realists, Dubček finally resigned as first secretary of the CC CPCz.

Of course, Dubček was still a member of the Presidium of the CC CPCz, because of his new office—Chairman of the Federal Assembly of the CSSR. It was in this period that he took one the most controversial steps of his career—namely signing, together with two other *'Men of January'*, Černík and Svoboda) Act 99/1969, which was aimed against *'anti-Socialist elements'*. It was on the basis of this law that dissidents were persecuted later in 1970 and 1980. Dubček claimed that this was not a law, but only a *'measure of the Presidium of the Federal Assembly'* and it was thus approved by this body, not him. Though he presided over this body, he allegedly did not vote on this bill (drafted by Husák's Presidium of the CC CPCz). Dubček later sought to explain the situation: "My great error was that I signed the law at all. Signing laws, I must say, was the chairman's routine task, whether

---

20 Doskočil, Z. *Duben 1969: Anatomie jednoho mocenského zvratu*. Brno: Doplněk, 2006, p. 37–39.

they approved of the laws or not. But this was not a routine situation, and I should have refused to sign it. But it was a hectic, nervous moment; I was completely isolated there and at the time I did not think through the consequences. I'll never stop regretting it. I am not trying to excuse myself; I can only explain the situation.[21"].

But Dubček did not remain Chairman of the Federal Assembly for long. As normalization proceeded, the realists (led by Husák), who were suddenly getting along with the former dogmatists, needed Dubček less and less every day. Eventually, they resorted to a historically tried and true method: getting rid of a troublesome politician by '*expelling*' him to the diplomatic service. Dubček accepted the post of Czechoslovak Ambassador to Turkey, claiming that he did so because his ill wife could not bear hearing the accusations made against him in the press and in public. The new leadership of the CPCz hoped that Dubček would leave the country for good; indeed, they were thinking of ways to prevent him from returning. But after the adventurous journey, he managed to come back to Czechoslovakia, only to endure the torment of being expelled from the Party in June 1970 and then banished to the fringes of society, yet continuing, by simply existing, to be a blot on the consciences of the '*new masters*' of '*normalized*' Czechoslovakia.

Free but still a prisoner

Dubček was later expelled from the Revolutionary Trades Union Movement, the Union of Antifascist Fighters and even from the Huntsmen's Association. The secret police followed him everywhere, even when he went to his father's and brother's graves. Nevertheless, as early as in 1970, he wrote two protest letters to Husák, in which he pointed out the violation not only of his personal freedom, but also of the lawfulness of these actions in general.[22] Later, in 1974, he sent a long letter of criticism to the Federal Assembly of the CSSR and to the

---

21   Dubček, A. *Nádej zomiera posledná*. Bratislava: Nová Práca, 1993, p. 250-251.
22   Laluha, I. *Alexander Dubček, politik a jeho doba*. Bratislava: Nová Práca, 2000, p. 93.

Slovak National Council (SNC; the Slovak legislature), where he analyzed the web of power that sprawled over the everyday life of the citizens of Czechoslovakia. In the conclusion of this letter, he wrote: *"It is a violation of human rights."*²³ Dubček thus became one of the first Czechoslovak dissidents unequivocally to define their concern with civil and human rights—three years before the issuing of the Charter 77 human rights document and establishment of the movement of the same name. Later, a group of dissidents formed around him, including Ivan Laluha, Vladimír Krajčí, Hvezdoň Kočtúch, Ján Uher, Jozef Baník, and Milan Strhan.

The milestone of Dubček's dissident activity was in November 1988, when one of the oldest universities in the world, Bologna, awarded him an honorary doctorate. This was great acknowledgement not only of Dubček but also of the whole reformist and democratic movement in Czechoslovakia. In his speech at the ceremony, Dubček mentioned the need for a *'common European home'*, which contributed to his image as a politician of European dimensions.²⁴ The activities that he later undertook at home contributed to the collapse of the totalitarian régime in late 1989.

After the fall of the totalitarian régime

Amongst historians, political scientists, and other observers, the Czechoslovak presidential election in December 1989 and Dubček's role in this historic event will obviously be discussed for a long time. The suggestion that Dubček should be President of Czechoslovakia in late December 1989 had already appeared at the beginning of the year, in the dissident organization Obroda (Rebirth). Naturally, back then, nobody knew how politics would develop in Czechoslovakia at the end of the year, which is why Dubček was regarded as a candidate of the civil opposition even in socialist Czechoslovakia on the condition

---

23 Žatkuliak, J., Laluha, I. (eds.) *Alexander Dubček.Od totality k demokracii: Prejavy, články a rozhovory*. Bratislava: Veda, 2002, p. 234–246.

24 Žatkuliak, J., Laluha, I. (eds.) *Alexander Dubček.Od totality k demokracii: Prejavy, články a rozhovory*. Bratislava: Veda, 2002, p. 281–288.

that he would not aspire to the post of General Secretary of the CC CPCz and since it was clear that his political profile in 1989 went significantly beyond the CPCz Action Programme of 1968. This proposal was also agreed to by Václav Havel in a private conversation with two representatives of Obroda, Věněk Šilhán and Miloš Hájek.[25] And it was perhaps this that made Dubček willing to stand for President also after the events of November 1989. It was only later that the Civic Forum changed its position and, its counterpart in Slovakia, the Public against Violence (Verejnosť proti Násiliu—VPN) was of the same opinion. Instead, Havel became the president of Czechoslovakia, and it was allegedly his wish that Dubček become the chairman of the Federal Assembly.[26]

Dubček did not accept his followers' proposal to create a political party of his own, he did not join the Social Democratic Party, and declined an offer to join the Slovak Communist Party. He sincerely assumed that the era of civil movements that aimed to bring society to democracy had arrived.[27] Maybe that is why he let himself be put on the candidates list of the Public against Violence, which had before the first free elections, in June 1990, the preferences only 9.6 per cent, which meant fifth place in Slovakia, thus *'pulling the thorn out of the foot'* of the movement.[28] Dubček, who was then the most popular politician, has significantly contributed to the victory of the Public against Violence in Slovakia, even if the Public against Violence had not supported him in his ambition to become President of the Republic. Thus for a short time the Public against Violence attacks on Dubček and the reformers of 1968 had been postponed.

---

25 Šilhan V. 'K Alexandru Dubčekovi', in Bárta, M., Hoppe, J. (eds) *Úloha Alexandra Dubčeka v moderních dějinách Československa*. Brno: Masaryková dělnická akademie, 2002, p. 126.
26 Šilhan V. 'K Alexandru Dubčekovi', in Bárta, M., Hoppe, J. (eds) *Úloha Alexandra Dubčeka v moderních dějinách Československa*. Brno: Masaryková dělnická akademie, 2002, p. 127.
27 Laluha, I. *Alexander Dubček, politik a jeho doba*. Bratislava: Nová Práca, 2000, p. 115.
28 Laluha, I. *Alexander Dubček, politik a jeho doba*. Bratislava: Nová Práca, 2000, p. 115.

After the breakup of the Public against Violence and the creation of the Movement for a Democratic Slovakia (Hnutie za demokratické Slovensko), in 1991, Dubček did not become a member of either. He remained independent, and assumed that as Chairman of the Federal Assembly his influence would be more effective. The truth is that by that time real power was moving away from him and, moreover, the process of his transformation from reform Communist to Social Democrat was finishing. *"We all very much appreciate that at heart you are a Social Democrat"*, the chairman of the Social Democratic Party of Slovakia, Boris Zala (b. 1954), wrote to him in a letter in which he invites Dubček to join the party and become part of its leadership.[29] Dubček had come full circle. He had returned to where his father hailed from. Moreover, he was chosen to be the Deputy Chairman of the Socialist International at the next conference of its executive bodies.

All the expectations of Slovak and European Social Democrats about Dubček's future political work, and also those of the Slovak people about whether he would become the first president of the Slovak Republic after the dissolution of the federation, died with Dubček on 7 November 1992 in consequence of injuries sustained in a car crash. He died tragically, similarly to two other great Slovaks, Ľudovít Štúr and Milan Rastislav Štefánik (1880–1919). That is probably why suspicions of foul play immediately arose. This version of his death, however, is not in keeping with Czechoslovak political culture, and it was probably the result of a set of unfortunate coincidences and an astonishing lack of thoroughness in its investigation.

Dubček in the eyes of the Slovak public today

Dubček is one of those Slovak politicians who considerably influenced developments and ways of thinking on the Slovak political scene. At the same time, however, he was a political personality, with an influence beyond the borders of Czechoslovakia. In this respect, he was unrivalled. But what do Slovaks think about him today? A leading

---

[29] Laluha, I. *Alexander Dubček, politik a jeho doba*. Bratislava: Nová Práca, 2000, p. 118.

Slovak sociologist Ľudmila Benkovičová sought to answer this question with public opinion research carried out by the Institute of Political Science at the Slovak Academy of Science in collaboration with the Department of Research on Media of Slovak Radio in late June 2004. The representative sample of the Slovak population comprised 2,244 respondents aged 14 and older.[30]

It is symptomatic that today citizens of Slovakia appreciate Dubček's humanity (35 per cent), honesty (32 per cent), decency (32 per cent), and understanding for the common people (28 per cent). If we take the average of these figures, which would give us a figure for his whole character as a symbol, we get 31.75 per cent, which is close to one third of the Slovak population. And that is truly important, because more than a third of the respondents (38.7 per cent) and therefore more than a third of the Slovak population see Dubček as a synonym of 1968, the year of a genuine attempt to democratize socialism of the Soviet type in Czechoslovakia.[31] The most important thing is that one third of today's adult Slovak population has personal experience of 1968 with its illusions, hopes, and consequences. About 1.5 million Slovaks today were teenagers and young men and women back then, intensely perceiving the atmosphere not only in their immediate proximity, but also throughout society, and these experiences will remain with them for the rest of their lives. That is why this segment of the Slovak population is a relevant source of personal information about this important Slovak politician.

These facts also explain the interest in the life and work of Dubček. According to the results of the public opinion research, 37 per cent of the respondents have a lively interest in Dubček even today;

---

30   Benkovičová, Ľ. 'Alexander Dubček očami verejnosti', in Laluha, I, Petrovičová, E., Pekník, M. (eds.) *Alexander Dubček politik, štátnik, humanista*. Bratislava: Veda, 2009, p. 302-16.
31   Although Dubček was an extraordinarily active and influential politician in 1989, Slovak society, as reflected in this research, is mostly unaware of this (4.3 per cent). See Benkovičová, Ľ. 'Alexander Dubček očami verejnosti', in Laluha, I, Petrovičová, E., Pekník, M. (eds.) *Alexander Dubček politik, štátnik, humanista*. Bratislava: Veda, 2009, p. 303-04.

62 per cent of those addressed, however, are not interested in his life and work. Characteristically, interest in Dubček increases the older the respondent is: among people 60 years old or more, 58 per cent of the respondents were interested in Dubček. By contrast, only 19 per cent of the respondents between 14 and 29 years of age are interested in him. The fact that the young generation of Slovaks is considerably indifferent (in this case, 80 per cent of those between 14 and 19 years old are not interested in him at all) should concern us. According to the research, it seems that the main cause is the schools, which teach little about Dubček or teach it poorly or both. Young people gain much more information from the mass media and also their families. Another, wider cause is the decrease of interest in the written word, in factual literature and in historical fiction in favor of action movies, dynamic '*play stations*', and other computer games.

Similarly, a third of the respondents reflects the weaker sides of Dubček's overall profile. In the research, there appear references to his political naivety, passivity, gullibility, not coping with the responsibilities of his position, or not showing himself to be a strong personality in some situations, for example, during the occupation by the Warsaw Pact armies in August 1968. It is interesting that the fact that Dubček was the key functionary of the Communist régime in Czechoslovakia disturbs only 6 per cent of addressed; it was irrelevant for almost 90 per cent of the respondents. An explanation may be that the public situates Dubček's activities amongst the attempts to change the totalitarian features of the Communist régimes in central Europe, which began with the redressing of injustices from the beginning of the Communist period. The research results confirm that a source of the tolerance of Dubček's Communist past is the fixed idea of the socialist period as a time when the social situation and everyday lives of most ordinary people were generally better than they are today.

It should be mentioned that a relatively large proportion of Slovaks (18 per cent) today blames Dubček for having betrayed the values of socialism and leading the country towards capitalism in 1968. It is an opinion that was widespread during normalization in the

1970s and 1980s, and was impressed into the minds of people primarily during the Party purges in the early 1970s. A smaller proportion of the population (13 per cent) claims that Dubček also represented a destabilizing and polarizing element of society at the time, and considers him a politician whose actions brought society into discord and instability. The circumstances of his death in a car accident are part of the legend. A third of the people addressed (35 per cent) agreed with the statement that the car crash was an unfortunate accident. The opposite opinion was expressed by 59 per cent of those addressed. The official investigation into the car accident and the conclusions of the investigation seemed for most Slovaks to have been insufficient, unconvincing, and not trustworthy. Two thirds of those asked were critical of the work of the investigating bodies and think that the investigation was lax. The public reactions to the car accident are, however, one of the indicators of Dubček's greatness and importance for Slovak society. He thus belongs to the great figures of modern Slovak history (together with Štúr and Štefánik), whose deaths remain, even decades later, veiled in mystery and legend, figures about whom it is said that they died unnecessarily and mainly because they had defended the interests of Slovakia and its people.

When it comes to an appreciation of this important modern Slovak politician the prevailing belief is he is appreciated mainly by ordinary Slovaks. Slovak politicians appreciate him less, but that is understandable: during the bitter struggle for power after the fall of the Communist régime, one of the characteristic features of members the centrist and right-wing political parties used to be their negative attitude to Dubček, who in the 1950s and 1960s had been a prominent member of the Communist ruling structures and after 1989 definitely a left-wing politician, leaning towards Social Democracy. The often emphasized fact that in Slovakia almost only the older generation is interested in him suggests that interest in Dubček will continuously decline there. From that, stems the common view that Dubček is far more appreciated abroad than at home, because in Slovakia only the positive features of his character come to the fore: his humanity, honesty, bravery, decency, and unprecedented courage to act in the heat of the struggle for democracy, against the leader of Communist totalitarianism, the Soviet Union and its political leadership. The petty disputes among Slovak politicians and political parties are in this case of absolutely no interest to people abroad.

Alexander Dubček, a Czechoslovak Politician

Oldřich Tůma[1]
The Academy of Sciences of the Czech Republic

Abstract: This paper focuses on the role of Czechoslovak Communist politician Alexander Dubček, one of the preponderant figures of the Prague Spring of 1968. While in Slovakia Dubček is often cherished as a national hero of sorts, Czechs tend to be more critical of his role in politics. Interestingly, this is not due to any inter-national hostility, as Czechs understand Dubček as a figure of their own history. The paper analyses key political and cultural circumstances that engendered this 'cool', rather critical attitude in comparison with the importance attributed to Dubček in the Slovak discourse.

In the Czech historical consciousness, amongst historians and the general public, Alexander Dubček (1921–1992) clearly holds a more problematic place and is seen more critically than he generally is in Slovakia. There are many reasons for that, but among them is not the fact (or mainly the fact) that Dubček was ethnically a Slovak; Czechs do not perceive Dubček as an historical figure of a nation different from their own.

To think about the perception of Dubček in the Czech historical consciousness properly—and particularly to compare the Czech perception of him with the Slovak, the most important factor is probably that Czechs (and this is true of historians, journalists, and above all the general public) did not perceive him, nor do they now perceive him as a Slovak politician, or at least not primarily as a Slovak politician. That does not mean that they would like to appropriate Dubček or even do not know he was a Slovak. (Non-Czechs and non-Slovaks, even comparatively renowned historians and journalists, sometimes think he is a Czech politician.) Mainly it has to do with his being perceived as a 'one of ours', that is, a local politician in the broader, Czechoslovak sense. It is symptomatic that in the Czech Wikipedia entry,

---

1   Email: tuma@usd.cas.cz.

Dubček is described as a 'Czechoslovak and a Slovak politician' whereas in the Slovak Wikipedia entry he is listed as a 'Slovak politician'.[2]

For Czechs, as is well known, it was not particularly difficult to accept a Czechoslovak identity (as a kind of slightly broader Czech identity). As long as the shared state existed, that is until 1 January 1993, Czechs perceived not only politicians of Slovak origin but also, for example, sportsmen and sportswomen, artists, and other Slovak public figures to be their own, not foreign. The situation was of course somewhat different concerning those politicians who made Slovak-related topics (including relations with the Czechs, and the standing of Slovakia in the common state, the division of the shared state) leitmotifs of their political careers. The leading figures in the Slovak efforts to achieve autonomy or independence in the interwar and war years, Andrej Hlinka (1864–1938), Jozef Tiso (1887–1947), and most recently, for example, the key Slovak politicians during the division of Czechoslovakia after the Changes of 1989, Ján Čarnogurský (b. 1944) and Vladimír Mečiar (b. 1942), are certainly perceived by Czechs as mainly Slovak politicians and therefore foreign. But the Slovak politicians who did not pursue that objective, or for whom it was less pronounced, are perceived more or less neutrally together with other Czechoslovak politicians (that is, predominantly Czech politicians), whether positively or negatively. Two starkly different examples are Milan Rastislav Štefánik (1880–1919), who together with Tomáš Garrigue Masaryk and Edvard Beneš helped to establish an independent Czechoslovakia in 1918, and Jozef Lenárt (1923–2004), a long-standing senior Communist functionary. Not even Gustáv Husák (1913–1991), who in a certain period, particularly during his mercurial rise to the top of power in Czechoslovakia, between August 1968 and April 1969, played the Slovak card in a high-stakes game, is perceived primarily as a Slovak politician. Other determining factors come to the fore in his case – namely, he is perceived, regardless of nationality (ethnicity),

---

2   Online: http://sk.wikipedia.org/wiki/Alexander_Dubček, [accessed 10 April 2013].

firstly as the main actor and symbol of 'normalization' policy, which ensured the re-establishment of hard-line Communism in the period from early 1969 to late 1989, and this is perceived negatively in the Czech historical memory. This is, incidentally, attested to by the public-opinion polling results published in this volume.

In January 1968, it was surely noted among Czechs, that Dubček is a Slovak. It was noted with interest and perhaps also with a bit of surprise, for it was the first time in the fifty years of the existence of Czechoslovakia that the most important position of power in the state was held by a Slovak. In Prague, a joke was going round at the time, which well illustrates this surprise and interest, neither of which was, however, clear-cut or at all hostile: 'Do you know what ÚV KSČ [Central Committee of the Czechoslovak Communist Party] means? Už Vládnou Konečně Slováci Čechům [The Slovaks are finally ruling the Czechs].' The philosopher and literary critic Milan Šimečka (1930–1990) even made the joke the title of his article in the second issue of the restored *Literární listy* (Literary News) in early March 1968 — and for the amazed public that was one of the most convincing pieces of evidence that censorship was truly no longer working.[3] But events were then moving quickly and other things were now important, so that Dubček's Slovak origin no longer played almost any role at all.

If we were to summarize the Czech view of Dubček, we would need a whole range of terms, from initial, let's say, polite interest in early 1968, through growing goodwill during the spring, to admiration and almost adoration, which at the tensest moment, in August 1968, was surely identical with the view from Slovakia, through growing embarrassment mixed with some pity, all the way to a comparatively critical attitude. These different views of Dubček alternated with each other, but with the distance of time they have now come to exist simultaneously.

The Czech view of Dubček went through a development that took the form of hyperbole and was actually repeated twice, first in

---

3   "Už vládnou konečně Slováci Čechům" in *Literární listy* 1 (2), 7 March 1968, p. 1.

1968–69 and then in 1989–92. Today's view is differentiated and certainly not as admiring as some of the views of him in Slovakia. The 2009 book *Zastavte Dubčeka!* (Stop Dubček!),[4] by Jozef Banáš (b. 1948), a Slovak politician and writer, tells Dubček's life story in the form of belle-lettres. It is actually a hagiography, with all the attributes of that genre — also with a reference to how women and girls admired Dubček's well-built body at the swimming pool. This sort of book probably finds few readers amongst Czechs, for they would read it with growing mistrust. Indeed, a book of this nature is hard to imagine having been written about any politician, let alone a Czech one, because Czechs have a more detached and perhaps more suspicious and ironic attitude to their politicians (and even their historic figures) than Slovaks do. Not even the writer Lenka Procházková's (b. 1951) novel about the self-immolation of the student Jan Palach (1948–1969) presents its protagonist to the readers as straightforwardly positive[5] as Banáš does with his Dubček. At least, one exception, however, does come to mind — namely, the novel about the Mašín brothers, Josef (b. 1932) and Ctirad (1930–2011), who in the early 1950s tried to organize resistance to the Communist régime, killed several people in the process, and eventually shot their way through East Germany to West Berlin, and it presents its heroes one-dimensionally. This work employs an interesting literary devise whereby in their imagined musings, the Mašín brothers — like Banaš's Dubček — react to future doubts and criticisms of their deeds, which will be expressed only decades later. The Mašín brothers are, however, a completely different kind of historical figure, desperados, not politicians. And the author, Jan Novák (b. 1953), is perhaps more American than Czech, having left his native Bohemia at the age of sixteen and having had attended American schools and universities.[6]

If we had to sketch out the curve of the development of the view of Dubček, we would therefore have to begin with a mixture of the

---

4   Banáš, J. *Zastavte Dubčeka!* Bratislava: Ikar, 2009.
5   Procházková, L. *Slunce v úplňku: Příběh Jana Palacha.* Prague: Prostor, 2008.
6   Novák, J. *Zatím dobrý.* Brno: Petrov, 2004.

curiosity and uncertainty felt by Czechs when he first entered the public eye in January 1968. Dubček, who had up to that point held various political positions in Slovakia, was not well known in Prague at the time. But public curiosity was soon superseded by growing interest and support. In Bohemia and Moravia, in the spring months of 1968, Dubček became the same symbol as he was in Slovakia, standing for reform, the almost universally popular attempt to turn the existing political system into something more rational and humane. And he also became the embodiment of almost unrealistic hopes and expectations. The growth in his popularity (which is verifiable in the public opinion polls that were carried out) was the result of a combination of various factors: support for the policies that he represented in the eyes of the public, but certainly also thanks to the way he acted in public, his personal traits, and charisma. As a public figure (and that need not mean as a politician too), Dubček was undoubtedly strikingly different, in a highly positive sense, from the Communist apparatchiks before and after him.

In the eyes of the Czech public even Dubček's Slovak language gained him greater goodwill, for it enhanced the impression of something new, special, and different, which everyone must have noticed in comparison with the unpopular Antonín Novotný (1904–1975), whom he had taken over from in the post of First Secretary of the Czechoslovak Communist Party. In May at the latest, Dubček thus gained even more goodwill and support from the public because of the universally shared opinion that he was the one willing and able to advocate independence from the intensifying verbal attacks made against the reformists by Moscow, Warsaw, and East Berlin. We know today that this was more a matter of faith and illusion than a realistic assessment of the situation. And because of that external pressure the public was better able to forgive and explain the inconsistency and waffling that he demonstrated in the summer of 1968.

The intervention, the arrest and abduction, the lack of information, and the fears for Dubček's fate or life in the first days after 21 August then increased Dubček's popularity to utterly improbable heights. And it was only because, in the eyes of the public (including the Czech public) that he was endowed with the aura of a hero and martyr at the same time, that his teary-eyed speech after the signing of the Moscow Protocol and his return to Czechoslovakia on 27 August could have the effect that it had—namely, to reverse the atmosphere of deep suspicion and resistance to what had probably taken place in Moscow and what the Czechoslovak delegation had promised, even to compel the resigned acceptance of what a sobbing Dubček had urged the citizens of Czechoslovak—namely, the abandonment of open resistance and a return to normal life in an admittedly occupied country, but with the faith and hope that not everything was yet lost.[7] This faith was mainly based on confidence in Dubček as a person. One may recall, for instance, the words of Václav Havel (1936–2011) spoken during one of the last transmissions of a free, anti-occupation television station, broadcast from an improvised studio on the peak of Ještěd mountain in north Bohemia in August 1968: 'I, however, do not see the situation pessimistically. I think that the worst is behind us. The invasion, the aggression. And it is a matter of holding out and I actually believe in Dubček. He is a person—a politician—who is able to adapt to the situation, able to count on people.'[8]

With the growing number of repeated compromises or, rather, with the capitulation in the autumn of 1968 and the winter of 1968/69, uncertainty of course grew and so did the number of critical views of Dubček and his politics, which also had to be increased by the manner

---

[7] A recording of a speech by Alexander Dubček, regarding the conclusions of the Moscow talks, to the citizens of Czechoslovakia, broadcast by Czechoslovak Radio, on 27 August 1968, at about 17:30); Vondrová, J., Navrátil, J. (eds.) *Komunistická strana Československa. Kapitulace (srpen-listopad 1968)* Prameny k dějinám československé krize v letech 1967–1970, vol. 9/3), Prague and Brno: ÚSD and Doplněk, 2011, pp. 120–24. The written form of the speech cannot of course convey the emotion and urgency of that Dubček's words evoked. For the sound recording, see Janáč, M. (ed.) *Srpen 1968: 10 hodin komentovaných originálních nahrávek.* Prague: Radioservis and Český rozhlas, 2008, CD, track 30.

[8] Online: http://www.ceskatelevize.cz/vse-o-ct/historie/ceskoslovenska-televize/1968-1969/1968/vysilani-televizniho-studia-sever-27-srpna-1968/, [accessed 10 April 2013]

in which he gradually left the political stage and how he let himself be manipulated and accepted increasingly less important places, right to the bitter end, and his expulsion from the Party and exclusion from public life. But even his behaviour in late August 1969, when, as Chairman of the Federal Assembly, he took part in the Presidium's passing of 'Some Temporary Measures for Strengthening and Preserving Public Order', did not fundamentally harm his image, which was increasingly remote from reality. This legislation was an effective instrument of repression against the thousands of people who in the streets of Prague, Brno, and many other towns in the days of the first anniversary of the Soviet occupation were loudly voicing their resistance, for the last time, to the policy of normalization that was just starting — most often by cheering for Dubček.[9]

Dubček then soon completely vanished from public life and for the next two decades was present — from the perspective of the new Party leadership — only as a negative symbol of 1968 and as the object of sometimes very aggressive (albeit ultimately only verbal) attacks by the leaders of the normalization régime. Dubček's popularity was then far less the popularity of a specific person (let alone a politician) than the positive recollection of Dubček, yet because of that it was all the more the popularity of a symbol of a vaguely defined antithesis to the rhetoric of the normalization régime and actually the antithesis of the wretched present in general. He was definitely not perceived as a symbol of opposition or resistance.

In this period as well, however, critical assessments of Dubček's role in politics in 1968 and 1969 were already beginning to appear in samizdat and in exile publications. One need only recall, for example, the articles by the doyen and most respected representative of the Czech exiles, Pavel Tigrid (1917–2003),[10] or by Petr Pithart (b. 1941) at

---

9   § 99/1969 Sb. Zákonné opatření předsednictva Federálního shromáždění o některých přechodných opatřeních nutných k upevnění a ochraně veřejného pořádku. See Tůma, O., et al *Srpen '69: Edice dokumentů*. Prague: ÚSD and Maxdorf 1996, pp. 17–18 and 269–71.
10   Tigrid, P. *Kvadratura kruhu: Dokumenty a poznámky k československé krizi 1968–1970*. Paris and New York: Edice Svědectví, 1970.

home, who, in an essay[11] written to mark the tenth anniversary of the Prague Spring, presented — well before the collapse of the Communist régime enabled unfettered historical research in Czechoslovakia — the most profound and comprehensive Czech analysis of the events of 1968. Critics at home and in exile judged Dubček's politics in 1968 as random and improvised, and believed that his tactics of calming Czechoslovakia's alarmed 'allies' and later interventionists by trying to convince them that neither the Communist régime nor the Party's monopoly on power were threatened, while ensuring the public that there was no danger of outside interference in Czechoslovak affairs, could not succeed. They reproached Dubček for having been unable or even unwilling after the occupation began in August to rely on the support offered him by the Czech and the Slovak public even months later, and for having chosen instead the behind-the-scenes politics of compromise, which was, they argued, nothing more than gradual capitulation. Ultimately, they argued, he was actually a co-creator of the grim reality of the years of re-established hard-line Communism.

Dubček the man, rather than just the symbol, did not reappear in the Czech public eye till the late 1980s. It was essentially a repeat of that curve of interest and goodwill, though with less intensity and a less concentrated form than twenty years before. His journey to the University of Bologna, which the régime permitted him to undertake in autumn 1988, to be awarded an honorary degree, the interviews that he gave to Hungarian Television and the Voice of America,[12] which were broadcast in the spring and summer of 1989, were all perceived as serious signs that things were truly beginning to change, and that it might be worthwhile for people to become involved in politics again. But even at that time, except for some groups, Czechs generally did not perceive Dubček as a potential political leader. The second peak in his popularity came on Friday, 24 November 1989, when, after

---

11   Pithart, P. *Osmašedesátý*. Prague: Rozmluvy, 1990.
12   For the interview that Dubček gave to Hungarian television in April 1989, see Žatkuliak, J., Laluha, I. (eds.) *Alexander Dubček. Od totality k demokracii: Prejavy, články a rozhovory*. Bratislava: Veda, 2002, pp. 293-98.

more than twenty years' absence, he spoke publicly in Prague. He gave his speech on Wenceslas Square, on the fifth day of the Velvet Revolution, when anti-régime demonstrations by hundreds of thousands of people were being held on the square every afternoon. (In Bratislava, Dubček had appeared on Slovak National Uprising Square [náměstí Slovenského národného povstania] the day before.) The introductory sentence of his speech from the balcony of the Melantrich publishing house, 'My dear people of Prague, I love you and you know it', truly called forth a storm of emotion and enthusiasm.[13] But this time, it was superseded by a quick sobering up. Dubček's speech at the even larger demonstration, on Letná Plain, Prague, on Saturday, was a bit disappointing and a bit boring, and certainly did not present a clear political programme. The rapid developments at the end of the year and especially in the first half of 1990 did not yet, from the Czech perspective, sideline Dubček, and his actions as Chairman of the Federal Assembly were perceived until 1992 more with a growing sense of his being out of place and embarrassing. Incidentally, an alleged agreement, of December 1989, between Havel and Dubček, whereby Havel would vacate the office of president for Dubček after the general elections of 1990,[14] is often discussed. Whatever the truth of that agreement may be, it would have been impracticable in the summer of 1990 – the political atmosphere in Bohemia and Moravia had changed so much that Dubček would have been totally unacceptable

---

[13] The text of the speech is printed in the daily *Svobodné slovo*, 25 November 1989, and is republished Otáhal, M., Sládek, Z. (eds.) *Deset pražských dnů (17.–27. listopad 1989): Dokumentace*. Prague: Academia, 1990, pp. 463–64. The volume *Alexander Dubček. Od totality k demokracii*, a representative Slovak selection of Dubček's speeches, articles, and interviews does not include this speech. It does, however, include the speech given in Bratislava, on 23 November 1989. See *Alexander Dubček. Od totality k demokracii*, pp. 320–21. Dubček's speech on Wenceslas Square, Prague, is not listed in either the large Slovak bibliography of Dubček's appearances in the mass media, Šváčová, S., et al (eds.) *Alexander Dubček v slovenskej a českej tlači: Personálna bibliografia*. Bánská Bystrica: Štátna vedecká knižnica, 2007.

[14] See, for example, most recently, Suk, J. *Politika jako absurdní drama: Václav Havel v letech 1975–1989*. Prague: Paseka, 2013, pp. 400–02.

as president. (It is pointless to say that the reason was not because he was a Slovak, but because he was a former top-ranking Communist.)

In 1990–92, the assessment of 1968 (and therefore also of Dubček) became one of the fields on which the battle over the orientation of Czechoslovak (or rather Czech) politics, economics, and foreign affairs was fought. The struggle over radical economic reform, the establishment of a standard Western-style political system based on parties, entry into NATO, and so forth, the struggle over the orientation and control of the Civic Forum, and then also the dual between the new, right-wing political parties, the Civic Democratic Party (Občanská demokratická strana) and the Civic Democratic Alliance (Občanská demokratická aliance) on the one hand and the centrist Citizens' Movement (Občanské hnutí) on the other, in which a number of former Sixty-eighters were active, became, among other things, a struggle over the various assessments of 1968. In the political debates, in the mass media, and to a certain extent also amongst historians, the Prague Spring then became somewhat of a victim of the collateral damage of such a struggle. It was emphatically interpreted as a mere conflict within the Communist Party, a struggle for group interests, and in the best case as a quixotic attempt to reform the unreformable Communist system and perhaps thereby even to extend its life. Dubček was actually not the main target of such attacks, who were rather the real opponents on the Czech political scene, politicians with a somewhat different conception of the transformation from the one that was eventually put in place, people more or less linked with the Prague Spring (who had, moreover, been members of the Czechoslovak Communist Party before 1968), for example, Petr Pithart, Zdeněk Jičínský (b. 1929), Pavel Rychetský (b. 1943), and František Vlasák (1912–2005). But, thanks to the role he played in 1968, and also thanks to his existing position under the Constitution, Dubček was the most visible, and was sometimes attacked even beyond the bounds of decency.[15] Moreover, his current performance in politics, his indecision,

---

15   See, for example, Benčík, A. *Téma: Alexander Dubček*. Prague: Křesťanskosociální hnutí, 2012, pp. 302–04 and 308–10.

his fuzziness about what he actually represented, his uncertain position during the break-up of the Slovak democratic opposition during the Velvet Revolution (called the Public Against Violence; Verejnost proti násiliu—VPN), and so forth, did not help him to gain a particularly good name, certainly not from the Prague perspective. In early 1991, the most powerful grouping in the November 1989 revolution in Slovakia, VPN, split into the populist and nationalistically defined Movement for a Democratic Slovakia (Hnutie za demokratické Slovensko—HZDS) led by Mečiar (who was extraordinarily popular in Slovakia at the time) and, on the other hand, the liberal and pro-Czechoslovak Civic Democratic Union (Občanská demokratická únie). And Dubček somehow remained on the sidelines. No matter how much he was welcomed and fêted on his journeys abroad in 1990-92, in Prague he tended to be met only with attacks and some goodwill (in the form of pity) during his second term in office in the Presidium of the Federal Assembly.

After the division of Czechoslovakia, officially declared on 31 December 1992, Dubček, who had died almost two months before that, ceased to be an important topic of public discussion. He has, however, remained to this day an important topic of Czech historians. Here we find very different assessments of his historical role, ranging from the highly positive to the markedly critical. The first big 'post-November' work of Czech history devoted to the Prague Spring, which came out of the milieu of authors who in 1990-92 had been members of the Czechoslovak Federal Government Commission for the Analysis of the Historic Events of 1967 to 1970,[16] makes a largely positive assessment of the role of Dubček and other leaders of the 'process of rebirth' (*obrodný proces*). This is not the place to discuss the now huge number of publications devoted to the Prague Spring. It is reasonable to say that most Czech historians are more critical of Dubček than Slovak

---

16   Kural, V., Mencl, V., et al. *Československo roku 1968*, vols. I–II. Prague: Parta, 1993.

historians are.[17] They confirm, but now on the basis of thorough analysis and the interpretation of sources made accessible since the Changes of late 1989, the opinions expressed in exile publications and samizdat.[18] They also add more precise interpretations of Dubček's unfortunate role in the pacification of public resistance after the new leadership came to power in 1969, and also of Dubček's unpreparedness and unwillingness to participate in opposition activities at any time before the changes of 1989.[19] In this critical view of Dubček's historical role he is not perceived as a foreign politician. Even Jan Tesař (b. 1933), for example, who has sometimes used harsh words to describe Dubček, calling him a wretch (*ubožák*) and accusing him of Communist Party wickedness (*partajní podlost*), uses his criticism of Dubček to criticizes the Czech nation (but not the Slovak) and sets tasks for the Czech (but not the Slovak) 'national consciousness'.[20]

Also amongst some Czechs, however, Dubček — as a politician in the 1960s, as an opponent of the régime in the 1970s and 1980s, and again as a politician in the early 1990s — has his supporters. The most striking and steadfast of them is surely Antonín Benčík (b. 1926).[21]

---

17 For an example of a highly positive assessment, see Laluha, I. *Alexander Dubček, člověk a politik*. Bratislava: Nová práca, 2000, and Laluha, I., Petrovičová, E., Pekník, M. (eds.) *Alexander Dubček politik, štátnik, humanista*. Bratislava: Veda 2009.

18 This has probably been most systematically analyzed by Jitka Vondrová. See, for example, her introductions to volumes of the monumental edition of documents, *Prameny k dějinám československé krize*, published by the Institute of Contemporary History, Prague, over the last twenty years. See, in particular, vol 9, pts 1–4 of Moravec, J., Navrátil, J., Vondrová, J. (eds.) *Komunistická strana Československa*. vol. 9, pt 1. Prague and Brno: ÚSD and Doplněk, 1999, 2000, 2001, and 2003, and pts 1–4 of Navrátil, J., Vondrová, J. (eds.) *Mezinárodní souvislosti československé krize*, Prague and Brno: ÚSD and Doplněk, 1995, 1996, 1997, and 2011. See also the latest work by Vondrová, J. *Reforma? Revoluce? Pražské jaro 1968 a Praha*. Prague: ÚSD, 2013.

19 Among the many works concerned with this, see, for example, Suk, J. 'Alexander Dubček: Velký státník, nebo politický symbol? *Soudobé dějiny* 9, 2002, pp. 92–103.

20 Tesař, J. *Zamlčená diagnóza*. Prague: Triáda, 2003, p. 22.

21 In addition to the latest works (quoted in footnote 14), see, in particular, Benčík, A. *Utajovaná pravda o Alexandru Dubčekovi: Drama muže, který předběhl svou dobu*. Prague: Ostrov, 2001. For the author's response to critical reviews of his book, see Benčík, A. 'Obrazy historie z petřínského bludiště: Několik poznámek a úvah nad recenzí knihy o Alexandru Dubčekovi', *Soudobé dějiny* 9, 2002, pp. 620–38.

Benčík has resolutely defended his hero again and again. In the details and in particular questions he has often argued against Dubček's critics, past and present, accusing them of mistakes or even conscious bias. It remains a question, however, whether he has, for all the details, always been able to perceive the context, the connections, and the point. A nice example is the matter of Dubček and his alleged planning of measures, in 1968, for the internment of opponents to reform. Vasil Bilak (1917–2014), one of the main figures in the leadership of the Czechoslovak Communist Party who worked with the Kremlin in preparing the intervention and was later the *éminence grise* and one of the most powerful men of the Czechoslovak régime after 1969, said in a 1985 interview with the West German weekly *Der Spiegel*: 'everything was already prepared in early August 1968, to set up concentration camps in Czechoslovakia for opponents of the right-wing forces [that is, of the reformers]'.[22] Dubček protested vehemently and wrote to *Der Spiegel*, explaining that what Bilak had said was untrue, and that, on the contrary, 'a proposal had been drafted for the political isolation of persons in the event of open opposition to socialism', for the leadership of the Czechoslovak Communist Party conceive right-wing danger and antisocialist statements to be their main problem.[23] Benčík recapitulates this matter in detail[24] and triumphantly demonstrates that Bilak had lied and Dubček had told the truth. Undoubtedly, Benčík is correct. But it remains a question why today, almost a quarter of a century after the collapse of the Communist régime, the argument that he did nothing in the summer of 1968 against traitors and conspirators who had helped foreign powers to orchestrate the occupation of their own country, but wanted to have people coming out 'against socialism' interned, should help Dubček's reputation.

---

22 "Unsere Löwe ist noch immer ein Löwe". Der Prager ZK-Sekretär Vasil Bilak über die Politik der Tschechoslowakei, *Der Spiegel*, 28 October 1985, p. 167–174, reprinted as Rozhovor soudruha V. Bilaka pro časopis Der Spiegel in *Rudé právo*, 30 October, 1985, pp. 1 and 7.
23 Published in Czech (Vyjádření Alexandera Dubčeka k interview Vasila Bilaka v časopise Der Spiegel) in *Listy* XV, 6 (December 1985), p. 7.
24 Benčík, A. *Téma: Alexander Dubček*, pp. 136–40.

It is hard to rid oneself of the impression that a more positive view of Dubček tends to be shared by historians who are close to him in age and opinion. In this connection, I recall, for instance, a conference held by the Institute of Contemporary History together with the Masaryk Academy of Labour (today the Masaryk Academy of Democracy) to mark Dubček's eightieth birthday (had he lived). Also in the statements of experienced professional historians and masters of their craft it was sometimes clear what an important role former personal contacts and shared life experiences in general played in their assessments of Dubček.[25]

In sum: amongst Czechs, Alexander Dubček is today perceived without any particular emotion; indeed, he is even perceived with cool indifference, albeit in various ways. He is seen as part of the Czechs' own history, while at the same time probably not as an historical figure that the Czechs would boast about. But perhaps that corresponds completely to the way the Czechs now look at their own history, that is, with a certain suspicion and aloofness, and certainly without any of the undue excitement or enthusiasm with which previous generations experienced them.

---

25 Bárta, M., Hoppe, J. *Úloha Alexandra Dubčeka v moderních dějinách Československa: Sborník z konference.* Prague: Masarykova dělnická akademie, 2002.

'Havel on Wawel!' or a Prophet is Not without Honour, but in His Own Country

Paweł Ukielski[1]
Polish Academy of Sciences

Abstract: The paper examines the representations of the former dissident, Czechoslovak and later Czech president Václav Havel in the Polish public discourse. Although Havel remains a relatively controversial figure in the Czech and Slovak republics, his public image in Poland is unequivocally positive. The article specifically investigates how meaning is attributed to Havel in Polish public sphere with respect to three key dimensions of his persona — the dissident, the playwright and the president.

This essay on the Polish perspective on Václav Havel was initially prepared for the conference 'My Hero, Your Enemy', held in Prague on 1–3 December 2011. Shortly after the conference, we heard the news that Havel had died at his Hrádeček country house. His death was inevitably followed by numerous articles, reminiscences, and biographies throughout the Polish mass media. These did not, however, change the main theses of the conference paper; indeed, they tended to be 'conclusive evidence' of them.

When discussing Havel, one basic statement needs to be made. He is not a typical hero. He is not an 'enemy' of any nation or society. And since he is not even controversial in Poland, or any other Visegrád country, the title of the conference does not quite apply to him (or he is not quite suitable as a topic for the conference). One could object that in this case the perspective should be the other way round, since Havel always had more critics in the Czech Republic than in Poland. Nevertheless, how Poles perceive one of the most important Czechs of the last century remains highly interesting and worthy of analysis.

The former Czechoslovak and Czech president is widely known in Poland. Indeed it is fair to assume that he is the most recognizable

---

1   Email: ukielski@ipn.gov.pl.

Czech there. Moreover, this popularity goes together with a liking and admiration for him, even with envy of him. Havel became widely known in Poland during the 'Velvet Revolution' of November and December 1990, and soon turned into a something of an idol. Once he had been elected President, many Poles began to call for 'Havel na Wawel!'[2], that is to say, 'We want to have such a president as well'. As the novelist Krzysztof Masłoń has aptly pointed it out: 'at the turn of the century we envied Czechs the most: the beer, the literature [...], the cinema and, lastly, Václav Havel'.[3]

Havel's image in Poland has three basic features, which are easy to discern even in almost any encyclopaedia entry. Let us consider the Polish Wikipedia entry: 'A Czech writer and a playwright, an anti-Communist activist, the ninth and the last president of Czechoslovakia (1989–92) and the first president of the Czech Republic (1993–2003)'.[4] The emphasis is slightly different in an encyclopaedia published by PWN: 'A Czech politician, a playwright, and an essayist; one of the initiators of Charter 77, persecuted; in November 1989, he was among the leaders of the Civic Forum; from December 1989 to July 1992, was President of Czechoslovakia and from 1993 to 2003, President of the Czech Republic.'[5] In a six-volume encyclopaedia from the same publisher, the entry is similar but adds the information that Havel took part in the 'Prague Spring' of 1968 and was banned from publishing or having his plays staged.[6]

From these entries, we can state the main themes present in probably every account of Havel in Poland: Havel, the dissident, Havel, the president, and Havel, the writer.

---

2   A Polish slogan, popular in the early 1990s, meaning 'we want Havel to rule Poland' (Wawel is the castle in Cracow, where the kings of Poland had their seat).
3   Masłoń, K. 'Rozluźnione obyczaje Vaclava Havla', *Rzeczpospolita*, 1 September 2007.
4   Online: http://pl.wikipedia.org/wiki/V%C3%A1clav_Havel [Accessed 16 February 2012].
5   *Encyklopedia Popularna PWN*. Warsaw: PWN, 2006 (33rd edn), p. 306.
6   *Nowa encyklopedia powszechna PWN*, vol. 2. Warsaw: PWN, 1995, p. 715.

Havel, the Dissident

Havel's activities in the Czechoslovak anti-Communist opposition are the most discussed topic in every account of Havel. He is described mostly as the main figure of the opposition among the Czechs who are generally not noted to be keen on this kind of activity. His role in the establishment of the 'Charter 77' human-rights movement and his famous essay 'The Power of the Powerless' is almost always recalled. Probably no Havel biography or essay about him omits information about his years in prison. The story of Havel, the opposition member, has been developed for many years by his Polish friends and colleagues from Havel's years of work with the editor-in-chief of *Gazeta Wyborcza*, Adam Michnik. A crucial part of the Havel story in Poland therefore is the cooperation between Charter 77 and the Workers' Defence Committee (KOR) in the late 1970s or the contacts in 'Polish-Czechoslovak Solidarity' in the 1980s.

The most comprehensive narrative in Polish historiography was by Michnik in his foreword to the first edition of Havel's essays, published in late 2011. He begins with the meeting of Polish and Czech dissidents on Śnieżka/Sněžka Mountain, on the Polish-Czech border, in 1978. It was, Michnik writes, 'an important meeting, symbolic confirmation of the shared aspirations and values of the democratic opposition in Poland and Czechoslovakia'.[7] And he states that Havel 'defies all labelling: he was not a rebel Communist or a Roman Catholic, not conservative, or liberal, or Social Democrat'.[8] Michnik then analyzes Havel's principle writings, calling, for example, Havel's letter to Husák an open challenge to dictatorship. And he notes: 'Havel resisted the temptation to leave the country. He chose the fate of a man on the margins, a spiritual man (Patočka's definition), a dissident, risking future imprisonment or annihilation.'[9]

---

7   Michnik, A. 'Wielka historia Václava Havla', in V. Havel, *Siła bezsilnych i inne eseje*. Warsaw: Agora, 2011, p. 9.
8   Ibid., p. 10.
9   Ibid., p. 14.

In his analysis, Michnik says that many of Havel's ideas were 'close to ideas of people associated with the Workers' Defence Committee, mainly Kuroń's ideas. There were, however, differences too.'[10] According to Michnik, Havel was very open-minded, which could be perceived as one of the most crucial attributes of Havel's dissident thought: 'I think that for my dissident friends and for me as well this dissident philosophy about life was enough. But not for Havel. He was contending not only with the Communist dictatorship, but also with the evils of contemporary civilization.'[11] And, what is especially important for Michnik, 'Havel knew, and wrote, that the status of the dissident might lead one to conform to the 'gregarious behaviour' of one's own environment, making their enemies (for example, the Communists) into devils and themselves into angels. For Havel, the enemy was not the Communists, but the Communist system.' And he adds: 'Havel never was a primitive anti-Communist';[12] every human being was for him a distinct world, worthy of fair consideration.'[13]

Havel, the President

As the head of the state, Havel was repeatedly criticized by his compatriots while abroad his image was almost immaculate. In Polish accounts of his four presidential terms, his vision, authority, erudition, and ability to act above party politics are his most emphasized traits. Another key element of the narrative is Havel's 'informality'; it is often pointed out that he tried to avoid being enclosed in the 'gilded cage' of power, which he had criticized so often. The third aspect of his image as president is Havel's relations all over the world, not only in political and diplomatic circles, but also in the world of show business

---

10   Ibid., p. 16.
11   Ibid., p. 20.
12   Michnik writes *jaskiniowy antykomunista*, literally a 'cave anti-Communist', a term used by many Poles to describe in an emotionally negative way someone in favour of settling old scores with the Communist régime and functionaries.
13   Michnik, 'Wielka historia', pp. 19–20.

(particularly his friendship with Mick Jagger and Frank Zappa). Several titles of Polish articles from recent years depict Havel, the President, in the best possible light: 'A Philosopher at the Castle'[14], 'A Philosopher-King,[15] and 'A President That Remained Human'.[16]

The 'human face' of Havel as President has been frequently discussed. In an article published in *Polska. The Times* newspaper, Anna Dudek wrote: 'A president always with a cigarette, wearing a casual sweater. A president, whose secretary was a hippie famous for her huge funny earrings that didn't go with her clothes. A head of the state darting through the corridors of the presidential palace on a scooter, rushing from one appointment to another.' And she aptly sums it up: 'the dissident that became a politician, but never lost touch with the things that had been essential in his life before he became one of the most eminent politicians of post-war Europe—the theatre, the fascinating world of underground Prague culture.' Then she describes Havel's friendship with Frank Zappa and the astonishing decision to make him an adviser, and Havel's relations with the Rolling Stones: 'Havel's magnetic personality attracted not only world leaders (he could meditate with the Dalai Lama for hours and take Bill Clinton to jazz concerts), but also international superstars. And vice versa, there is the famous scene during an official visit in 1995, when Havel deep in talks with Mick Jagger, the frontman of the Rolling Stones, ignored dignitaries waiting for a greeting.'[17]

It has frequently been argued that Havel entered high-level politics by accident. Michnik states: 'Havel was not a typical politician. He was striking in his idealism, truthfulness, and courage in withstanding public adoration. He was implementing policies stemming from the belief that though "none of us—as an individual—can save the world as a whole; [...] each of us must behave as if it were in his

---

14 Sierszuła, B. 'Filozof na Hradzie', *Rzeczpospolita*, 18 January 2003.
15 Geremek, B. 'Król-filozof', *Gazeta Wyborcza*, 22 October 2004.
16 Szczygieł, M. 'Prezydent, który pozostał człowiekiem,' *Gazeta Wyborcza*, 21 August 2007.
17 Dudek, A. 'Miłośnik rocka w teatrze polityki', *Polska. The Times*, 19 December 2011.

power to do so'".[18] And he says: 'Havel was a special kind of politician, like Martin Luther King, Mahatma Gandhi, Nelson Mandela, Andrei Sakharov, and Jacek Kuroń; in politics he was a man of testimony, a great moral authority of his times.'[19]

But this was, in Michnik's opinion, the main problem for Havel, the president. He writes: 'The story of Havel's life until 1 January 1990 was like a wonderful fairy tale with a miraculous ending. Many of us, yesterday's dissidents, thought in a similar way — since it had been so far, so good, it should now also continue that way [...] But soon the fairy tale was over.'[20] And in his obituary for Havel, Michnik states: 'he soon went from being an idol to being the object of a witch-hunt. It was organized by Czech philistines, whom Havel called čecháčkové, people who are full of hatred towards every dissident.'[21]

Aleksander Kwaśniewski, the former president of Poland, pointed out a paradox that was strictly bound up with Havel the politician. 'Havel found it hard to be in politics. It was not his world. Aggression and ruthlessness hurt him. [...] The fact that despite all his aversion to politics and political parties he managed to remain president for so long is another Havel paradox. He was the president of Czechoslovakia and the Czech Republic, and was thus in politics for a long time, from late 1989 to 2003, holding the highest office for fourteen years. His dislike of politics meant that he left no successor, either in the personal or political sense.'[22]

Havel, the writer

The question of Havel's contribution to literature is the least discussed. But the fact that he is well known as a writer (with most attention paid

---

18   Michnik, 'Wielka historia', p. 38.
19   Ibid., pp. 36–37.
20   Ibid., p. 25.
21   Michnik, A. 'Jak uderzenie w twarz drzwiami w przeciągu', *Gazeta Wyborcza*, 19 December 2011.
22   Kwaśniewski, A. 'Mam nadzieję na hawlizm', *Gazeta Wyborcza*, 19 December 2011.

to his plays in the style of the Theatre of the Absurd) perfectly complements Havel's image as a moral and intellectual authority. His plays and in particular his essays, are often put into the context of his dissident activity. It is interesting, however, that in Poland most of his plays were published only in samizdat in the 1980s, never by the state-owned publishing houses. Noticeable publicity accompanied the first 'post-presidential' Havel writings, *Prosím, stručně* (published in English as *To the Castle and Back* and in Polish as *Tylko krótko, proszę*) and the play *Odcházeni* (*Leaving*), performed at the Teatr Ateneum, Warsaw, as *Odejścia*.

This part of Havel's activity was discussed after his death. In the article 'Mąż stanu, co nie stronił od kultury' (A statesman who did not shun the arts), Bożydar Brakoniecki points out that according to theatre historians Havel wrote several dozen plays, but emphasizes that Havel's essays and poetry are no less interesting.[23]

Andrzej Jagodziński, a member of the Polish opposition to the Communist régime, and an interpreter of Havel's literary works, said:

> He was the most important Czech playwright of the 1960s, one of the creators of the Theatre of the Absurd phenomenon. His plays, staged at the Divadlo Na zábradlí, Prague, [...] made a great impression. Havel received many awards in this field. His plays were staged all over the world. [...] In 1968, the barriers went back up. Václav Havel was no longer an officially acceptable writer. His books were withdrawn from libraries and nothing of his was published. For a fiction writer or poet, it is difficult to write only for 'the drawer' or to be published only in samizdat; for a playwright it is a tragedy. Without contact with an audience, a play does not exist; even if perfectly written, it is still only half of what it should be. From 1968 to late 1989, Vaclav Havel saw none of his plays staged.[24]

This aspect of Havel's work is strongly emphasized in the PWN encyclopaedias, especially in the extended, six-volume *Nowa encyklopedia*

---

23   Brakoniecki, B. 'Mąż stanu, co nie stronił od kultury', *Polska. The Times*, 19 December 2011.
24   Jagodziński, A. 'Czechypogrążone w smutku i żałobie. Vaclav Havel nie żyje', online: http://wiadomosci.onet.pl/raporty/vaclav-havel-nie-zyje/czechy-pograzone-w-smutku-i-zalobie-vaclav-havel-n,2,4975521,wiadomosc.html, [Accessed: 18 December 2011].

powszechna PWN. The greater part of the entry describes his literary achievements.[25]

Immaculate Havel?

In each of the 'incarnations' we have discussed, Havel is presented in Poland almost as unimpeachable. No serious criticism of him as a Czech politician and a playwright appears in the Polish public discourse. The only variable that might be different is the intensity of delight, ranging from almost unconditional adoration to a far more moderate and balanced picture, with slightly demythologizing elements.

An example of the first approach is an article by Piotr Nowina-Konopka, who wrote with praise after Havel's second (and last) presidential term: 'It remains only to admit that the Czechs (or actually the Czechs and the Slovaks) gave the world a politician of unusually great dimensions, and to congratulate them for it. We can only congratulate them for having raised the standards much higher than in other democracies today. And we can only regret that someone like Vašek Havel is not born every day.'[26] Nowina-Konopka goes even beyond the praise we have discussed so far, calling Havel 'a great dissident', 'a great president', and 'a great writer'.

Enthusiastic opinions of him were also, understandably, heard after Havel's death. In the obituary published a few hours after the sad news had arrived, one of the biggest Polish information websites wrote: 'Havel was one of the greatest people in the modern history of the Czech Republic and Czechoslovakia. An intellectual who was first denounced, but then managed to bring down the Communist régime in his country. He was and a thinker who had the courage to lead his country.'[27] And Andrzej Grajewski wrote: 'A seeker after the truth has died, one of the most courageous people I have ever known, but also

---

25 *Nowa Encyklopedia*, p. 715.
26 Nowina-Konopka, P. 'Cytat dyplomatyczny', *Wprost* 4, 2003.
27 *Vaclav Havel nie żyje*, online: http://wiadomosci.wp.pl/kat,1356,title,Vaclav-Havel-nie-zyje,wid,14093128,wiadomosc.html?ticaid=1e4cb [Accessed: 18 December 2011].

a man who was very modest, one of the greatest friends of Poland, an irreplaceable authority, not only for Czechs and Slovaks, but for all Europeans.'[28]

In contrast to Nowina-Konopka's views of Havel, stands for example Krzysztof Masłoń. He claims that *To the Castle and Back* 'is worth reading, mostly to get some critical distance from our long-term admiration'. But he attempts to demythologize Havel, albeit gently, remaining full of appreciation and understanding for what makes Havel, as he himself writes, 'an idol of a considerable part of the Polish intelligentsia, regardless of whom we would call an intellectual'. Masłoń explains the enthusiasm for Havel of those Poles who long to have a president of that calibre, rather than Jaruzelski and Wałęsa, who, from that Polish perspective, are weak compared to the Czechoslovak (and then Czech) head of state.

Masłoń's main criticism in his article is made in three points. First, he argues, Havel was always overrated (both with regard to his literary talent and his foreign-language skills). Second, the Czechs, who know Havel best, happen to be, Masłoń claims, highly critical of him. And last, he considers ethical aspects (mainly the question of Havel's relationship with his future second wife while his first wife, Olga, was still alive). Even this criticism is restrained, with evident kindness towards Havel, who has, the author admits, his shortcomings and is not quite as ideal as he is often made out to be, but still deserves a great deal of respect and appreciation.[29]

Polish controversies around Havel

Serious controversies and criticism concerning Havel appeared in Poland only once. It was in 2007, after he stated: 'you should conduct free

---

28 Grajewski, A. 'Zawszemówił z wielkim respektem o transcendentnym wymiarze życia. Przyjaźnił się z wieloma chrześcijanami', online: http://wpolityce.pl/wydarzenia/20052-zawsze-mowil-z-wielkim-respektem-o-transcendentnym-wymiarze-zycia-przyjaznil-sie-z-wieloma-chrzescijanami, [Accessed: 18 December 2011].

29 Masłoń, 'Rozluźnione obyczaje Vaclava Havla'.

elections as soon as possible. It would be in the best interest of Poland, if international observers were invited to those elections'.[30] This remark was made after two years of rule in Poland by the right-wing coalition led by PiS, in the face of early parliamentary elections. It was made at the presentation of the Polish translation of Havel's *To the Castle and Back, Tylko krótko, proszę*, in Cracow.

The remark was met with widespread puzzlement in Poland, and Havel quickly realized that he had blundered and tried to soften the point of his words, asserting that the invitation of international observers was something usual and that he had never meant to imply that Polish democracy was threatened: 'if my aside was understood by anyone as an attack on Polish democracy, or as questioning it, or even as an insult to the Poles, then I am truly sorry about that and apologize'.[31] Something else that might come as a bit of a surprise to certain people is that Polish reactions were also very moderate. The main wave of criticism was directed at the people associated with *Gazeta Wyborcza* and the former Freedom Union, who were frequently perceived, or presented, as the true source of Havel's words. Havel himself was treated as their tool, and, unaware of the real situation in Poland, had allegedly allowed himself to be manipulated by his friends, mainly Michnik.

This perspective appears, for example, in Rafał Ziemkiewicz's article, who writes: 'If there were a decoration for meddling in other people's business in a manner that combined opinion untainted by understanding, together with the subtlety of a bull in a china shop, it would definitely be called The Havel Award'. But he also offers an explanation: 'on the one hand, he had Michnik, who instead of talking about Havel's book, spent the whole time talking about the authoritarian tendencies of the Kaczyński brothers and a coup d'état they had

---

30 Quoted in Armata, J., Niemczyńska, M. 'Mądry człowiek w ciężkich czasach', *Gazeta Wyborcza Kraków* 4 September 2007.
31 Jagodziński, A. 'Vaclav Havel: My zawsze zapraszamy obserwatorów', *Gazeta Wyborcza*, 5 September 2007.

planned, and, on the other hand, he had Senator Kazimierz Kutz expressing, with a serious face, his fear that Adam was going to go to jail again. And in front of them they had *Gazeta Wyborcza* readers applauding the spectacle.'[32]

This article reveals an interesting attitude towards Havel, which was, or is still, held by Polish right-wing politicians and intellectuals close to them. Although ideologically close to Michnik (who is fundamentally criticized by the Polish right-wing), Havel has never been attacked or even criticized from that side. His name has of course appeared much less often in conservative periodicals than it has in *Gazeta Wyborcza*, but when it does appear there, it does so in a largely positive context.

This view is supported by an analysis of articles from *Nasz Dziennik*, a daily newspaper with a clearly national profile connected with the political tradition of the pre-war National Democrats (*Narodowa Demokracja*, also known by its initials as 'endecja'). Havel's name has rarely appeared in this paper, and practically no article has been directly about him. Sometimes, however, his name has been used to strengthen the credibility of opinions presented there: 'See, even Havel, far from us from ideologically, holds a similar view'. This was how the Czech president was depicted as a supporter of the vetting legislation (*lustrace*) and de-Communization, when the newspaper quoted his words: 'from the history of our country we know that it was always up to us, when we believed that it did not matter what had been and that we should not be interested in it. [...] There is a great need in society to deal with this past, to dismiss people who terrorized the nation and obviously infringed human rights. They should be ousted from their jobs.' This was contrary to what was being said by the Polish élites of the transition period: 'in Poland at this time it was affirmed that it was impossible to carry out vetting and it was proclaimed that "everybody was implicated". The post-Communists

---

32 Ziemkiewicz, R. 'Czas wrzeszczących staruszków', *Rzeczpospolita* 7 September 2007.

with the help of the so-called "post-Solidarity left-wing" worked out a method of retaining their influence during the transition period.[33]

Havel's attitude towards vetting was, however, much more complicated and complex than this. After his death, one short sentence was published in the same newspaper, without further explanation: 'but he was an opponent of settling scores with the Communist past.'[34] Michnik too found it hard to comprehend Havel's opinion on the matter: 'In August 1990, he said, to the surprise of many of his friends, 'our revolution is not finished yet', since the 'tentacles of invisible mafias are hidden' behind the troubles of everyday life — they try to 'take over assets that do not belong to them, to establish suspected joint-stock companies and search ways to locate safely capital gathered illegally. Such tentacles are entwining invisibly our whole economy.' Those opinions were amazing. In the language of those days it meant calling for purges, creating the atmosphere of fear of omnipresent enemy. [...] Several times I wondered whether Havel's true belief was hidden in those words of 'unfinished revolution' and 'invisible tentacles' or whether it was only a tactic, adopting radical populists' catchwords to give those threateningly sounding platitudes different content.'[35]

Other examples of *Nasz Dziennik*'s endeavouring to 'use' Havel's authority in the internal Polish political debate are of a similar nature. Havel's criticism of 'vulgar realism'[36] in Czech politics was contrasted to the approach of Polish supporters of the 'Czech way': 'the most preposterous sounding was Konwicki's moaning that we did not ulti-

---

33   Jackowski, J. M. 'Tylko pełna jawność', *Nasz Dziennik* 3–4 February 2007.
34   Falkowski, P. 'Vaclav Havel nie żyje', *Nasz Dziennik,* 19 December 2011.
35   Michnik, 'Wielka historia', pp. 27–28.
36   Havel wrote about this term: 'I mean realism characterized by the attitude: "a bird in the hand is worth two in the bush" [...] I am talking about the "realism" of the Czech deputies in the Austrian parliament with their deals and timid concessions, about the "realism"'of Beneš during the Munich crisis, Hacha's "realism" and his conception of Bohemia as an oasis of calm in a stormy Europe, about the "realism" of Beneš's and Gottwald's servile Stalinist orientation after the war, about the "realism" of Husak's consolidation'. Quoted in Nowak, J. R. 'Antynarodowa publicystyka "Wprost"', *Nasz Dziennik* 29 August 2007.

mately get "nice, Czech characteristics" (meaning extreme opportunism and conformism to the power), while the leading Czechs reject those traits as being extremely unacceptable'.[37] Havel was also quoted to strengthen criticism of the Russo-German Baltic gas pipeline project. In November 2007, *Nasz Dziennik* wrote: 'In October this year, the governments of Estonia and Finland, and even [...] the former Czech president, Vaclav Havel, took a critical position towards Nord Stream. In the best interest of everyone, one should not, ignore the fact that a country called Poland is located between Germany and Russia. [...] We did not take down the "Iron Curtain" to erect a new one, based on oil and gas supplies—said Havel in an interview for the *Koelnischer Rundschau* daily'.[38]

Havel, a friend of Poland

We now come to another part of the story. Havel was often perceived and described as a friend of Poland, a man who for many years had special relations with the country of the Czechs' northern neighbours. Just after Havel's death, the lead article on page one of the newspapers *Polska Times* was entitled: 'Havel, a Great Man Has Passed Away. A Hero of the Czech Republic, A Friend of Poland, Has Died at the Age of 75.' Then we read: 'Václav Havel was a special person for the Poles and a great friend of Poland. The friendship began with clandestine meetings with members of the Polish opposition in the mountains on the Czech-Polish border in the 1980s. His friendship with Adam Michnik is well known. In 2005, at the invitation of Jolanta and Aleksander

---

37   Ibid.
38   Tomczyk, P. 'Kto popiera gazociąg?', *Nasz Dziennik*, 2 November 2007.

Kwaśniewski, Havel and his wife were guests in Jurata [a Polish seaside resort].[39] His friendship with Poland was emphasized also in *Super Express*, a Polish tabloid. Havel's obituary there was entitled: 'Vaclav Havel, a Great Friend of Poland, Has Passed Away'.[40]

This feature occurs also in President Bronisław Komorowski's speech about Havel after his death. The Polish head of state emphasized: 'we should remember Václav Havel also because in everything he did he was always a faithful friend of Poland and the Poles. He was a man who, cultivating solidarity in practice, which was both human and democratic in general and Polish-Czech in partiular.' He decided also to put the flags on the Presidential Palace and Belweder Palace at half mast in honour of Havel.[41] Similar remarks, signed by Minister Radosław Sikorski, were posted on the website of the Polish Ministry of Foreign Affairs. Sikorski added: 'To commemorate Havel, on Monday, 19 December, all meetings in the Council of the European Union, during the Polish presidency, will begin with a minute of silence.'[42]

I would add just one more comment, from Havel's friend, Andrzej Grajewski: 'Václav Havel was a friend of the Poles. For many he was an inspiration when he helped to get Charter 77 going. Some activities of the Polish movement in opposition to the Communist régime in the late 1970s were inspired by his great essay *The Power of the Powerless*, where he presents the idea of a non-violent movement of resistance to totalitarian systems.'[43]

---

39   Rogacin, W. 'Odszedł Havel, wielki człowiek: Bohater Czech, przyjaciel Polski, zmarł w wieku 75 lat', *Polska. The Times*, 19 December 2011.
40   Skowron, M. 'Odszedł Vaclav Havel, wielki przyjaciel Polski', *Super Express*, 19 December 2011.
41   Website of the Polish President, online: http://www.prezydent.pl/aktualnosci/wydarzenia/art,2055,havel-byl-zawsze-przyjacielem-polski-i-polakow.html, [Accessed: 12 March 2012].
42   Website of the Polish Ministry of Foreign Affairs, online: http://www.msz.gov.pl/Zmarl,Vaclav,Havel,47594.html, [Accessed: 12 March 2012].
43   Grajewski, 'Zawszemówił'.

Havel honoured

This short preview of opinions, articles, and analyses has sought to show the special Polish attitude towards Havel. It gives a thumbnail sketch of him as seen through Polish eyes. This picture based on opinions must be supplemented, since apart from the good opinion people had of him 'from the Left to the Right', Havel was also repeatedly honoured in Poland. This was done by authorities at different levels and by several institutions. A short enumeration of the most important distinctions would include orders, honorary degrees, and honorary citizenships:

Orders
Order of the White Eagle (1993)

Honorary degrees in Poland
Wrocław University (1992)
Warsaw University (2004)

Honorary citizenship
Wrocław (2001)

Awards
Jan Nowak-Jeziorański Prize (2009); Man of the Year of Central Europe and Eastern Europe, from the European Forum, Krynica (2007); Laurels of Competence and Abilities awarded by the Regional Chamber of Commerce and Industry, Katowice (2005); and the Medal of St George, awarded by the *Tygodnik Powszechny* weekly (2003)
First Decade of the *Gazeta Wyborcza* Award (1999)

This short list of Havel's main distinctions and awards from Poland clearly shows how esteemed the former Czech president has been there. The best quip is perhaps Kwaśniewski's, who, while President of Poland, remarked during the ceremony at which Warsaw University awarded Havel an honorary degree. 'I envy you a bit', he said to Havel. 'No Polish politician will ever hear so many warm words from a department of history dean at any Polish institution of higher learning'.[44] Most likely the same could be said about Havel and the deans of the departments of history in Czech universities.

---

[44] K. Z., 'Havel pielgrzym i doktor h.c.', *Rzeczpospolita*, 22 October 2004.

Wałęsa's Absence from Czech Society

Tomáš Zahradníček[1]
The Academy of Sciences of the Czech Republic

Abstract: This paper focuses on the public representation of Polish dissident and former president Lech Wałęsa—or conspicuous lack of it. It first examines Wałęsa's image in the press of Communist Czechoslovakia in the context of general lack of information about Polish uprising and the Solidarity movement. The author then focuses on Wałęsa's absence from the post-Communist discourse, salient in the context of popularity of Czech dissidents in the other countries of the Eastern bloc.

It requires a good deal of detective work to trace the presence of Lech Wałęsa (b. 1943) in Czech discourse. Writers such as Václav Havel (1936–2011) left behind visible traces in countries other than their own in the form of translations of their works and quotable words. More often than not, their writing is consciously aimed not only at the local audience but also beyond national borders. The power of popular leaders such as Wałęsa lies in their interaction with their home audience. I will therefore discuss Wałęsa's absence in the Czech Republic more than his presence. I will also discuss how many important Polish events were 'lost in translation' into Czech, and how this loss was possibly greater than in translation into other languages. I will begin with Wałęsa, the leader of Solidarity, before moving on to Wałęsa, the President.

Wałęsa's most important absence is his first, in 1980–81. While the West kept an eye on the Polish uprising as if it were a TV series filmed before a live audience, Czech and other east European societies perceived it as an uprising that they could only read about or listen to radio coverage. Television is unmatched in mediating experiences and emotions. Because of television—and during the first Solidarity (1980–81) foreign TV crews had a lot of freedom—the story of Solidarity resonated even in Western circles that normally did not follow foreign

---

1 Email: zahradnicek@usd.cas.cz

affairs. The Polish uprising was popular in the West and Wałęsa contributed to that greatly — his face, his gestures, and even his Black Madonna of Częstochowa lapel pin became familiar images in the West. Television, a medium in which what one says is less important than how one says it, was conveying around the world an image of Wałęsa as a charismatic leader of the working classes — an image to which most citizens of the Eastern Bloc had never been exposed.

In the Czech milieu, the images of Polish events in writing prevailed. In those narratives Wałęsa's role was diminished, regardless of whether one is talking about the official Czechoslovak press, samizdat, or exile publications. He figures neither as the central villain in the propaganda against Solidarity, nor as an example to follow. Certainly the name Lech Wałęsa and a few biographical lines or short commentaries, and his words and deeds, did appear many times, but most frequently he was cast in the role of the first among many Polish worker-rebels.

For the state-controlled press, the ruling Polish United Workers' Party (PSDS) was the main culprit of the Polish 'carnival'. The PSDS was blamed for the bad economic policy that had resulted in social tension. It was also criticized for 'bad ideological work' and thereby enabling the growth of opposition activities or, in the language of the Czech Communist daily, *Rudé právo*, of groups of ideological saboteurs (*ideodiverzní skupiny*) linked with the Western secret services, which were allegedly taking advantage of the situation. This scheme reduced Wałęsa to a pawn on a chessboard. The main pieces, according to the Communist mass media, were the leading figures of the Workers' Defence Committee (KOR), Jacek Kuroń and Adam Michnik.[2] This was in line with the efforts of the Polish government to dis-

---

2   One of the first Czech articles demonstrating this propaganda line is 'Jaké jsou cíle nepřátel lidového Polska. Odmaskovali se' (What Are the Aims of the Enemies of the People's Poland: They've Been Dropped Their Masks), *Rudé právo*, 27 September 1980, p. 6.

tinguish between the good and the bad rebels, and it also corresponded better with the practice of journalists, who preferred writer-heroes whose works they could quote from.

Wałęsa fared no better in the opposition press. The key question of why the Poles rebelled and the Czechs did not was generally answered with reference to either cultural or social differences. The former recalled the tradition of Polish uprisings which has fascinated certain Czech intellectuals since the first half of the nineteenth century. The argument that the Poles were rebelling because they were Poles and the Czechs were remaining passive because they were Czechs had very little impact and required no real knowledge of the situation of their neighbour to the north.[3] The exploration of the social differences was more interesting. Under the impression of the Polish events, Czech sociologists in uncensored, samizdat publications were stressing the special nature of Communist rule in Czechoslovakia with its high level of income equality, exceptional even in the Eastern Bloc: three quarters of all employees were receiving more or less equal wages. Skilled labour had good reason to be dissatisfied, but unskilled workers did not feel poor. These sociological studies are possibly the most relevant part of the contemporaneous debates about Solidarity and they present a challenge to today's historians to write a comparative study of wage policies.[4] Nevertheless, this analysis was presented in abstract terms, leaving no space for a story about an individual.

We should also try to settle the question of whether most Czechs supported Solidarity. The answer is 'yes' and 'no'. In order to find out anything of importance, we have to ask a different question—namely, which kinds of reactions can we document with certainty? It is not

---

[3] 'For those who know Polish history, there is no need to worry about them,' wrote the journalist Jiří Lederer, considered the leading expert on Poland in the Czech opposition of the 1970s. Lederer, J. *Mé Polsko: 200 let boje proti cizí nadvládě*. Cologne: Index, 1982, p. 232.

[4] Strmiska, Z. *Sociální systém a strukturální rozpory společnosti sovětského typu: Projekt analýzy*. Cologne: Index, 1983; Klofáč, J. *Sociální struktura ČSSR a její změny v letech 1945-1980*. Cologne: Index, 1985.

hard to identify basic reactions and their dynamics, which, interestingly enough, correspond with Polish reactions to the Prague Spring of 1968. I will outline them only briefly: (1) delight that something is finally happening; (2) malicious joy that Moscow is having troubles with a neighbour; (3) jealousy that the neighbour is getting all the attention, and the related question of the importance of the event (the Poles were interpreting the Prague Spring as delayed destalinization with excellent public relations, whereas the Czechs looked at Solidarity as the politicization of the fact that Polish workers do not want to work); (4) fear of the consequences based on the realization that neither the victory nor the defeat of the Prague Spring or Solidarity would bring any benefits to the neighbouring society and would most likely result in its increased state surveillance, which is exactly what happened in both cases.[5]

For Czech society in 1980–81, Wałęsa remained hidden behind the barrier of television censorship. For the Western media, the events around Solidarity were personified by Wałęsa. He received little attention, however, either from people in the opposition or from Czechoslovak state propaganda; to the sociologists, he appeared to be an accidental figure, not an active agent of historical events. Many Czechs had no clear idea who Wałęsa actually was, as was noted with surprise by a Czech émigré after his return to his homeland in 1990.[6]

From the first absence of Wałęsa, others naturally followed. Czech society after the Changes beginning in 1989 continued to know little about Wałęsa; indeed, they had little need for him. It had its own stories of victory about the Prague Spring, Charter 77, and the Velvet Revolution that brought Havel to presidential office within a few weeks. Seen from Prague, Poland, with President General Wojciech

---

5   The Polish doubts about the Prague Spring are discussed in, Zahradníček, T. *Polské poučení z pražského jara: Tři studie z dějin politického myšlení 1968–1981*. Prague: ÚSD AV ČR, 2011; the Czechoslovak response to Solidarity is presented in Kobus, A. *Czechosłowacja wobec narodzin, rozwoju i delegalizacji "Solidarności" (1980–1982)*. Toruń: Adam Marszałek, 2006.
6   Jan Čulík in an interview with Grzegorz Musiał about Czechoslovak-Polish relations: 'Šance střední Evropy', *Respekt*, 5 December 1990, p. 13.

Jaruzelski, suddenly looked like a country lagging behind. When Havel arrived in Warsaw as a guest of Jaruzelski in January 1990, he did not find time to travel to Gdańsk to meet the leader of Solidarity, Wałęsa, and vice versa. The two leaders met later, on Sněžka mountain, on the Czech-Polish border, to correct the bad impression that the visit had left.

The first post-Communist months were a difficult period for Czech-Polish relations. President Havel energetically announced reforms of international organizations and was accepted abroad as a speaker for the whole region. In practical terms, however, the number of unresolved matters between the two new governments grew. In particular, the opening up of the borders did not happen as fast as was hoped, and the Czechs began to indicate that they were made uneasy by being neighbours with a country with such high debts and generally in economic turmoil. *Gazeta Wyborcza*, a left-leaning Polish newspaper established and edited by Adam Michnik, began to write about the end of the dreams of central Europe.[7] Yet if we reflect on what happened after the First and Second World Wars, how quickly conflict emerged between the new élites of the two states who had, just a few weeks before assuming office, spoken so poetically and sincerely about friendship, we have to admit that in 1990 no serious harm was done. Immediately after Wałęsa's election, the three central European presidents—Árpád Göncz, Václav Havel, and Lech Wałęsa—met in Visegrád, and regional cooperation was finally given its impetus.

Three heroes in three presidential offices were a true luxury for the region. Havel, Wałęsa, and Göncz each represented three different national stories about the road away from Communism, stories which competed with, rather than complemented, each other. The presidents tried to maintain good relations, but inevitably got in each other's way. To give an example: the current state of the Havel–Wałęsa competition for honorary doctorates as of November 2011 is 46:45 for Havel, yet we have to note that Havel received two doctorates from Poland and

---

7 Quoted in ibid.

Wałęsa none from the Czech Republic.[8] I do not want to exaggerate the importance of mathematical methods in historiography, but the result is more than telling.

Neither Wałęsa's struggle for the presidency nor his period in office found few supporters in Prague. An emotional link with the leader of Solidarity was missing. Common sense dictated that the best neighbour is a predictable neighbour. Consequently, the Czech press in 1990 sympathized with Tadeusz Mazowiecki's candidacy and in 1995 with Aleksander Kwaśniewski, though in the latter case the attitude of the Czech press was more ambivalent. We may say in general that the Czech public adopted the *Gazeta Wyborcza* view because it was perfectly understandable and its editor-in-chief, Michnik, was considered a guarantee of truthfulness.[9] The Czech reaction was special in the sense that in 1991 the nascent political parties were noticeably nervous about the consequences of Wałęsa's success in establishing strong presidential rule. They were afraid it could be contagious and that Wałęsa could, by his example, strengthen similar ambitions in Havel.[10] This fear, however, was assuaged by the summer of 1992. After the break-up of Czechoslovakia, Havel was a far weaker player in internal politics, which was given by the Constitution of the new Czech Republic.

I would sum up the question by putting forward two theses: (1) in the period of the first Solidarity, Wałęsa was far less present in Czech discourse compared to his presence in the discourse in the West. I would explain this as being the result of different information flows

---

8 'Václav Havel Library, Awards—Honorary Doctorates', online: http://www.vaclavhavel-library.org/en/vaclav-havel/awards/doctorates, [accessed 1 December 2011]; *Wikipedia, List of awards and honors received by Lech Wałęsa*, online: http://cn.wikipedia.org/wiki/, [accessed 1 December 2011].

9 'I admit that I trust Michnik a priori. He has proved himself many times,' said Zdeněk Urbánek, a writer and s close friend of Havel, in response to Michnik's article, 'My Vote against Wałęsa.' Urbánek, Z. 'Kolik svobody uneseme', *Lidové noviny*, 24 November 1990, p. 8.

10 Explicitly, for instance, in an interview with a Social Democratic deputy of the Federal Assembly, who was a professor of constitutional theory, František Šamalík, in *Právo lidu*, 18 January 1992, p. 4.

and the difference between images of the Polish uprising, which result from the difference between visual and print media. (2) As the leader of the second Solidarity and as the Polish President, Wałęsa was outshined by the Czechs' own symbolic hero, Havel.

As I noted at the beginning of this essay, given the subject, I have had to dwell more on Wałęsa's absence than his presence. But I believe that this has not been a futile enterprise, and that this perspective has shed some light on certain aspects of Czech-Polish relations in recent decades.

Summary:
Factors Driving Nation Building Processes after 1918 and Their Implications

Magdalena M. Baran, PhD[1]

Central Europe is a strange place, somewhere between East and West. A place which means today something more than just Visegrad but is historically connected with it Austria. This is a place where, according to various definitions, can be found many nations, and thus many languages and cultures, which are somehow interconnected. The place is understood as a point of view from which people — maybe a little differently — looked and still look at Europe, at the same time finding their place in it and telling their own Central European history. Here it is understood that this history — however we look at it — "is not a theater which takes place at the front of our eyes, only the responsible implementation of the relationship, which is man. History — wrote Czech philosopher Jan Patočka — is not the view, but the responsibility". It is also full of dilemmas about all small and great affairs for which we are responsible.

An so... over the past 100 years Visegradd is looking for its identity. Countries — for years pushed to the margins of Europe — seek their own place. The most important role in these activities is not accounted for by professional politicians, but by intellectuals, who not only allowed these nations to remember their European origin, but also did not allow Europe to forget about fellow citizens that firstly had to renew their own countries, nations, and societies, and then, for years, were locked behind the Iron Curtain. Without their writings, it

---

1   Email: magdalena.baran@gmail.com

is difficult to imagine today's Visegrad — modern, involved in European policy and European intellectual life. But to understand the history of the so called Visegrad Group — a block of four such a different countries — we need to look back, to the sources of their modern identity.

In our considerations we could follow one of the paths given by intellectuals such as Czesław Miłosz, Jenő Szűcs, Milan Kundera and many others. Following Szűcs, we can think of the orgins of Central Europe, seeing it as extended between the borders of the empire of Charlemagne, and the eastern borderlands of the Polish Kingdom (in the time of Jagiellonian dynasty, XVI century) and the Kingdom of Hungary (during a similar period). Here the whole europeanization of the Slavic "no man's land" began around the year 1000 CE, and for 600 years it followed the path determined by the culture of the West. A similar approach can be found in the analyses of Milan Kundera. In his essay "Kidnapped West or the Tragedy of Central Europe", Kundera asks: "What is Europe for Hungarian, Czech or Pole?" and he indicates the origin of these nations, placing them in a greater Europe, rooted in the Roman and Christian world. Kundera sees that Central European nations have participated in all phases of its history. He emphasizes the fact that "for them — these nations — the word 'Europe' is not a phenomenon of the geographical sphere, but is a spiritual concept, synonymous with the word 'West'". However, defining Europe — for Europe — a writer reminds us that it was divided since the beginning. Kundera understands Europe as stretched between the two ends. On one hand, it was dominated by the legacy of ancient Rome, but on the other hand came to influence the Byzantine Empire. A breakdown of this resulted in different religions (Roman Catholic and Orthodox), alphabets (Latin and Cyrillic), styles of governance, and finally culture itself, and Kundera has no doupts that all those factors shaped the identity of the peoples of this continent. The question is, what has happened on the border of the clash of those influences, and therefore in the part that we know as Central Europe? At the border, which — according to Kundera — became particularly clear

SUMMARY 397

after 1945, were formed no longer two, but now three Europes. This is the same border that we want to see existing a bit earlier, in 1918, just after the Great War that somehow gave back countries to their nations, but at the same time forced them to restore thinking and build new society, bearing in mind that the most important question is the one about their own identity.

To see things more clearly it might be good to go back to a spirit of Central Europe, seen by Czesław Miłosz in his book *Native Realm*. Miłosz is the one who sees the common characteristics that creates one region. This book "was written because of a desperate desire to communicate to the western reader some data, to explain what is the phenomenon of the origin of the other, poorer parts of Europe". However, for Miłosz the most important seems to be the identity of the historical phenomenon known as Mitteleuropa, which consists of something more than individual countries. What counts here is the fate of community, culture, and story creating an overall vision. "I decided to write a book about an Eastern European, born around the time when crowds in Paris and London cheered in honor of the first airmen, a man who less than anyone is German in notions of order and possesses the Russian *ăme slave* " — wrote Czesław Milosz. "This book — wrote years after Csaba Kiss — introduces us to the thicket of Central European dilemmas, which crosses the borders of languages, religions and cultures". With this dilemma we opened the discussion, inviting intellectuals of todays Central Europe to think together about our orgins.

We all agree that after the Great War Europe underwent fundamental changes. Not only the balance of power on the continent was new, but renewal required also a new way of thinking about politics, society and citizenship. That novelty was experienced especially in the countries of the former Austro-Hungarian Empire. Central Europe emerged from the war completely transformed. Some nations regained their independence, while others finally felt its taste, yet others had to deal with a new statehood, embedded within boundaries other than those they expected. Thus, the concept of the state and nation became fundamental. Citizens and governments of Central Europe had to answer the questions: What does the concept of the nation mean? What are its roots? What are its elements? Who belongs to the nation, who does not, and who can or should be excluded from it, and why? And finally: to what extent do the boundaries of the concepts of nation and state overlap and how can they peacefully coexist? Among the answers to the above questions appears the concept of nationalism. This chapter will focus on the role of nationalism as a constitutive element of new states in Central East Europe and on key events and ideologies and the impact of the events of 1918 on the political culture of new national states. Professor Dorota Pietrzyk-Revees, from the Jagiellonian University in Krakow considers civic and ethnic nationalism and the identity formation of Central European societies in the interwar period, re-examining the distinction between civic and ethnic nationalisms and its application to the Central European context after the First World War. Professor Miklós Zeidler from the Hungarian Academy of Sciences analyses the influence of historical revisionism and commemoration rituals on the process of Hungarian nation-building. Finally, professor Ivo Budil from the University of West Bohemia asks about the history of modern Central Europe, and, by using anthropological tools, looks at the emergence of totalitarianism and its related ideologies in the region of Central Europe. All three essays look at Central Europe, bearing in mind the term "identity" – the one that was inherited by generation of 1918, but also the one that had to be discovered, re-newed, re-thought and re-built after the experience of the Great War.

Persons who became myths

Paul Gradvohl[1]
University of Warsaw

The specific place taken by "historical characters" turned into myths partly shaped the relations of various neighboring countries and people. There is no doubt that collective identities in Central Eastern Europe are built not only on the grounds of big abstract national tales, but also resort to personification, casting heroes out of historical figures. This is probably why the examples chosen for presentation at the panel II at the conference were overwhelmingly political (Štefánik, Esterházy, Mikó, Piłsudski, Masaryk), and included a historian (Krofta) who was also an ambassador and Foreign Affairs minister, not as a myth, but as a key interpreter of Czechoslovak (and Czech) national identity. The only type of identity considered here was national identity. Thus the scope of the presentations was limited. Nevertheless the confrontation of the various points of views helped to unveil certain Central European idiosyncracies.

A first glimpse at the six heroes named above demonstrates that the implicit assumption of the title of this panel, one person is equivalent to one myth, is mistaken. The French major, and finally general, Milan Rastislav Štefánik, has been portrayed as a successful Czechoslovak politician and a martyr Slovak, possibly the victim of a plot. So one person means several heroes. The fate of minority Hungarian politicians, one in Slovakia and the other in Romania, helps to face the ambiguities of national politics abroad and underlines an unsolved contradiction: leaders of minority groups were to be suspected both by majority politicians in the country in which they were born and lived and, in this case, by the Hungarian government, to be out of control and follow unclear agendas under pressure from various hidden

---

1   E-mail: paul.gradvohl@uw.edu.pl.

sources. Both heroes and antiheroes according to nationalists, they occupied an ambivalent, if not downright dubious, position. So these heroes necessarily became fragile myths, constantly under suspicion.

Considering Masaryk and Piłsudski as flag bearers of national philosophies means discarding all hopes of a strictly national perspective. Basically, it even means deriving the national philosophy of an anti-German politician from a German *Weltanschauung*. These heroes are therefore partially deceiving their people, a quite puzzling predicament when national discourses supposedly draw on autochthonous intellectual tradition. Beyond any philosophical analysis, the various and more or less compatible strata of national discourses show the grey zones of legitimation constructs. And when deciphering Krofta's Czechoslovak nation-building endeavor, the fuzzy nature of the Czech or Czechoslovak nation is highlighted.

All four approaches question the essentialism underlying contemporary nationalism. All national heroes mentioned here, supposed to personify their (sole) nation, cannot in fact satisfy expectations. Neither ideological coherence, nor personal roots, seem to guarantee national purity or justify a specific place for our heroes. Nevertheless, here they stand and some of them still have currency as part of a national pantheon, even if the Czechoslovak nation is no longer promoted by a state apparatus. Various governments of the regions stress their Christian roots and keep silent about the diversity of the inhabitants of their own countries over the centuries. So, silently the spatial rooting of nations becomes a source of doubt, and national heroes lack the nationally exclusive color one could attribute to them.

On these grounds, we ought to stress the lack of coherence of these myths, and to question the relationship between (in)coherence and efficiency as far as national heroes are concerned. Obviously, discourses and images about persons are to be derived from the illusion of unity relying on the assumption of the identity of a person with himself or herself. But men and women are not identical to themselves through time. And the collective « us » is not an obvious fact, all the more so because to distinguish what is interior from what is exterior is not easy. Let us only recall Krofta's case with Germans, Hungarians and even Slovaks, which underlines the complexity of the intellectual task undertaken by modern nation builders.

People and lands are manifold, and ever-changing. Notwithstanding all the ambivalences mentioned above, none of our heroes came to terms with his double or multiple identities. The social production of historical characters, and even more so of heroes, when confronted with disrupted realities, is not to be oversimplified. Our conference opposed heroes, friends and enemies, and the national identities of neighbors. What we could learn here is that even persons serving as national heroes are no exception to the rule of transformation and the multiplicity of layers of each personality. Apparently, propaganda cannot totally eradicate the ever-springing consciousness of the multiple faces of each individual.

But strangely, religion and the figure of Christ, so central to European discourses about heroes, were not mentioned, even though purgatory was mentioned. The least Catholic figure, as duly recounted, was Piłsudski. The difficult connection between religion and nation in Central Europe, as elsewhere, opposes universal values and national discourses, and results in silence about Jews and their place in these societies. A similar silence concerns women and the overview of our debates shows how difficult it is to embed national myth building in social dynamics and to escape the attractiveness of victimization. The haphazard selection of elements included in the imaginary biographies of national heroes seems to produce uncertain effects. The social efficiency of historical heroes is therefore highly unstable and friable not only because of the changes of history and politics, but also thanks to the structural incoherence of the characters used as heroes. Once again, Central Eastern Europe is not so atypical, and, for example, the acute vision of the posthumous fate of minority leaders simply adds new shades to the image of weak states and puzzled societies, conscious that their fate largely depends on external factors.

How to teach history today?

Summary of the Working Group

Andrea Pető[1]
Central European University, Budapest

After 1989, the collapse of communism brought a zeal for reform in the teaching of history. The rewriting of curriculum and textbooks were informed by the desire to teach a "different history" than during communism. Very few would argue against replacing the monolithic presentation of political history with new narratives and methods. There were taboo topics such as Shoah or Gulag that needed to be incorporated in the curriculum. The question this panel examined was how these challenges have or have not been met especially in the digital age.

The panelists presented their projects in this framework trying to respond to the question of what the students/users learn, and how they apply that new, critical knowledge.

Martin Šmok from the Shoah Foundation Prague[2] represented an institution which hosts the largest digital archive of Shoah testimonies. The 52 000 interviews are indexed and searchable by keywords. The new program, called I-Witness is offering users the chance to edit a film of their own from those testimonies. The Foundation is mostly active in secondary level education and in making attempts to integrate new types of sources: digitalized testimonies in teaching the Shoah. The challenge of language is very much present as only testimonies that were given in Czech can be used.

Štěpán Černoušek[3] represented the project Gulag.cz. They built a webpage where they mapped the gulag system in the Soviet Union.

---

1 E-mail: petoa@ceu.hu.
2 Web page: sfi.usc.edu.
3 Web page: gulag.cz.

The memory-activists identified sites online using google view and documented the sites. The webpage consists of the story of the gulag system as well as a virtual museum. The sites are not only difficult to access due to their distance but also because of the political situation. The virtual museum replaces the "factual museum" and makes it real. The reconstructivist perspective of this project recreates a virtual space representing a real space which was destroyed intentionally or by neglect. The exhibition is interactive and the program is informed by the different computer games.

Karina Hořeni represented the Institute for the Study of Totalitarian Regimes[4], which is creating an educational web-platform about the history of communism in the Czech Republic. The project "Socialism Realized- The Czechoslovak Past 1948-1989" is a multimedia educational tool. The educational material contained in the tool is based on archival material, films and other types of media, and is based on constructivist didactics, encouraging students to be active in the process of making history.

Marton Liska, a secondary school teacher from Budapest, shared his experience of a field trip to Heroes' Square. The square as an actual space for memory and memorialization is a proper site to talk about how in different historical periods this space was used by different actors to promote their agenda.

Fedor Blaščák, a philosopher from Bratislava explained the memory walk organized every year to Žilina. The memory walks are important pedagogical tools as the participants learn by doing the same route as the former deportees.

The five presentations addressed similar theoretical issues:

Redefinition of space is happening as a form of rediscovery. The potential is (as it was pointed out in the discussion) that spaces are connected to narratives such as during the memory walk or the digital interactive plan for the gulag. The stories are based on previous canonized knowledge therefore critical positioning is crucial. The fact that

---

4   Web page: www.ustrcr.cz.

certain issues and topics have been forgotten or omitted should not be the basis of new hegemonic knowledge production. The topography of space is based on discussion and interrogation of the different memory levels, which is easier with *digital resources*. Digital technology offers access but at the same time creates another interpretive framework. The online availability of resources allows for experimentation with innovative teaching practices, which provide students with opportunities to engage in new forms of critical analysis and to create their own narratives about complex topics. One of the aims of reforming history teaching after 1989 was *to teach competing narratives* instead of one monolithic story. The politics of the archives like the Shoah Foundation which consciously rejected interviews with perpetrators, or the virtual museum of the gulag—which also lacks the perspective of the perpetrators—can hinder real understanding. This is also connected to the issue of *multiple perspectives*. This challenges traditional information flows and classroom dynamics; and the constructivist approach to teaching and learning gradually replaces information transmission. The politics of selectivity as far as editing the archive is concerned also needs to be studied. One example can be the indexing of "rape" in the Shoah Visual History Archive collection. In the mid-1990s when the testimonies were recorded rape was an issue which was still taboo so no questions were asked by the interviewer. Today's users are interested in this issue therefore they need to find euphemistic terms among the index terms like "sexual assault" or listen to stories and label those stories as rape themselves. The multi perspective approach for teaching history includes not only direct channeling of knowledge to the users but also includes criticism and meta-analysis of the source material by the users. *Participation* is the key issue as there is not much novelty in digital sources if they are used the same way as printed textbooks: as the source of the only and ultimate knowledge. These resources are creating space for multimedia learning—learning from words and pictures, which means that the visual narrative is a subject of study and is itself a subject of transformation.

Interactivity has a limit, as it is only possible to the extent that programmers make it possible. In the case of the Shoah Visual History Archive the users are expected to watch a film before starting their video editing assignment about responsible editing. The students are actively engaged in editing and recreating a narrative from the testimony of the survivors. The digital teaching material of the "Socialism Realized- The Czechoslovak Past 1948-1989" is in production now so one can only hope that it moves beyond the one directional communicational pattern. In case of memory walks the personal contacts and communication between the teacher and the students are crucial. Visiting and seeing the space give authenticity to the experience.

The projects presented offered different learning outcomes. The first result is that users learn about events, facts and personalities who were previously not part of the historical canon. Focusing on testimonies of everyday people or places which have been consciously destroyed provide factual knowledge. Members of the panel asked the question how this data would contribute to *creating a new narrative*. Here digital technology is playing an important role which should not only be about using the screen as a sheet of paper but as a medium which is creates *transferable digital historical literacy*. The purpose of these projects is teach skills which are transferable during everyday communication. That is how our history becomes our present. The panelists agreed that digital technology offers us the chance to teach history in a new way, and that it depends on us if we use that chance for the benefit of all or not.

What is the role of history in contemporary political discourses?

Summary of the Working Group

Dominika Kasprowicz[1]
Pedagogical University of Cracow

History, understood very widely as an aggregate of past events, is one of many tools available for the persuasive construction or deconstruction of certain communities. This obvious truth has also been acknowledged in representative democracies, where the biggest agents that rely and depend on electoral communities (voters) use a "record of past events and times" to communicate effectively. It is worth noting that the political establishment and its discourse should be seen at the same time as a product of history and its craftsman, which is manifested in the day-to-day political *praxis* and long-term strategies of political parties and their leaders.

Political discourse is "full of history": the narratives that come from the sphere of politics are imbued with symbols of the past that presuppose communal awareness and the ability of people to think of them as one of *us*. 'We' are the people who have inherited a shared body of values and perspectives on the world, setting the boundaries of what is relevant and acceptable for the relevant group of members, as opposed to those outside. It applies to the processes of the formation of political institutions people sharing the same core ideologies and aims act together in order to secure group interest and — later on — political communication with a wider audience. One of the main objections to politicians in that regard is the practice of employing double-standards with respect to covering history, basically using it as a propagandistic tool in societies, camouflaging the bad deeds of

---

1   E-mail: d_kasprowicz@wp.pl.

business and government, even as they claim to be objective and neutral depositories. This has become one of the main concerns directed towards post-authoritarian regimes with relatively weak civil societies and politically dependent universities and religious institutions.

Central-Eastern Europe, a region consisting of a few sovereign post-communist nation-states, shares common denominators, including experience of 20th century authoritarianism followed by parallel patterns of political transformation, while at the same time has highly particular collective identities and historical trajectories. This creates a unique ground for (comparative) analysis of political messages, and for contrast with other European cases.

The importance of learning our lessons from the past in times of an evident crisis of the European sense of community is growing, and the notion of 'we-ness' is again a hotly debated topic, both academically and politically. The participants of the working group entitled: "What is the role of history in contemporary political discourses?" discussed current political and cultural institutions as critically important for creating a sense of collective identity and its extension into the future of societies. This was carried out from a multi-disciplinary perspective, including political science and history, as well as educational studies.

The remarks from the historiographic perspective given by Peter Bugge (Copenhagen University) started out from a crucial distinction between the "past" and "history" and their mutual relations. The "past" was defined as "everything that has happened and is no more". On the contrary, "history" was understood as "a set of conventions about how the past should be constructed and re-constructed and results of these (adapted) conventions". Acknowledgement of this relativism, the fact that history is a process that can be designed or re-designed by members of a society and politicians themselves, is an important starting point in any discussion of history in politics and vice versa. As mentioned by Bugge: "For politicians, the use of history is a tool to gain political legitimacy (…) and we should not blame politicians, it is a part of their game". The important question that arises concerns the role of historians confronted with the political use of history. In his speech, Bugge underlined the importance of a critical approach to the epistemological foundations of the political use of history and the tasks historians should undertake. The latter include a critical distance towards concepts such as nation, totalitarianism, our heroes, etc. and making the tools of designing and redesigning history visible. In other words, the first conclusion and proposal calls on historians to become watch-dogs of politicians and political discourses on history and not to marginalise personal experiences and history of communities other than national ones.

The Polish case, presented by Łukasz Jasina (Polish History Museum, Warsaw), was used to depict several modes of political actions in the sphere of history, with special attention given to reconciliation and museums serving as tools in that processes. The power of the institution of the museum to construct meaning positions and identities through the use of objects was portrayed by the list of currently open exhibitions at the Polish History Museum, the Warsaw Uprising Museum etc., all dedicated to traumatic and constitutive events for the national myth, seeming to deny the argument that truth and understanding of the past is deemed possible only through a very fixed notion of identity.

The topic of history being re-written and used by institutional agents was continued by Raluca Bigu (University of Bucharest), who drew attention to the Romanian Orthodox Church and its relations with the establishment and exploitation of history. The presented research results were based on discourse analysis, mainly of religion textbooks. Teaching religion in this case proves to be a key element of building national identity in Romania and similarly to the political elites, the Orthodox Church extensively used notions of history in order to gain the label of "national religion". The symbolic figures put in the analysed materials were charismatic leaders, whose most important assets, in the light of the discourse, were patriotism or devotion ("heroes of the nation", "martyrs of the faith") that mixed together in the new category of "martyrs of the nation" and later on were legitimised by the state.

The catalogue of wide range instruments that serve political discourses on history was completed by Ágnes Tamás (University of Szeged) in her presentation of political caricatures in the Austro-Hungarian empire. The historical narration on losses and gains of territories — a topic sensitive in the international relations within the CEE region — was a central point of the presentation. The content of newspapers, caricatures pointing to the unfairness of peace treaties, depicted by the symbolic act of eating, the motif of amputation (doctor-patient situations), or the suffering of Christ. The allegories used in comic papers proved to be powerful and universal tools replicated through the region and throughout different time periods.

How to ask about the V4 identity from historical and contemporary point of view?

Michal Vít[1]
EUROPEUM Institute for European Policy

The question of the (non-) existence of the V4 identity regularly becomes the object of interest of various expert discussions. The demand for a satisfactory answer can be detected not only in the individual V4 countries, but also among other actors attempting to define and interpret the V4 region. Historians emphasize the role of the middle ages in forming a Central European consciousness and the role of the Habsburg monarchy as the initiating integrative element. In the larger consciousness of current society a V4 identity is constituted through the interaction of three phenomena – the common communist experience, to some extent forced cooperation, and subsequently common integration efforts with regard to the EU and NATO. In the last decade the phenomenon of a political demand arose, one that amounts to a need for common integration and a common search for interests. It is possible to identify the latter element as dominant in mutual integration efforts in the last 25 years. The existence of a political demand and its role in the creation of a V4 identity is a very interesting element in the process of the creation and shaping of a V4 identity – it amounts to a top-down process, with a common political effort and the declaration of common goals serving as its basis. As such, it may be considered as embodying the same, often criticized approach used in the creation of a European identity at the EU level. This gives rise to several fundamental questions of interpretation: What are the fundamental elements of the V4 identity and in what ways is it being formed?

---

1   Email: mvit@europeum.org

Turning to the genesis of the conception of identity in the V4 region, it is possible to conclude that elements generally considered as identity forming are to a large degree absent. Is it possible to talk about the countries' *shared* culture? Is it possible to find a *shared* geographic unit, as is the case with Scandinavian or Alpine identity? Can we speak of sharing a language or certain linguistic elements? Because the answers to these questions tend to be negative, while in the political context we need to rather talk of the existence of a political V4 identity or at least a demand for such an identity. What elements substitute the creation of identity in the absence of the more basic elements mentioned above?

The process of identity creation has to overcome the various forms of incongruity that exist in the relevant region. The V4 region is a suitable and telling example — the political motive for the creation of a common identity highlights a naturally occurring disharmony. We may observe the mutual exchange of ideas on the various elements which would serve as the basis for a common identity. The divergent understanding and interpretations of the inter-war period in the respective V4 countries serves as a classical example of the difficulties inherent in the attempts at a common interpretation of the year 1918. The conceptions are hardly comparable — the developments marking the year are understood as the culmination of democratization efforts (in the case of Czechoslovakia), national-ethnic liberation (in the case of Poland), but also the defeat of national pride (in the case of Hungary). Yet the process of identity creation may be under way only under the condition that harmony in interpretation is gradually attained. In other words, only when a common approach to perceiving and assessing concrete phenomena is achieved, can we talk about the possibility for a common identity. Yet it is always the case that such process has to be goal-directed and purposeful.

Given the absence of a shared culture and language, it is necessary to ask what can substitute these elements in terms of identity-creation (as this process is generally accomplished through the search for common elements). These can empirically exist in the real world (such as economic ties or interconnected infrastructure) or abstract (such as political allegiance). With a deeper investigation into the genesis of the notion of identity and its use, it is possible to understand it as an organic aspect of society. It is developed under the conditions of the natural environment of shared culture, language, or ethnicity. On the other hand, an extreme use of identity may lead to the birth of nationalism. If it is the case that identity construction is artificial, that is, one that has not emerged from the bottom up, then such identity may serve to legitimize a political construct. To a large extent, that is the case in V4 identity construction.

In the case of V4 identity, its construction is not *entirely* artificial — it has not emerged without any links to historical and social developments. In the case of the V4 region, what undoubtedly constitutes this naturally existing connection is the post-war development of the respective V4 societies — not only their shared communist past, but also the subsequent common interest in the form of the countries' integration into NATO and the EU. In fact, it could be argued that it was precisely this shared experience that became one of the main factors constituting the current shape of V4 identity. In other words, we may primarily speak of a political and ideological aspect of this identity that contributes towards the sense of togetherness in the region. Other aspects of the V4 identity are only secondary. Serving a supporting function, they are the following:

a) The first is the geographic location linking the East with the West. At the same time, this geographic aspect may be considered as limited by the lack of clarity regarding the notion of "Central Europe." Where exactly can we find its borders? Are the cultural or historical frontiers salient? The issue with the fluid concept of Central Europe aside, this idea also has the function of refusing the label of "Eastern Europe" — which we can observe as a case of delimitation vis-a-vis the outside.

b) This is related to another aspect — conceiving of Central-Europeanness as a phenomenon delineated primarily not in geographic terms, but as a cultural space between the East and the West. What is at its center is a continuing discussion and negotiations over mutual influence, the adoption of culture and social norms—not only inside the V4 region but also from the outside. Through the consolidation of an idea of Central-Europeanness the aim is not only to achieve certain neutrality in the context of advancing globalization, but also to take advantage of it in cementing this shared awareness.

c) This awareness strengthens another aspect, the shared legacy of communism. The prevailing negative connotations with regard to this period underscore the role of this element.

d) Associated with the legacy of the past is another element—the legacy of Austria-Hungary that tends to be often recalled. This nostalgic heritage becomes particularly evident in the heart of the V4 region most directly affected by Austrian influence. This heritage is still sustained by historical art monuments, architecture, existing links in infrastructure, as well as cuisine. Especially in Krakow—close to the geographic center of Europe—it is possible to observe the nostalgia that characterizes reminiscing about the Habsburg monarchy. Instead of fulfilling its original functions, the infrastructure that used to connect the different parts of the monarchy has in the past twenty-five years been marked by the organization of events where nostalgia for the monarchy often plays out.

The V4 region may be thus generally characterized as containing elements that help constitute, but also disrupt the creation of a common V4 identity. To support the creation of a V4 identity, it is therefore important to facilitate the integration of elements and fields that are not the object of excessive pressures or great expectations. In other words, integration should take place in areas that enable a natural contact between individual countries, such as cooperation in science, culture or tourism.

In a search for a similar geographic entity that latently contributes towards the birth of a regional identity, it is possible to look to the Scandinavian cooperation between Denmark, Norway, Sweden and, somewhat detached, Finland. The similarities in language, culture and to some extent also the geographical character of these countries provided a framework for a much wider regional cooperation, the dissolving of common frontiers and an intensive sense of individual regional affiliation towards the rest of the region. It is precisely such natural, broad allegiance that serves as an essential factor in successful identity-creation. From the perspective of choosing the development of integrative elements the V4 identity, if perceived through the lens of the Scandinavian identity formation, may be understood to be at the beginning of its development and subsequent gradual consolidation.

Looking over the developments over the 20th century, the recent decision to strengthen the V4 identity in the region may be described as successful. We can observe a gradual approximation of countries that share a similar historical heritage — this cooperation above all illustrates that it is possible to overcome differences in understanding of the formative period of their nation-states. In the current context where the broader EU integration project is often being called into question, it is possible to pinpoint another positive development — regional consciousness is being artificially solidified without necessarily provoking aggressive criticism.

The existence of a V4 identity can be undoubtedly be disputed, as can the forms of its manifestations. This text was not meant to provide a comprehensive account of the phenomenon, but rather to sketch out the potential categories for additional observation and further analysis.

Bibliography

Ablonczy, B. *Teleki Pál*. Budapest: Osiris, 2005.

Ádám, M. *Ki volt valójában Edvard Beneš?* Budapest: Gondolat Kiadó, 2009.

Albert, R. 'Le poirier de Petőfi. Un modèle des cultes littéraires hongrois' in *L'écrivain et ses demeures, Rapport final*, 2003. Available on-line: http://www.cultu recommunication.gouv.fr/Disciplines-et-secteurs/Patrimoine-ethnologique/Tr avaux-de-recherche/Rapports-de-recherche/Liste-par-mots-cles/%28offset% 29/16 [accessed: 28 April 2014].

Alexander, J. C. 'Cultural Pragmatics: Social Performance between Ritual and Strategy'in Alexander, J. C., Giesen, B., Mast, J. L. (eds.) *Social Performance: Symbolic Action, Cultural Pragmatics and Ritual*. New York: Cambridge University Press, 2006, p. 32.

Alexander, J., et al. *Cultural Trauma and Collective Identity*. Berkeley: University of California Press, 2004.

Alexander, J., Eyerman, R., Breese, E. *Narrating Trauma: On the Impact of Collective Suffering*. Herndon: Paradigm, 2011.

Anderson, B. *Imagined Communities: Reflections on the Origin and Spread of Nationalism*. London & New York: Verso, 2006.

Angyal, B. *Dokumentumok az Országos Keresztényszocialista Párt történetéhez (1918–1935)*. Somorja–Dunaszerdahely: Fórum Kisebbségkutató Intézet-Lilium Aurum, 2003.

Angyal, B. *Érdekvédelem és önszerveződés. Fejezetek a csehszlovákiai magyar pártpolitika történetéből*. Galánta-Dunaszerdahely: Fórum Kisebbségkutató Intézet-Lilum Aurum, 2002.

Archives du ministère des Affaires Étrangères, Paris, CPC 1914–1940, Z-Europe, Tchécoslovaquie, Vol. 8, Letter from 6. 5. 1919, N° 103.

Arendt, H. *Původ totalitarismu*. Prague: OIKOYMENH, 1996.

Armata, J., Niemczyńska, M. 'Mądry człowiek w ciężkich czasach', *Gazeta Wyborcza Kraków* 4 September 2007.

Ash, T. G. 'Does Central Europe Exist?', *The New York Review of Books*, 9 October 1986, p. 46.

Assmann, A. *Der lange Schatten der Vergangenheit: Erinnerungskultur und Geschichtspolitik*. Bonn: Bundeszentrale für politische Bildung, 2007.

Atllanka. Stránky pravicově konzervativní politiky. Available on-line: http://www.at llanka.net/index.php [accessed 13 August 2012].

Auer, S. *Liberal Nationalism in Central Europe*. London: Routlege, 2004.

Baert, P. *The Existentialist Moment: The Rise of Sartre as a Public Intellectual*. Cambridge: Polity, 2015.

Bajcsy-Zsilinszky, E. 'Egy közigazgatási gyakornok', *Budapesti Hírlap*, 1914.01.25, 1914, pp. 1-2.

Bajcsy-Zsilinszky, E. *Egyetlen út a magyar paraszt*. Budapest: Kelet Népe, 1938.

Bajcsy-Zsilinszky, E. *Helyünk és sorsunk Európában*. Budapest: Gergely, 1941.

Bajcsy-Zsilinszky, E. *Mátyás király*. Budapest: Athenaeum, 1939.

(Bajcsi-)Zsilinszky, E. 'Rana Rupta', *Szózat*, 1925.03.22, 1925, pp. 1-2.

Bajcsy-Zsilinszky, E. *Transsylvania. Past and future*. Geneva: Kundig, 1944.

Bakoš, V. 'K Tisovej koncepci národa a nacionalizmu', in Bystrický V., Fano, Š. (eds), *Pokus o politický a osobný profil Jozefa Tisu*, pp. 275-86.

Balázs, S. *Mikó Imre. Élet- és pályakép*. Kolozsvár: Polis, 2003.

Bán, A. D. *PAX BRITANNICA – Wartime Foreign Office Documents regarding Plans for Postbellum East Central Europe*. Boulder: Columbia University Press, 1997.

Banáš, J. *Zastavte Dubčeka!* Bratislava: Ikar, 2009.

Bánffy, M. *They were counted*. London: Everyman's Library, 2013.

Barcs, S. 'A dráma sodrában' in Vigh, K. (ed.) *Kortársak Bajcsy-Zsilinszky Endréről*. Budapest: Magvető, 1984.

Bárdi, N. 'Egy magyar girondista Erdélyben' in Mikó, I. *Az erdélyi falu és a nemzetiségi kérdés*. Csíkszereda: Pro Print, 1998, pp. 5-33.

Bárdi, N. *Otthon és haza. Tanulmányok a romániai magyar kisebbség történetéből*. Csíkszereda: Pro Print, 2013.

Barsch, A. *The Danube Basin and the German Economic Sphere*. Boulder: Columbia University Press, 1943.

Bárta, M., Hoppe, J. *Úloha Alexandra Dubčeka v moderních dějinách Československa*: Sborník z konference. Prague: Masarykova dělnická akademie, 2002.

Bartha, Á. 'Tojástánc a populizmusok körül: A magyar népi mozgalom fogalmi keretei és regionális dimenziója', *Múltunk*. 59 (4), 2014, pp. 58-105.

Bartha, Á., Szilágyi, Zs. 'Történelmi tapasztalat mint mentális valóság. A történelemoktatás és a történetírás néhány kérdése a személyes emlékezet tükrében', *Forrás*, Vol. 43(2011), No. 7-8, pp. 225-242.

Bartůšek, J. *Generál M. R. Štefánik*. Prague: Československá grafická unie, 1938.

Beck, J. *Ostatni raport*. Warsaw: Państwowy Instytut Wydawniczy, 1987, p. 50.

Békés, C. (ed.) *Evolúció és revolúció: Magyarország és a nemzetközi politika 1956-ban*. Budapest: 1956-os Intézet and Gondolat, 2007.

BIBLIOGRAPHY 419

Békés, C. *Az 1956-os forradalom a világpolitikában*. Budapest: 1956-os Intézet, 2006.

Benčík, A. 'Obrazy historie z petřínského bludiště: Několik poznámek a úvah nad recenzí knihy o Alexandru Dubčekovi', *Soudobé dějiny* 9, 2002, pp. 620-38.

Benčík, A. *Téma: Alexander Dubček*. Prague: Křesťanskosociální hnutí, 2012.

Benčík, A. *Utajovaná pravda o Alexandru Dubčekovi: Drama muže, který předběhl svou dobu*. Prague: Ostrov, 2001

Bencsik, G. *Horthy Miklós: A kormányzó és kora*. Budapest: Magyar Mercurius, 2001.

Beneš, E. 'Postwar Czechoslovakia', *Foreign Affairs*, April, 1946, pp. 397-410.

Beneš, E. 'The New Central Europe', *Journal of Central European Affairs*: Vol.I.1, April, 1941, p. 2.

Beneš, E. 'The New Slav Policy', *Free World*, May 1944.

Beneš, E. 'The Organization of Postwar Europe', *Foreign Affairs*, January, 1942, pp. 226-242.

Beneš, E. *Memoirs of Dr. Eduard Benes: From Munich to New War and New Victory*, transl. G. Lias, London and Boston: George Allen and Unwin and Houghton Mifflin, 1954.

Beneš, E. *Paměti: Od Mnichova k nové válce a k novému vítězství*. Prague: Orbis, 1948.

Beneš, E. *Šest let exilu a druhé světové války: Řeči, projevy a dokumenty z r. 1938-1945*. Prague: Družstevní práce, 1946

Beneš, E. *Úvahy o slovanství*. Prague: Čin, 1947.

Beneš, Z. *Historický text a historická kultura*. Prague: Karolinum, 1995.

Benkovičová, Ľ. 'Alexander Dubček očami verejnosti', in Laluha, I, Petrovičová, E., Pekník, M. (eds.) *Alexander Dubček politik, štátnik, humanista*. Bratislava: Veda, 2009.

Benz, W. 'Der Generalplan Ost. Zur Germanisierungspolitik des NS-Regimes in den besetzten Ostgebieten 1939-1945' in *Die Vertreibung der Deutschen aus dem Osten*. Frankfurt: Fischer, 1985, pp. 39-48.

Berecz, J. 'Gondolatok a nemzet és a munkásmozgalom történetéről', *Társadalmi Szemle* 6, 1986, pp. 3-13.

Berend, I. *Decades of Crisis: Central and Eastern Europe Before World War II*. Berkeley: University of California Press, 1998.

Bibó, I. *Misère des petits États d'Europe de l'Est*. Paris: L'Harmattan, 1986.

Biernacki, L. *Ksiądz Józef Tischner, czyli Sumienie "Solidarności"*. Gdańsk: Wszechnica Solidarności

Billig, M. *Banal Nationalism*. London, Thousand Oaks, and New Delhi: Sage, 1995.

Blondel, J. *Political Leadership*. London: Sage, 1987, p. 13.

Böhm, V. *Két forradalom tüzében*. Munich: Verlag für Kulturpolitik, 1923.

Borsody, S. *The Tragedy of Central Europe: The Nazi and Soviet Conquest of Central Europe*. New York: Collier Books, 1962.

Bottoni, S. 'Népszolgálat mint politikai játszma. Mikó Imre és a román állambiztonság, 1948-1971' in Bárdi, N., Filep, T., Lőrincz D. J. (eds.) *Népszolgálat. A közösségi elkötelezettség alakváltozatai a Magyar kisebbségek történetében*. Bratislava: Kalligram, 2015, pp. 187-231.

Bourdieu, P. *Teorie jednání*. Prague: Karolinum, 1998.

Brakoniecki, B. 'Mąż stanu, co nie stronił od kultury', *Polska. The Times*, 19 December 2011.

Brandes, D. *Cesta k vyhnání 1938-1945: Plány a rozhodnutí o 'transferu Němců' z Československa a z Polska*. Brno: Prostor, 2002.

Brandes, D. *Exil v Londýně 1939-1943: Velká Británie a její spojenci Československo, Polsko a Jugoslávie mezi Mnichovem a Teheránem*. Prague: Karolinum 2003.

Brandes, D. *Sudetští Němci v krizovém roce 1938*. Prague: Argo, 2011.

Breuilly, J. *Nationalism and the State*. 2nd ed., Manchester: Manchester University Press, 1993.

Brown, D. 'Are there good and bad nationalisms?', *Nations and nationalism* 5 (2), 1999, pp. 281–302.

Brown, M. D. *Dealing with Democrats: The British Foreign Office and the Czechoslovak Émigrés in Great Britain, 1939 to 1945*. Frankfurt am Main: Peter Lang, 2006.

Brubaker, R. 'Nationhood and the National Question in the Soviet Union and Post-Soviet Eurasia: An Institutionalist Account', *Theory and Society* 23 (1994), pp. 47-78.

Brubaker, R. 'The Manichean Myth: Rethinking the Distinction between 'Civic" and 'Ethnic' Nationalism', in Kriesi, H., et al. *Nation and National Identity: the European experience in Perspective*. Zurich: Ruegger, 1999, pp. 55-72.

Brykczynski, P. 'A Poland for the Poles? József Piłsudski and the Ambiguities of Polish Nationalism', *PRAVO: The North American Journal For Central European Studies* 1:1, pp. 1-20.

Buchner, Wł. 'Czechy a Polska', *Mucha*, No. 40, 30September 1938, p. 2.

Bucur, M. 'Birth of a Nation. Commemorations of December 1. 1918 and National Identity in Twentieth Century Romania' in: Bucur, M., Wingfeld, N. (eds.) *Staging the Past: The Politics of Commemoration in Habsburg Central Europe, 1848 to the Present*. West Lafayette: Purdue University Press, 2001, pp. 286-323.

Bucur, M. *Heroes and Victims. Remembering War in Twentieth Century Romania*. Bloomington: Indiana University Press, 2008.

Budil, I. *Triumf rasismu*. Prague: Triton, 2015.

Budil, I. *Úsvit rasismu*. Prague: Triton, 2013.

Burke, P. 'A történelem mint társadalmi emlékezet', *Regio*, 1 (2001), pp. 3–21.

Burmeister, H.-P. (ed.) *Mitteleuropa, Traum oder Trauma*. Bremen: Temmen, 1988.

Burns, J. M. *Leadership*. New York: Harper and Row, 1978.

Bútora, M., Bútorová, Z. (eds.) *Slovensko rok po: Cesty a križovatky nového štátu očami jeho obyvateľov*. Prague: SLON, 1994.

Buzinkay, G. 'A trianoni békeszerződés és a magyar liberális sajtó', *Médiakutató*, Vol. 12. (4), 2011, p. 105.

Calleo, D. *The German Problem Reconsidered: Germany and the World Order, 1870 to the Present*. Cambridge: Cambridge University Press, 1978.

Canetti, E. *Crowds and Power*. London: Phoenix Press, 2000.

Canovan, M. *Nationalism and Political Theory*. Cheltenham: Edward Elgar, 1996.

Čarnogurský, J. *Videné od Dunaja*. Bratislava: Kalligram, 1997, Doc. 3, pp. 122–24.

Čarnogurský, P. *Svedok čias*. Bratislava: USPO Peter Smolík, 1997.

Carsten, F. L. *The Rise of Fascism*. Berkeley: University of California Press, 1982.

Čechura, J., Čechurová, J. *Korespondence Josefa Pekaře a Kamila Krofty*. Praha: Karolinum, 1999.

České slovo, No. 151, 4 June 1942.

Chlebowczyk, J. *Między dyktatem, realiami a prawem do samostanowienia: prawo do samookreślenia i problem granic we wschodniej Europie Środkowej w pierwszej wojnie światowej oraz po jej zakończeniu*. Warszawa: PWN, 1998.

Chodorkowski, J. *Niemiecka doktryna gospodarki wielkiego obszaru (Grossraumwirtschaft) 1800–1945*. Wroclaw: Zakład Narodowy im. Ossolińskich, 1972.

Clementis, V. *Odkazy z Londýna*. Bratislava: Obroda, 1947.

Coakley, J. 'Mobilizing the Past: Nationalist Images of History', *Nationalism and Ethnic Politics*, 10 (4), 2004, pp. 531–560.

Codogni, P. 'Aktywność społeczna w Polsce w 1956 roku: Obszary i kulminacje', in Szymoniczek, J., Król, E. C. (eds.) *Rok 1956 w Polsce i jego rezonans w Europie*. Warsaw: Instytut Studiów Politycznych PAN, 2009, pp. 174–190.

Codogni, P. 'Gesellschaftliche Aktivitäten in Polen im Jahre 1956: Bereiche und Höhepunkte', in Szymonicek, J., Król, E.C. *Das Jahr 1956 in Polen Und Seine Resonanz in Europa*. Warsaw: Instytut Studiów Politycznych PAN, 2010.

Codogni, P. 'La différenciation du communism: Le cas de la Pologne', in Mink, G., Lazar, M., Sielski, M. (eds.) *1956, une date europeenne*. Paris: Noir sur blanc, 2010, pp. 217-223.

Codogni, P. *Rok 1956*. Warsaw: Prószyński i Spółka, 2006.

Cole, A. 'Studying Political Leadership: The Case of François Mitterrand', *Political Studies*, XLII, 1994, pp. 453-468.

Collins, R. *Interaction Ritual Chains*. Princeton & Oxford: Princeton University Press, 2004.

Cornelius, D. *In Search of the Nation. The New Generation of Hungarian Youth in Czechoslovakia 1925-1934*. Boulder: Co. East European Monographs, 1998.

Coudenhove-Kalergi R.N., *Crusade for Pan-Europe*. New York: Putnam, 1943.

Coudenhove-Kalergi, R. N. *Pan-europa*. Wien: Paneuropa Vlg., 1923.

Csepeli, Gy. *National Identity in Contemporary Hungary*, Boulder: Social Science Monographs, 1997.

Čulen, K. *Po Svatoplukovi druhá naša hlava: Život Dr. Jozefa Tisu*. Middletown, PA.: Prvá katolícka slovenská jednota, 1947.

Čulen, K. *Zločin vo fundamente: Svedectvo o Štefánikovej smrti*. Bratislava: Lúč, 2009.

Davies, N. *Europe – A History*. Oxford: Oxford University Press, 1997.

Deák, L. (ed.) *Súčasníci o Trianone*. Bratislava: Kubko Goral, 1996.

Deák, L. *Politický profil Jánoša Esterházyho*. Bratislava: Kubko Goral, 1995.

Deák, L. *Slovensko v politike Maďarska v rokoch 1938-1939*. Bratislava: Veda, 1990.

Deák, L. *Zápas o strednú Európu 1933-1938*. Bratislava: Veda, 1986.

Declaration of the History Institute of the Slovak Academy of Sciences: http://www.histo ry.sav.sk/esterhazy.htm [accessed 10 October 2012].

Dedina, S. *Edvard Beneš – der Liquidator: Dämon des Genozids an den Sudetendeutschen, Totengräber der tschechoslowakischen Demokratie: zeitgeschichtlicher Roman*. Eichendorf: Eichendorf Verlag, 2000.

Dedina, S. *Edvard Beneš – likvidátor: dokumentární román*. Prague: Annonce, 2003.

Dejmek, J. 'Kroftovo chápání sudetoněmecké otázky a její vyústění', *Acta universitatis Carolinae. Philosophica et historica* 5, 1991, p. 33-49.

Dejmek, J. *Edvard Beneš: Politická biografie českého demokrata*. Prague: Karolinum, 2006 and 2008.

Dejmek, J. *Historik v čele diplomacie. Studie z dějin československé zahraniční politiky v letech 1936-1938*. Praha: Karolinum, 1998.

Dérer, I. *Slovenský vývoj a luďácká zrada: Fakta, vzpomínky a úvahy*. Prague: Kvasnička a Hampl, 1946.

Dernői Kocsis, L. *Bajcsy-Zsilinszky*. Budapest: Kossuth, 1966.

Dmowski, R. *Polityka polska i odbudowanie państwa*. Warsaw: Nakładem Spółki Wydawniczej Niklewicz, 1926.

Doblhoff, L. *Horthy Miklós*. Budapest: Athenaeum,1939.

Domnitz, C. *Zápas o Benešovy dekrety před vstupem do Evropské unie: Diskuse v Evropském parlamentu a v Poslanecké sněmovně Parlamentu ČR v letech 2002–2003*. Prague: Dokořán, 2007.

Doskočil, Z. *Duben 1969: Anatomie jednoho mocenského zvratu*. Brno: Doplněk, 2006.

Drtina, P. *Československo můj osud 1*, Prague: Melantrich, 1991.

Drtina, P. *Československo můj osud 2*, Prague: Melantrich, 1992.

Dubček, A. *Nádej zomiera posledná*. Bratislava: Nová Práca, 1993.

Ducháček, M. *Václav Chaloupecký. Hledání československých dějin*. Praha: Karolinum, 2015.

Dudek, A. 'Miłośnik rocka w teatrze polityki', *Polska. The Times*, 19 December 2011.

Ďurčanský, F. *Právo Slovákov na samostatnosť vo svetle dokumentov. Biela kniha I*. Buenos Aires: Slovenský oslobodzovací výbor, 1954.

Ďurica, M. S. 'Dr. Joseph Tiso and the Jewish Problem in Slovakia', *Slovakia*, 3–4, 1957, pp. 1–22

Ďurica, M. S. *Jozef Tiso 1887–1947: Životopisný profil*. Bratislava: Lúč, 2006.

Durkheim, É. *The Elementary Forms of Religious Life*. New York: The Free Press, 1995.

Edelsheim Gyulai, I. *Becsület és kötelesség*, 2 volumes, Budapest: Európa, 2006, 2007.

Egry, G. 'Endangered by alienation? Raising a minority elite between nationalizing higher education systems: the new generation of Hungarians in interwar Romania' in Heppner H., Bieber F. (eds.) *Societal Evolution or Social Ruin? Universities and Elite Formation in Central, Eastern and Southeastern Europe*. Vienna-Berlin: LIT Verlag, 2015, pp. 39–59.

Egry, G. 'Megoldás vagy halogatás? A román királyi doktatúra és a magyar kisebbség, 1938–1940', *Limes*, 1/2007, pp. 65–78.

Egry, G. 'Nép, nemzet, állam, népszolgáló közösségkép és közösségszervezés az erdélyi magyar politikában, 1918–1944' in: Bárdi, N., Filep T., Lőrincz D. J. (eds.) *Népszolgálat. A közösségi elkötelezettség alakváltozatai a Magyar kisebbségek történetében*. Bratislava: Kalligram, 2015, pp. 48–71.

Egry, G. *Az erdélyiség "színeváltozása". Kísérlet az Erdélyi Párt ideológiájának és identitáspolitikájának elemzésére, 1940–1944*. Budapest: Napvilág Kiadó, 2008.

Egry, G. *Etnicitás, identitás, politika. Magyar kisebbségek a nacionalizmus és a regionalizmus között Romániában és Csehszlovákiában, 1918-1944*. Budapest: Napvilág, 2015.

Eiler, F. *Kisebbségvédelem és revízió. Magyar törekvések az Európai Nemzetiségi Kongresszuson (1925-1939)*. Budapest: Gondolat-MTA Etnikai és Nemzeti Kisebbségkutató Intézet, 2007.

Encyklopedia Popularna PWN. Warsaw: PWN, 2006.

Fabian, J. 'Analýza masových oznamovacích prostriedkov (1967-1970)' in *Slovenská spoločnosť v krízových rokoch 1967-1970*. Bratislava: Politologický cabinet SAV, 1999, pp. 132-135.

Fabricius, M., Hradská, K. (eds.) *Jozef Tiso: Prejavy a články*, vol. 2 (1938-44). Bratislava: Academic Electronic Press, 2007.

Fałkowska-Warska, M. 'Die Geschichte aus der Perspektive der Bürger der Visegrád-Staaten — Verklärung der Vergangenheit oder gesellschaftliche Amnesie?' Available on-line: www.laender-analysen.de/polen/pdf/PolenAnalysen102.pdf [accessed 9 June 2012].

Falkowski, P. 'Vaclav Havel nie żyje', *Nasz Dziennik*, 19 December 2011.

Fazekas C. 'Prohászka Ottokár és a "hungarizmus" fogalmának genezise', *Múltunk*, 2/2015, pp. 4-34.

Feierabend, L., K. *Politické vzpomínky*, vol. 3, (1982). Brno: Atlantis, 1996.

Ferencová, M. 'Od ľudu k národu: Vytváranie národnej kultúry v etnografickej produkcii v socialistickom Československu a Maďarsku', *Etnologické rozpravy* 2 (2006), pp. 104-133.

Ferko, M., Marsina, R., Deák, L. *Starý národ — mladý štát*. Bratislava: Litera, 1994.

Filip, O. *Sousedé*, Brno: Host, 2003.

Findor, A. '(De)constructing Slovak National Mythology', *Sociológia* 2 (2002), pp. 195-208.

Findor, A. *Začiatky národných dejín*. Bratislava: Kalligram, 2011.

Findor, A., Kiliánová, G., Macho, P. 'Symbolické aspekty národnej identity', in Kiliánová, G., Kowalská, E., Krekovičová, E. (eds.) *My a tí druhí v modernej spoločnosti*. Bratislava: Veda, Vydavateľstvo SAV, 2009, pp. 285-337.

Franzen, K. E., Schulze Wessel, M. (eds.) *Opfernarrative: Konkurrenzen und Deutungskämpfe in Deutschland und im östlichen Europa nach dem Zweiten Weltkrieg*. Munich: Oldenbourg, 2012.

Frieder, E. *Z denníku mladého rabína*. Bratislava: SNM, Oddelenie židovskej kultúry, 1993.

Friszke, A. 'Polski październik 1956 r. z perspektywy pięćdziesięciolecia', in Rowiński, J. (ed.) *Polski Październik 1956 w polityce światowej*. Warsaw: PISM, 2006, p. 315.

Gál, É., Hegedűs, A. B.,Litván, G., Rainer, J. M. (eds.) *A "Jelcin-dosszié": Szovjet dokumentumok 1956-ról*. Budapest: Századvég—1956-os Intézet, 1993.

Gati, C. *Vesztett illúziók: Moszkva, Washington, Budapest és az 1956-os forradalom*. Budapest: Osiris, 2006.

Gawroński, J. *Moja misja w Wiedniu 1932–1938*. Warsaw: PWN, 1965.

Geiss, I. *Die deutsche Frage 1806–1990*. Mannheim: BI Taschenbuch, 1992.

Gergely, J. *A keresztényszocializmus Magyarországon 1903–1923*. Budapest: Akadémiai Kiadó, 1977.

Girard, R. *O původu kultury*. Brno: Centrum pro studium demokracie a kultury, 2008.

Gołębiewicz, M. (undated) 'Śledztwo w sprawie katastrofy w Gibraltarze'. Available on-line: http://ipn.gov.pl/wydzial-prasowy/komunikaty/b [accessed: 28 April 2014].

Gomułka, W. 'Droga demokratyzacji jest jedyną drogą prowadzącą do zbudowania najlepszego w naszych warunkach modelu socjalizmu. Przemówienie Władysława Gomułki wygłoszone na VIII. Plenum KC PZPR', *Trybuna Ludu*, 21 October 1956, p. 3.

Gomułka, W. 'Sytuacja w partii i w kraju. Referat tow. Władysława Gomułki na X Plenum KC PZPR', *Trybuna Ludu*, 26th October 1957, p. 3.

Gosztonyi, P. *A kormányzó, Horthy Miklós*. Budapest: Téka, 1990.

Grabski, S. *Pamiętniki, Vol. 2*. Warsaw: Czytelnik, 1989, pp. 191–92.

Grajewski, A. 'Zawszemówił z wielkim respektem o transcendentnym wymiarze życia. Przyjaźnił się z wieloma chrześcijanami', online: http://wpolityce.pl/wyd arzenia/20052-zawsze-mowil-z-wielkim-respektem-o-transcendentnym-wymia rze-zycia-przyjaznil-sie-z-wieloma-chrzescijanami, [accessed 18 December 2011].

Green, A. *Education, Globalization and the Nation State*. New York: St. Martin's Press, 1997.

Gruša, J. *Beneš jako Rakušan*, Brno: Barrister & Principal, 2011.

Gyárfášová, O. *Visegrad Citizens on the Doorstep of the European Union*. Bratislava: Institute for Public Affairs, 2003.

Gyárfášová, O., Krivý, V., et al. *Krajina v pohybe: Správa o politických názoroch a hodnotách ľudí na Slovensku*. Bratislava: Inštitút pre verejné otázky, 2001.

György, P. *Néma hagyomány*, Budapest: Magvető, 2000.

Gyurgyák, J. *Magyar fajvédők*. Budapest: Osiris, 2012.

Hahn, E., Hahn, H. *Die Vertreibung im deutschen Erinnern: Legenden, Mythos, Geschichten*. Paderborn: Ferdinand Schöningh, 2010.

Halecki, O. *The Limits and Divisions of European History*. New York: Sheed & Ward, 1950.

Hampl, S., Vinopal, J., Šubrt, J. 'Reflexe novodobých českých dějin, sametové revoluce a současného vývoje v názorech veřejnosti', *Naše společnost* (CVVM Sociologického ústavu AV ČR), Vol., 9, No. 1, 2011, pp. 19-29.

Hanak, H. 'The New Europe, 1916-20', *The Slavonic Review*, Vol. 39, 1960/61, pp. 368-399.

Hankiss, E. *Hongrie. Diagnostiques. Essai en pathologie social.* Geneva: Georg, 1990.

Hantos, E. *Der Weg zum neuen Mitteleuropa.* Berlin: Mitteleuropa Verlag Berlin, 1933.

Harris, E. *Nationalism: Theories and Cases.*Edinburgh: Edinburgh University Press, 2009.

Haslinger, P. 'The Nation, the Enemy, and Imagined Territories: Slovak and Hungarian Elements in the Emergence of a Czechoslovak National Narrative during and after WWI', in Wingfield, N. (ed.) *Creating the Other: The Causes and Dynamics of Nationalism, Ethnic Enmity, and Racism in Eastern Europe.* Oxford and New York: Berghahn, 2001.

Hauner, M. 'Mitteleuropa' in *Encyclopedia of Contemporary German Culture.* London: Routledge, 1998.

Hauner, M. *Hitler. A Chronology of His Life and Time.* London: Macmillan, 2005.

Hauner, M. *What is Asia to us? Russia's Asian Heartland Yesterday and Today.* London: Unwin & Hyman, 1990.

Heckenast G., Incze, M., Karácsonyi, B., Lukács, L., Spira, Gy. *A magyar nép története*, Budapest: Művelt Nép, 1953.

Heiber, H. 'Der Generalplan Ost', *Vierteljahrshefte für Zeitgeschichte*, 6, 1958, pp. 319-320.

Heim, H. *Monologe im Führer-Hauptquartier 1941-1944.* Hamburg: A. Knaus, 1980.

Heinsohn, G. *Lexikon der Völkermorde.* Hamburg: Rowohlt, 1988.

Herzeg, F. *Horthy Miklós.* Budapest: Singer es Wolfner, 1939.

Hillgruber, A. *Germany and the Two World Wars.* Cambridge: Harvard U.P, 1987.

Hitler, A. *Mein Kampf.* Munich: Franz Eher Vlg., 1927.

Hobsbawm, E. 'The new threat to history', *The New York Review of Books*: December 16, 1993, p. 62.

Hobsbawm, E. *The Age of Extremes.* London: Michael Joseph Publs., 1994.

Hodža, M. *Federation in Central Europe.* London: Jarrolds Limited, 1942.

Hodža, M. *Szövetség Közép-Európában: Gondolatok és visszaemlékezések.* Bratislava: Kalligram, 2004.

Hodža, M., Lukáč, P. (ed.) *Federácia v Strednej Európe a iné štúdie.* Bratislava: Kalligram, 1997.

Hoensch, K. 'National-sozialistische Europapläne im Zweiten Weltkrieg' in Plaschka R. G. (ed.) *Mitteleuropa-Konzeptionen in der Ersten Hälfte des 20. Jahrhunderts*. Vienna: Verlag der österreichischen Akademie der Wissenschaften, 1995, pp. 307–25.

Hoffmann, G., Hoffmann, L. *Katolícka cirkev a tragédia slovenských židov v dokumentoch*. Partizánske: G-print, 1994.

Hoffmann, L. 'Katolícka cirkev a tragédia slovenských Židov', *Kultúrny život*, 7 June 1968.

Holotík, Ľ. *Štefánikovská legenda a vznik ČSR)*. Bratislava: SAV, 1958.

Horváth, M. *1956 hadikrónikája*. Budapest: Akadémiai Kiadó, 2003.

Horváth, S. F. *Elutasítás és alkalmazokodás között. A romániai magyar kisebbségi elit politikai stratégiái (1931–1940)*. Csíkszereda: Pro Print, 2007.

Hrnko, A. 'Nežný prevrat, alebo revolúcia?', *Slovenské pohľady* 11, 1999, p. 66.

Hroch, M. 'Historické vědomí a potíže s jeho výzkumem dříve i nyní', in Šubrt, J. (ed.) *Historické vědomí jako předmět badatelského zájmu: teorie a výzkum*. Kolín: Nezávislé centrum pro studium politiky, 2010.

Hubenák, L. (ed.), *Riešenie židovskej otázky na Slovensku 1939–1945*. Dokumenty II. Bratislava: Slovenské národné múzeum, Historické múzeum, Oddelenie židovskej kultúry, 1994.

Huntington, S. P. 'The Clash of Civilizations?', *Foreign Affairs*, Summer 1993, pp. 22–49.

Huntington, S. *The Clash of Civilizations and the Remaking of World Order*. New York: Simon and Schuster, 1996.

HVG.hu: 'A külügy elítélte a kassai Esterházy-szobor megrongálását.' Available on-line: http://hvg.hu/vilag/20110328_eliteltek_esterhazy_szobor [accessed 7 October 2012].

Illyés, G. *Zsilinszky 1886–1986*. Budapest: Hazafias Népfront–Bajcsy-Zsilinszky Endre Emlékbizottság, 1986.

Irzykowski, K. *Dzienniki*, Vol. 2: *1916–1944*. Cracow: Wydawnictwo Literackie, 2001, p. 347.

Jablonický, J.*Glosy o historiografii SNP*.Bratislava: NVP International, 1994.

Jackowski, J. M. 'Tylko pełna jawność', *Nasz Dziennik*, 3–4 February 2007.

Jagodziński, A. 'Czechypogrążone w smutku i żałobie. Vaclav Havel nie żyje', online: http://wiadomosci.onet.pl/raporty/vaclav-havel-nie-zyje/czechy-pograzone-w-smutku-i-zalobie-vaclav-havel-n,2,4975521,wiadomosc.html, [accessed 18 December 2011].

Jagodziński, A. 'Vaclav Havel: My zawsze zapraszamy obserwatorów', *Gazeta Wyborcza*, 5 September 2007.

Jáki, L. (ed.) *Érettségi tételek történelemből, 1851–1949*. Budapest: OPKM, 2000.

Janáč, M. (ed.) *Srpen 1968: 10 hodin komentovaných originálních nahrávek*. Prague: Radioservis and Český rozhlas, 2008.

Janek, I.'A Magyarországgal szembeni szlovák propaganda és revíziós elképzelések 1939-1941 között', *Limes* 1 (2010), pp. 25–40.

Jankowiak, S. 'Poznański Czerwiec 1956 — Kon', in Szymoniczek, J., Król, E. C. (eds.) *Rok 1956 w Polsce i jego rezonans w Europie*. Warsaw: Instytut Studiów Politycznych PAN, 2009, p. 11.

Jarosz, D. *Polityka władz komunistycznych w Polsce w latach 1948-1956 a chłopi*. Warsaw: DiG, 1998.

Jászi, O. 'Central Europe and Russia', *Journal of Central European Affairs*, April, Vol. V.1, 1945, pp. 1–16.

Jászi, O. 'The Choices of Hungary', *Foreign Affairs*, April, Vol. 24.3, 1946, pp. 453–465.

Jászi, O. 'The Future of Danubia', *Journal of Central Europan Affairs*, July,Vol. I.2, 1941, p. 128.

Jászi, O. *Magyar kálvária – magyar föltámadás*. Budapest: Magyar Hírlap Könyvek, 1989.

Jaworski, R. 'Die aktuelle Mitteleuropadiskussion in historischer Perspektive', *Historische Zeitschrift*, No. 247, 1987, pp. 529–550.

Jaworski, R. 'Tomáš G. Masaryk versus Friedrich Naumann. Zwei Europavisionen im Ersten Weltkrieg' in Pousta, Z., Seifter, P., Pešek, J. (eds.) *Setkání, Begegnung. Sborník k 65.narozeninám Jana Křena*. Prague: Karolinum, 1996, pp. 123–34.

Joachimsthaler, A. *Breitspurbahn. Das Projekt zur Erschließung des groß-europäischen Raumes 1942-1945*. Munich: Herbig, 1985.

Joch, R. 'Edvard Beneš se zasloužil o stát.'Available on-line: http://www.kcpry marov.estranky.cz/clanky/vyznamne-osobnosti/roman-joch-do-diskuse_-edv ard-benes-se-zaslouzil-o-stat-___.html [accessed 13August 2010].

John, M. *Milan Rastislav Štefánik. Život a smrt národního hrdiny*. Olomouc: Votobia, 2000.

Johnson, O. V. 'Begetting & Remembering: Creating a Slovak Collective Memory in the Post-Communist World', in Kopeček, M. (ed.) *Past in the Making: Historical Revisionism in Central Europe after 1989*. Budapest and New York: CEU Press, 2008, pp. 129-143.

Kaiser G. *Nehéz hőskölteményt nem írni. Az Országos Kereszténységszocialista Párt kezdetei*. Dunaszerdahely: Media Nova, 2014.

Kaiserová, K., Kaiser, V. (eds.) *Dějiny města Ústí nad Labem*. Ústí nad Labem: Město Ústí nad Labem, 1995.

Kamenec, I. *Tragédia politika, kňaza a človeka: Dr. Jozef Tiso 1887-1947*. Bratislava: Archa, 1998.

Kamiński, M. K. 'Czy Edvard Beneš mógł być dla Polski wiarygodnym partnerem?', *Arcana*, 4/1997, pp. 126-131.

Kaminski, M. K. E. *Benes kontra gen. W. Sikorski*. Warsaw: Neriton, 2005.

Kamiński, M. K. *Edvard Beneš we współpracy z Kremlem: Polityka zagraniczna władz czechosłowackich na emigracji 1943-1945*. Warsaw: Neriton, 2009.

Káša, P. 'Román Tisícročná včela ako slovenský obraz "fin de siècle"', *Acta Universitatis Palackianae Olomucensis* 5 (2007), pp. 155-160.

Kautský, E. K. *Kauza Štefánik: legendy, fakty a otázniky okolo vzniku Česko-Slovenskej republiky*. Martin: Matica slovenská, 2004.

Kedourie, E. *Nationalism*. Oxford: Blackwell, 1993.

Kerecsényi, Z. *Az utolsó nyár: Bajcsy-Zsilinszky Endre életének utolsó szakaszairól, valamint magyar antifasiszta ellenállásról*. MEASZ-Bajcsy-Zsilinszky Emlékbizottság, 2013.

Kerepeszki, R. 'Nationalist Masculinity and Right-Wing Radical Student Movements in Interwar Hungary: The Case of the Turul Association', *Hungarian StudiesReview*, 1/2014, pp. 61-88.

Keynes, J.M. *The Economic Consequences of the Peace*. London: Penguin, 1988.

King R., Stone D. *Hannah Arendt and the uses of history: imperialism, nation, race, and genocide*. New York: Berghahn Books, 2007.

Kirschbaum, J. M. 'Dr. Joseph Tiso: The Prelate-Politician who Died on the Gallows for His People', *Slovakia* vol. 22 (45), 1972, pp. 5-20.

Kirschbaum, J., M. *My Last Diplomatic Report to the President of Slovakia*. Furdek: Jednota, 1972

Kiss, B. 'Államfordulat Nyitrán 1918-1923', *Kisebbségkutatás*, 2/2008.

Kiss, J. 'Szlovákia helye és szerepe Milan Hodža geopolitikai koncepciójában (I-II.)', *Fórum* (2/2004), pp. 83-96. and (3/2004), pp. 85-103.

Kiss, J. *Fajvédelemtől a nemzeti demokráciáig: Bajcsy-Zsilinszky Endre politikai tervei a trianoni Magyarország megújulására (1918-1932)*, PhD thesis, 2007. Available on-line: https://dea.lib.unideb.hu/dea/bitstream/handle/2437/79674/ertekezes_ magyar.pdf?sequence=7 [accessed: 28 August 2015].

Klimek, A. *Velké dějiny zemí Koruny české XIII (1918-1929)*. Prague and Litomyšl: Paseka, 2000.

Klofáč, J. *Sociální struktura ČSSR a její změny v letech 1945-1980*. Cologne: Index, 1985.

Kmet, M. 'Híd a magyar-szlovák kulturális kapcsolatokban', *Barátság*, Vol. 16 (2009), No. 3, pp. 6099-6101.

Kő, A. 'Horthy Miklós szobra Szegeden?', *Magyar Nemzet*, 18 June 2007.

Kobus, A. *Czechosłowacja wobec narodzin, rozwoju i delegalizacji "Solidarności" (1980–1982)*.Toruń: Adam Marszałek, 2006.

Kohn, H. *Nationalism: Its Meaning and History*. Princeton: N.J. Van Nostrand, 1955.

Kohn, H. *The Idea of Nationalism: A Study of Its Origins and Background*. New York: The Macmillan Company, 1944.

Kollai, I. 'A szlovák középiskolai történelemtankönyvek összehasonlító jellegű bemutatása', in Hornyák, Á., Vitári, Z. (eds.) *A magyarságkép a közép-európai tankönyvekben a 20. században*, Pécs: Pécsi Tudományegyetem, 2009, pp. 283–319.

Komarnicki, T. (ed.) *Diariusz i teki Jana Szembeka (1935–1945), Vol. I*. London: Polish Research Center, 1964.

Komarnicki, T. (ed.) *Diariusz i teki Jana Szembeka (1935–1945), Vol. II*, London: Polish Research Center, 1965.

Komarnicki, T. (ed.) *Diariusz i teki Jana Szembeka (1935–1945), Vol. IV*, London: Polish Research Center, 1972.

Konrád, G. *Antipolitik. Mitteleuropäische Meditationen*. Frankfurt: Suhrkamp, 1985.

Kopeček, M., Kunštát, M. 'Tzv. Sudetoněmecká otázka v české akademické debatě po roce 1989', *Český a slovenský zahraniční časopis*, No. 9, 2006. Available on-line: http://www.cs-magazin.com/index.php?a=a2006091039 [accessed 11 June 2012].

Kornat, M. (ed.) *Polskie Dokumenty Dyplomatyczne, 1938*. Warsaw: PISM 2007.

Körösényi, A. 'Political Leadership: Between Guardianship and Classical Democracy', For the ECPR Workshop on ,*Political Leadership: a Missing Element in Democratic Theory*', Helsinki, 7–12 May 2007.

Körösényi, A. 'The Impact of Crises and States of Emergency on Political Leadership', Paper presented at the 7th ECPR General Conference, Section on *Elites and Transatlantic Crisis*, Bordeaux, 4–7 September 2013, pp. 5–31.

Kováč, D. 'Identita a národ', in Kiliánová, G., Kowalská, E., Krekovičová, E. (eds.) *My a tí druhí v modernej spoločnosti*. Bratislava: Veda, Vydavateľstvo SAV, 2009, pp. 338–342.

Kováč, D. 'M. R.Štefánik a dialektika dejín', *Literárny týždenník*, 28 April, 1989, p. 10.

Kováč, D. *Štefánik a Janin. Príbeh priateľstva(Štefánik and Janin. The Story of a Friendship)*. Bratislava: Dilema, 2001.

Kozicki, S. *Pamiętnik 1876–1939*. Słupsk: Wydawnictwo Naukowe Akademii Pomorskiej, 2009.

Král, V. *Intervenční válka československé buržoazie proti Maďarské sovětské republice v roce 1919*. Prague: ČSAV, 1954.

Krekovič, E., Mannová, E., Krekovičová, E. (eds.) *Mýty naše slovenské*. Bratislava: AEP, 2005.

Krekovičová, E. 'Identity a mýty novej štátnosti na Slovensku: Náčrt slovenskej mytológie na prelome tisícročia', *Slovenský národopis* 2 (2002), pp. 147-170.

Křesadlo, J. *Fuga trium*, Brno: Host, 1992.

Krivý, V. *Kolektívne identity na súčasnom Slovensku: Pramenná publikácia dát zo sociologického výskumu*.Bratislava: SAV, 2004, pp. 24-25.

Krivý, V. *Politické orientácie na Slovensku a skupinové profily*. Bratislava: Inštitút pre verejné otázky, 2000.

Krofta, K *Národnostní vývoj zemí československých*. Praha: Orbis, 1934.

Krofta, K. 'Rádlova Válka Čechů s Němci', *Národnostní obzor 1*, 1930

Krofta, K. 'Tři úvahy o 28. Říjnu', in Krofta, K. *Byli jsme za Rakouska... Úvahy historické a politické*. Prague: Orbis, 1936, p. 612.

Krofta, K. *Čechové a Slováci před svým státním sjednocením*. Praha: Orbis, 1932.

Krofta, K. *Čechy a Německo v dějinném vývoji*. Praha: Orbis, 1938.

Krofta, K. *Čtení o ústavních dějinách slovenských*, Praha: Nákl. Klubu historického, 1924;

Krofta, K. *Das Deutschtum in der tschechoslowakischen Geschichte*. Praha: Orbis, 1935.

Krofta, K. *Die Deutschen in Böhmen*. Praha: Orbis, 1924.

Krofta, K. *Die Deutschen in der Tschechoslowakei*. Praha: Deutschpolitisches Arbeitsamt, 1928.

Krofta, K. *Němci v československém státě*. Praha: Orbis, 1937.

Krofta, K. *O úkolech slovenské historiografie*, Bratislava: Academia, 1925.

Krofta, K. *Výchova k státnosti*, Praha: Masarykův lidovýchovný ústav, 1935.

Kšiňan, M. 'Metamorfózy Štefánikovej slovenskosti' in Čaplovič, M., Ferenčuhová, B. and Stanová, M. (eds.) *Milan Rastislav Štefánik v zrkadle prameňov a najnovších poznatkov historiografie*. Bratislava: Vojenský historický ústav, 2010, pp. 97-115.

Kühl, J. *Föderationspläne im Donauraum und in Ostmitteleuropa*. Munich: Oldenbourg, 1958.

Kuklík, J. *Mýty a realita tak zvaných Benešových dekretů*. Prague: Linde, 2002.

Kulesza, W. T. 'Myśl Polityczna Józefa Piłsudskiego', *Przegląd Historyczny* 74 (1), 1983, pp. 49-73.

Kundera, M. 'The Tragedy of Central Europe', *The New York Review of Books*, 26 April, 1984, pp. 33-38.

Kural, V., Mencl, V., et al. *Československo roku 1968 (1)*, Prague: Parta, 1993.

Kural, V., Mencl, V., et al. *Československo roku 1968 (2)*, Prague: Parta, 1993.

Kurcyusz, J. Na przedpolu Jałty: Wspomnienia z tajnej służby w dyplomacji. Katowice: Societas Scientiis Favendis Silesiae Superioris—Instytut Górnośląski, 1995, pp. 371-372.

Kuzio, T. 'The myth of the civic state: a critical survey of Hans Kohn's framework for understanding nationalism', *Ethnic and Racial Studies* 25 (1), 2002, pp. 20-39.

Kwaśniewski, A. 'Mam nadzieję na hawlizm', *Gazeta Wyborcza*, 19 December 2011.

Laluha, I. *Alexander Dubček, člověk a politik*. Bratislava: Nová práca, 2000.

Laluha, I. *Alexander Dubček, politik a jeho doba*. Bratislava: Nová Práca, 2000.

Laluha, I., Petrovičová, E., Pekník, M. (eds.) *Alexander Dubček politik, štátnik, humanista*. Bratislava: Veda, 2009.

Lange, K. 'Der Terminus 'Lebensraum' in Hitlers 'Mein Kampf', *Vierteljahrshefte für Zeitgeschichte*, Vol. 13, 1965, pp. 426-437.

Le Goff, J. *Paměť a dějiny*. Praha: Argo, 2007.

Lederer, J. *Mé Polsko: 200 let boje proti cizí nadvládě*.Cologne: Index, 1982.

Legięć, J. *Człowiek w filozofii pracy Józefa Tischnera*. Katowice: Księża Sercanie,2012.

Lehman, H. G. *Der Reichsverweser-Stellvertreter*, Mainz: Hase 81 Koehler, 1975.

Lendl, E. *Die mitteleuropäische Kulturlandschaft im Umbruch der Gegenwart*. Marburg: Elwert, 1951.

Lettrich, J. *Dejiny novodobého Slovenska*. Bratislava: Archa, 1993.

Lévai, J. *A hősök hőse...! Bajcsy-Zsilinszky Endre, a demokrácia vértanúja*. Budapest: Müller Károly Könyvkiadóváll, 1945.

Lipták, L *Storočie dlhšie ako sto rokov*. Bratislava: Kalligram, 2011.

Lipták, L. *Slovensko v dvadsiatom storočí*. Bratislava: Kaligram, 2011.

Litvan, G. (ed.) *O.Jászi: Homage to Danubia*. Lanham: Rowman & Littlefield, 1995.

Litván, G. 'A Nagy Imre-csoport kialakulása és tevékenysége', *Társadalmi Szemle*, vol. 47(1992), no. 6, pp. 89-95.

Litván, G. *Jászi Oszkár*. Budapest: Osiris, 2003.

Livezeanu, I. *Cultural Politics in Greater Romania. Regionalism, Nation-Building and Ethnic Struggle 1918-1930*. Ithaca–London: Cornell University Press, 1995.

Londák, M., Londáková, E., Sikora, S. *Predjarie: Politický, ekonomický a kultúrny život na Slovensku v rokoch 1960-1967*. Bratislava: Veda, 2002.

Lőrincz, G. 'Az áruló', *Forrás*, 30 (12), 1998.

Lukáč, P. *Milan Hodža v zápase o budúcnosť strednej Európy 1939–1944*. Bratislava: Veda, SAV, 2005.

Lukes, S. 'Political Ritual and Social Integration', *Sociology* 9, 1975, pp. 289–308.

Machcewicz, P. *Polski rok 1956*. Warsaw: Oficyna Wydawnicza – Mowia Wieki, 1993.

Macho, P. 'Národný hrdina a politika. Štefánik medzi čechoslovakizmom a autonomizmom', *Človek a spoločnosť* 7 (3), 2004.Available on-line: http://www w.saske.sk/cas/archiv/3-2004/index.html [accessed 24 July 2015].

Macho, P. 'Poznámky k výskumu kolektívnych identít v 19. a 20. storočí na Slovensku', *Historický časopis*. 52 (2), 2004, pp. 353–362.

Mackinder, H. *The Democratic Ideals and Reality*. New York: H. Holt and company, 1919.

Macůrek, J. *Dějiny Maďarů a Uherského státu*. Prague: Melantrich, 1934.

Madajczyk, P. 'Gomułka – dwie odmienności od linii stalinowskiej', in Szymoniczek, J., Król, E. C. (eds.) *Rok 1956 w Polsce i jego rezonans w Europie*. Warsaw: Instytut Studiów Politycznych PAN, 2009, pp. 56–70.

Magyar, S. *Álmodni mertünk. Harc a levegőért*. Budapest: Műegyetemi Sportrepülő Egyesület, 1941.

Majewski, P. M. 'Freimaurer, Feigling, Russophiler, Intrigant. Edvard Beneš in den Augen den Polen 1918–1945', in *Edvard Beneš: Vorbild und Feindbild: politische, historiographische und mediale Deutungen*. Göttingen: Vandehoeck & Ruprecht, 2013, pp. 71–91.

Malfatti, A. (ed.) *Esterházy János emlékkönyv*. Budapest: Századvég. Pol. Isk. Alapítvány, 2001

Manuscript. 28. fond. 178, 214, 217. Hungarian National Library.

Manuscript. 28. fond. 59. Hungarian National Library.

Mark, J. *The Unfinshed Revolution: Making Sense of the Communist Past in Central Eastern Europe*. New Haven: Yale University Press, 2010.

Masaryk, T.G. *Nová Evropa: Stanovisko slovanské*. Brno: Doplněk, 1994.

Masłoń, K. 'Rozluźnione obyczaje Vaclava Havla', *Rzeczpospolita*, 1 September 2007.

Materski, W., Wosik, E. (eds.) *Katyń-Dokumenty ludobójstwa... przekazane Polsce 1992r.*Warsaw: Instytut Studiów Politycznych, 1992.

Matis, H. 'Wirtschaftliche Mitteleuropa-Konzeptionen in der Zwischenkriegszeit' in Plaschka R. G. (ed.) *Mitteleuropa-Konzeptionen in der Ersten Hälfte des 20. Jahrhunderts*. Vienna: Verlag der österreichischen Akademie der Wissenschaften, 1995, pp, 229–255.

Matula, V. (ed.)*25 rokov československo-maďarskej historickej komisie*. Bratislava: Veda, 1985.

Mentzel, P. C. 'Nationalism, Civil Society, and the Revolution of 1989', *Nations and Nationalisms*, Vol. 18, No. 4, 2012, p. 628.

Merhout, C., Němec, B. *Československá národní čítanka. Sborník k desátému výročí Republiky československé*. Praha: Státní nakladtelství, 1928.

Meyer, H.C. *Mitteleuropa in German Thought and Action*. The Hague: M. Nijhoff, 1955, p. 246.

Michela, M. 'Functions of the Myth of "National Oppression" in Slovak Master Marrative, 1918-1945', in Szarka, L. (ed.) *A Multiethnic Region and Nation-State in East-Central Europe: Studies in the History of Upper Hungary and Slovakia from the 1600s to the Present*. Boulder: Social Science Monographs, 2011, pp. 253-68.

Michela, M. 'Okupácia, či návrat?', *História: revue o dejinách spoločnosti*, 6 (2007), pp. 42-43.

Michela, M., Csaba, Z. (eds.) *Magyarország felbomlása és a trianoni békeszerződés a magyar és szlovák kolektív emlékezetben 1918-2010*, LIMES: *Tudományos szemle* 4 (2010) and 1 (2011).

Michnik, A. 'Jak uderzenie w twarz drzwiami w przeciągu', *Gazeta Wyborcza*, 19 December 2011.

Michnik, A. 'Wielka historia Václava Havla', in V. Havel, *Siła bezsilnych i inne eseje*. Warsaw: Agora, 2011.

Miklós, Á. K. 'A népszolgálat és a hetvenes évek romániai magyar irodalmának nemzedéki vitái' in Bárdi N., Filep T., Lőrincz D. J. (eds.) *Népszolgálat. A közösségi elkötelezettség alakváltozatai a Magyar kisebbségek történetében*. Bratislava: Kalligram, 2015, pp. 232-248.

Milward, A. *The German Economy at War*. London: Athlone Press, 1965.

Milward, A. *War, Economy and Society, 1939-1945*. Berkeley: University of California Press, 1979.

Mináč, V. *Dúchanie do pahrieb*. Bratislava: Smena, 1970.

Molnár, I. *Esterházy János élete és mártírhalála*. Budapest: Nemzeti Könyvtár, 2013.

Mommsen, W. J. 'Die Mitteleuropaidee und -Planungen im Deutschen Reich vor und während des Ersten Weltkrieges' in Plaschka R. G. (ed.) *Mitteleuropa-Konzeptionen in der Ersten Hälfte des 20. Jahrhunderts*. Vienna: Verlag der österreichischen Akademie der Wissenschaften, 1995, pp. 3–24.

Moravec, J., Navrátil, J., Vondrová, J. (eds.) *Komunistická strana Československa*. Prague and Brno: ÚSD and Doplněk, 1999

Morawski, K. *Tamten brzeg: Wspomnienia i szkice*. Warsaw: Editions Spotkania, 1996.

Mucha No. 43, 21 October 1938.

Mucha, No. 15, 10 April 1925.

Mucha, No. 25, 1 June 1937.

Mucha, No. 41, 7 October 1938.

Mucha, No. 47, 18 November 1921.

Mucha, No. 5, 4 December 1936.

Murányi, G. 'Bajcsy-Zsilinszky Endre 1935-ös fordulata: tisztességtelen ajánlat', *HVG*, 32 (49), 2010, pp. 40–41.

Murín, K. *Spomienky a svedectvo*. Hamilton, Ont.: Zahraničná Matica slovenská, 1987.

Nagy, I. *"A magyar nép védelmében": Vitairatok és beszédek 1955–1956*. Paris: Magyar Füzetek, 1984.

Nagy, I., Vida, I. (ed.) *Snagovi jegyzetek: Gondolatok, emlékezések 1956–1957*, ed. Budapest: Gondolat, 2006.

Národnie noviny, 17. 2. 1939.

Năstasa L. *Antisemitismul universitar in România (1919–1938). Mărturi documentare*. Cluj: ISPMN, 2011.

Naumann F. *Mitteleuropa*. Berlin: Georg Reimer, 1915.

Naumann, F. *Was wird aus Polen?* Berlin: Georg Reimer Vlg., 1917.

Navrátil, J., Vondrová, J. (eds.) *Mezinárodní souvislosti československé krize*, Prague and Brno: ÚSD and Doplněk, 1995, 1996, 1997, and 2011.

Největší Čech. Available on-line: http://www.ceskatelevize.cz/specialy/nejvet sicech/oprojektu_top100 [accessed 11June 2012].

Nemeček, J. *Od spojenectví k roztržce 1939–1945*. Prague: Academia, 2003.

Nemere, I. *Bajcsy-Zsilinszky Endre magánélete*. Budapest: Anno, 2003.

Nieguth, T. 'Beyond dichotomy: concepts of the nation and the distribution of membership', *Nations and nationalism* 5 (2), 1999, pp. 155–173.

Nolte, E. *Der europäische Bürgerkrieg 1917–1945. Nationalsozialismus und Bolschewismus*. Berlin: Herbig, F. A., 1987.

Nora, P. 'Between Memory and History: Les Lieux de Mémoire', *Representations*, No. 26, Special Issue: Memory and Counter-Memory (Spring, 1989), pp. 8–9.

Nora, P. *Emlékezet és történelem között*. Budapest: Napvilág Kiadó, 2008.

Novák, J. *Zatím dobrý*. Brno: Petrov, 2004.

Novota, M. *Údery pod pás*. Banská Bystrica: M. Novota, 2006.

Nowa encyklopediapowszechna PWN, vol. 2. Warsaw: PWN, 1995, p. 715.

Nowak, J. R. 'Antynarodowa publicystyka "Wprost"', *Nasz Dziennik* 29 August 2007.

Nowak, J. R. 'Antynarodowa publicystyka "Wprost"', *Nasz Dziennik* 29 August 2007.

Ogurčáková, J. 'Odhaľovanie Esterházyho busty v Košiciach sa skončilo bitkou'. Available on-line: http://kosice.korzar.sme.sk/c/5806387/odhalovanie-esterhazyho-busty-v-kosiciach-sa-skoncilo-bitkou.html [accessed 7 October 2012].

Olivová, V. *Dějiny první republiky*. Prague: Karolinum, 2000.

Otáhal, M., Sládek, Z. (eds.) *Deset pražských dnů (17.–27. listopad 1989): Dokumentace*. Prague: Academia, 1990.

Otčenášová, S. *Schválená minulosť: Kolektívna identita v československých a slovenských učebniciach dejepisu*. Košice: FF UPJŠ, 2010.

Overy, R. J. *War and Economy in the Third Reich*. Oxford: Clarendon Press, 1995, p. 227.

Paczkowski, A. *Pół wieku dziejów Polski 1939–1989*. Warsaw: Wydawnictwo Naukowe PWN, 1995, p. 318.

Paderewski, I., Janowska, H. (eds.) *Archiwum Polityczne Ignacego Paderewskiego*, Vol. II: *1919–1921*. Wrocław: Zakład Narodowy im. Ossolińskich, 1973–1974.

Paksa, R. *A Magyar szélsőjobboldal története*.Budapest: Jaffa Kiadó, 2012.

Pálffy, Z. 'The Dislocated Transylvanian Student Body and the Process of Hungarian Nation-Building after 1918' in Trencsényi, B. et al (eds.) *Nation-Building and Contested Identities. Romanian and Hungarian Case Studies*. Budapest–Iaşi: Regio Books–Polirom, 2001, pp. 179–196.

Pallos, L. 'Területvédő propaganda Magyarországon 1918–1920', Part 1, *Folia Historica*, vol. 24, 2005–2006, pp. 33–93.

Pallos, L. 'Területvédő propaganda Magyarországon 1918–1920', Part 2, *Folia Historica*, vol. 26, 2008–2009, pp. 37–74.

Pándi, L. *Köztes-Európa, 1756–1997(kronológia)*. Budapest: Teleki László Alapítvány, 1999, pp. 174, 186, 254.

Partsch, J. *Central Europe*. New York: D. Appleton, 1903.

Partsch, J. *Mitteleuropa*. Gotha: J. Perthes, 1904.

Paučo, J. (ed.), *Dr. Jozef Tiso o sebe*. Passaic, NJ: Slovenský katolícky Sokol, 1952.

Paučo, J. *Slováci a komunizmus*. Middletown, PA: Jednota Press, 1957.

Paučo, J. *Tak sme sa poznali: Predstavitelia Slovenskej republiky v spomienkach*. Middletown, PA.: Jednota Press, 1967.

Pauer, J. *Praha 1968:Vpád Varšavské smlouvy, pozadí – plánování – provedení*. Prague: Argo, 2004.

Payne, S. *A History of Fascism, 1914–45*. London: Routledge, 1995.

Pekar, M. 'Maďari a maďarská menšina na Slovensku v slovenských učebniciach dejepisu po roku 1989', in Šutaj, Š., et al. *Maďarská menšina na Slovensku po roku 1989*. Prešov: Universum, 2008, pp. 184-199.

Pekár, M. 'Neznalosť a konfrontácia: Dve podoby pozostatkov kontroverzných slovensko-maďarských vzťahov 1939-1945', in Šutaj, Š. (ed.) *Národ a národnosti na Slovensku v transformujúcej sa spoločnosti – vzťahy a konflikty*. Prešov: Universum, 2005, pp. 127-31.

Pešek, J. *Nástroj represie a politickej kontroly: Štátna bezpečnosť na Slovensku 1953-1970*. Bratislava: Veda, 2000.

Picker, H. (ed.) *Hitlers Tischgespräche im Führer-hauptquartier, 1941-1942*. Stuttgart: Seewald, 1965.

Pilch, J. *Horthy Miklós*. Budapest: Athenaeum, 1928.

Piłsudski, J. *Wybór Pism*. Warszawa: Zakład Narodowy im. Ossolińskich, 1999.

Pintér, I. (ed.) *Bajcsy-Zsilinszky Endre 1886-1986. Tudományos tanácskozás születésének centenáriuma alkalmából*. Budapest: Hazafias Népfront-TIT, 1986.

Písecký, F. *Generál M. R. Štefánik*. Prague: Svaz národního osvobození, 1929.

Pithart, P. *Osmašedesátý*. Prague: Rozmluvy, 1990.

Plamenatz, J. 'Two types of Nationalism' in Kamenka, E. (ed.) *Nationalism: The nature and evolution of an idea*. Canberra: Australian National University Press, 1973, pp. 23-36.

Podolský, P. *Slobodomurárstvo – nešťastie našej doby*. Bratislava: Magnificat, 2007. Available on-line: http://www.magnificat.sk/htm02/sbm2.pdf [accessed: 8 March 2009].

Polakovič, Š. *Z Tisovho boja*.Bratislava: Vydavateľstvo HSĽS, 1941.

Polonsky, A. *Politics in Independent Poland 1921-1939*. Oxford: Oxford University Press, 1972.

Pragier, A. *Czas przeszły dokonany*. London: Bolesław Świderski, 1966, pp. 624-25.

Pravda o rodu Kinských. Available on-line: http://www.knize-kinsky.cz [accessed 13 August 2012].

Pravda, 6. 5. 1947.

Pricker, D. P. *Georges Clemenceau. Politikai életrajz*. Budapest: Gondolat, 1988.

Procházková, L. *Slunce v úplňku: Příběh Jana Palacha*. Prague: Prostor, 2008.

Prosto z Mostu, No. 43, 2 October 1938.

PSP ČR. *Minutes from the meeting of the NS RČS, on 26 October 1921*. Available on-line: www.psp.cz [accessed 7 October 2012].

Pusztaszeri, L. 'Egy élet Magyarországért', in Vuray G. (ed.) *Vitéz nagybányai Horthy Miklós élete képekben*. Budapest: Faktor, 1993.

Raczyński, E. *W sojuszniczym Londynie: Dziennik ambasadora Edwarda Raczyńskiego 1939-1945*. London: Niezależna Oficyna Wydawnicza "Nowa", 1997, p. 107.

Rainer, J. M. *Nagy Imre: Politikai életrajz*, vol. 1 *(1896-1953)*; Budapest: 1956-os Intézet, 1996-99.

Rainer, J. M. *Nagy Imre: Politikai életrajz*, vol. 2 *(1953-1958)*. Budapest: 1956-os Intézet, 1996-99.

Ránki, G. (ed.) *Magyarország története 1918-1919, 1919-1945*. Budapest: Akadémiai, 1976.

Rašla, A. 'Legendy o Tisovi' in Bystrický, V., Fano, Š. (eds), *Pokus o politický a osobný profil Jozefa Tisu*, pp. 140-43.

Rašla, A. *Zastupoval som československý štát: Vyznanie*. Prešov: Privatpress, 1999.

Rataj, M. *Pamiętniki 1918-1927*. Warsaw: LSW, 2011.

Reich, W. *The Mass Psychology of Fascism*. New York: Orgone Institute Press, 1980.

Renner, K. *'Deutschland, Österreich und die Völker des Ostens'*. Berlin: Verlag für Sozialwissenschaft, 1922.

Rhodes, R. A. W., t' Hart, P. 'Puzzles of Political Leadership', in Rhodes, R. A. W., t'Hart, P. (eds.) *The Oxford Handbook of Political Leadership*. Oxford: Oxford University Press, 2014, pp. 1-27.

Ricoeur, P. *Interpretation Theory: Discourse and The Surplus of Meaning*. Fort Worth: The Texas Christian University Press, 1976.

Ripka, H. *East and West*. London: Lincolns-Praeger, 1944.

Ripka, H. *Russia and the West*. London: *New Europe Forum, 1942; idem, Small and the Great Nations*. London: Czechoslovakia MFA Information Service, 1944.

Ripka, H. *The Central European Observer*, London: 30 May, 1941.

Ripp, Z. '1956 emlékezete és az MSZMP', *Múltunk*, vol. 47 (2002), no.1, pp. 146-71.

Ripp, Z. 'A pártvezetés végnapjai', in Horváth, J., Ripp, Z. (eds.) *Ötvenhat októbere és a hatalom*. Budapest: Napvilág, 1997, pp. 169-314.

Ripp, Z. 'Az ötvenhatos hagyományok és a politika', *Mozgó Világ*, vol. 29 (2003), no. 8, pp. 15-26.

Ripp, Z. 'Hungary's Part in the Soviet-Yugoslav Conflict, 1956-58', *Contemporary European History*, vol. 7 (1998), no. 2, pp. 197-225.Rogacin, W. 'Odszedł Havel, wielki człowiek: Bohater Czech, przyjaciel Polski, zmarł w wieku 75 lat', *Polska. The Times*, 19 December 2011.

Rojek, W. (ed.) *Dokumenty Rządu RP na obczyźnie:Suplementy do tomów I-VIII protokołów posiedzeń Rady Ministrów Rzeczypospolitej Polskiej, październik 1939-sierpień 1945*. Cracow: Oficyna Wydaw.-Drukarska Secesja, 2010.

Romsics, G. *Nép, nemzet, birodalom. A Habsburg Birodalom emlékezete a német, osztrák és magyar történetpolitikai gondolkodásban, 1918-1941*. Budapest: ÚMK, 2010.

Romsics, I. 'A magyar birodalmi gondola' in: Romsics, I. *A múltról a mának. Tanulmányok és esszék a magyar történelemről*. Budapest: Osiris, 2002, pp. 121-159.

Romsics, I. 'Történelem és emlékezet', *Heti Világgazdaság*, 10 July 1999.

Rowley, D. G. 'Giuseppe Mazzini and the democratic logic of nationalism', *Nations and Nationalism* 18 (1), 2012, pp. 39-56.

Rudé Právo, 24. 5. 1927.

Rudlinský, J. F. *Československý štát a Slovenská republika*. München: Akademischer Verlag Dr. Peter Belej, 1968.

Rupnik, J. *Jiná Evropa*. Prague: Prostor, 1992.

Rupnik, J. *The Other Europe: The Other Europe: The Rise and Fall of Communism in East-Central Europe*, New York: Pantheon, 1989.

Rüsen, J. 'Was ist Geschichtskultur?,' in Füssmann, K. (ed.) *Historische Faszination: Geschichtskultur heute*, Cologne: Böhlau, 1994, pp. 3-26.

Rychlík, J.'František Vnuk a tzv. slovenský pohľad na dejiny', *Kultúrny život* 25 (36), 1991, p. 4

Rychlík, J. 'Ideové základy myšlení Jozefa Tisa a jejich politický dopad', in Bystrický, V., Fano, Š. (eds) *Pokus o politický a osobný profil Jozefa Tisu, Bratislava*: Slovak Academic Press, 1992, pp. 263-74.

Rychlík, J. 'K otázke postavenia českého obyvateľstva na Slovensku v rokoch 1938-1945', *Historický časopis* vol. 37 (3), 1989, pp. 405-10.

Rychlík, J. 'National Consciousness and Social Justice in Historical Folklore', in Hoerder, D., Rößler, H. (eds), *The Roots of the Transplanted*, vol. 2. Boulder: East European Monographs, 1994

Rychlík, J. 'Situace v Protektorátu Čechy a Morava v roce 1939 a na počátku roku 1940 ve zprávách Generálního konzulátu Slovenské republiky v Praze', *Český časopis historický* vol. 109 (4), 2011, pp. 716-38.

Rychlík, J. 'Vznik Slovenského státu a česká společnosť' in Bystrický, V., Michela, M., Schvarc, M. (eds), *Rozbitie alebo rozpad?Historické reflexie zániku Česko-Slovenska*. Bratislava: Veda, 2010, pp. 392-405

Rychlík, J. *Češi a Slováci ve 20. století: Česko-slovenské vztahy 1945-1992*. Bratislava: Academic Electronic Press, 1998

Rychlík, J. *Rozpad Československa: Česko-slovenské vztahy 1989–1992*. Bratislava: Academic Electronic Press, 2002

Rychlíková, M., Rychlík, J. 'Problémy výzkumu transmise lidové kultury', *Národopisný věstník československý*, vol. 2 (1985), no. 44, pp. 85–93.

Rys, J. *Židozednářství – metla světa*. Prague: Nákladem zednářské korespondence, 1938.

Sakmyster, T. *Admirális fehér lovon*. Budapest: Helikon, 2001.

Šalda, F. X. Dr. *Edvard Beneš ve fotografii: Historie velkého života*, Prague: Orbis, 1936.

Šalda, F. X. *Nový prezident: Značka E. B.* Prague: Společnost F.X. Šaldy, 1993.

Šalda, F. X.*Nový prezident: Značka E. B. Šaldův zápisník* 8 (193536), No. 4 and 5, pp. 91–95.

Sallai, G., Szarka, L. 'Önkép és kontextus: Magyarország és a magyarság történelme a szlovák történetírásban a 20. század végén', *Regio* 2 (2000), pp. 71–107.

Sándor, J. *Vitéz nagybányai Horthy Miklós, Magyarország kormányzója és népe az Árpádházi királyok vérében.*Budapest: Szerző, 1938.

Schiller, F., von Goethe, J. W. *Xenien*. Leipzig: Weber, 1852.

Schlögel, K. *Die Mitte liegt ostwärts. Die Deutschen, der verlorene Osten und Mitteleuropa*. Berlin: Siedler Verlag, 1986.

Schmidtmyer, A. *Der Weg der Sudetendeutschen. Ein Volksbuch*. Karlsbad-Drahowitz. Leipzig: Adam Kraft Verlag, 1938.

Schmitt, C. 'Pojęcie Polityczności', in *Teologia polityczna i inne pisma*. Kraków: Znak, 2000.

Schöpflin, G. *Nations, Identity, Power*. London: Hurst, 2002.

Schultz, H.-D. 'Deutschlands "natürliche" Grenzen', *Geschichte und Gesellschaft*, No. 15, 1989, pp. 248–281.

Schumpeter, A. J. *Capitalism, Socialism and Democracy*. New York: Harper & Row, 1942.

Sebestény, S. 'Bajcsy-Zsilinszky "nemzeti demokrácia" felfogása', *Elmélet és Politika*, 1982/1, pp. 67–73.

Segeš, D.—Herter, M.—Bystrický, V. (eds.) *Slovensko a Slovenská otázka v poľských a maďarskychdiplomatickych dokumentoch v rokoh 1938–1939*. Bratislava: Spoločnosť Pro Historia, 2012.

Seibt, F. *Německo a Češi: Dějiny jednoho sousedství uprostřed Evropy*. Prague: Academia 1996.

Sennett, R.*Razem. Rytuały, zalety i zasady współpracy*. Warszawa: Muza SA, 2013.

Sezimovo Ústí. Webové stránky. Available on-line: http://www.sezimovo-usti.c z/_turista/ben_vila.php [accessed 11 June 2012].

Shulman, S. 'Challenging the Civic/Ethnic and West/East Dichotomies in the Study of Nationalism', *Comparative Political Studies* 35 (5), 2002, pp. 554–585.

BIBLIOGRAPHY 441

Sikora, S. *Rok 1968 a politický vývoj na Slovensku*. Bratislava: Pro Historia, 2008.

Šilhan V. 'K Alexandru Dubčekovi', in Bárta, M., Hoppe, J. (eds) *Úloha Alexandra Dubčeka v moderních dějinách Československa*. Brno: Masaryková dělnická akademie, 2002.

Simon, A. 'Maďarská komunita, štátna moc a 15. marec v období prvej Československej republiky', in Macho, P. et al., *Revolúcia 1848/49 a historická pamäť*. Bratislava: Historický ústav SAV, 2012, pp. 95–107.

Simon, A. *Egy politikus a történeti tények tükrében (interjú)*. Available on-line: www.ujszo.com/napilap/interju/2015/04/04/egy-politikus-a-torteneti-tenye k-tukreben [accessed 21 March 2016].

Simon, A. *Egy rövid esztendő krónikája. A szlovákiai magyarok 1938-ban*. Somorja: Fórum Kisebbségkutató Intézet, 2010.

Šimončič A., Polčín, J. *Jozef Tiso, prvý prezident Slovenskej republiky*. Bratislava: Zväz slovenských knihkupcov, 1941.

Sirácky, A. *Klerofašistická ideológia ľudáctva*. Bratislava: Slovak Academy of Sciences, 1955.

Skirmunt, K. *Moje wspomnienia 1866–1945*. Rzeszów: Wydaw.Wyższej Szkoły Pedagog., 1997, p. 121.

Skowron, M. 'Odszedł Vaclav Havel, wielki przyjaciel Polski', *Super Express*, 19 December 2011.

Slovák, 4. 5. 1939.

Slovensko proti revízii Trianonskej smluvy, Bratislava: Slovenská odbočka čsl. národnej rady, 1929, p. 45.

Slovenský biografický slovník, vol. 6. Martin: Matica slovenská, 1994.

Slovenský národný archiv, ÚV KSS – tajomníci, A. Dubček, c. no. 2380.

Smith, A. D. *The Ethnic Origins of Nations*. Oxford: Blackwell, 1986.

Smith, W. D. *The Ideological Origins of Nazi Imperialism*. New York: Oxford University Press, 1986.

Smolec, J., Sokol, L., Vasiľková, Ľ. (eds) *Proces s dr. J. Tisom: Spomienky obžalobcu Antona Rašlu a obhajcu Ernesta Žabkayho*.Bratislava: Tatrapress, 1990.

Snyder, T. *Bloodlands. Europe between Hitler and Stalin*. New York: Basic Books, 2010.

Spahn, M. 'Mitteleuropa', *Volk und Reich*. Berlin: Politische Monatshefte, 8., 1925.

Sperfeld, E. *Arbeit als Gespräch: Józef Tischners Ethik der Solidarność*. Freiburg/München: Karl Alber, 2012.

Sperber, D. 'Anthropology and Psychology: Towards an Epidemiology of Representations', *Man*, New Series, vol. 20 (Mar., 1985), no. 1, pp. 82–85.

Starzeński, P. *Trzy lata z Beckiem*. Warsaw: PAX, 1991, p. 53.

Stegmann, N. (ed.) *Die Weltkriege als symbolische Bezugspunkte: Polen, die Tschechoslowakei und Deutschland nach dem Ersten und Zweiten Weltkrieg.*Praha: MÚA, 2009.

Štovíček, I., Valenta, J. *Czechoslovak-Polish Negotiations 1939-1944*. Prague: Karolinum 1995.

Strmiska, Z. *Sociální systém a strukturální rozpory společností sovětského typu: Projekt analýzy.*Cologne: Index, 1983

Studnicki, W. *Polen im politischen System Europas*. Berlin: Mittler, 1935.

Šubrt, J., Vinopal, J. 'K otázce historického vědomí obyvatel České republiky', *Naše společnost* (periodical of the CVVM Sociologického ústavu AV ČR), Vol. 8, No. 1, 2010, pp. 9-20.

Suk, J. 'Alexander Dubček: Velký státník, nebo politický symbol? *Soudobé dějiny* 9, 2002, pp. 92-103.

Suk, J. *Politika jako absurdní drama: Václav Havel v letech 1975-1989*. Prague: Paseka, 2013

Suppan, A. 'Mitteleuropa-Konzeptionen zwischen Restauration und Anschluss' in Plaschka R. G. (ed.) *Mitteleuropa-Konzeptionen in der Ersten Hälfte des 20. Jahrhunderts*. Vienna: Verlag der österreichischen Akademie der Wissenschaften, 1995, p. 195.

Suppan, A., Vyslonzil, E. (eds.) *Edvard Beneš und die tschechoslowakische Außenpolitik 1918-1948*. Frankfurt am Main: Peter Lang, 2002.

Šváčová, S., et. al. (eds.) *Alexander Dubček v slovenskej a českej tlači: Personálna bibliografia*. Banská Štiavnica: Štátna vedecká knižnica, 2007.

Sweet, P. 'Recent German Literature on Mitteleuropa', *Journal of Central European Affairs*. III.1, 1943, pp. 1-24.

Szarka, L. 'Kisebbségvédelem, autonómia és revízió: Esterházy János szerepe a csehszlovákiai magyar politika alakításában 1932-1938', *Történelmi Szemle*, 3/2013, pp. 425-450.

Szczygieł, M. 'Prezydent, który pozostał człowiekiem,' *Gazeta Wyborcza*, 21 August 2007.

Szereda, V., Rainer, J. M. *Döntés a Kremlben, 1956*. Budapest: 1956-os Intézet, 1996.

Szereda, V., Sztikalin, A. (eds.) *Hiányzó lapok 1956 történetéből*. Budapest: Móra, 1993.

Szinai, M., Szűcs, L. (eds), *Horthy Miklós titkos iratai*. Budapest: Kossuth, 1972.

Szirtes Jóvérné, Á. *Történelem IV*. Budapest: Tankönyvkiadó, 1982.

Szostek, A. *Pogadanki z etyki*. Częstochowa: Tygodnik Katolicki Niedziela, 1998.

Talpassy, T. *A reggel még várat magára*. Budapest: Gondolat, 1981.

Tamás, Á. 'Serbs, Croatians and Romanians from Hungarian and Austrian Perspectives. Analysis of Caricatures from Hungarian and Austrian Comic Papers', in Demski, D., Baraniecka-Olszewska, K. (eds) *Images of the Other in Ethnic Caricatures of Central and Eastern Europe*. Warsaw: Polish Academy of Sciences, 2010, pp. 272-297.

Tamir, Y. *Liberal nationalism*. Princeton: Princeton University Press, 1995.

Tigrid, P. *Kvadratura kruhu: Dokumenty a poznámky k československé krizi 1968-1970*. Paris and New York: Edice Svědectví, 1970.

Tikovský, V. 'Osudy a náhody', *Hlas revoluce* 3, 1987.

Tilkovszky, L. (ed.) *Bajcsy-Zsilinszky irataiból*. Békéscsaba: Békés Megyei Tanács Tudományos-Koordinációs Szakbizottsága, 1986.

Tilkovszky, L. (ed.) *Bajcsy-Zsilinszky. Írások tőle és róla*. Budapest: Kossuth, 1986.

Tischler, J. 'Wladyslaw Gomulka und Imre Nagy (Der Verhältnis zwieschen beiden Staatsmännern im Lichte ausgewählter Dokumente und Erinnerungen 1956-1958)', in Hahn, H., Olschowsky, H. (eds.) *Das Jahr 1956 in Ostmitteleuropa*. Berlin: Akademie Verlag, 1996, pp. 146-61.

Tischler, J. 'Poland and Hungary in 1956', in Congdon, L., Király, B. K., Nagy, K. (eds.) *1956: The Hungarian Revolution and War for Independence*. New York: Atlantic Research and Publications, 2006, pp. 95-127.

Tischler, J. *Rewolucja Węgierska 1956 w polskich dokumentach*. Warsaw: Instytut Studiów Politycznych Polskiej Akademii Nauk, 1995.

Tischner, J. *Idąc przez puste błonia*. Kraków: Znak, 2000.

Tischner, J. *Polski kształt dialogu*. Kraków: Znak, 2002.

Tiso, J. *Ideológia Slovenskej ľudovej strany*. Prague: Tiskový odbor ÚSČS, 1930.

Todorov, T. *Mémoire du mal, tentation du bien*. Paris: Robert Laffont, 2000.

Tomaszewski, J. 'Edvard Beneš w opiniach polskich dyplomatów', *Mówią wieki* 4-5, 1997.

Tomczyk, P. 'Kto popiera gazociąg?', *Nasz Dziennik*, 2 November 2007.

Tóth, D. (ed.), *Tragédia slovenských Židov*.Banská Bystrica: Múzeum SNP, 1992.

Tóth, L. (ed.) *Bajcsy-Zsilinszky Endre. Emlékfüzet születésének 100. évfordulójára*. Budapest: Hazafias Népfront-Szarvasi Városi Tanács, 1986.

Trevor-Roper, H. (ed.) *Hitler's Table Talk 1941-1944*. London: Weidenfeld & Nicolson, 1973.

Tůma, O. et al *Srpen '69: Edice dokumentů*. Prague: ÚSD and Maxdorf 1996, pp. 17-18 and 269-71.

Uhl, H. 'Memory Culture — Politics of History: Some Reflections on Memory and Society', in Wahnich, S., Lášticová, B., Findor, A. (eds.) *Politics of Collective Memory*. Vienna: LIT, 2008, pp. 57-65.

Üldözöttek védelmében. Documentary. Available on-line: http://www.youtube.com/wa tch?v=8WmoH4ckmS4 [accessed 10 October 2012].

Unger, M. *A történelmi tudat alakulása középiskolai történelemkönyveinkben a századfordulótól a felszabadulásig.* Budapest: Tankönyvkiadó, 1977.

Ungváry, K. 'A Kormányzó 139 éves', *Népszabadság,* 12 February 2007.

Urbánek, Z. 'Kolik svobody uneseme', *Lidové noviny,* 24 November 1990.

Ursíny, J. *Z môjho života.* Martin: Ústav T. G. Masaryka and Matica slovenská, 2000.

Vajda, B. 'Magyarságkép a csehszlovákiai történelem tankönyvekben 1950-1993', in Hornyák, Á, Vitári, Z. (eds.) *A magyarságkép a közép-európai tankönyvekben a 20. században.* Pécs: Pécsi Tudományegyetem, 2009, pp. 259-82.

Város, M. *Posledný let generála Štefánika.* Bratislava: Obzor, 1991.

Vásárhelyi, M. 1977, *A lord és a korona.* Budapest: Kossuth, 1977.

Verheyen, D., Soe, C. (eds.) *The Germans and Their Neighbors.* Boulder: Westview, 1993.

Vigh, K. 'Bajcsy-Zsilinszky Endre szerepe a népi mozgalmakban', *Hitel,* 18 (1), 2005, pp. 80-88.

Vigh, K. *Bajcsy-Zsilinszky Endre külpolitikai nézeteinek alakulása.* Budapest: Akadémiai, 1979.

Vigh, K. *Bajcsy-Zsilinszky Endre külpolitikája.* Budapest: Mundus, 2002.

Vigh, K. *Bajcsy-Zsilinszky Endre. 1886-1944, A küldetéses ember.* Budapest: Szépirodalmi, 1992.

Vilikovský, P. 'Le panthèon slovaque' in Servant, C. – Boisserie, É. (eds.) *La Slovaquie face à ses héritages.* Paris: L'Harmattan, 2004.

Vincent, A. *Nationalism and Particularity.* Cambridge: Cambridge University Press, 2002, p. 142.

Vnuk, F. 'Ľudová strana v slovenskej politike', *Alamanach Slováka v Amerike* 1968.

Vnuk, F. *Dokumenty o postavení katolíckej církvi na Slovensku v rokoch 1945-1948.* Martin: Matica slovenská, 1998.

Vnuk, F. *Neuveriteľné sprisahanie.* Middletown, PA: Jednota, 1964.

Voegelin, E. *Modernity without Restraint: The Political Religions; The New Science of Politics; And Science, Politics and Gnosticism.* London: The University of Missouri Press, 2000, p. 54.

Vondrová, J. *Reforma? Revoluce?Pražské jaro 1968 a Praha.* Prague: ÚSD, 2013.

Vondrová, J., Navrátil, J. (eds.) *Komunistická strana Československa. Kapitulace (srpen-listopad 1968)* Prameny k dějinám československé krize v letech 1967-1970, vol. 9/3), Prague and Brno: ÚSD and Doplněk, 2011.

Vonyó, J. 'Zsilinszky és a zsidókérdés' in Vonyó, J. *Jobboldali radikálisok Magyarországon, 1919-1944: tanulmányok, dokumentumok.* Pécs: Kronosz, 2012, pp. 56-71.

Vörös, L. *Analytická historiografia versus národné dejiny: "Národ" ako sociálna reprezentácia.* Pisa: Edizioni Plus and Pisa University Press, 2010.

Walicki, A. 'Intellectual Elites and the Vicissitudes of the 'Imagined Nation' in Poland', *East European Politics and Societies* 11 (2), pp. 227-253.

Wandycz, P. *Czechoslovak-PolishConfederation and the Great Powers 1940-43.* Bloomington: Indiana University Press, 1956.

Ward, J. M. *Priest, Politician, Collaborator: Jozef Tiso and the Making of Fascist Slovakia.* Ithaca-London: Cornell University Press, 2013.

Weber, M. Economy and Society: An Outline of Interpretive Sociology. Berkeley & Los Angeles: University of California Press, 1978, pp. 1111-1156.

Weger, T. 'Češi a Němci v ČSR 1918-1938 – dějiny a vzpomínání' in Kasper, T., Kasperová, D. Češi, Němci, židé v národnostním Československu.Liberec: Technická univerzita v Liberci, 2006, pp. 11-18.

Weger, T. 'Das Hussitenstereotyp in sudetendeutschen völkischen Diskurs' in Dimitrów, E., et al. *Deutschlands östliche Nachbarschaften.* Frankfurt am Main: Peter Lang, 2009, s. 585-608.

Weger, T. '*Volkstumskampf* ohne Ende? Sudetendeutsche Organisationen, 1945-1955. Frankfurt am Main: Peter Lang, 2008, p. 124.

Witos, W. *Dzieła wybrane, t. 3:Moja tułaczka w Czechosłowacji.* Warsaw: LSW, 1995.

http://www.wszechnica.solidarnosc.org.pl/?page_id=1410, Accessed on: September 7, 2015.

Wojtecki, A. *Sprawa Europy Srodkowej.* Warsaw: Skład główny Gebethner i Wolff, 1939.

Wysocki, A. *Tajemnice dyplomatycznego sejfu. Warsaw: Książka i Wiedza,* 1988.

Zahradníček, T. *Polské poučení z pražského jara: Tři studie z dějin politického myšlení 1968-1981.* Prague: ÚSD AV ČR, 2011.

Žatkuliak, J., Laluha, I. (eds.) *Alexander Dubček.Od totality k demokracii: Prejavy, články a rozhovory.* Bratislava: Veda, 2002.

Zbyszewski, W. A. *Gawędy o ludziach i czasach przedwojennych.* Warsaw: Czytelnik, 2000.

Zeidler, M. (ed.) *Trianon: Nemzet és emlékezet.* Budapest: Osiris, 2003, pp. 709-819.

Zeidler, M. 'A Magyar Revíziós Liga', *Századok,* vol. 131, no. 2, pp. 303-351.

Zeidler, M. *A magyar irredenta kultusz a két világháború között.* Budapest: Teleki László Alapítvány, 2002.

Zeidler, M. *A revíziós gondolat.* Bratislava: Kalligram, 2009.

Zeman, Z. *Edvard Beneš – politický životopis*. Prague: Mladá fronta, 2009

Zeune, A.*Gea – Versuch einer wissenschaftlichen Erdbeschreibung*. Berlin: Wittich, 1808.

Zubrzycki, G. 'The Classical Opposition Between Civic and Ethnic Models of Nationhood: Ideology, Empirical Reality and Social Scientific Analysis', *Polish Sociological Review* 3 (139), pp. 275-295.

Zvara, J. *Maďarská menšina na Slovensku po roku 1945*. Bratislava: Epocha, 1969.

Index

1

1848 80, 104, 133, 161, 246, 278
1991 Visegrad Declaration 15

A

Alexander, J. C. 40
Anders, Władysław 162
Anderson, Benedict 41
Anderson, Benedict 41, 166
Anschluss 59, 62, 147, 177, 183, 187
anthropology 101
    anthropological methods 101
    anthropological perspective 104
    anthropological thinking 101
anti-revisionism 188
anti-Semitism 103
Aryan ideology 105
assimilationist 124
Austro-Hungarian empire 16, 40, 49, 120, 145, 151, 159, 177, 183, 188, 259, 399, 412
Austro-Hungarian Monarchy 177, 183, 188
authoritarianism 122, 410
awakening 164

B

Baert, Patrick 41
Benárd, Ágost 181
Beneš Decrees 15, 276
biologized 104
Blondel, Jean 47
Brauner 164
Burns, James MacGregor 45
Bútora, Martin 17, 229

C

Čelakovský 164

Central Europe (Mitteleuropa) 5, 6, 9, 11, 12, 14, 15, 16, 17, 20, 22, 23, 26, 31, 32, 33, 34, 35, 39, 45, 49, 50, 51, 52, 53, 54, 55, 56, 57, 59, 60, 61, 62, 63, 64, 65, 66, 67, 68, 69, 70, 71, 72, 73, 75, 76, 99, 101, 102, 103, 106, 119, 120, 121, 123, 124, 125, 126, 127, 128, 145,146, 147, 149, 150, 151, 153, 161, 168, 173, 249, 387, 397, 398, 399, 401, 403, 405, 413, 415
Černák, Matúš 154
Chaloupecký, Václav 168
Chamberlain, Houston Stewart 105, 302
charismatic personalities 40
Cisleithania 164, 167
civic identity 121
civic rights 121
civil society 36, 121, 346
Clemenceau, France Georges 181, 184, 185, 186, 187
Clinton, Bill 16, 377
Codreanu, Corneliu Zelea 103
Cole, Alistair 44
collective desires 104
collective imagination 104, 105
collective memory 75, 76, 77, 78, 84, 131, 138, 164, 241, 270
Collins, Randall 42, 43
colonialism 102, 105, 170
Comenius 80, 90, 163, 168, 341
Commonwealth of the Two Nations 125
communism 22, 31, 103, 314, 327, 405, 406, 416
crisis of legitimation 40
cultural sociology 39
cultural unity 120
Czech gentry at White Mountain 163
Czechoslovak identity 152, 167, 170, 175, 360

Czechoslovak nation 41, 155, 163, 166, 172, 173, 244, 284, 300, 402
Czechoslovak Republic 80, 81, 154, 158, 163, 164, 166, 171, 197, 210, 211, 218, 243, 251, 271, 273, 337, 339, 340
Czechoslovak Society for the Study of Minority Issues 171
Czechoslovakia 12, 13, 22, 24, 28, 29, 30, 58, 62, 63, 69, 70, 71, 82, 84, 119, 128, 146, 151, 153, 154, 155, 159, 160, 161, 163, 165, 169, 171, 172, 173, 179, 186, 191, 192, 193, 195, 196, 197, 199, 201, 206, 209, 210, 215, 216, 217, 219, 220, 221, 222, 226, 229, 231,233, 235, 244, 245, 246, 247, 272, 274, 277, 283, 284, 286, 287, 288, 290, 291, 293, 294, 295, 296, 297, 298, 299, 300, 301, 304, 305, 333, 338, 339, 340, 342, 345, 346, 347, 348, 350, 351, 353, 354, 355, 360, 361, 364, 366, 369, 371, 374, 375, 378, 380, 389, 391, 394, 414

D

democracy 46, 47, 48, 121, 128, 173, 193, 223, 245, 281, 291, 323, 328, 332, 333, 352, 357, 382
distinction between civic and ethnic nationalism 119, 121, 123, 128, 400
civic nationalism 119, 122, 124, 125, 127
ethnic nationalism 6, 52, 119, 122, 126, 128, 129, 400
Dmowski, Roman 123, 124, 285
Dobrovský 164
Drasche-Lázár, Alfréd 181
Dubček, Alexander 7, 81, 82, 85, 96, 161, 337, 338, 339, 340, 341, 342, 343, 344, 345, 346, 347, 348, 349, 350, 351, 352, 353, 354, 355, 356, 359, 360, 361, 362, 363, 364, 365, 366, 367, 368, 369, 370, 371, 372
Durkheim, Émile 42, 43

E

East-Central Europe (Ostmitteleuropa) 49, 54, 55, 60, 68, 69, 71, 244, 249, 325
Eastern and Central Europe 119
eastward expansionism (Drang nach Osten) 49
Emanuel III, Victor 184
Emperor Charles IV 170
Enlightenment 26, 103, 105, 121
essentialism 402
Esterházy 35, 235, 236, 242, 252, 401
ethnic homogeneity 103
ethnic nationhood 174
ethnic variant 125
ethnic/national category 129
ethnically heterogeneous state 168
ethno-cultural identity 126

F

fascism 102, 103, 235
Ferdinand, Frank 158
Freemasons 158, 159, 286, 290, 297

G

Gajda, Radola 154, 159
General Ištók 154
George of Poděbrady 165
German Volk 41
Germanism, 106
Germany 12, 14, 24, 49, 50, 51, 52, 53, 54, 57, 58, 59, 60, 61, 62, 64, 65, 67, 68, 69, 72, 105, 137, 143, 146, 147, 169, 175, 177, 184, 192, 193, 195, 196, 199, 216, 222, 225, 227, 247, 274, 284, 286, 287, 290, 333, 339, 362, 385
Gömbös, Gyula 93, 103, 142, 144
Great Moravian Empire 163
Great War 12, 24, 26, 28, 29, 54, 57, 60, 120, 127, 142, 164, 191, 268, 399
Gulag 68, 405

H

Habermas, Jürgen 40

Habsburg 50, 51, 58, 62, 146, 165, 245, 256, 258, 413, 416
Hadúr 103
Hart, Paul 'T 44, 47
Havel, Václav 7, 16, 23, 34, 40, 46, 80, 84, 85, 90, 91, 212, 214, 352, 364, 367, 373, 374, 375, 376, 377, 378, 379, 380, 381, 382, 383, 384, 385, 386, 387, 388, 389, 392, 393, 394, 395
Havlíček 164
Henlein 27, 170, 197, 199, 220
Herzl, Theodor 41
historical consciousness 75, 76, 78, 79, 105, 239, 359
Hitler, Adolf 13, 28, 29, 35, 40, 41, 47, 55, 57, 62, 63, 64, 65, 66, 67, 69, 70, 105, 134, 169, 175, 192, 199, 218, 219, 220, 222, 225, 226, 235, 248, 261, 265, 281
Hlinka, Andrej 97, 154, 191, 192, 199, 208, 217, 360
Holocaust 67, 102
Horthy, Miklós 6, 7, 45, 83, 93, 134, 138, 142, 144, 196, 209, 222, 225, 235, 236, 237, 242, 244, 245, 246, 247, 250, 251, 252, 253, 255, 256, 257, 258, 259, 260, 261, 262, 263, 264, 265, 266, 267, 268, 269, 270
Hungarian Red Army 186
Hus, Jan 80, 85, 90, 163, 165, 171
Hussite period 167
Hussitism 171

I

Identity 5, 6, 32, 107, 125, 136, 151, 163, 237, 242, 250
identity formation 119, 120, 121, 128, 400, 417
illiberal nationalism 127
imagined communities 41, 166, 243
imperialism 55, 56, 102, 168, 263
inclusive 121, 124
Intermarium 60, 123
International Visegrad Fund (IVF) 17, 18

J

Jungmann 164

K

Kállay government 148
Katyń 68, 70, 162, 313
Kollár 164
Körösényi, András 45, 46, 47
Krofta, Kamil 6, 163, 164, 165, 168, 171, 172, 173, 174, 401, 402, 403

L

leader democracy 46
leaders 16, 40, 43, 45, 46, 47, 48, 54, 69, 132, 156, 197, 201, 202, 220, 232, 256, 257, 267, 278, 292, 310, 312, 313, 326, 327, 328, 333, 334, 348, 365, 369, 374, 377, 389, 393, 401, 403, 409, 411
leadership 45, 46, 47, 48, 54, 60, 149, 192, 200, 276, 311, 317, 326, 327, 328, 330, 331, 332, 339, 342, 343, 345, 346, 348, 350, 353, 365, 370, 371
Legion of Archangel Michael 103
liberal nationalism 122, 127
liberalism 121, 193, 293
Lloyd George, David 179, 183, 185

M

Magyar, Mihály 134, 135, 136, 143, 144, 148, 182, 244, 257, 268, 270, 327
Marianne 179
Masaryk, Tomáš Garrigue 26, 27, 33, 40, 41, 55, 58, 61, 64, 80, 81, 85, 90, 96, 152, 153, 155, 156, 159, 160, 163, 165, 179, 271, 272, 273, 275, 277, 278, 281, 286, 287, 360, 372, 401, 402
meaning negotiation 43, 44
Meinecke 173
Michael the Austrian 184
Michael the German 184
Michal the Hungarian 179, 186

Mimetic Rivalry 5, 101
modern totalitarianism 102
multiethnic and multicultural 126
multiethnicity 13, 53, 59
multinational societies 120
multinational states 103, 120
Mussolini 134, 135, 146, 169, 218, 261, 292
myths 7, 18, 43, 84, 139, 161, 237, 401, 402

N

Nagy, Mihály 7, 81, 92, 182, 263, 323, 324, 325, 326, 327, 328, 329, 330, 331, 332, 333, 334
Napoleon 47
Národnostní obzor (National Horizon) 171, 173, 174
Narodowa Demokracja (National Democracy) 123, 383
nation state 120, 122, 128, 166, 169, 177
nation state building 128
national awakening 120
national concept of the state 170
national consciousness 126, 174, 370
national identities 127, 151, 162, 403
nation-state building 120
Nazism 12, 55, 64, 66, 68, 69, 71, 103, 105, 149, 195, 199, 216, 218, 227, 229, 251, 267, 268, 275, 278, 290, 339
New Cultural History 101
nominal nations 120

O

other Europe 49, 410

P

Palacký 164, 167
Paris peace treaties 169
Parler, Peter 170
particularism 125
Party of Racial Defence 103
Pekař, Josef 165
Pellé, Maurice 186

performance 39, 41, 42, 48, 136, 149, 285, 301, 368
Petőfi, Sándor 161, 162
Philistines 179
Piłsudski, Józef 40, 45, 60, 81, 123, 124, 125, 129, 209, 290, 291, 294, 296, 401, 402, 403
Pittsburgh Agreement 27, 153
Polish Republic 119
Polish-Lithuanian Commonwealth 123, 126
political culture. 102
political leadership 39, 44, 45, 48, 357
political radicalization 102
political science 39, 48, 410
politics of selectivity 407
Polonization 123
Přemyslid Bohemia 165
propaganda 25, 55, 58, 123, 134, 136, 137, 152, 177, 187, 224, 229, 232, 246, 255, 258, 266, 275, 295, 297, 303, 317, 318, 390, 392, 403

R

racist ideology 102
Rádl, Emanuel 29, 35, 163, 172, 173, 174
Rašín, Alois 159
rationalism 103
Reich, Wilhelm 40, 56, 62, 63, 64, 65, 66, 67, 150, 197, 219, 223, 225, 226, 227, 275, 278, 292
Renner, Karl 56, 182
revisionist policy 169
revivalist 164
Rhodes, Roderick A. W. 44, 47
Rieger 164
ritual 39, 42, 43, 44, 131, 400

S

Saint Wenceslas 90, 165
Samson 179
Schumpeter, Joseph 46
secessionist movements 122
Shoah 405, 407
Sikorski, Władysław 70, 162, 300, 386

Slovak People's Party 152, 191, 217, 218
Slovak war-time state 44
social Darwinism 106
Sólyom, László 46
South Tyrolese Germans 169
Stalin, Joseph 13, 35, 47, 67, 68, 69, 70, 261, 278, 279, 304, 310, 312, 338, 341
Štefánik, Milan Rastislav 6, 81, 82, 96, 151, 152, 153, 154, 155, 156, 157, 158, 159, 160, 161, 162, 202, 353, 356, 360, 401
stereotypes 23, 75, 89, 177, 178, 202, 294, 303, 305
Štúr, Ľudovít 82, 96, 161, 337, 338, 353, 356
Sudeten German identity 170
Sudetendeutsche Heimatbewegung 170
Švehla, Antonín 28, 159

T

Tiso, Jozef 6, 44, 83, 84, 85, 96, 97, 154, 191, 192, 193, 194, 195, 196, 197, 198, 199, 200, 201, 203, 204, 205, 206, 207, 208, 210, 211, 212, 214, 215, 216, 217, 218, 219, 220, 221, 222, 223, 224, 225, 226, 227, 228, 229, 230, 231, 232, 233, 360
totalitarianism 101, 102, 218, 357, 400, 411
totalitarian movements 103
transactional leader 45
transformational leader 17, 45
Treaty of Saint-Germain 182
Treaty of Trianon 59, 131, 132, 133, 136, 138, 146, 149, 177, 181, 187, 237, 258, 271
Tuka, Vojtěch 154, 193, 196, 214, 227

Turanians 103

U

United Nations 12, 225
universalism 125

V

Vaida-Voevod, Alexandru 179
Venus of Milo 184, 185
virtual museum 406, 407
Visegrad 9, 10, 11, 14, 15, 16, 17, 18, 22, 23, 28, 36, 79, 107, 118, 242, 397, 398
Visegrad meeting 18
von Tepl, Johannes 170

W

Wałęsa, Lech 7, 40, 46, 81, 84, 94, 95, 381, 389, 390, 391, 392, 393, 394, 395
Western Balkans 15
White Mountain 165, 167
Wilson, Woodrow 25, 26, 27, 28, 122, 127, 179, 183, 185

Y

Yugoslavia 12, 32, 50, 58, 62, 119, 147, 148, 179, 263, 264

Z

Žantovský, Michael 17
Zbraslav Chronicle 174
Zion 41
Žitavský, Petr 174
Žižka, Jan 80, 90, 163, 165, 171

SOVIET AND POST-SOVIET POLITICS AND SOCIETY

Edited by Dr. Andreas Umland

ISSN 1614-3515

1 *Андреас Умланд (ред.)*
   Воплощение Европейской
   конвенции по правам человека в
   России
   Философские, юридические и
   эмпирические исследования
   ISBN 3-89821-387-0

2 *Christian Wipperfürth*
   Russland – ein vertrauenswürdiger
   Partner?
   Grundlagen, Hintergründe und Praxis
   gegenwärtiger russischer Außenpolitik
   Mit einem Vorwort von Heinz Timmermann
   ISBN 3-89821-401-X

3 *Manja Hussner*
   Die Übernahme internationalen Rechts
   in die russische und deutsche
   Rechtsordnung
   Eine vergleichende Analyse zur
   Völkerrechtsfreundlichkeit der Verfassungen
   der Russländischen Föderation und der
   Bundesrepublik Deutschland
   Mit einem Vorwort von Rainer Arnold
   ISBN 3-89821-438-9

4 *Matthew Tejada*
   Bulgaria's Democratic Consolidation
   and the Kozloduy Nuclear Power Plant
   (KNPP)
   The Unattainability of Closure
   With a foreword by Richard J. Crampton
   ISBN 3-89821-439-7

5 *Марк Григорьевич Меерович*
   Квадратные метры, определяющие
   сознание
   Государственная жилищная политика в
   СССР. 1921 – 1941 гг
   ISBN 3-89821-474-5

6 *Andrei P. Tsygankov, Pavel
   A.Tsygankov (Eds.)*
   New Directions in Russian
   International Studies
   ISBN 3-89821-422-2

7 *Марк Григорьевич Меерович*
   Как власть народ к труду приучала
   Жилище в СССР – средство управления
   людьми. 1917 – 1941 гг.
   С предисловием Елены Осокиной
   ISBN 3-89821-495-8

8 *David J. Galbreath*
   Nation-Building and Minority Politics
   in Post-Socialist States
   Interests, Influence and Identities in Estonia
   and Latvia
   With a foreword by David J. Smith
   ISBN 3-89821-467-2

9 *Алексей Юрьевич Безугольный*
   Народы Кавказа в Вооруженных
   силах СССР в годы Великой
   Отечественной войны 1941-1945 гг.
   С предисловием Николая Бугая
   ISBN 3-89821-475-3

10 *Вячеслав Лихачев и Владимир
   Прибыловский (ред.)*
   Русское Национальное Единство,
   1990-2000. В 2-х томах
   ISBN 3-89821-523-7

11 *Николай Бугай (ред.)*
   Народы стран Балтии в условиях
   сталинизма (1940-е – 1950-е годы)
   Документированная история
   ISBN 3-89821-525-3

12 *Ingmar Bredies (Hrsg.)*
   Zur Anatomie der Orange Revolution
   in der Ukraine
   Wechsel des Elitenregimes oder Triumph des
   Parlamentarismus?
   ISBN 3-89821-524-5

13 *Anastasia V. Mitrofanova*
   The Politicization of Russian
   Orthodoxy
   Actors and Ideas
   With a foreword by William C. Gay
   ISBN 3-89821-481-8

14   Nathan D. Larson
Alexander Solzhenitsyn and the
Russo-Jewish Question
ISBN 3-89821-483-4

15   Guido Houben
Kulturpolitik und Ethnizität
Staatliche Kunstförderung im Russland der
neunziger Jahre
Mit einem Vorwort von Gert Weisskirchen
ISBN 3-89821-542-3

16   Leonid Luks
Der russische „Sonderweg"?
Aufsätze zur neuesten Geschichte Russlands
im europäischen Kontext
ISBN 3-89821-496-6

17   Евгений Мороз
История «Мёртвой воды» – от
страшной сказки к большой
политике
Политическое неоязычество в
постсоветской России
ISBN 3-89821-551-2

18   Александр Верховский и Галина
Кожевникова (ред.)
Этническая и религиозная
интолерантность в российских СМИ
Результаты мониторинга 2001-2004 гг.
ISBN 3-89821-569-5

19   Christian Ganzer
Sowjetisches Erbe und ukrainische
Nation
Das Museum der Geschichte des Zaporoger
Kosakentums auf der Insel Chortycja
Mit einem Vorwort von Frank Golczewski
ISBN 3-89821-504-0

20   Эльза-Баир Гучинова
Помнить нельзя забыть
Антропология депортационной травмы
калмыков
С предисловием Кэролайн Хамфри
ISBN 3-89821-506-7

21   Юлия Лидерман
Мотивы «проверки» и «испытания»
в постсоветской культуре
Советское прошлое в российском
кинематографе 1990-х годов
С предисловием Евгения Марголита
ISBN 3-89821-511-3

22   Tanya Lokshina, Ray Thomas, Mary
Mayer (Eds.)
The Imposition of a Fake Political
Settlement in the Northern Caucasus
The 2003 Chechen Presidential Election
ISBN 3-89821-436-2

23   Timothy McCajor Hall, Rosie Read
(Eds.)
Changes in the Heart of Europe
Recent Ethnographies of Czechs, Slovaks,
Roma, and Sorbs
With an afterword by Zdeněk Salzmann
ISBN 3-89821-606-3

24   Christian Autengruber
Die politischen Parteien in Bulgarien
und Rumänien
Eine vergleichende Analyse seit Beginn der
90er Jahre
Mit einem Vorwort von Dorothée de Nève
ISBN 3-89821-476-1

25   Annette Freyberg-Inan with Radu
Cristescu
The Ghosts in Our Classrooms, or:
John Dewey Meets Ceauşescu
The Promise and the Failures of Civic
Education in Romania
ISBN 3-89821-416-8

26   John B. Dunlop
The 2002 Dubrovka and 2004 Beslan
Hostage Crises
A Critique of Russian Counter-Terrorism
With a foreword by Donald N. Jensen
ISBN 3-89821-608-X

27   Peter Koller
Das touristische Potenzial von
Kam''janec'–Podil's'kyj
Eine fremdenverkehrsgeographische
Untersuchung der Zukunftsperspektiven und
Maßnahmenplanung zur
Destinationsentwicklung des „ukrainischen
Rothenburg"
Mit einem Vorwort von Kristiane Klemm
ISBN 3-89821-640-3

28   Françoise Daucé, Elisabeth Sieca-
Kozlowski (Eds.)
Dedovshchina in the Post-Soviet
Military
Hazing of Russian Army Conscripts in a
Comparative Perspective
With a foreword by Dale Herspring
ISBN 3-89821-616-0

29 Florian Strasser
    Zivilgesellschaftliche Einflüsse auf die
    Orange Revolution
    Die gewaltlose Massenbewegung und die
    ukrainische Wahlkrise 2004
    Mit einem Vorwort von Egbert Jahn
    ISBN 3-89821-648-9

30 Rebecca S. Katz
    The Georgian Regime Crisis of 2003-
    2004
    A Case Study in Post-Soviet Media
    Representation of Politics, Crime and
    Corruption
    ISBN 3-89821-413-3

31 Vladimir Kantor
    Willkür oder Freiheit
    Beiträge zur russischen Geschichtsphilosophie
    Ediert von Dagmar Herrmann sowie mit
    einem Vorwort versehen von Leonid Luks
    ISBN 3-89821-589-X

32 Laura A. Victoir
    The Russian Land Estate Today
    A Case Study of Cultural Politics in Post-
    Soviet Russia
    With a foreword by Priscilla Roosevelt
    ISBN 3-89821-426-5

33 Ivan Katchanovski
    Cleft Countries
    Regional Political Divisions and Cultures in
    Post-Soviet Ukraine and Moldova
    With a foreword by Francis Fukuyama
    ISBN 3-89821-558-X

34 Florian Mühlfried
    Postsowjetische Feiern
    Das Georgische Bankett im Wandel
    Mit einem Vorwort von Kevin Tuite
    ISBN 3-89821-601-2

35 Roger Griffin, Werner Loh, Andreas
    Umland (Eds.)
    Fascism Past and Present, West and
    East
    An International Debate on Concepts and
    Cases in the Comparative Study of the
    Extreme Right
    With an afterword by Walter Laqueur
    ISBN 3-89821-674-8

36 Sebastian Schlegel
    Der „Weiße Archipel"
    Sowjetische Atomstädte 1945-1991
    Mit einem Geleitwort von Thomas Bohn
    ISBN 3-89821-679-9

37 Vyacheslav Likhachev
    Political Anti-Semitism in Post-Soviet
    Russia
    Actors and Ideas in 1991-2003
    Edited and translated from Russian by Eugene
    Veklerov
    ISBN 3-89821-529-6

38 Josette Baer (Ed.)
    Preparing Liberty in Central Europe
    Political Texts from the Spring of Nations
    1848 to the Spring of Prague 1968
    With a foreword by Zdeněk V. David
    ISBN 3-89821-546-6

39 Михаил Лукьянов
    Российский консерватизм и
    реформа, 1907-1914
    С предисловием Марка Д. Стейнберга
    ISBN 3-89821-503-2

40 Nicola Melloni
    Market Without Economy
    The 1998 Russian Financial Crisis
    With a foreword by Eiji Furukawa
    ISBN 3-89821-407-9

41 Dmitrij Chmelnizki
    Die Architektur Stalins
    Bd. 1: Studien zu Ideologie und Stil
    Bd. 2: Bilddokumentation
    Mit einem Vorwort von Bruno Flierl
    ISBN 3-89821-515-6

42 Katja Yafimava
    Post-Soviet Russian-Belarussian
    Relationships
    The Role of Gas Transit Pipelines
    With a foreword by Jonathan P. Stern
    ISBN 3-89821-655-1

43 Boris Chavkin
    Verflechtungen der deutschen und
    russischen Zeitgeschichte
    Aufsätze und Archivfunde zu den
    Beziehungen Deutschlands und der
    Sowjetunion von 1917 bis 1991
    Ediert von Markus Edlinger sowie mit einem
    Vorwort versehen von Leonid Luks
    ISBN 3-89821-756-6

44 *Anastasija Grynenko in Zusammenarbeit mit Claudia Dathe*
Die Terminologie des Gerichtswesens der Ukraine und Deutschlands im Vergleich
Eine übersetzungswissenschaftliche Analyse juristischer Fachbegriffe im Deutschen, Ukrainischen und Russischen
Mit einem Vorwort von Ulrich Hartmann
ISBN 3-89821-691-8

45 *Anton Burkov*
The Impact of the European Convention on Human Rights on Russian Law
Legislation and Application in 1996-2006
With a foreword by Françoise Hampson
ISBN 978-3-89821-639-5

46 *Stina Torjesen, Indra Overland (Eds.)*
International Election Observers in Post-Soviet Azerbaijan
Geopolitical Pawns or Agents of Change?
ISBN 978-3-89821-743-9

47 *Taras Kuzio*
Ukraine – Crimea – Russia
Triangle of Conflict
ISBN 978-3-89821-761-3

48 *Claudia Šabić*
"Ich erinnere mich nicht, aber L'viv!"
Zur Funktion kultureller Faktoren für die Institutionalisierung und Entwicklung einer ukrainischen Region
Mit einem Vorwort von Melanie Tatur
ISBN 978-3-89821-752-1

49 *Marlies Bilz*
Tatarstan in der Transformation
Nationaler Diskurs und Politische Praxis 1988-1994
Mit einem Vorwort von Frank Golczewski
ISBN 978-3-89821-722-4

50 *Марлен Ларюэль (ред.)*
Современные интерпретации русского национализма
ISBN 978-3-89821-795-8

51 *Sonja Schüler*
Die ethnische Dimension der Armut
Roma im postsozialistischen Rumänien
Mit einem Vorwort von Anton Sterbling
ISBN 978-3-89821-776-7

52 *Галина Кожевникова*
Радикальный национализм в России и противодействие ему
Сборник докладов Центра «Сова» за 2004-2007 гг.
С предисловием Александра Верховского
ISBN 978-3-89821-721-7

53 *Галина Кожевникова и Владимир Прибыловский*
Российская власть в биографиях I
Высшие должностные лица РФ в 2004 г.
ISBN 978-3-89821-796-5

54 *Галина Кожевникова и Владимир Прибыловский*
Российская власть в биографиях II
Члены Правительства РФ в 2004 г.
ISBN 978-3-89821-797-2

55 *Галина Кожевникова и Владимир Прибыловский*
Российская власть в биографиях III
Руководители федеральных служб и агентств РФ в 2004 г.
ISBN 978-3-89821-798-9

56 *Ileana Petroniu*
Privatisierung in Transformationsökonomien
Determinanten der Restrukturierungs-Bereitschaft am Beispiel Polens, Rumäniens und der Ukraine
Mit einem Vorwort von Rainer W. Schäfer
ISBN 978-3-89821-790-3

57 *Christian Wipperfürth*
Russland und seine GUS-Nachbarn
Hintergründe, aktuelle Entwicklungen und Konflikte in einer ressourcenreichen Region
ISBN 978-3-89821-801-6

58 *Togzhan Kassenova*
From Antagonism to Partnership
The Uneasy Path of the U.S.-Russian Cooperative Threat Reduction
With a foreword by Christoph Bluth
ISBN 978-3-89821-707-1

59 *Alexander Höllwerth*
Das sakrale eurasische Imperium des Aleksandr Dugin
Eine Diskursanalyse zum postsowjetischen russischen Rechtsextremismus
Mit einem Vorwort von Dirk Uffelmann
ISBN 978-3-89821-813-9

60   Олег Рябов
     «Россия-Матушка»
     Национализм, гендер и война в России XX
     века
     С предисловием Елены Гощило
     ISBN 978-3-89821-487-2

61   Ivan Maistrenko
     Borot'bism
     A Chapter in the History of the Ukrainian
     Revolution
     With a new introduction by Chris Ford
     Translated by George S. N. Luckyj with the
     assistance of Ivan L. Rudnytsky
     ISBN 978-3-89821-697-5

62   Maryna Romanets
     Anamorphosic Texts and
     Reconfigured Visions
     Improvised Traditions in Contemporary
     Ukrainian and Irish Literature
     ISBN 978-3-89821-576-3

63   Paul D'Anieri and Taras Kuzio (Eds.)
     Aspects of the Orange Revolution I
     Democratization and Elections in Post-
     Communist Ukraine
     ISBN 978-3-89821-698-2

64   Bohdan Harasymiw in collaboration
     with Oleh S. Ilnytzkyj (Eds.)
     Aspects of the Orange Revolution II
     Information and Manipulation Strategies in
     the 2004 Ukrainian Presidential Elections
     ISBN 978-3-89821-699-9

65   Ingmar Bredies, Andreas Umland and
     Valentin Yakushik (Eds.)
     Aspects of the Orange Revolution III
     The Context and Dynamics of the 2004
     Ukrainian Presidential Elections
     ISBN 978-3-89821-803-0

66   Ingmar Bredies, Andreas Umland and
     Valentin Yakushik (Eds.)
     Aspects of the Orange Revolution IV
     Foreign Assistance and Civic Action in the
     2004 Ukrainian Presidential Elections
     ISBN 978-3-89821-808-5

67   Ingmar Bredies, Andreas Umland and
     Valentin Yakushik (Eds.)
     Aspects of the Orange Revolution V
     Institutional Observation Reports on the 2004
     Ukrainian Presidential Elections
     ISBN 978-3-89821-809-2

68   Taras Kuzio (Ed.)
     Aspects of the Orange Revolution VI
     Post-Communist Democratic Revolutions in
     Comparative Perspective
     ISBN 978-3-89821-820-7

69   Tim Bohse
     Autoritarismus statt Selbstverwaltung
     Die Transformation der kommunalen Politik
     in der Stadt Kaliningrad 1990-2005
     Mit einem Geleitwort von Stefan Troebst
     ISBN 978-3-89821-782-8

70   David Rupp
     Die Rußländische Föderation und die
     russischsprachige Minderheit in
     Lettland
     Eine Fallstudie zur Anwaltspolitik Moskaus
     gegenüber den russophonen Minderheiten im
     „Nahen Ausland" von 1991 bis 2002
     Mit einem Vorwort von Helmut Wagner
     ISBN 978-3-89821-778-1

71   Taras Kuzio
     Theoretical and Comparative
     Perspectives on Nationalism
     New Directions in Cross-Cultural and Post-
     Communist Studies
     With a foreword by Paul Robert Magocsi
     ISBN 978-3-89821-815-3

72   Christine Teichmann
     Die Hochschultransformation im
     heutigen Osteuropa
     Kontinuität und Wandel bei der Entwicklung
     des postkommunistischen Universitätswesens
     Mit einem Vorwort von Oskar Anweiler
     ISBN 978-3-89821-842-9

73   Julia Kusznir
     Der politische Einfluss von
     Wirtschaftseliten in russischen
     Regionen
     Eine Analyse am Beispiel der Erdöl- und
     Erdgasindustrie, 1992-2005
     Mit einem Vorwort von Wolfgang Eichwede
     ISBN 978-3-89821-821-4

74   Alena Vysotskaya
     Russland, Belarus und die EU-
     Osterweiterung
     Zur Minderheitenfrage und zum Problem der
     Freizügigkeit des Personenverkehrs
     Mit einem Vorwort von Katlijn Malfliet
     ISBN 978-3-89821-822-1

75 Heiko Pleines (Hrsg.)
Corporate Governance in post-
sozialistischen Volkswirtschaften
ISBN 978-3-89821-766-8

76 Stefan Ihrig
Wer sind die Moldawier?
Rumänismus versus Moldowanismus in
Historiographie und Schulbüchern der
Republik Moldova, 1991-2006
Mit einem Vorwort von Holm Sundhaussen
ISBN 978-3-89821-466-7

77 Galina Kozhevnikova in collaboration
with Alexander Verkhovsky and
Eugene Veklerov
Ultra-Nationalism and Hate Crimes in
Contemporary Russia
The 2004-2006 Annual Reports of Moscow's
SOVA Center
With a foreword by Stephen D. Shenfield
ISBN 978-3-89821-868-9

78 Florian Küchler
The Role of the European Union in
Moldova's Transnistria Conflict
With a foreword by Christopher Hill
ISBN 978-3-89821-850-4

79 Bernd Rechel
The Long Way Back to Europe
Minority Protection in Bulgaria
With a foreword by Richard Crampton
ISBN 978-3-89821-863-4

80 Peter W. Rodgers
Nation, Region and History in Post-
Communist Transitions
Identity Politics in Ukraine, 1991-2006
With a foreword by Vera Tolz
ISBN 978-3-89821-903-7

81 Stephanie Solywoda
The Life and Work of
Semen L. Frank
A Study of Russian Religious Philosophy
With a foreword by Philip Walters
ISBN 978-3-89821-457-5

82 Vera Sokolova
Cultural Politics of Ethnicity
Discourses on Roma in Communist
Czechoslovakia
ISBN 978-3-89821-864-1

83 Natalya Shevchik Ketenci
Kazakhstani Enterprises in Transition
The Role of Historical Regional Development
in Kazakhstan's Post-Soviet Economic
Transformation
ISBN 978-3-89821-831-3

84 Martin Malek, Anna Schor-
Tschudnowskaja (Hrsg.)
Europa im Tschetschenienkrieg
Zwischen politischer Ohnmacht und
Gleichgültigkeit
Mit einem Vorwort von Lipchan Basajewa
ISBN 978-3-89821-676-0

85 Stefan Meister
Das postsowjetische Universitätswesen
zwischen nationalem und
internationalem Wandel
Die Entwicklung der regionalen Hochschule
in Russland als Gradmesser der
Systemtransformation
Mit einem Vorwort von Joan DeBardeleben
ISBN 978-3-89821-891-7

86 Konstantin Sheiko in collaboration
with Stephen Brown
Nationalist Imaginings of the
Russian Past
Anatolii Fomenko and the Rise of Alternative
History in Post-Communist Russia
With a foreword by Donald Ostrowski
ISBN 978-3-89821-915-0

87 Sabine Jenni
Wie stark ist das „Einige Russland"?
Zur Parteibindung der Eliten und zum
Wahlerfolg der Machtpartei
im Dezember 2007
Mit einem Vorwort von Klaus Armingeon
ISBN 978-3-89821-961-7

88 Thomas Borén
Meeting-Places of Transformation
Urban Identity, Spatial Representations and
Local Politics in Post-Soviet St Petersburg
ISBN 978-3-89821-739-2

89 Aygul Ashirova
Stalinismus und Stalin-Kult in
Zentralasien
Turkmenistan 1924-1953
Mit einem Vorwort von Leonid Luks
ISBN 978-3-89821-987-7

90 Leonid Luks
Freiheit oder imperiale Größe?
Essays zu einem russischen Dilemma
ISBN 978-3-8382-0011-8

91 Christopher Gilley
The 'Change of Signposts' in the Ukrainian Emigration
A Contribution to the History of Sovietophilism in the 1920s
With a foreword by Frank Golczewski
ISBN 978-3-89821-965-5

92 Philipp Casula, Jeronim Perovic (Eds.)
Identities and Politics During the Putin Presidency
The Discursive Foundations of Russia's Stability
With a foreword by Heiko Haumann
ISBN 978-3-8382-0015-6

93 Marcel Viëtor
Europa und die Frage nach seinen Grenzen im Osten
Zur Konstruktion ‚europäischer Identität' in Geschichte und Gegenwart
Mit einem Vorwort von Albrecht Lehmann
ISBN 978-3-8382-0045-3

94 Ben Hellman, Andrei Rogachevskii
Filming the Unfilmable
Casper Wrede's 'One Day in the Life of Ivan Denisovich'
Second, Revised and Expanded Edition
ISBN 978-3-8382-0044-6

95 Eva Fuchslocher
Vaterland, Sprache, Glaube
Orthodoxie und Nationenbildung am Beispiel Georgiens
Mit einem Vorwort von Christina von Braun
ISBN 978-3-89821-884-9

96 Vladimir Kantor
Das Westlertum und der Weg Russlands
Zur Entwicklung der russischen Literatur und Philosophie
Ediert von Dagmar Herrmann
Mit einem Beitrag von Nikolaus Lobkowicz
ISBN 978-3-8382-0102-3

97 Kamran Musayev
Die postsowjetische Transformation im Baltikum und Südkaukasus
Eine vergleichende Untersuchung der politischen Entwicklung Lettlands und Aserbaidschans 1985-2009
Mit einem Vorwort von Leonid Luks
Ediert von Sandro Henschel
ISBN 978-3-8382-0103-0

98 Tatiana Zhurzhenko
Borderlands into Bordered Lands
Geopolitics of Identity in Post-Soviet Ukraine
With a foreword by Dieter Segert
ISBN 978-3-8382-0042-2

99 Кирилл Галушко, Лидия Смола (ред.)
Пределы падения – варианты украинского будущего
Аналитико-прогностические исследования
ISBN 978-3-8382-0148-1

100 Michael Minkenberg (ed.)
Historical Legacies and the Radical Right in Post-Cold War Central and Eastern Europe
With an afterword by Sabrina P. Ramet
ISBN 978-3-8382-0124-5

101 David-Emil Wickström
Rocking St. Petersburg
Transcultural Flows and Identity Politics in the St. Petersburg Popular Music Scene
With a foreword by Yngvar B. Steinholt
Second, Revised and Expanded Edition
ISBN 978-3-8382-0100-9

102 Eva Zabka
Eine neue „Zeit der Wirren"?
Der spät- und postsowjetische Systemwandel 1985-2000 im Spiegel russischer gesellschaftspolitischer Diskurse
Mit einem Vorwort von Margareta Mommsen
ISBN 978-3-8382-0161-0

103 Ulrike Ziemer
Ethnic Belonging, Gender and Cultural Practices
Youth Identitites in Contemporary Russia
With a foreword by Anoop Nayak
ISBN 978-3-8382-0152-8

104 Ksenia Chepikova
‚Einiges Russland' - eine zweite
KPdSU?
Aspekte der Identitätskonstruktion einer
postsowjetischen „Partei der Macht"
Mit einem Vorwort von Torsten Oppelland
ISBN 978-3-8382-0311-9

105 Леонид Люкс
Западничество или евразийство?
Демократия или идеократия?
Сборник статей об исторических дилеммах России
С предисловием Владимира Кантора
ISBN 978-3-8382-0211-2

106 Anna Dost
Das russische Verfassungsrecht auf dem Weg zum Föderalismus und zurück
Zum Konflikt von Rechtsnormen und -wirklichkeit in der Russländischen Föderation von 1991 bis 2009
Mit einem Vorwort von Alexander Blankenagel
ISBN 978-3-8382-0292-1

107 Philipp Herzog
Sozialistische Völkerfreundschaft, nationaler Widerstand oder harmloser Zeitvertreib?
Zur politischen Funktion der Volkskunst im sowjetischen Estland
Mit einem Vorwort von Andreas Kappeler
ISBN 978-3-8382-0216-7

108 Marlène Laruelle (ed.)
Russian Nationalism, Foreign Policy, and Identity Debates in Putin's Russia
New Ideological Patterns after the Orange Revolution
ISBN 978-3-8382-0325-6

109 Michail Logvinov
Russlands Kampf gegen den internationalen Terrorismus
Eine kritische Bestandsaufnahme des Bekämpfungsansatzes
Mit einem Geleitwort von Hans-Henning Schröder
und einem Vorwort von Eckhard Jesse
ISBN 978-3-8382-0329-4

110 John B. Dunlop
The Moscow Bombings of September 1999
Examinations of Russian Terrorist Attacks at the Onset of Vladimir Putin's Rule
Second, Revised and Expanded Edition
ISBN 978-3-8382-0388-1

111 Андрей А. Ковалёв
Свидетельство из-за кулис российской политики I
Можно ли делать добро из зла?
(Воспоминания и размышления о последних советских и первых послесоветских годах)
With a foreword by Peter Reddaway
ISBN 978-3-8382-0302-7

112 Андрей А. Ковалёв
Свидетельство из-за кулис российской политики II
Угроза для себя и окружающих
(Наблюдения и предостережения относительно происходящего после 2000 г.)
ISBN 978-3-8382-0303-4

113 Bernd Kappenberg
Zeichen setzen für Europa
Der Gebrauch europäischer lateinischer Sonderzeichen in der deutschen Öffentlichkeit
Mit einem Vorwort von Peter Schlobinski
ISBN 978-3-89821-749-1

114 Ivo Mijnssen
The Quest for an Ideal Youth in Putin's Russia I
Back to Our Future! History, Modernity, and Patriotism according to *Nashi*, 2005-2013
With a foreword by Jeronim Perović
Second, Revised and Expanded Edition
ISBN 978-3-8382-0368-3

115 Jussi Lassila
The Quest for an Ideal Youth in Putin's Russia II
The Search for Distinctive Conformism in the Political Communication of *Nashi*, 2005-2009
With a foreword by Kirill Postoutenko
Second, Revised and Expanded Edition
ISBN 978-3-8382-0415-4

116 Valerio Trabandt
Neue Nachbarn, gute Nachbarschaft?
Die EU als internationaler Akteur am Beispiel ihrer Demokratieförderung in Belarus und der Ukraine 2004-2009
Mit einem Vorwort von Jutta Joachim
ISBN 978-3-8382-0437-6

117 Fabian Pfeiffer
Estlands Außen- und Sicherheitspolitik I
Der estnische Atlantizismus nach der
wiedererlangten Unabhängigkeit 1991-2004
Mit einem Vorwort von Helmut Hubel
ISBN 978-3-8382-0127-6

118 Jana Podßuweit
Estlands Außen- und Sicherheitspolitik II
Handlungsoptionen eines Kleinstaates im
Rahmen seiner EU-Mitgliedschaft (2004-2008)
Mit einem Vorwort von Helmut Hubel
ISBN 978-3-8382-0440-6

119 Karin Pointner
Estlands Außen- und Sicherheitspolitik III
Eine gedächtnispolitische Analyse estnischer
Entwicklungskooperation 2006-2010
Mit einem Vorwort von Karin Liebhart
ISBN 978-3-8382-0435-2

120 Ruslana Vovk
Die Offenheit der ukrainischen
Verfassung für das Völkerrecht und
die europäische Integration
Mit einem Vorwort von Alexander
Blankenagel
ISBN 978-3-8382-0481-9

121 Mykhaylo Banakh
Die Relevanz der Zivilgesellschaft
bei den postkommunistischen
Transformationsprozessen in mittel-
und osteuropäischen Ländern
Das Beispiel der spät- und postsowjetischen
Ukraine 1986-2009
Mit einem Vorwort von Gerhard Simon
ISBN 978-3-8382-0499-4

122 Michael Moser
Language Policy and the Discourse on
Languages in Ukraine under President
Viktor Yanukovych (25 February
2010–28 October 2012)
ISBN 978-3-8382-0497-0 (Paperback edition)
ISBN 978-3-8382-0507-6 (Hardcover edition)

123 Nicole Krome
Russischer Netzwerkkapitalismus
Restrukturierungsprozesse in der
Russischen Föderation am Beispiel des
Luftfahrtunternehmens "Aviastar"
Mit einem Vorwort von Petra Stykow
ISBN 978-3-8382-0534-2

124 David R. Marples
'Our Glorious Past'
Lukashenka's Belarus and
the Great Patriotic War
ISBN 978-3-8382-0574-8 (Paperback edition)
ISBN 978-3-8382-0675-2 (Hardcover edition)

125 Ulf Walther
Russlands "neuer Adel"
Die Macht des Geheimdienstes von
Gorbatschow bis Putin
Mit einem Vorwort von Hans-Georg Wieck
ISBN 978-3-8382-0584-7

126 Simon Geissbühler (Hrsg.)
Kiew – Revolution 3.0
Der Euromaidan 2013/14 und die
Zukunftsperspektiven der Ukraine
ISBN 978-3-8382-0581-6 (Paperback edition)
ISBN 978-3-8382-0681-3 (Hardcover edition)

127 Andrey Makarychev
Russia and the EU
in a Multipolar World
Discourses, Identities, Norms
With a foreword by Klaus Segbers
ISBN 978-3-8382-0629-5

128 Roland Scharff
Kasachstan als postsowjetischer
Wohlfahrtsstaat
Die Transformation des sozialen
Schutzsystems
Mit einem Vorwort von Joachim Ahrens
ISBN 978-3-8382-0622-6

129 Katja Grupp
Bild Lücke Deutschland
Kaliningrader Studierende sprechen über
Deutschland
Mit einem Vorwort von Martin Schulz
ISBN 978-3-8382-0552-6

130 Konstantin Sheiko, Stephen Brown
History as Therapy
Alternative History and Nationalist
Imaginings in Russia, 1991-2014
ISBN 978-3-8382-0665-3

131 Elisa Kriza
Alexander Solzhenitsyn: Cold War
Icon, Gulag Author, Russian
Nationalist?
A Study of the Western Reception of his
Literary Writings, Historical Interpretations,
and Political Ideas
With a foreword by Andrei Rogatchevski
ISBN 978-3-8382-0589-2 (Paperback edition)
ISBN 978-3-8382-0690-5 (Hardcover edition)

132 Serghei Golunov
The Elephant in the Room
Corruption and Cheating in Russian Universities
ISBN 978-3-8382-0570-0

133 Manja Hussner, Rainer Arnold (Hgg.)
Verfassungsgerichtsbarkeit in Zentralasien I
Sammlung von Verfassungstexten
ISBN 978-3-8382-0595-3

134 Nikolay Mitrokhin
Die "Russische Partei"
Die Bewegung der russischen Nationalisten in der UdSSR 1953-1985
Aus dem Russischen übertragen von einem Übersetzerteam unter der Leitung von Larisa Schippel
ISBN 978-3-8382-0024-8

135 Manja Hussner, Rainer Arnold (Hgg.)
Verfassungsgerichtsbarkeit in Zentralasien II
Sammlung von Verfassungstexten
ISBN 978-3-8382-0597-7

136 Manfred Zeller
Das sowjetische Fieber
Fußballfans im poststalinistischen Vielvölkerreich
Mit einem Vorwort von Nikolaus Katzer
ISBN 978-3-8382-0757-5

137 Kristin Schreiter
Stellung und Entwicklungspotential zivilgesellschaftlicher Gruppen in Russland
Menschenrechtsorganisationen im Vergleich
ISBN 978-3-8382-0673-8

138 David R. Marples, Frederick V. Mills (eds.)
Ukraine's Euromaidan
Analyses of a Civil Revolution
ISBN 978-3-8382-0660-8

139 Bernd Kappenberg
Setting Signs for Europe
Why Diacritics Matter for European Integration
With a foreword by Peter Schlobinski
ISBN 978-3-8382-0663-9

140 René Lenz
Internationalisierung, Kooperation und Transfer
Externe bildungspolitische Akteure in der Russischen Föderation
Mit einem Vorwort von Frank Ettrich
ISBN 978-3-8382-0751-3

141 Juri Plusnin, Yana Zausaeva, Natalia Zhidkevich, Artemy Pozanenko
Wandering Workers
Mores, Behavior, Way of Life, and Political Status of Domestic Russian Labor Migrants
Translated by Julia Kazantseva
ISBN 978-3-8382-0653-0

142 David J. Smith (eds.)
Latvia – A Work in Progress?
100 Years of State- and Nation-Building
ISBN 978-3-8382-0648-6

143 Инна Чувычкина (ред.)
Экспортные нефте- и газопроводы на постсоветском пространстве
Анализ трубопроводной политики в свете теории международных отношений
ISBN 978-3-8382-0822-0

144 Johann Zajaczkowski
Russland – eine pragmatische Großmacht?
Eine rollentheoretische Untersuchung russischer Außenpolitik am Beispiel der Zusammenarbeit mit den USA nach 9/11 und des Georgienkrieges von 2008
Mit einem Vorwort von Siegfried Schieder
ISBN 978-3-8382-0837-4

145 Boris Popivanov
Changing Images of the Left in Bulgaria
The Challenge of Post-Communism in the Early 21st Century
ISBN 978-3-8382-0667-7

146 Lenka Krátká
A History of the Czechoslovak Ocean Shipping Company 1948-1989
How a Small, Landlocked Country Ran Maritime Business During the Cold War
ISBN 978-3-8382-0666-0

147 Alexander Sergunin
Explaining Russian Foreign Policy Behavior
Theory and Practice
ISBN 978-3-8382-0752-0

148 Darya Malyutina
Migrant Friendships in
a Super-Diverse City
Russian-Speakers and their Social
Relationships in London in the 21st Century
With a foreword by Claire Dwyer
ISBN 978-3-8382-0652-3

149 Alexander Sergunin, Valery Konyshev
Russia in the Arctic
Hard or Soft Power?
ISBN 978-3-8382-0753-7

150 John J. Maresca
Helsinki Revisited
A Key U.S. Negotiator's Memoirs
on the Development of the CSCE into the OSCE
With a foreword by Hafiz Pashayev
ISBN 978-3-8382-0852-7

151 Jardar Østbø
The New Third Rome
Readings of a Russian Nationalist Myth
With a foreword by Pål Kolstø
ISBN 978-3-8382-0870-1

152 Simon Kordonsky
Socio-Economic Foundations of the
Russian Post-Soviet Regime
The Resource-Based Economy and Estate-Based Social Structure of Contemporary Russia
With a foreword by Svetlana Barsukova
ISBN 978-3-8382-0775-9

153 Duncan Leitch
Assisting Reform in Post-Communist Ukraine 2000–2012
The Illusions of Donors and the Disillusion of Beneficiaries
With a foreword by Kataryna Wolczuk
ISBN 978-3-8382-0844-2

154 Abel Polese
Limits of a Post-Soviet State
How Informality Replaces, Renegotiates, and Reshapes Governance in Contemporary Ukraine
With a foreword by Colin Williams
ISBN 978-3-8382-0845-9

155 Mikhail Suslov (ed.)
Digital Orthodoxy in the Post-Soviet World
The Russian Orthodox Church and Web 2.0
With a foreword by Father Cyril Hovorun
ISBN 978-3-8382-0871-8

156 Leonid Luks
Zwei „Sonderwege"? Russisch-deutsche Parallelen und Kontraste (1917-2014)
Vergleichende Essays
ISBN 978-3-8382-0823-7

157 Vladimir V. Karacharovskiy, Ovsey I. Shkaratan, Gordey A. Yastrebov
Towards a New Russian Work Culture
Can Western Companies and Expatriates Change Russian Society?
With a foreword by Elena N. Danilova
Translated by Julia Kazantseva
ISBN 978-3-8382-0902-9

158 Edmund Griffiths
Aleksandr Prokhanov and Post-Soviet Esotericism
ISBN 978-3-8382-0903-6

159 Timm Beichelt, Susann Worschech (eds.)
Transnational Ukraine?
Networks and Ties that Influence(d) Contemporary Ukraine
ISBN 978-3-8382-0944-9

160 Mieste Hotopp-Riecke
Die Tataren der Krim zwischen Assimilation und Selbstbehauptung
Der Aufbau des krimtatarischen Bildungswesens nach Deportation und Heimkehr (1990-2005)
Mit einem Vorwort von Swetlana Czerwonnaja
ISBN 978-3-89821-940-2

161 Olga Bertelsen (ed.)
Revolution and War in Contemporary Ukraine
The Challenge of Change
ISBN 978-3-8382-1016-2

162 Natalya Ryabinska
Ukraine's Post-Communist Mass Media
Between Capture and Commercialization
With a foreword by Marta Dyczok
ISBN 978-3-8382-1011-7

163 Alexandra Cotofana,
James M. Nyce (eds.)
Religion and Magic in Socialist and
Post-Socialist Contexts I
Historic and Ethnographic Case Studies of
Orthodoxy, Heterodoxy, and Alternative
Spirituality
With a foreword by Patrick L. Michelson
ISBN 978-3-8382-0989-0

164 Nozima Akhrarkhodjaeva
The Instrumentalisation of Mass
Media in Electoral Authoritarian
Regimes
Evidence from Russia's Presidential Election
Campaigns of 2000 and 2008
ISBN 978-3-8382-1013-1

165 Yulia Krasheninnikova
Informal Healthcare in Contemporary
Russia
Sociographic Essays on the Post-Soviet
Infrastructure for Alternative Healing
Practices
ISBN 978-3-8382-0970-8

166 Peter Kaiser
Das Schachbrett der Macht
Die Handlungsspielräume eines sowjetischen
Funktionärs unter Stalin am Beispiel des
Generalsekretärs des Komsomol
Aleksandr Kosarev (1929-1938)
Mit einem Vorwort von Dietmar Neutatz
ISBN 978-3-8382-1052-0

167 Oksana Kim
The Effects and Implications of
Kazakhstan's Adoption of
International Financial Reporting
Standards
A Resource Dependence Perspective
With a foreword by Svetlana Vlady
ISBN 978-3-8382-0987-6

168 Anna Sanina
Patriotic Education in
Contemporary Russia
Sociological Studies in the Making of the
Post-Soviet Citizen
With a foreword by Anna Oldfield
ISBN 978-3-8382-0993-7

169 Rudolf Wolters
Spezialist in Sibirien
Faksimile der 1933 erschienenen
ersten Ausgabe
Mit einem Vorwort von Dmitrij Chmelnizki
ISBN 978-3-8382-0515-1

170 Michal Vít,
Magdalena M. Baran (eds.)
Transregional versus National
Perspectives on Contemporary Central
European History
Studies on the Building of Nation-States and
Their Cooperation in the 20th and 21st Century
With a foreword by Petr Vágner
ISBN 978-3-8382-1015-5

ibidem.eu